CAMBRIDGE LIBRAR

Books of enduring sch

CW01510255

Medieval His...,

This series includes pioneering editions of medieval historical accounts by eye-witnesses and contemporaries, collections of source materials such as charters and letters, and works that applied new historiographical methods to the interpretation of the European middle ages. The nineteenth century saw an upsurge of interest in medieval manuscripts, texts and artefacts, and the enthusiastic efforts of scholars and antiquaries made a large body of material available in print for the first time. Although many of the analyses have been superseded, they provide fascinating evidence of the academic practices of their time, while a considerable number of texts have still not been re-edited and are still widely consulted.

Court Rolls of the Manor of Wakefield

The detailed records of the proceedings of the manorial court of Wakefield provide a unique insight into medieval life and commerce, the many legal disputes arising, and the mechanisms for resolving them. The manor court met every three weeks, as well as holding additional courts, or 'tourns', at various locations around the West Riding of Yorkshire. Recognising the historical significance of these exceptionally complete court records for one of the largest manors in England, in 1901 the Yorkshire Archaeological Society began publishing them as part of its Record Series. Up to 1945, five volumes appeared that span the years 1274–1331. Edited by William Paley Baildon (1859–1924) and published in 1906, Volume 2 contains the surviving court rolls for the years 1297–8 and 1306–9. The editor's introduction provides an explanation of the workings of the court and the content of the rolls, the texts of which are given in English translation.

Cambridge University Press has long been a pioneer in the reissuing of out-of-print titles from its own backlist, producing digital reprints of books that are still sought after by scholars and students but could not be reprinted economically using traditional technology. The Cambridge Library Collection extends this activity to a wider range of books which are still of importance to researchers and professionals, either for the source material they contain, or as landmarks in the history of their academic discipline.

Drawing from the world-renowned collections in the Cambridge University Library and other partner libraries, and guided by the advice of experts in each subject area, Cambridge University Press is using state-of-the-art scanning machines in its own Printing House to capture the content of each book selected for inclusion. The files are processed to give a consistently clear, crisp image, and the books finished to the high quality standard for which the Press is recognised around the world. The latest print-on-demand technology ensures that the books will remain available indefinitely, and that orders for single or multiple copies can quickly be supplied.

The Cambridge Library Collection brings back to life books of enduring scholarly value (including out-of-copyright works originally issued by other publishers) across a wide range of disciplines in the humanities and social sciences and in science and technology.

Court Rolls of the Manor of Wakefield

VOLUME 2: 1297 TO 1309

EDITED BY
WILLIAM PALEY BAILDON

CAMBRIDGE UNIVERSITY PRESS

Cambridge, New York, Melbourne, Madrid, Cape Town,
Singapore, São Paolo, Delhi, Mexico City

Published in the United States of America by Cambridge University Press, New York

www.cambridge.org
Information on this title: www.cambridge.org/9781108058629

© in this compilation Cambridge University Press 2013

This edition first published 1906
This digitally printed version 2013

ISBN 978-1-108-05862-9 Paperback

The Anniversary Reissue of Volumes from the Record Series of the Yorkshire Archaeological Society

To celebrate the 150th anniversary of the foundation of the leading society for the study of the archaeology and history of England's largest historic county, Cambridge University Press has reissued a selection of the most notable of the publications in the Record Series of the Yorkshire Archaeological Society. Founded in 1863, the Society soon established itself as the major publisher in its field, and has remained so ever since. The *Yorkshire Archaeological Journal* has been published annually since 1869, and in 1885 the Society launched the Record Series, a succession of volumes containing transcriptions of diverse original records relating to the history of Yorkshire, edited by numerous distinguished scholars. In 1932 a special division of the Record Series was created which, up to 1965, published a considerable number of early medieval charters relating to Yorkshire. The vast majority of these publications have never been superseded, remaining an important primary source for historical scholarship.

Current volumes in the Record Series are published for the Society by Boydell and Brewer. The Society also publishes parish register transcripts; since 1897, over 180 volumes have appeared in print. In 1974, the Society established a programme to publish calendars of over 650 court rolls of the manor of Wakefield, the originals of which, dating from 1274 to 1925, have been in the safekeeping of the Society's archives since 1943; by the end of 2012, fifteen volumes had appeared. In 2011, the importance of the Wakefield court rolls was formally acknowledged by the UK committee of UNESCO, which entered them on its National Register of the Memory of the World.

The Society possesses a library and archives which constitute a major resource for the study of the county; they are housed in its headquarters, a Georgian villa in Leeds. These facilities, initially provided solely for members, are now available to all researchers. Lists of the full range of the Society's scholarly resources and publications can be found on its website, www.yas.org.uk.

Court Rolls of the Manor of Wakefield, 1297–1309
(Record Series volume 36)

The Wakefield manorial court rolls span more than six centuries from 1274 to 1925, making them one of the most comprehensive series now in existence, and the Yorkshire Archaeological Society has been engaged in their publication and preservation for more than a century. The manor of Wakefield was one of the largest in England, covering a huge area of the West Riding of Yorkshire, although it was divided into many sub-manors. The actual area over which the court had jurisdiction during the centuries for which the records survive was approximately 90 square miles. The records of the manor's property transactions, agricultural business and law enforcement are an important source for legal, social and economic historians.

In 1898, several members of the Society provided a fund to employ Miss Ethel Stokes, a leading London record agent, to produce translations of the earliest surviving rolls. Three years later, the first of five volumes devoted to these early rolls appeared in the Society's Record Series, edited by a young legal scholar, William Paley Baildon. A London-based barrister, proud of his Yorkshire ancestry, he was one of the eleven founder members of the Selden Society and had begun his secondary career as a record scholar under the guidance of F.W. Maitland.

This is the second of the five volumes, the others being 29, 57, 78 and 101. It contains translations of the surviving rolls for 1297–8 and the three years 1306–9, with an introduction describing the contents of the rolls in the first two volumes. The court rolls published here are held by the Society and have the references MD225/1/24, 32, 33 and 34.

COURT ROLLS
OF THE MANOR OF WAKEFIELD.

VOL. II.

THE YORKSHIRE
ARCHÆOLOGICAL SOCIETY.

FOUNDED 1863.   INCORPORATED 1893.

RECORD SERIES.
VOL. XXXVI.
FOR THE YEAR 1906.

COURT ROLLS
OF THE
MANOR OF WAKEFIELD.
VOL. II.
1297 to 1309.

EDITED BY

WILLIAM PALEY BAILDON, F.S.A.

PRINTED FOR THE SOCIETY.

1906.

PRINTED BY

J. WHITEHEAD AND SON, ALFRED STREET, BOAR LANE,

LEEDS.

INTRODUCTION.

THE first volume of these Court Rolls ended with the Court held on the Vigil of St. Matthew the Apostle, that is September 20th, 1297; the present volume ends with the corresponding Court in 1309. There is, however, an unfortunate gap between 1298 and 1306, for which period the rolls are missing.

In 1309 a suit was adjourned because the rolls were wanting (ii, 194); and again at a later Court because the rolls had not been found (ii, 199).

It appears from this that the missing rolls were lost or destroyed at an early date.

As stated in the Introduction to vol. i (p. xvii), the Earl of Surrey had been appointed Keeper of Scotland in 1296. His services there are incidentally mentioned more than once in this volume. Thus, in 1298 a suit against Richard de Colley is adjourned until Richard's return from Scotland (p. 27); in the same year John de Holne was sued for the value of a sheep carried off in Scotland in 1295-6 (p. 38).

John de Warenne, Earl of Surrey, died on September 27th, 1304. The year is given in the *Complete Peerage* as 1305, but this appears to be an error. On October 16th, 1304, the King gave leave to the executors of the Earl's will to dispose of his lands in Norfolk for a term of ten years, notwithstanding certain defects in the will[1]; and on December 10th, 1304, mention is made of "John de Warenna, late Earl of Surrey."[2] These items seem conclusive as to the year. The inquisition taken after his death, if any, has not been preserved. This is most unfortunate, as we might have had some interesting details of the Yorkshire property.

The Earl's only son, William de Warenne, died in his father's lifetime, on December 15th, 1285, having been killed in a tournament held at Croydon.

John de Warenne, only son of the above William, therefore succeeded to the title and estates of his grandfather. He was born on June 29th, 1286,[3] and was therefore under age when his grandfather

---

[1] Patent Roll.   [2] *Ibid.*   [3] *Complete Peerage.*

died.   Here again the proof of age on his attaining twenty-one is
most unfortunately not forthcoming.   He was knighted on May 22nd,
1306, and from that year until 1335 he was almost constantly
employed in public service of some sort.

His services in the Scotch wars are incidentally mentioned several
times in this volume.

In 1311 the Earl had a grant of the Castle and Honour of the
Peak, in Derbyshire, which has a remote local bearing.   The family
of Peck was for several centuries one of the most noted in
Wakefield, and I think there is little doubt that the Peter del Peak,
mentioned on p. 10, etc., is the ancestor of the Pecks, and that he
was a Derbyshire man from the Peak.

In the same way, Thomas de Dorking, p. 33, etc., must have come
from the Earl's Surrey manor, and Peter Llewelyn from one of the
Welsh estates.   Such migrations of individuals owing to feudal
relationships are by no means uncommon, but it is not often that
they can be traced so distinctly.

Apart from these Court Rolls, there is but little to record of the
manor of Wakefield during the period covered by this volume.   The
Patent Rolls throw no light, nor do the Close Rolls so far as they
are printed; there is one more volume of the Close Rolls for the
reign of Edward I yet to be issued.

The indefatigable Watson prints a translation of a confirmation
by Earl John to the Burgesses of Wakefield, of which the following
is a note[1]:—

"His temporal grants, which I have seen any account of, are, that
he confirmed to the free-burgesses of Wakefield, and their heirs, their
privileges, and granted them to be toll free in all his lands, for all
wares, merchandise of their own manufacture, and that they should
not be obliged to answer at any court but his, called Burman Court,
in Wakefield, unless for trespasses against himself; and that whatsoever
goods should be bought of any burgess for him, or his use, at certain
rates, should be paid for within forty days; the pawnage for every hog
to be twopence, and for a pig one penny.   They were also to have
commonage for all cattle but goats, in all his woods, moors, &c.,
except the new and old park, and the great meadow (only not in
fawning time).   They might likewise inclose, and hedge their corn
ground, and fright away his deer from thence, without horn.   Witnesses,
John de Nevil, Hugh de Eland, William son of William, Roger son

---

[1] Watson's *Memoirs of the Ancient Earls of Warren and Surrey*, 1782, vol. ii,
p. 59.

of Thomas, Peter son of Thomas, knights, John de Doncaster, John Curson, Peter de Stamford, Tho. de Heton, Adam de Pontefract. Dated at Coningsburgh, Oct. 5, 1 Edw. II."

Watson, contrary to his usual practice, gives no authority for this charter, nor any text save the above rather inept translation; it seems evident, therefore, that he had not seen the original document and had no copy of it. Nevertheless, there are internal indications that his note was taken from a genuine charter, and I see no reason why it should not be accepted as such.

We are now in a position to give some account of these Court Rolls generally, but I must preface my remarks with the statement that they do not profess to be a treatise on manorial courts at large; and, as I presume the bulk of my readers are not lawyers, I have endeavoured to keep as free from legal technicalities as possible.

THE COURT BARON AND CUSTOMARY COURT.

It is commonly said that a manor with freehold and copyhold tenants has two courts, the Court Baron and the Customary Court, the former for the freeholders and the latter for the copyholders. At a later date than that with which we are now dealing, the title or heading frequently runs "Court Baron and Customary Court" of A. In these rolls we have no trace of any such arrangement, unless the plea of a free man, that he was not bound to answer at the Court held at Rastrick, is an indication that this was a Customary Court (ii, 7).

The principal Court was held at Wakefield every three weeks, "from three weeks to three weeks," as it was often quaintly expressed; but there was a certain amount of elasticity, and when a feast day or other cause made the normal day inconvenient, the interval might be shortened or lengthened.

In addition to those at Wakefield, twice a year Courts were held at Kirkburton and Rastrick, and occasionally at Brighouse and Halifax; these were generally in May and October.

The Steward was the presiding officer at these Courts, but in his absence the deputy-steward officiated. Apparently he had less power than the Steward, for matters were often adjourned until the Steward himself could be present.

The business transacted was of a very miscellaneous nature, and may be divided roughly into three classes, (*a*) transactions relating to the holding and transfer of land, (*b*) litigation, and (*c*) manorial offences.

Practice. The practice of the Court followed generally that of the King's Courts. We do not hear of any writ, but there must have been a summons of some sort, and it was probably in writing.

If the defendant did not appear he was first attached and then distrained, but certain excuses for non-appearance were allowed, such as sickness, being on the King's service, or the bad state of the roads; these were called "essoigns."

An essoign could not be made after a default (i, 238), and was vitiated if the person essoigning was seen in Court (i, 254). If a plaintiff who had made essoign was afterwards seen in Court, he was liable to have judgment given against him on the ground of non-prosecution (i, 206).

An essoign from suit apparently was good for other matters at the same Court. A. sued B. for assault; B. had essoigned from suit, and the question arose whether that was a good essoign against A. or not. At the next Court it was ordered that B. should be summoned, which seems to answer the question in the affirmative (i, 156).

The pleading, like that in the King's Courts, was of a highly technical nature, and any departure from the proper form was fatal to either side. Several instances of this are worth noting. A defendant "denies everything against Richard de B. and his suit"; the plaintiff was not Richard de B., but Thomas his man, and judgment was given for him on this slip (i, 88). A plaintiff does not name the day nor the hour when certain goods were alleged to have been stolen: his claim failed accordingly (i, 104). A. charged B. with assault and carrying off his bow and arrows; B. pleaded that he was not bound to answer, because he was charged with two offences, one of which might be true and the other false (ii, 15).

When the defendant had appeared and had pleaded successfully, he could claim to have a jury or he could wage his law. The wager of law consisted in finding a certain number of persons, "compurgators," who swore that they believed his statement to be true. In the King's Courts the number of compurgators was invariably eleven, and this was called "waging his law twelve-handed," the twelfth hand being the defendant's own. In these rolls the number of compurgators is often less than twelve, but there does not seem to have been any uniform rule in this respect; in Manorial Courts the six-handed wager seems to have been common, and probably in this manor, where no number is mentioned, the wager was to be six-handed, that is, the defendant and five compurgators. A wager of law "with the third hand," that is, with two compurgators, occurs in a plea of debt (i, 88); another (i, 199).

A defendant asked for "a free law because he is free" (ii, 20); probably a wager of law with free men is meant.

A wager of law by a woman with women was held bad (i, 194, 212).

A withdrawal from a wager of law was an admission of the point as to which the law was waged; the defaulter also incurred a fine (i, 297).

If the plaintiff abandoned his claim without license he incurred a fine; but a "license of concord," as it was termed, was commonly asked for and obtained on payment of a small fee. The "love-day, which occurs so frequently, was an adjournment for the purpose of seeing if an agreement could be effected.

Either party could demand a jury, and as a general rule a fee was paid by the person making the demand.

The number of jurors as a rule was twelve, but there appears to have been an appeal in some cases from 12 jurors to 24, and from 24 to 48. The custom in this respect is shown by the report of a case at the Court held on Friday after the feast of St. Lucy the Virgin, 4 Edw. III (13 Dec., 1330), in which Walter Gunn sued Richard Bunny for land, &c., in the graveship of Alvirthorpe, and claimed the benefit of a verdict of twelve jurors given at a previous Court. Richard Bunny defended, and said that he was not bound to answer, because at another Court it was found by an attaint (*attincta*) of twenty-four jurors on the said jury of twelve that the latter had made a false oath, and Richard was accordingly to recover seisin. He also said that it was not consonant with the law or the custom of the manor to make further inquisition in pleas of land than by an attaint of twenty-four, and he demanded judgment. Walter replied that with land held in bondage at the will of the lord, the lord of his special grace, notwithstanding the common law, can grant to such tenants at will an attaint on an attaint, to inquire more truly regarding the tenants' right (*attinctam super attinctam pro jure tenencium verius inquirendo*), and thereupon he produced a certain close letter from Earl Warenne directed to Sir Simon de Baldrestoun, Steward of his lands in the county of York, directing the Steward to summon before him forty-eight of those who best knew the truth of the matter, and put them on their oath concerning the right of the said Walter. By virtue of which command order was given for forty-eight men of the nearest graveships to come to the next Court to inquire as above.

Where a plaintiff demanded a jury he was allowed to pay for it with a condition that if his claim failed the payment should be taken in lieu of any amercement (i, 174). In this case there were thirteen jurymen.

An appeal from an attaint of twenty-four was decided by a jury of twenty-four, summoned from five graveships (ii, 100).

The Earl's men could only be sued in the Earl's Court, and a plaintiff infringing this was fined (i, 86., etc.).

It was also a serious manorial offence to sue in any other court for a matter within the jurisdiction of the Manor Court (i, 283).

Chattering in court was punished by fine.

On one occasion the Court at Burton was held in the church (i, 148; see *post*, p. xxv).

The Borough or "Burman" Court claimed jurisdiction where the defendant was a burgess, or where the assault complained of was committed in the town (i, 262, 264).

A plea of assault, apparently committed in the borough of Wakefield, was remitted to the Borough Court, as pertaining to the farmers of the ville (i, 178).

A judgment of this court was pleaded in the Manor Court (i, 206).

THE COURT LEET OR TOURN.

The Court Leet, unlike the Court Baron, is not an integral part of a manor, but a franchise which can only belong to a subject by direct grant from the Crown. No such grant is known in connection with the manor of Wakefield, but we must presume that it was included in the original grant of the manor to the Warennes, some time after the completion of the Domesday Survey (i, *intro.*, pp. v, vi), and certainly prior to 1121. It was missing in 1280, for the Earl of that date was unable to produce it at the *Quo warranto* proceedings, and was forced to plead prescription (*ibid.*, pp. xi–xv). As the manor had belonged to Edward the Confessor and was still in the possession of the Crown at the time of Domesday, it seems probable that the Leet jurisdiction had belonged to it from an early period.

The Court Leet was a criminal court, and had an extensive jurisdiction in minor offences. It was held twice a year and no oftener by virtue of Magna Charta, c. 35, once after Easter and once after Michaelmas.

As a general rule, one of the principal functions of the Leet was the View of Frank Pledge, and it is somewhat remarkable that in these rolls there is no reference to it.

The Steward was the sole judge, and in matters within the jurisdiction of the Leet he had powers equal to those of the Justices of the Bench.

The Tourns, as here recorded, do not seem to have kept very strictly to Leet business. We find matters adjourned from the Courts to the Tourns, and from the Tourns to the Courts, in a way that appears to be somewhat irregular.

The criminal jurisdiction of the Tourn was not limited to tenants of the manor. Two strangers [*extranei*] were ordered to be attached for mutual bloodshed (i, 282). Though not so stated, it perhaps may be presumed that the assault was committed within the manor.

A plaintiff was amerced for bringing an accusation of robbery, "which this court cannot judge" (i, 145). The accused was not a tenant of the manor, and this is probably the point intended; there are many cases of robbery dealt with without question, but these may have been all concerning tenants of the manor.

In one case (i, 127, 130) at the Tourn at Wakefield there were two juries, one "from within," and the other "from without." There is no explanation that I can suggest, and it does not occur again.

Slander cases are very numerous. Most of them are of a commonplace nature, such as calling a man a thief or a usurer, or a woman a harlot, or such like vulgar abuse. But a few are very curious and difficult to understand. For instance, A. says that B.'s father "was buried at Agbrigg" (i, 164). Some insult is clearly lurking in the words, though we lack the clue. It has been suggested that as Agbrigg was the meeting-place of the Wapentake Court, malefactors may have been buried there in early times. The existing "Gallows Hill," nearer the town of Wakefield, may have been a later place of execution.

In another case the slander consisted in calling the plaintiff "Robert the Brus" (ii, 71).

MANORIAL OFFICERS.

The Steward was the principal manorial officer, and presided over the Courts. There is considerable evidence that some of his work was done by deputy, for we find adjournments "until the Steward comes." These may, however, refer to the "Chief Steward," *capitalis seneschallus*, who is only mentioned once. This was in 1307, when a matter was respited "till the coming of Sir John de Nevill, the Chief Steward" (ii, 68), the Steward at that time being William de Wakefield (ii, 61).

Any disrespect shown to the Steward was promptly punished; thus "contempt and despite shown to the Steward in open court" were met by a fine of 6s. 8d. (i, 114; see also 108).

The Serjeant. The Serjeant was appointed by the lord, and is frequently referred to as "the Earl's Serjeant" (i, 112). He seems to have been next in importance to the Steward.

There was a *bailiff;* also a *foreign bailiff,* who was concerned with matters that lay outside the manor (ii, 150).

Receiver. There is an appointment of a receiver by the Earl (i, 126); he found pledges that he would faithfully answer for all receipts, payments and expenses, so that he was clearly the Earl's treasurer. He is not mentioned again in that capacity.

Collector for pannage. It is doubtful whether this was a permanent or temporary office (i, 92). It is not mentioned elsewhere.

The Ale-tasters. These were probably appointed yearly, but are very seldom mentioned; their duties were to look after the assize of ale (i, 129). They are sometimes called the *ale-keepers* (i, 189).

There were other officers of the lord's who are not specifically designated. One, for instance, whose duty it was to sell the right to pasture in the lord's meadow after the hay was carried (i, 249).

The Foresters. There were several foresters in connection with the lord's forests; thus we have the foresters for Hipperholm and Shibden (i, 81).

They were appointed by the lord, and they were sworn to keep the Earl's forests and warrens and to present attachments (i, 81).

A curious contest arose as to the respective duties of the forester and the grave with regard to a nest of young hawks. It was held that the forester was responsible in the first place, and that he ought to appoint some one to take charge of it, who then became responsible for its safe keeping, while the grave was to pay the costs out of the lord's moneys. In this particular case the forester placed the grave in charge, the nest was stolen, and the grave was ordered to compensate the Earl for the value of the birds (i, 151).

The Graves. There were ten of these subordinate officers (i, 309), one for each graveship. In several respects each grave seems to have acted as a sort of under-steward in respect of his graveship,[1]

---

[1] In later times the graves took surrenders; see *post*, p. xxiii.

and he was a much more important officer than the *prepositus* of an ordinary manor. Wakefield, though in many respects treated as one manor, is much more like what in later times was called an Honour, that is, a collection of manors worked from a single centre. There are even some indications that the grave presided at the Graveship Courts in the absence of the Steward, for it is obvious that every Court must have had a president of some sort, and adjournments "till the Steward comes" are frequent. This is possibly the explanation of the plea of a defendant at a Court held at Rastrick, that he was a free man and not bound to answer at that Court (ii, 7).

The graves were chosen yearly, as a rule between Michaelmas and the end of the year; the elections, however, were not always entered in the earlier rolls.

The grave was elected by the graveship, that is, by the copyhold tenants in the graveship, who were collectively responsible to the lord for him; he was sworn to his office (i, 253).

Every tenant of villein or copyhold land was liable to serve the office in respect of his holding (ii, 81). At a later date we shall find that a rota was kept, and that the copyholders were strictly chosen in turn. It is probable that such an obviously convenient arrangement was also in use at the earlier period covered by these volumes, but there is no direct evidence of it. We find, however, that payments "not to be grave this year" are not infrequent, which certainly suggests a rota.

There is also the curious case (ii, 67) where A. sued B. for 4s. 2d. and 4s. under two agreements made in 31 and 32 Edward I, to the effect that B. would be grave for the whole community of the whole graveship of C. It looks as though the agreements were bonds to ensure B.'s filling the office, and it suggests that he was taking it out of turn.

If the person elected grave refused to act or to take the oath, he was liable to a considerable fine (i, 253).

Certain perquisites seem to have been attached to the office. He was entitled to part of the estreat of attachments of wood (i, 233).

The duties of the grave were multifarious, but are nowhere set out in detail; we can only ascertain them from scattered entries.

He had to keep his graveship faithfully, and to make attachments and presentments (i, 114).

The grave had to collect the lord's rents in his graveship, and was apparently held personally responsible for any deficit; see the case of the Wakefield fulling mill (i, 252).

A grave told the steward that a bovate of land was left altogether waste on the lord, and it was thereupon granted to someone else; when it was subsequently found that the mother of the late tenant was entitled to dower, the grave was fined 12*d*. (i, 283).

The grave had to attend the courts as representing his graveship (i, 88), and to summon jurors for inquisitions (i, 219); he seized land for rent in arrear (i, 250), and the forfeited chattels of fugitives (i, 85). On the retirement of the carpenter, he had to check the timber left in his graveship, and to make a tally of it (i, 114).

MANORIAL OFFENCES.

These were very numerous, and the bulk of them consisted in taking vert, dry wood, brushwood, ivy, ferns, rushes, broom, and the like, in the Earl's land. Taking apples occurs sometimes (i, 308).

Next, and still very numerous, are the cases of "escapes," that is, where various animals, horses, cattle, sheep, pigs, and so on, had got into the Earl's woods or crops and so done damage.

With these may be placed the cases of breaking the pale, which would in most cases be done for the purpose of getting into the park or other inclosures, or for letting animals in.

Poaching was a serious offence and fairly common, and to have one's dog caught with a hare, or even in the woods at all (i, 308), was to incur a considerable fine. Three men charged with a trespass in the forest, said that they sent their dogs to run in the common chase, and that one of the dogs ran into the Earl's liberty against their will, but did no harm; they were acquitted (i, 158).

All tenants were bound to do suit to the lord's mill, that is, to have their corn ground there, and the failure to do so, "withdrawing suit" as it was called, was punished by fine. Cases, i, 86, 107, 122, 128.

Digging stone on copyholds without license was another offence (i, 268, 274). And under this heading must be reckoned coal, which in one case is called *petram ad ardendam* (i, 268), and in other cases sea-coal, *carbones maritimos*, or *carbones maris*. A license to dig sea-coal was granted to Richard the Nailer (i, 96).

Offences in connection with ways and watercourses, though perhaps not, strictly speaking, manorial, may be referred to here. They include the obstruction of highways, the diversion or obstruction of footpaths, the making of new footpaths, and the diversion or obstruction of watercourses. With these we may group the cases where the right of way existed only in the "open time," that is, after the hay or corn was carried. We read of a road lawful for men in "close time," and for men and horses in "open time" (i, 247).

The lord's demesne meadow was exempt from the general rule as to pasturing in "open time" (i, 107).

THE FREEHOLD TENANTS AND THEIR LAND.

The services due from the freehold tenants were fealty, homage, suit of court, and reliefs, and, in some manors, rents of assize or quit-rents and heriots.

Freehold quit-rents were very common on north country manors, and although they do not appear very prominently on these rolls, there are a few instances.

A. held land of the manor and owed a rent, which was in arrear; his tenants in S. were apparently threatened with a distraint for their lord's rent, and they paid 2s. to have the rent levied equally from all their lord's tenants within the Earl's fee (ii, 2).

There is a good example of relief (i, 161); the heir of a deceased free tenant appeared and proved his age; he paid nothing for a relief because his guardian had paid it immediately on his father's death.

The lord was entitled to hold the land until the heir came and paid his relief (ii, 122).

The freehold tenants had to do suit at the Manor Court, and they were fined for default unless they had essoigned themselves by giving some reason for their absence which could be accepted by the Steward. A freeholder could appoint an attorney to do suit for him (i, 84, 91, 124, 147), and then the attorney was subject to the same necessity of doing suit or making essoign. Many freeholders paid a lump sum from time to time to be excused doing suit for a fixed period (i, 158).

The King occasionally respited suit or authorised the appointment of an attorney; this was probably when the tenant was going abroad or otherwise employed on the King's service (i, 158, 164).

Where a tenant owing suit of court had made default, distress could be levied on the goods of his under-tenant within the manor (i, 89, 136, 141). In this case it seems probable that the actual suitor had no goods within the manor on which a levy could be made; the distress would no doubt be made on the land in respect of which the suit was due.

The free tenants could only be sued in the Court Baron (to use a later term), that is, the court constituted with its proper 'homage' of other free tenants. These free suitors were the judges, and hence the doctrine is merely an application of the principle that every man must be tried by his peers. Thus, we find a man charged at the Court at Rastrick with wrongfully impounding sheep, pleading successfully that he was a freeman and not obliged to answer at that Court. He was ordered to come to the next Court at Wakefield (ii, 7). Evidently this particular court at Rastrick was a Customary Court.

But even the Court Baron had no jurisdiction to try a dispute as to a free tenement; the freeholder in such a case was not bound to answer except on the King's writ, that is, in the King's Courts (*e.g.* i, 157). This, however, was a personal privilege, which could be waived either actually or constructively.

A defendant pleaded that he was not bound to answer for his free tenement except by the King's writ. The Steward held that as he had previously recovered the land in that Court, he had submitted to the jurisdiction, and was bound to answer. He refused, and left the Court; and thereupon the Steward heard the case in his absence (ii, 100).

The freehold lands were transferred by grant or charter, which did not require to be enrolled. It is probable that, as in many other manors, a small fine had to be paid, but this is not quite clear. Many of the entries in this form—A. gives x*d.* for license to take *y* acres from B.—may relate to freeholds, but the surrenders of copyholds are also recorded in the same form in the earlier rolls, so that it is very difficult to distinguish them. (See i, 242, 260, 265.)

A free tenant who had sold freehold land by charter, could be sued in the Manor Court on his covenant to warrant (i, 84).

A free tenant could obtain the declaration of the Court as to the tenure of his holding; thus, we find a statement that A. holds freely a carucate of land in Wakefield, called Bothom (ii, 47).

The unusual term *frank-farmer* occurs only once (ii, 2); it seems to mean a freeholder who pays a free-rent. The word farmer as a rule means one who pays a farm, and is rarely used except for a leasehold or other limited interest; but in this case the payment of a relief seems to imply a freehold interest.

A. gave 4*s.*, because she was a free woman, to hold her dower for life; nevertheless she had to find a pledge that she would not remove her chattels from the lord's land (ii, 39).

This probably refers to the distinction made in most manors between dower in freeholds and in copyholds. In the former, the dower was usually for life; in the latter it was purely a matter of custom, and where it attached at all, it was as a rule during widowhood or chastity only.

Land might be specially placed under the lord's protection (ii, 152); the case is very obscure, and I confess that I do not clearly understand it.

FREE MEN AND VILLEIN LAND.

One of the most difficult questions in the history of our manorial system is that concerning the holding of copyholds by free men, and freeholds by men of villein status. So far as the present volumes are concerned, it would seem that, as a general rule, both free men and villeins were confined to their own class of land. Thus, A., against whom certain land had been recovered, went to the Earl, and complained that the land was "native land," and that the plaintiff was a free woman, and asked if the lord would allow his villein land to become hereditary in the hands of any free person. The lord thereupon caused A. to be re-seised of the land, because he was his "native" (ii, 81).

After land had been unoccupied for a long time, A., a free man, came and took it in Court; after his death it again was left unoccupied, and was granted to B. It was then claimed by A.'s heir, but his claim was disallowed on the grounds that B. had entry through the Earl, and that the heir was a free man while the land was villein land (ii, 82). The decision in this case was probably based on the lord's seizure and regrant.

A widow claimed as dower one-third of an acre of land. The defendant pleaded that the plaintiff was a free woman, and not a native, and that she did not reside within the fee, and therefore she ought not to have dower. The plaintiff was fined for a false claim (i, 306). Here, again, two reasons are given why the claim should not succeed, and it is by no means easy to assess their respective values. There were, apparently, some special customs regulating a widow's right to dower when she was not living within the manor (i, 242).

It is presented that R. is a clerk and the Earl's villein, inasmuch as his father was the Earl's native, yet he holds himself for a free man because he took free land with his wife in marriage (i, 120). At the next Court he admitted that he was a villein by birth, and gave 13s. 4d. as a recognition, and submitted to be thenceforth in the yoke of villeinage, paying 12d. a year (i, 125). We are not told what would happen if the heir of this self-confessed villein inherited the

b

free land. On the other hand, there are several cases quite incon-
sistent with those just cited.

A person gave 2s. for license to take a bovate of villein land and
4 acres of free land from the same person (i, 265). Here is a clear
sanction by the Court for the holding of free and villein land by the
same person. He was presumably a free man, for the following entry
seems to lay down the doctrine that free land made free men.

It was presented that J. was the Earl's villein, and yet held freehold
land in S.; he was to answer how and wherefore he went out from
villeinage into freedom (i, 116). No further details are recorded.

And the following, though not so explicit, apparently turns on the
same point:—

It was presented that a villein had bought a messuage with
buildings at Pontefract, a bovate of land with buildings at Barnsley,
and 3s. yearly rent at Skelmanthorpe (i, 242).

In another case A. B. gives 3s. for entry into a bovate of free
land and 12d. for license to take 4½ acres of native land; in each
case the previous tenant was A. B.'s father, who was still alive (i, 260).

THE VILLEIN TENANTS AND THEIR LAND.

The ordinary services of a copyholder were fealty, suit of court,
rents of assize, and heriots, all of which are found in the manor of
Wakefield. In addition to these were the customary services which
they owed for their lands; these will be dealt with later on.

The ordinary services mentioned above are all found in the manor
of Wakefield, and present no special features. The copyholder could
not do suit of court by an attorney, and the numerous fines for
default or for not coming no doubt refer in many cases to suit of
court. In most manors the copyholder could essoign as to suit, but
there is no clear instance of this in these rolls, and it may be
doubted if such a right was allowed by the custom of the manor.

Rents of assize are usually stated to be paid in respect of the
copyholds, but here we have a yearly payment to the lord which
seems to be more in the nature of an acknowledgment of villein
status by the individual (i, 116).

This payment is also called "the lord's aid" (ii, 81).

The degree of personal un-freedom attaching to villeins at this
period no doubt varied much in different manors. The subject is too
intricate to be discussed here, but I may point out the instances of
personal restriction (as apart from tenure) that we find in these rolls,

The principal and most irksome of these was that a villein could not remove either himself or his chattels from the manor without license. On several occasions pledges were exacted that chattels should not be removed (i, 252, 257). If the villein went away and refused to return, any chattels left in the manor could be seized, and he was liable to be arrested if found anywhere within the Earl's liberty (ii, 7).

Similarly, a villein's widow had to pay for license to remove (i, 256).

Villeins were not allowed to live in boroughs, and we have an interesting case of a villein who is presented for being a merchant of the borough of Wakefield (i, 131, 132).

A villein was not allowed to acquire land in another fee (i, 252), but he might have license to do so (i, 269).

An outsider wishing to settle in the manor had to obtain a license and pay a fee, and he might have to find pledges (i, 236).

A new man coming in paid 13s. 4d. to be under the protection of the Earl and bailiffs as to his land, and agreed to pay 6d. a year at the three terms usual in the Earl's fee (i, 116).

Another pays 12d. for license to enter the Earl's fee (i, 191).

If he came without license he was amerced (i, 212, 214; see also i, 203).

The case was the same where the outsider was marrying a female native; he paid a fee to come with his goods and chattels on to the Earl's land (ii, 192).

Might a man voluntarily become a villein? There is a case in 1286 which suggests this, but the proposition is full of difficulties. A. B. becomes the Earl's villein, and gives 2s. for license to marry C., daughter of D. E., and take her land to themselves and their heirs (i, 224). Apparently C. was the owner of copyhold land in her own right, and, as a native, she could not marry without the lord's consent. The difficulty lies with the intended husband. If he was already a villein it must have been on some other manor, and he must have obtained a license to remove, of which we have several examples in these rolls. But he may have been a free man, for instances are known of free men reducing themselves to the villein status.

The female villein was not allowed to marry without license; an infringement of this rule was punished by fine. The payment for such a license was called merchet, but the term is only once used in these rolls (i, 131), though the license to marry is common.

The widow of a villein apparently required a license to marry only if she wished to remove from the manor. Thus, a widow paid

3*s.* 4*d.* to marry off the lord's villein-land (ii, 168); another gave 4*s.* for license to remove from the Earl's land and to marry wherever she pleased (i, 256); a third gave 13*s.* 4*d.* for license to marry, to withdraw from the Earl's land, and to hold her dower so long as she did suit and service (ii, 49).

The special privilege with regard to the dower probably accounts for the large fine in the last case. An incoming widow paid only 2*s.* to have dower in her late husband's lands, on her finding pledges that she would bring her chattels on to the land, and would not live elsewhere without the Steward's license (i, 242).

A villein was distrained for selling his pigs, which he ought to have agisted (i, 240). It is difficult to say whether this refers to tenure or to personal status.

There is no "Custumal" of Wakefield Manor, that is, a code of customs, such as many manors possess; and so far as we have got, the rolls are very disappointing in their statements as to customs.

The most remarkable custom is that relating to the *legitimatio per subsequens matrimonium* (i, 212). This custom, as is well known, is the common law of Scotland at the present time.

As to legitimation of children born after troth plight but before marriage, in 1411 there was still a doubt whether troth-plight were not sufficient to legitimise the offspring. In vol. vi of *Papal Letters* (Rolls Series), page 210, is the following :—

3 id. April, 1411. To the Archbishop of Canterbury. Mandate, if he find to be true the statement made in the recent petition of Philip de Seint Martyn, clerk, of the diocese of Coutances,—viz. that the late Simon de Seint Martyn and the late Gillota Malcovenant contracted espousals, followed by copulation, but that before they proceeded to the solemnization of the marriage before the Church and before Philip was born, Simon died, wherefore Philip, who on account of the wars in those parts cannot with safety go to the ordinary, doubts whether an impediment of illegitimacy may not in future be brought against him—and if he find that there was no canonical impediment existing between Simon and Gillota at the time of the said espousals and copulation, or making it impossible for the marriage, had Simon lived, to be solemnized before the Church, to declare Philip legitimate and to have been procreated in lawful marriage.

In England the common lawyers appear to have rejected at an early date the rule of legitimation by subsequent marriage adopted by the Church, and this rejection was made definite by the Council of Merton (1236). Notwithstanding this rejection, it would appear from the Wakefield case that the rule of the Church still prevailed in that manor in the year 1286. There is a very able article by Sir Dennis FitzPatrick, K.C.S.I., on *Legitimation by Subsequent Marriage* in the *Journal of the Society of Comparative Legislation*, New Series, No. xiii. Reference also may be made to Maitland's *Canon Law in the Church of England*, chapter ii; Godolphin's *Repertorium Canonicum* (ed. 1680), chapter xxxv, "Of Bastards and Bastardy"; and the chapter on the same subject in Ayliffe's *Parergon Juris Canonici Anglicani*. See also Pollock & Maitland's *History of English Law*, i, 167 and 187; and ii, Book 2, chapter vii, on "Marriage."

Another custom of some rarity is that by which a father was heir to his son (i, 207). This did not become the general law of the land until the Wills Act of 1837.

A "custom of ploughing," a boon-work, was found by a jury in 1309; the jury found that a certain 12 acres owed 4*d.* a year for a whole plough and 2*d.* a year for half a plough (ii, 208). This is not very clear, but apparently it means that the custom of ploughing the lord's land had already been commuted for the money payment mentioned.

The copyhold tenants had to grind their corn at the lord's mill; it was therefore an offence to use hand-mills (ii, 8).

The villeins had to make the park pale (ii, 29).

The tenants, or some of them, were bound to collect "wood apples," *poma bosci*. These were real apples of some sort, perhaps crabs, for we are told that cyder was made from them (i, 252). A defaulter was fined 2*s.* (i, 258).

Driving the Wanlass. This custom consisted in driving the deer for the lord to shoot, "beating," as we should call it now-a-days. An interesting point was raised (i, 177) as to whether this custom could be exacted when the Earl himself was not present. Unfortunately there is no decision on the subject. There are two other instances, ii, 114, 177.

The tenants were not allowed to dig stones (i, 274) or coal (i, 268).

Swarms of bees belonged to the lord; if the tenant on whose land they were found wished to keep them, he had to pay their value to the lord (i, 293).

The lord was able by custom to grant the waste lands of the manor as copyholds; there are many grants of this "new land," as it was called. When essarted from the woods it was called "rodeland" (ii, 81).

The transfer of copyhold land is by surrender and admittance, that is, the tenant surrenders his holding to the lord, who admits the new tenant. As already stated, the earlier rolls do not record the transfer of copyholds in this form, and, with one exception, to be mentioned presently, it is not until we get nearly to the end of vol. ii that this becomes the common form of entry. I do not take this to mean that the form of transfer was in early times different from that of later times, but simply that the scribe who wrote the rolls deemed the simpler form of entry sufficient. The exception just referred to is in vol. i, p. 118. William son of Soignyf, being possessed of two bovates of land, had in open Court granted one to each of his sons; on the death of the father the sons pay relief, and the Steward grants seisin by the rod; the rod is described as being white at one end and black at the other, the white end being used for the lighter complexioned of the two brothers and the black end for the darker. The case is not very clear, but the action of the Steward and the use of the rod point to copyholds. However this may be, the fact of the rod being used at all seems to point to it as being the usual method for effectuating the surrender and admittance of copyholds. At a later date the tenants of copyhold land are sometimes referred to as "tenants by the rod."

A straw (attached to the writing of surrender) is now used in place of a rod, and surrenders may now be taken out of Court by any copyholder of the manor. The following is the formula:—

"You lift this surrender to me by this straw according to the custom of the manor of Wakefield for the purpose of passing (all your estate and interest in) the property comprised therein to the uses therein mentioned."

By the custom of the manor, a woman is entitled to her dower or freebench out of all copyhold lands of which her husband may have been seized in fee during the coverture, and whether alienated or not by the husband during his life, except with his wife's concurrence in the surrender, in which case the wife's right to freebench would be barred. It is necessary, however, for the wife in such case to be solely and separately confessed and examined by the Steward, apart from her husband, touching her knowledge of the surrender and her consent thereto. This was not always the practice, as appears by a case at the Court held 25th January, 7 Edward III (1333), of which the following is a note:—

ALVIRTHORP.—Alice formerly wife of Roger le Bordewright demands against Thomas son of Laurence, land, &c., in Alvirthorpe. Thomas says she can claim nothing, for she joined with her husband in surrendering the same in Wakefield Court. And the question is tried by a jury, who say that Roger (the husband) and Alice surrendered the land into the hands of John Attebarre the grave in Court, and he surrendered it into the hands of the Steward. Questioned as to whether Alice was examined by the Steward, or if it is the custom of the manor that she ought to be examined, they say no. It is therefore considered that Thomas shall go quit. Alice is in mercy for her false claim.

The custom, however, was quite clear, that a wife's dower (or freebench) could only be barred by her concurrence in the surrender. The following is a note of a case on the subject at a Halmote held at Wakefield on Wednesday after the feast of St. Swithin, 3 Edw. III (1328) :—

ALVIRTHORPE.—Margery formerly wife of Robert Gerbrod demands her dower in 10 acres at Alvirthorpe, sold by her late husband to John Attebarre, who resold to Adam le Bordwriht. Twelve jurors from four townships say that the custom of the manor is that from the time when any tenant by the rod sells or alienates any of the land so held, he is not responsible for any dower in such land so alienated, and cannot be called to warranty for livery of dower. Adam was to deliver her dower, because he then held the 10 acres.

In volume ii we find the common form, though it is never set out at full length, as it was in later times; A. surrenders to the lord to the use of B., who is thereupon admitted by the Steward.

Surrenders had to be made in Court; if made out of Court the surrenderor was fined (i, 279), or the land seized (ii, 188).

In a plea of land the plaintiffs alleged that the defendant had no entry save by a simple bargain made with their father out of Court, and without the lord's license, and that it was never surrendered in Court according to custom (ii, 100).

Where a man had taken land out of Court the lord apparently claimed the crop, and the purchaser paid a fine for entry (i, 162); he subsequently redeemed the crop (i, 176).

It was declared that a gift of [copyhold] land out of Court was invalid (i, 163), but a successful claimant on these grounds must make compensation for buildings erected and other expenses incurred by the purchaser out of Court (i, 164).

Any attempt on the part of a copyholder to alienate his land by charter caused a forfeiture. We have several cases of this. In one case (i, 88) a tenant sold certain native land by charter, and because he could not warrant it as free, according to his charter, without license of the Court, he was in mercy; he paid a fine of 6s. 8d., and was to possess his native land, that is, his copyholds, in peace thenceforward, without challenge. Nothing was said about the land attempted to be conveyed, but the grant was clearly void. Another case (i, 129) is a presentment by the jury on suspicion only; the parties are to be distrained to answer the charge.

Copyhold land might be voluntarily surrendered to the lord, and thereupon the liability of the tenant ceased in respect of it, and the lord could admit any one he pleased (i, 171).

It was forfeited for non-payment of the customary rent, or for non-performance of the services (i, 109). This is the explanation of the numerous cases of land "left waste on the lord." The other tenements of the same tenant were not affected (i, 275).

MISCELLANEOUS.

The following notes call attention to a variety of interesting entries which do not come under any of the foregoing headings.

Animals. Using animals without leave of the owner seems to have been fairly common. A complainant in 1286 alleged that the defendant had used four of his oxen in the Earl's hay wagon, and had also lent the plaintiff's mare to a third person to fetch salt from Manchester (i, 231). The salt would no doubt be from the Cheshire salt district.

Byrrelagh. A defendant charged with making an unlawful distress pleaded that he was distraining for a debt due to him by the judgment of the whole "Byrrelaghe" (ii, 48).

At a Halmote held at Brighouse on Wednesday after the Epiphany, 4 Edw. III (1330), Thomas son of Julian was in mercy for quitting the Halmote in contempt of the lord, and an inquisition found that the same Thomas allowed his cattle to graze in the herbage of the *Birefeld* contrary to the custom of *Bireleghe.* The Birefelds were the town fields or common fields, and were styled the Bierdoll fields (with some varieties of spelling) at Wakefield, Dewsbury, Elland, and Bierley. In the early rolls of Dewsbury Rectory Manor are many pains or bye-laws as to the Bierdoll fields in that manor.

Cattle. A. took a heifer from B., and was to have the milk and the calf; he used her for ploughing. He was ordered to give her back to the owner, and was fined 6*d.* (ii, 7).

The Earl's cattle were all marked with his mark (i, 97), and we find from a later entry that this was done by branding (ii, 37).

Church, Court held in (i, 148). The practice of using churches and churchyards for secular business must have been fairly common in the middle ages. Myrc's *Instructions for Parish Priests* (Early English Text Soc., vol. xxxi, p. 11, line 338) refers to it:—

> "Courte holdynge and suche maner chost,[1]
> Out of seyntwary put thow most;
> For Cryst hym self techeth us
> That holy chyrche ys hys hows,
> That ys made for no thynge elles
> But for to praye in, as the boke telles;
> There the pepulle schale geder with inne
> To prayen and to wepen for here synne."

The editor of that work, Mr. Edward Peacock, F.S.A., has an interesting note on the subject, from which I extract the following.

Games and other secular business were forbidden in churchyards by the Synod of Exeter, 1287 (Wilkins, *Concilia*, ii, 140). The holding of fairs and markets in churchyards was made illegal by the Statute of Winchester, 1285, 13 Edward I, c. vi. The practice, however, of using churches and churchyards for secular purposes continued to be common. Edward I received the oaths of the competitors for the Crown of Scotland in Norham Church. In 1326 the tythe corn of Fenham, Fenwick and Beele was collected in the chapel at Fenham, and at about the same period, when the monks of Holy Island found their grange would hold no more, they converted the chapel attached to their mance into a temporary tythe barn (Raine's *North Durham*, 82, 260). Law courts were held, books sold, and children taught in the porch of St. Peter's, Sandwich (Boys, *History of Sandwich*, 365). A manor court, called Temple Court, was held in the church of St. Mary and St. John Baptist, Dunwich, annually on the feast of All Souls (Gardner, *Dunwich*, 54).

Coal. It is interesting to note the use of coal in 1297, and, further, that it does not appear to have any distinctive name; it is simply "stone to burn." The offender sold it (i, 268).

---

[1] A.S. *ceást*, strife.

Common Fields. A good example of the difficulties attending the common field system occurs in vol. i, 261. A. having two bovates lying in scattered strips, sold one to B. and the other to C. C. complained that B. had taken the best strips. B. replied that he took what A. pointed out to him. The jury found for the plaintiff

Courts. A very interesting case is that against the Prior of Lewes (ii, 157). The jury at the Tourn at Halifax presented that the Prior was holding Courts there, sentencing the Earl's natives, appointing ale tasters, and generally acting as though he were lord of the liberty.

Crops. The heirs of a tenant claimed and recovered certain lands from the widow; on a dispute as to the right to the crops the jury found that the widow was entitled to the crop then on the land and to the next crop, on account of the benefit done to the land by the manure she had placed on it (i, 84).

A general rule was laid down with regard to crops, that an unsuccessful defendant in a claim for land should have any crops where he himself had sown the land (i, 148).

Game with Stones (i, 134). There is a reference to a similar game in Myrc's *Instructions for Parish Priests*. (Early English Text Soc., vol. xxxi, p. 11, line 330). The author is enjoining the proper use of church and churchyard, and forbidding the playing of games there:

> " Also wyth-ynne chyrche & seyntwary
> Do ry3t thus as I the say,
> Songe and cry and suche fare,
> For to stynte thow schalt not spare;
> Castynge of axtre & eke of ston,
> Sofere hem there to use non;
> Bal and bares and suche play,
> Out of chyrche3orde put a way."

The game mentioned in the text was probably some form of " Duck-stones"; a large number of references to this widely-spread game, with some description of how it was played in various parts, will be found in Wright's *Dialect Dictionary*, *s.v.* Duck.

Iron works. A certain amount of iron smelting was going on as early as 1284; Adam " le Blomer" of Heckmondwyke cut wood in Dewsbury Wood (i, 191), and his wife complained of a theft "at the forge in the great wood of Wakefield" (i, 212).

Mills. There is an interesting note of the letting of Soyland and Warley mills in 1307; the tenant paid only 40s. rent, but he was to repair the mills thoroughly, they being in bad condition (ii, 124).

A full account of the works at the mill and dam at Wakefield is given in 1308. The old mill was taken down and rebuilt, and the dam was remade (ii, 154).

The keeper of the windmill was presented for dealing falsely with the stones in order to steal the flour of the customary tenants; as he lived out of the fee, nothing was done (i, 129).

Oats. There is a curious case where the defendant is alleged to be bound in a certain quantity of oats and the profits thereof for ten years (i, 232). This is not very clear, but apparently the defendant had been set up with a stock of oats, which was to be repaid, with "interest" in kind, at the end of ten years.

Oven. A license to build a common oven was granted in 1298 (ii, 53). There must, one would think, have been an oven prior to this date; perhaps the license was for a second one.

Plebicite. With regard to the trespass of cattle in the common fields in close time, it would seem that the tenants had some power to assess damages without coming to the Court. This, at any rate, is the construction I place upon the curious entry respecting a sum of 5*d.* awarded *per communitatem plebiceti* (i, 279).

Pledges. If a horse was taken in pledge, the person taking it had no right to use it for his own purposes (i, 274).

Where a person had no money to pay a fine and could not find anyone as pledge, he or she (it is generally she) was allowed to deposit some chattel as security. There are instances of tunics, smocks, and coverlets thus deposited, and in one or two cases mere "promises" are recorded.

Ploughing. A case occurs of using a mare as part of a plough-team (i, 297).

Pontefract. The proximity of the Earl of Lincoln's important fee at Pontefract was a source of constant trouble. It must have been a great temptation to the lawlessly inclined, to make a raid in the enemies' territory and slip back over the border. The procedure in such cases probably varied with the state of local amenities at the moment. A bad feeling between the two Earls would account for a case like the following :—

The jury found that A. drew blood from B., in consequence of which B. lost his arm. But B. belonged to the Earl of Lincoln's liberty, "therefore nothing is done" (ii, 45).

At other times the respective Stewards seem to have been quite ready to help each other by arresting malefactors, or even by trying them.

When the jury found that A. had stolen an ox of the Countess of Lincoln's, he was ordered to be arrested (ii, 53).

A plea of trespass was adjourned until the Steward of Pontefract had been spoken with (i, 102).

Where the Earl of Lincoln's tenants had committed trespasses in the manor of Wakefield, an arrangement was made that they should be tried before the Steward of Pontefract (i, 104, 119).

Tithe. The Vicar of Halifax tried to extort more tithes from his parishioners than he was entitled to. He could legally claim one calf in ten, and it appears that by custom one was payable if there were only seven calves. He claimed one out of six, and apparently (for the text is not very clear) one out of every six. The Rector did likewise in the case of lambs, and the victims complained that they could get no remedy except through the Earl's bailiffs (i, 173).

Treasure trove. There is one case of this, but unfortunately no details are given (i, 131).

War. There are several cases of persons charged with returning from the Scotch war without license (i, 253, 257). It is difficult to see what this had to do with the Court of the manor, but there it is.

Words of Court, verba de curia or *verba curie* (i, 25 ; ii, 34). See *Select Pleas in Manorial Courts* (Selden Society, ii, 186, 187).

For the sake of saving space, a certain amount of compression has been used.

All essoigns are from suit of Court, unless otherwise stated, and the fact that this is "for the first time," or as the case may be, is omitted.

In transfers of land, a surrender to A. B., unless qualified, means "to A. B. and his heirs for ever."

In litigation, the commencement is always given, also essoigns ; but mere records of default, where the case is not advanced, are mostly omitted. These are fairly numerous.

The text has been prepared by Miss Stokes, and checked with the Rolls by myself. I have added a full Index of Subjects to both volumes.

The thanks of the Society are again due to the Countess of Yarborough, the Lady of the Manor.

As before, I have much pleasure in recording my obligation to Messrs. Stewart and Chalker, the Stewards of the Manor, to Mr. Gascoigne and Mr. Milner, and especially to Mr. S. J. Chadwick, F.S.A., for much kind assistance.

W. PALEY BAILDON.

LINCOLN'S INN.

APPENDIX.

NOTES AND OBSERVATIONS OF ANTIQUITIE CONCERNYNGE THE VACCARIE OF SALTONSTALL IN SOWERBYESHIER.

[Copied from an old MS. on parchment (? *temp.* James I), at the Rolls Office, Wakefield.]

Sowerbyshier was a severall Jurisdiction or Libertie within the Mannor of Wakefeilde, beinge in tymes paste accounted as a Forreste or Freechase; & replenished with deere; yt conteyned in it all those Towneshippes & Hamlettes which nowe be within the Leete or Turne Holden at Halifax. There was a Castell at Sowerbye & Courts kept there, but it is thought that the eldest Rooles be all burnied. But since the tyme of Kinge Henrie the Sixte the Courtes holden for Sowerbye have bene holden at Sandall & Wakefeilde.

This Sowerbieshier was parcell of the possessiones of the Earles of Warrenne & Surreye & there were diverse vaccaries therein, & namely these, Cromptonstall, Ferneside, Oversaltonstall, Nethersaltonstall, Hadershelfe, Baitinges & Mancanholes, all knowne by meates & boundes, at the which Cattell were norished and bredd, as may appeare as well by diverse surveyes hadd & taken in the tyme of the Earle Warrenne, & these vaccaries were in demesne to the said Earles under this title.

Tenementa que sunt in manu domini in dominico.

Oversaltonstall.

Anno regni Regis Edwardi filii Regis Edwardi Tertio. Apud Oversaltonstall est locus unius Vaccarie et sunt ibidem una parva domus in qua firmarius illius vaccarie solebat manere, una bovaria et una Grangia ad fenum imponendum et sunt ibidem triginta acre prati et pasture unde xv possunt falcari quolibet anno et xv acre iacent ad pasturam vitulorum. Et possunt ibidem sustineri unus taurus et triginta vacce cum vitulis de exitu si habeant hussetum in hyeme prostratum pro sustentacione eorundem. Et ille locus oportet includi quolibet anno cum bona sepe et illa sepes costabit Domino quolibet anno octo solidos, et si Dominus voluerit dimittere illum locum ad firmam potest dimitti per annum pro xl. s.

Netalsaltonstall [*sic*].

Apud Netalsaltonstall est quidam Locus qui potest sustinere in hyeme xxiiij averia et ibidem solebant averia ille [*sic*] sustinere in hyeme, et sunt ibidem xxx acre prati ad falcandum ad sustentacionem dictorum averiorum. Et in estate debent dicta averia removeri ab illo loco usque alium locum vocatum le Baitinges et ibidem sustinere in estate. Et plura averia possunt sustinere ibidem in eadem pastura ad valentiam unius marce per annum. Et si dominus voluerit dimittere ad firmam Locum de Netalsaltonstall potest dimitti ad firmam per annum ad xliij^s viij^d. Et si voluerit dimittere Locum de Baytinges ad firmam potest dimittere illum Locum pro xxvj^s viij^d.

In Rotulis Compoti Instauratoris de Sowerbyeshier tempore Ed. I. And the officers of these vaccaries were called *Instauratores* and did give their yearly accounts of the Revenues of their Cattell as the Graves did give of their Rents at every Audicte to the Officers of the Earlewarrenne.

These vaccaries were letten forth by copies to Tenantes & a yearly rent reservid, not by nomber of acres, but as parcells of grounds lyinge within knowne meates & lymites; & although the first grauntes thereof, by reason of the lacke of the Rooles, cannot be shewed, yeat it is easie to be sene by those copyes that followe that they never had contents of acres but of a lymitted boundary; and there is some of these copies yeat extaunte although the Rooles be perished.

It should seme that the first grauntes made by Copye of Saltonstall (which was in the latter end of the Reigne of Kinge Edward the Second as it should séeme) were made upon Divition of the whole into sex equall partes, & everye parte was called a sextondole of Saltonstall; & it seemeth by sundrie accountes that diverse of the surname of the Saltonstall were officers of the Earle Warrenne for Saltonstall, & to them was diverse partes thereof graunted.

Anno Domini 1343. Die Veneris proxime post festum Apostolorum Petri et Pauli anno xvij Ed. III.

Johannes de Brounehirste reddit in Curia duas partes sexte partis de Saltonstall una cum Revertione tertie partis dicte sexte partis que Isabella mater dicti Johannis tenet nomine dotis. Que concesse sunt, videlicet medietatem Johanni filio Thome de Saltonstall et aliam medietatem Ricardo filio Thome de Saltonstall et Willielmo de Saltonstall. Tenendum sibi et heredibus suis &c.

e Rotulis in Custodia Thome Talbott in Turri Londoniensi. Note that John, the last Earl Warrene, died in die Sabati in festo commemorationis Sancti Pauli anno 21 Ed. III, so that thereby it is manifest that the vaccarye of Saltonstall was demised by Copye before the Lordshippe of Wakefeild came to the possession of the Crowne.

Notes of Surrenders made of that parte of Saltonstall which was late Richard Saltonstall's,

Anno 6 Hen. IV. Ricardus Saltonstall sursum reddit duas sextas partes de Saltonstall et dimidiam sexte partis prout iacet inter Blakebrooke, Deyesclough, aquam de Luddingdene et Hoorestones cum pertinentiis in Sowerbye ad opus Ricardi Saltonstall et heredum suorum &c.

And by the same bounderies have all the copies ever since passid without any content or number of acres.

15 Ed. IV. For this Richard, 10 April, 15 Ed. IV, surrendered the same Landes by the same names & bounded as aforesaid to Gilberte Saltonstall, his sonn, &c.

Which Gilbert, 7 July, 23 Hen. VII, surrendered the same lands by the same names & bounderies to Richard Saltonstall, his sonn.

30 Hen. VIII. After the death of which Richard, sonn of Gilberte, Richard Saltonstall, sonn & heir of the same Richard, 21 April, 30 Hen. VIII, made fyne of Heriot for the same lands lyinge within the same bounderies.

40 Eliz. This last Richard had issue Gilberte, which Gilberte dyed in the lyfe of his father, haveinge issue Samuell, which Samuel, after the death of Richard his grandfather, made fyne of heriote for the same landes by the same name & boundaryes, viz.: 21 July, 40 Elizabeth, in whose laste fyne there is insertid theise wordes, "Salvo jure Domine Regine in eisdem si quid habet."

Wakefield Court Rolls.

ROLL FOR 25 AND 26 EDWARD I, 1297–8.

[NOTE.—This roll has a piece torn lengthwise off the right hand side, the damage extending about 12 inches down. The top of the roll has served as cover, so that the writing is in parts illegible.]

[COURT held on] Friday next after the Feast of S. Dionysius [the Areopagite] [Oct. 3rd], in the year abovesaid [1297].

Cartewrth mill is let to Jordan the Milner.

ESSOIGNS.—William and John Scot, William Herloc, Alan Almot, attorney of Lady Margaret de Nevill . . . . Richard de Stanley [?] . . . . The essoigners are Richard the Cobbler of Northmanton, Robert de Heton, Robert de Donecastre, Robert the Clerk of Sandale, and Thomas de Schipeden.

. . . .

Richard Suart . . . .

. . . . Jacke Blade v. Richard s. of Ivo, for seizing 2 cows, value 15s.

William de Locwode offers himself against Walter de Tofteclive [?], who is to be distrained.

Nicholas [?] de Caylli gives 8d. to have respite of suit of court until Michaelmas.

HIPERHOLME.—John Maufe v. Hugh de Presteley, for 7s 6d.,— 3s. for an over-tunic of cameline [de camelino], 2s. for a quarter of oats . . . . . 12d. for a heifer [juvenca] sold him in 21 Edw. I. Deft. fails to find surety for waging his law; he is fined 3d. as if undefended [?].

John Maunsel gives 6d. for license of concord with Magge wife of Richard the Pindere of Ossete.

SANDALE.—Robert de la Grene of Crigeliston v. Emma wife of Adam s. of Penne, for an old cart, which she sold him for 6d., which the Court assigns to him, fining her 6d. Pledge, John Monk.

. . . . Adam Gerbot sues John, his brother, saying that he demised him ½ acre of land for 6 years before he surrendered it to

A

Ed[usa] da. of Richard Broun, whereof Richard Gerbot . . . .
They refer to the verdict of Richard Gerbot. He confirms the plt.,
who is to recover; deft. fined 6*d*.

WAKEFEUD.—John son and heir of John Wytlof pays 6*d*. relief
on the land his father held in the Graveship of Thornes [*Spinetum*].
Pledge, Thomas s. of Henry.

THORNES [SPINETUM].—Adam s. of Walter gives 2*s*. for license to
take a bovate of land in Thornes [*Spinetum*] from John s. of John
Witlof, for . . . . . . years.

SANDALE.—William de Chyvet gives 2*s*. for license to take a
bovate of land in le Neubigg' from Robert s. of Adam de Neubi[gg'],
for ever. Pledge, John Monk.

. . . . William the Milner *v*. Alexander s. of Adam the Milner,
for trespass. Pledge, John le Barn.

William de Coppeley, distrained for trespasses in Soureby Forest
by 20*s*. owed him by Robert Talvace, was called upon at each Court
last year to come and make satisfaction, etc.; but refused to come.
The said 20*s*. is therefore to be levied from said Robert Talvace.
Pledges, John de Trimigham, Peter Swerd, Hugh the Carter of
Horbiry, and John de Heptonstall.

Ralph brother of Thomas de Hopton to be attached for arresting
a person within the Earl's liberty by night, and taking him to the Earl
of Lincoln's liberty.

Henry de Lepton's tenement is in the Earl's hand because he is
dead. John, his son and heir, pays 8*d* relief; he is now 12 years
old, a frank-farmer [*francus firmarius*], and pays 12*d*. for respite of
suit of Court till he is of age.

STAYNELANDE.[1]—All Thomas de Thorneton's tenants in Staynland
give 2*s*. for help to levy the rent of the said Thomas, their lord, on
all his tenants everywhere in the Earl's fee. Pledges, William del
Helywell and Henry Fraunceis.

A stray heifer [*juvenca*] was delivered to Hugh de Lictheseles, the
lord's pewterer [*stannarius*], and the bailiff presents that Elias s. of
Ivo de Werloweley took it out of the lord's keeping, and sold it.
He is attached by William, his brother.

SANDALE.—Elias and Maude de Wadethorp [?] give 12*d*. for
license to take half the land in that place, formerly held by their
father and mother, from John Munk and Alice his wife, for ever.
Pledge, Robert the Clerk.

---

[1] Added in a later hand.

John Munk has license to take a small piece of meadow at *le Fulewell* and another at Sandalker for his life, from the said Elias and Maude, who are to do service.

John de Thornhill gives 4s. for respite of suit till Michaelmas. Robert de Hoderode, the like.

HOLNE.—Elias At-well [*ad fontem*] is fined 6*d.* for breaking the branches of an oak, etc.

Thomas Warin, Robert Strik, Adam s. of Nelle, William s. of Richard, Adam s. of Nelle de Scoles, Thomas de Berniclif, and William Strekeys, fined for the like.

Cicely de Honlay, for escape of a horse, 6*d.* Pledge, Simon de Holne.

Adam de Dalton, Thomas s. of Roger, Hugh de Cartewrth, Adam del Dounes, Richard del Dounes, Margery da. of Geoffrey, Alice da. of Luke, and Joan wife of Hugh, 3*d.* each, for collecting nuts.

SOURBY.—Adam s. of Robert del Lone, Alice and Ellota daughters of Henry de Holgate, Magota wife of Ivo del Hole and Nalle his sister, Maude wife of the Fuller, Alice da. of Eve de Northland, and the daughter of Maude de Stockes, fined for the like. Pledges, John s. of Jordan and Adam Migge.

HIPERUM.—John de Bristall, for vert, 6*d.* Pledge, Walter de Eurum.

John del Wytehill, the like. Pledge, Richard de Bosco.

Richard de Bosco, for a branch blown down by the wind, 3*d.*

William Swyer, Peter de Sutheclyf, John de Astay and Henry de Coppelay, fined for escape of pigs. Pledge, John del Rede.

TOURN there the Sunday following, etc. [1297].

JURORS.—Robert de Wyrumthorp, Baudewyn de Seyvill, Thomas de Wyttelay, William de Dewysbyry, Maurice de Eckeleshill, John de Toftclyf, Michael de Flocketon, Robert de Wodehusme, German s. of Philip, John de la Sale, Henry Eril, and Henry de Swynlington.

Richard Broun of Heton does not come, because he is on the Earl's service.

Ellen wife of Hugh Jordan of Normanton brewed weak beer, fine 6*d.*

Peter Shepherd [*bercarius*], Parson of Emmelay, and Henry the Milner of Emmelay, drew blood from one another. Henry fined 6*d.*, and both to be attached.

Henry de Wilkeshesik of Bretton, and Robert Aleyn are fined 6*d.* for not coming.

The said Robert is a baker, and does not take a weight from anyone [? *qui non capit pondus aliquo*]; fine 6*d.*

Agnes wife of William Burnell, the like, 6*d.*

Thomas Saunfayl, fined 6*d.* for not coming.

Amabel Quen of Bretton and John Batty, for brewing weak beer, fines 6*d.* and 3*d.*

Robert, for the like, three times, 6*d.*

William s. of William, Peter his son, and Thomas Luvecok of Bretton, were sworn and did not present these defaults; fines 3*s.*

Richard s. of Broun of Alverthorpe took one of Adam Gerbode's sheep and cut off its ears.

Maude widow of Gerbode, for marrying without license, 12*d.*

John With-the-hounds [*cum canibus*], for marrying his daughter without license, 6*d.*

Adam Brodto is attached for petty larcenies of geese and fowls.

Alice daughter of Henry Sampson of Gildusme broke into the barn of Master John, Rector of the Schools [*Rectoris Scolarum*] of Wakefeud, at Toftclyf, and stole 16 fleeces [*pelles lanutas*]. She is to be arrested.

John de Toftclyf's wife drew blood from Michael Dodeman, fine 2*s.*

After the affray between John Scot of Dewysbyry and Roger the Fuller of Mirfeud,[1] several men, viz. Adam de Hopton, Henry s. of Sir John de Heton, Matthew le Hunte, Henry the Porter, and others unknown, came with Roger the Fuller, broke open the door of William the Fuller of Dewysbyry, and searched his house; they then went to Wodekirk, and searched the house of Stephen the Shepherd [*bercarius*], where they found William Scot, and wounded him, etc. They are to be attached.

The wife of William the Clerk of Dewysbyry, for weak beer, 3*d.*

Agnes de Bretton unjustly raised the hue after Henry de Swynlington for carrying away corn which he had sown on land that she claims, which is the Earl's villein-land. She is to come before the Steward.

Robert the Tailor [*cissor*] justly raised the hue after Lance s. of Symon, for following Robert from Westgate to his lodging [*ospitium*], and felling him with a stick in front of the door; Robert drew blood from Lance in defending himself, cutting his foot with a sword whilst he lay on the ground.

---

[1] Vol. i, pp. 302, 303, 305.

William Wlmere raised the hue without reason on William de Castelford, John le Boteller, and John de Fery, for distraining on him for a common amercement imposed on all the town.

Gilbert the Tinckeler raised the hue justly on John the Coupere, for wounding him in the head with a sword.

Amice Ragge habitually raises a cry and hue at night, without cause, to the constant annoyance of all the neighbours.

COURT at Birton on Monday after the Feast of St. Wilfrid [Oct. 12th], in the year of King Edward abovesaid [1297], and in the time of the aforesaid [Steward].[1]

HOLNE.—Magge wife of Warin sues William son of the Grave for ⅓ of a bovate of land, as her dower. Deft. says that she has no claim to dower therein, because Matthew,[2] her former husband, lost the land under an inquisition before Alexander Lucas, then Steward, and he refers to the Rolls, which prove it to be the case. Her fine is forgiven, because she is poor.

Juliana widow of William the Milner gives 12d. for help to recover her dower in 9 acres of land from Hugh s. of Richard. He is present, and agrees to give it her. She does service, etc., therefor. Pledge, John s. of Hugh de Littlewode.

Marg[aret] widow of Nicholas s. of Hugh pays 6d. to recover dower in 6 acres from the said Hugh, who consents, etc.

Robert de Mirefeud sues Peter de Rodewode for trespass. Pledge, William de Castelford. Plt. says that the deft. had agreed with him to mow his meadow for a week at 3d. a day; deft. says that the arrangement was for one day only, on which day he did not come; he is to pay damages, fine 3d. Pledge, Thomas de Billeclif.[3]

Elias de Schelf admits owing Diota da. of Matthew de Gris (represented by Thomas s. of Fernhoule), 2s. 9d. Pledge, John s. of Richard del Rodes. Fine 12d.

Gilbert de Alstanley sues John de Holne for carrying away his hay and corn, etc. An inquisition is ordered for the next Court at Wakefield.

---

[1] Probably John de Doncaster; see vol. i, p. 288, and *post*, Court held on May 2nd.

[2] Warin *struck out.*

[3] This case is very obscure. I suggest that the action was of the class known at a later date as "trespass on the case." Apparently the defendant had undertaken to mow the plaintiff's meadow, and had failed to do so.

Thomas de Meltham gives 6*d* for an inquisition as to whether
Gilbert de Alstanley and Adam de Cartewrth were pledges for William
le Parmenter for 22*s*. on account of cattle sold him. An inquisition
finds that they were not.

An inquisition finds that John de Thwong struck Richard de
Thwong, and broke the heads of Hugh del Hole and Adam
Strekayse. He must pay damages, and 3*d*. fine for each offence. It
is found that they assaulted him only in self-defence, so he is fined 3*d*.
for false claim. Pledge, Thomas Ferenhoule.[1]

TOURN there the same day.

JURORS.—Henry de Schelfley, John de Ryley, Henry de Birton,
Robert s. of Malle de Schepeley, John Wyther, John s. of Quenilda,
Adam de Heley, Adam Cusin, Thomas Brid, Richard s. of Robert de
Thwong, Hanne s. of the Grave, and Nicholas Keneward.

HOLNE.—Christiana de Ecclisley, Emma le Baggere, Alice Fox,
Magota de Birton, Matthew Marsh's wife, William Skinner's wife,
Thomas Ferenhoule, Maude da. of Thomas, Peter le Breus, Robert
s. of Molle, Adam s. of Emma, and Robert del Scoles, brew and sell
contrary to the assize. Fined 6*d*. each.

Robert del Merse drew blood from Margery, mother of the
chaplain. To be attached.

Adam Strekayse, the like from John de Thwong, 6*d*.

Robert Stirk, the like from John del Dam, 6*d*.

John Birstall gives 6*d*. to take a bovate of waste land in
Uverthwong, which is one rood short; he is therefore to have a rood
that Ric. Don left unoccupied on the Earl's hands, until that land is
taken by someone else. To hold to him and his heirs for ever.
Pledge, Richard de Thwong.

COURT at Rastrick on the Tuesday following, etc.

John Fox comes and wages his law on behalf of Adam his son,
and goes quit.[2]

An inquisition of the neighbours finds that Thomas de Hopton
is guilty of the charge against him.[2] Fine 6*s*. 8*d*. Pledges, John Fox
and Henry de Fekesby.

---

[1] See vol. i, p. 304.   [2] See vol. i, p. 308.

RASTRIK.—Alexander s. of Adam the Milner gives 6d. for license of concord with Richard Knot in a plea of trespass. His fine for the like with William the Milner is pardoned, because he is poor.

Ellen da. of Maude de Fekesby sues Henry de Fekesby for a tenement in Fekesby, formerly held by Peter de Fekesby as her inheritance; an inquisition finds that Peter was a bastard, and therefore she has no right in the same. The tenement is taken into the lord's hand till enquiry be made how Henry had entry.

John le Barn, attorney of Thomas his son, v. Henry s. of Thomas, for impounding his sheep. Deft. says he is a freeman, and not obliged to answer in this Court. He is to come to the next Court at Wakefield.

A quarter of a bovate of land, left on the Earl's hands by Celia [sic] da. of Richard de Thothill, is granted to Richard de Thothill till the said Cecilia [sic] comes; if she does not come, to hold to him and his heirs. Fine for entry 6d. Pledge, Adam the Grave.

An inquisition finds that Matthew de Thohill [sic] harnessed to a plough a heifer [juvenca] which he took from Malina de Fekesby for first issue [pro primo exitu], viz. milk and calf; she is to have the heifer back again, as he used her for labour, and he is fined 6d.

HIPERUM.—William s. of Nalke, the Earl's villein [villanus], left the Earl's land, and would not return with his chattels; and an acre of oats he had sown on Henry de Hiperum's land was taken into the lord's hand by the Serjeant of the Liberty. This was sold by William del Both, the Grave, for 2s., without leave. He is to account for the 2s., and is fined 12d.

RASTRIK.—A hog, sow and 2 young pigs [porcelli], thought to be strays, are in the custody of Adam Fraunceis of Staynland. Further enquiry is to be made, and he is to bring them to the next Court at Wakefield.

————

TOURN there the same day.

JURORS.—John de Querneby, John le Barn, John le Flemeng, Thomas de Dalton, Alexander del Frith, John the Clerk of Hertesheved, John de Percy, John del Rode, Adam de Locwode, John de Locwode, Henry de Hiperum, and John de la Haye.

HIPERUM.—Richard Boton drew blood from Henry de Wycthon [?].

RASTRIK.—John de Barkesey, the like from John s. of John de Barkesey, fine 6d.

HIPERUM.—Richard Boton and Maude, his mother, the like from Adam s. of Ivo.

Geoffrey the Colyer raised the hue after William the Grave of Hiperum, for distraining him in 6*d*. in which he was amerced for his cattle found in the Earl's wood, where he had no common.

Eva del Brok has hand-mills [*molas manuales*] to the prejudice of the lord; they are to be taken into the Earl's hand; she is attached to answer therefor at the next Court at Wakefield. Fine 6*d*.

COURT at Halifax on Wednesday following, etc.

Adam de Hudresfeld gives 3*s*. for help to recover two cows which were in the custody of Hugh de Lictheselis. Pledge, John de Querneby.

Soureby. John de Miggeley *v*. William Wiltibigche; pledge, Roger Rotel. He says that Eva, his [deft.'s] wife, sold him a calf and the milk of a cow for 2*s*., and then took the calf and impounded it. An inquisition find for the plt., fine 6*d*. Pledge, William the Grave.

Thomas le Crouder and Malina de Horton recovered ⅓ of a bovate of land in Soureby from Robert s. of William de Saltonstal, as dower. They are two terms' rent in arrear. Being asked whether they wished to hold it any longer, they come before the Steward and say they do not. William [*sic*] may hold in peace.

William le Vacher and Juliana, his wife, *v*. John de Miggeley, say that he is ousting them from a rood of land, with buildings, in Soureby, which belongs to them and the heirs of Juliana. John says that his brother, who was the right heir of the said land, sold it to him. An inquisition is called of the neighbours, viz. Hugh de Lictheseles, Richard s. of Thomas, Richard Hodde, Hanne de Ludingden, Hannecok de Soland, Roger s. of Amabel, Thomas Lilie, John s. of Richard, Richard s. of Alice, Nelle the Milner, Hanne s. of William, and William s. of Thomas, who say that Juliana, mother of the plt. Juliana, acquired the said land before Robert Wade married her, and that Juliana, the plt., is the right heir; she is therefore to recover seisin. John is fined 6*d*. Pledge, William the Grave.

Saltonstall.—William s. of Thomas de Saltonstall gives 5*s* to take 1½ bovates of land in Saltonstall (bought by the Earl from Sir John de Horbiry) to himself and his heirs for ever, at 7*s*. 5*d*. rent. Pledge, Richard de Saltonstall. And if it be found that the rent was higher in Sir John de Horbiry's time, he will pay more.

Richard de Saltonstall gives 5*s*. to take 2½ bovates of the same land, at 9*s*. 11*d*. rent.

ALVIRTHORPE.—Malle widow of Gerbot *v.* William s. of John Hoskel, for debt. Pledge, Philip the Grave.

William s. of John *v.* the said Malle, regarding an agreement. Pledge, John s. of Walter de Flanshowe.

TOURN there the same day.

JURORS.—Henry de Rissewrth, Richard del Dene, Thomas de Langefeud, William de Herteley, William de Stodley, Richard de Waddeswrth, John de Haldewrth, Thomas de Connhall, John de Wylley, Hugh s. of Reyner, John the Harpur, and Hugh s. of Nalle de Northland.

SOUREBY.—Thomas s. of Michael de Hillingwrth is obstructing a way that used to be open in open times.

John s. of John de Holgate drew blood from John Stebing. Fine 6*d.*

Maude wife of the Fuller was indicted for stealing, and is now a resident; she is therefore to be attached. She afterwards broke open a box [*huchia*] and stole 6*d.*

A box [*huchia*] was stolen from William the Milner's house, and found in the house of Nicholas de Werloweley, who is to be attached.

William s. of Agnes drew blood from John s. of John de Halifax. He is pardoned by the Steward.

Juliana wife of Thomas of the Hall, the wife of Gilbert, and of Jordan Spini, brewed and sold beer contrary to the assize. Fines 6*d.* each.

John de Tofteclyve *v.* Walter, his brother, for trespass. Pledge, William de Locwode.

Thomas de Schepeley *v.* Thomas de Hopton, for trespass. Pledge, Henry the Serjeant. He is attached by Henry de Schelfley.

Thomas de Hopton *v.* Thomas Badde of Schepeley, for debt. Pledge, John Fox. He is attached by Thomas de Schepeley.

THORNES.—Richard Gerbot *v.* Philip Wlf, for debt. Pledge, Philip de Mora.

Matthew de Bosco *v.* Thomas de Coppeley, for trespass. Pledge, William son in law of the Chaplain.

SANDAL.—Agnes widow of Thomas Erneburg *v.* Thomas s. of Thomas Pelle [?], for trespass. Pledge, Robert de Donecastre. He is attached by John the Grave.

HOLNE.—Nicholas Keneward *v.* Adam s of Adam de Wlvedale, for heymsoken and assault. Pledge, William s. of the Grave. He is attached by Jordan the Milner. Nicholas also sues Adam s. of Nelle de Wlvedale, Thomas s. of Warin, and John, his brother, for the like. Attached by Adam Cusin.

John Warin *v.* Nicholas Keneward, Nicholas, John, John,[1] and Adam, his sons, for assault. Pledge, Adam Cusin.

Peter del Peck sues Robert Strike for the like. Pledge, John Waryn.

Thomas Warin and John, his brother, *v.* Adam del Scoles, for the like. Pledge, Adam Cusin. He is attached by John del Scoles.

COURT there[2] on Friday after the Feast of All Saints [Nov. 1] in the year abovesaid, etc. [1297].

ESSOIGNS.—Maude de Birstall, from suit of Court by Robert the Cobbler. Pledge, Robert de Mirefeud.

John de Trimigham, the like, by Richard the Serjeant. Same pledge.

Alan Almod, attorney of Lady Margaret de Nevill, the like, by William de Mirefeud. Same pledge.

Edmund le Normaund, the like, by John Patrik. Pledge, John de Haldewrth.

Richard de Staneley, the like, by Robert de Ledes. Pledge, John de Flemeng.

William de Schipeden, the like, by Thomas de Schipeden. Pledge, Robert de Wyrunthorpe.

John de Crosland, the like, by John Gurdon. Pledge, John de Haldewrth.

Thomas de Thorneton, the like, by John s. of Hugh. Pledge, Robert de Wyrunthorpe.

William Scot, deft., against Roger the Fuller, in a plea of trespass, by William de Locwode. Pledge, John de Tofteclive. The same William, plt. against the same Roger, by John Patrike. Pledge, William de Locwode.

John Scot and William Herloc against the same Roger, by Richard de Wlvedale and John de Tofteclyve.

John Calf against Robert the Harpur, by John Patrik. Pledge, Henry Calf.

---

[1] Written on an erasure.　　[2] *Sic ;* but probably at Wakefield.

Richard Suart against Richard de Sausemer, by Richard de Erdesley. Pledge, Robert de Wyrunthorpe. Also against Adam s. of Wymark de Erdesley, by Elias de Ossete, his father. Pledge, John de Tofteclyve.

Nicholas de Bateley, against the same Adam, by Richard de Erdeslawe. Pledge, Robert de Wyrunthorpe.

Thomas Badde against Thomas de Hopton, by Henry de Schelfley. Pledge, Thomas de Schepeley.

William de Locwode and Walter de Tofteclyve have a love-day.

Thomas de Schepeley, plt. against Thomas de Hopton, makes his statement against him not in the manner prescribed in the words of the law; so the deft. goes quit, and plt. fined 6d.

Adam le Corker brought an ox for sale to Wakefield market, the Friday after Michaelmas, and Adam de Gildeste [Gildstead] claimed [quesivit] the ox, for which he [Adam le Corker] was arrested, and has been in prison ever since. Adam [de Gildeste] now comes and charges him [Adam le Corker] with stealing the ox. The prisoner submits to the jurors named below, who acquit him. Adam de Gildestede [sic] is fined 3s. 4d. for a false claim.

Amabel of the parish of Gisburn, arrested on suspicion of [stealing] a carpet [tapeti] and other things, submits to the verdict of John de Haldewrth, Adam Hod, William del Okes, Richard de la Haye, John de la More, Peter Swerd, Robert de la Grene of Ossete, Adam Fraunceys, Henry Fraunceys, William de Hiperum, Robert del Westwode, and William del Heliwell, who say that she stole the goods, valued at 8½d., and because she is not bound to bear sentence for so much money [quia non tenetur ferre judicium pro tanta pecunia] she goes quit.

William de Hiperum, charged that he ought to have sent for a dog outside the Earl's liberty, to follow the blood which the said William found in Hiperum wood, admits that he did not. An inquisition is ordered for Rastrik Tourn.

SKYRECOTES.[1]—Matthew de Bosco v. Thomas de Coppeley, says that when his cattle were going to his common pasture in Coppeley-rodes, in the bounds of Skirecotes, Thomas drove 6 oxen and 5 cows to his manor [manerium] in Coppeley, and kept them there till delivered by the Earl's sworn bailiff, viz. the Grave of Soureby. He claims 100s. damages. Deft. says that the seizure was made because the cattle were grazing on his land sown with corn. An inquisition is ordered.

---

[1] In a later hand.

Adam Fraunceis of Staynland does not produce the two pigs at this Court, as ordered; he and his pledge, William de Heliwell, fined 2s.

SOUREBY.—Elias s. of Ivo pays 2s. to be in peace regarding a heifer concerning which he was charged. Pledge, William s. of Ivo.

SOUREBY.—The Grave of Soureby is to produce at the next Court a russet super-tunic, now in the custody of John de Stansefeud.

SANDAL.—Hugh Tubbing gives 12d. to take a bovate of land from Adam Tubbyng, his father, for ever. Pledge, John the Grave.

SOUREBY.—John le Baggere pays 13s. 4d. to be quit of the trespasses imputed to him in Soureby forest. Pledge, Alan s. of William de Heptonstall.

SANDALE.—William de Ossete gives 12d. for license to marry Ybbota del Overhalle of Sandale. Pledge, Robert the Clerk.

Peter the Shepherd gives 6d. for leave to buy a house from Geppe Strok, and to put it up [edificandi illam] at Milnethorpe. Pledge, John Monk.

STANLEY.—William s. of Adam Cote, for wood sold, 12d. Pledge, Hugh Kay.

Adam Spink, for vert, 4d. Pledge, Richard, his brother.

Nicholas de Bately, for vert, 12d. Pledge, John Thorald.

Adam Bullok, for an escape, 1d. Pledge, Philip Yssabell.

John s. of Philip de Wyrenthorpe, for nuts, 4d. Pledge, Roger Bele.

John Yssabell, for an escape, 3d. Pledge, Philip Yssabell.

Elias le Vacher of Rothewell, the like, 6d. Pledge, Richard del Bothem.

Richard del Bothem, the like, 1d. Pledge, John Cort.

WAKEFEUD.—The son of Richard s. of Hanne, for wood, 1d. Pledge, John s. of Sibbe.

Robert Dammesone, for vert, 2d. Pledge, Adam Gerbot.

Walter Apecok, for an escape, 6d. Pledge, Adam Hod.

SANDALE.—William de la Grene, for a purpresture on the Earl, 6d. Pledge, Robert de la Grene. The ditch [fossatum] to be destroyed.

The same William, for vert, 4d.

Richard s. of Hugh de Crigeliston, for an escape, 2d.

Henry North, the like, 2d. Pledge, Thomas s. of Bate.

OSSETE.—Adam Brown, the like, 2d. Pledge, Richard le [sic] Sausemer.

Robert del Wro of Horbiry, for wood, 2d. Pledge, Adam Tersy.

THORNES.—Thomas Vyrun, the like, 2d.   Pledge, Thomas the Smith

STANLEY.—The Grave of Rothewell, for putting 4 pigs to feed in the great wood without paying for them [*sine agistamento*], 12d. Pledges, Robert de Flansowe and Symon Tyting.

John Page's wife, for two pigs, 6d.   Pledge, Robert Estrild.

Richard the Forester's wife, for a sow and 6 young pigs, 6d. Pledge, Henry de Swynlington.

William the Stranger [*extraneus*],[1] for one pig, 3d.   Pledge, Richard le Lepore.

William de Lundo [?], for three hogs, 6d.   Pledge, Henry Schorthose.

Robert le Wyte of Metheley, for a pig and a little pig, 6d. Pledge, Hugh Skayf.

HOLNE.—William Strekayse, for an escape, 4d.   Pledge, John the Grave.

Thomas the Smith of Schepeley, the like, 1d.   Pledge, Nicholas s. of Nicholas.

Alice widow of William de Cardoil v. John Mollan and Robert de Wodhusme, for debt.

ALVIRTHORPE.—Malle widow of Gerbot v. William s. of John Hoskel, for 8d. he owes her according to the will of Gerbot, her husband.   The executors of Gerbot are called, and say that Gerbot forgave him the 8d. during his lifetime.   She is fined 3d.

Richard Gerbot gives 12d. for license to marry Margery, his daughter.   Pledge, Philip the Grave.

William s. of John is pardoned his fine for a false claim against Malle widow of Gerbot, because he is poor.

Richard Gerbot v. Philip Wlf, for 12d.; he acknowledges the debt and is fined 3d.

Robert s. of Symon v. Hugh s. of James, and Henry his son, for trespass; Hugh gives 3d. for license to agree.

THORNES.—Malina Lyleman v. Philip Wlf, for ⅓ of a rood of land as dower; he says that William Lyleman, her late husband, demised him the land for 6 years, for a sum of money paid; and it seems to him that Thomas, his son, ought to warrant the land for that term. Judgment accordingly.   Malina is to recover her dower from her said son.

SANDALE.—Beatrice widow of Payn de Crigeliston v. William de Colley, for ousting her from her dower in a toft and 18 acres of

---

[1] Or perhaps Le Strange, as a surname.

land in Crigeliston. He says that she is dowered therein under an agreement made between them in the presence of the neighbours, conditionally on her removing a house from that toft into another, he making the walls of the said house, and she giving him an acre of land, because he was bound to give her dower out of the whole land, and not out of any particular part of it. [? ; *per sic quod ipse deberet eam dotare semper versus solem integre et non particulariter.*] An inquisition is called of the neighbours, viz. Thomas s. of Robert, Thomas s. of Thomas Pelle, Robert de Donecastre, Thomas de Holgate, Robert s. of John, and John Cukewald, who confirm William. Beatrice is fined 3*d.*

STANLEY.—Thomas de Ludham gives 6*d.* to take all the arable and meadow land in Wyrunthorpe, held as dower by Margery widow of Adam Bulloc, for the term of her life, paying her 12*d.* a year, and doing service, etc.

Robert Daneis gives 18*d.* to take a bovate of land in Wodehalle from John Hockbeggere for ever.

SANDALE.—Agnes widow of Thomas Erneburg gives 6*d.* to agree with Thomas s. of Thomas s. of Penn. Pledge, John the Grave.

THORNES.—John Malin is elected Warrener of Thornes.

STANLEY.—Adam Nacke, elected Grave, gives 6*s.* 8*d.* not to be Grave this year.

ALVIRTHORPE.—Henry le Nunne *v.* William Attebarre, for trespass. Pledge, Robert s. of Ralph de Uchethorpe.

Alice widow of William de Cardoil *v.* John Mollan and Robert s. of Henry de Wodusme, for debt. Pledge, John de Donecastre.

ALVIRTHORPE.—Emma da. of Alexander Waltheu *v.* Mariota Bele, for trespass. Pledge, Adam Gerbot. Deft. attached by Roger le Bele.

SANDALE.—John le Permenter of Sandale *v.* William de la Grene, for trespass. Pledge, William de Castelford. Deft. is attached by Thomas s. of Bate.

William s. of William le Vacher and William de la Grene bring cross suits against one another for trespass.

All suits at the Tourns are adjourned until the coming of the Steward.

———

COURT there on Friday, the Eve of St. Andrew the Apostle [Nov. 30], in the year abovesaid, etc. [1297].

ESSOIGNS.—John le Flemeng, from suit of Court, by Richard the Serjeant. Pledge, John de la More.

Edmund le Normaund, the like, by Henry Waryn. Pledge, Peter Swerd.

John s. of John de Haldewrth, the like, by John del Stones. Pledge, Thomas de Thorneton.

Matthew de Bosco against Thomas de Coppeley, by William de Lyvereshcgge. Pledge, Thomas de Northland.

Thomas de Hopton against Thomas Badde, by Elias de Birton. Pledge, Robert de Mirefeld. And Thomas Badde by Roger the Fuller of Mirefeld. Pledge, Richard de Sausemer.

Walter de Tofteclyve against John his brother, by Adam s. of Wymark de Erdeslowe. Pledge, Richard de Sausemer.

William Scot gives 2s. to agree in two pleas with Roger the Fuller. Pledges, John de Tofteclive and Richard de Sausemer.

John Scot fined 2s. for refusing to wage his law against Roger the Fuller. He is to pay damages.

William Herloc wages his law and goes quit. Roger the Fuller is fined 12d. for a false claim. Pledge, William de Castelford.

Robert le Harpur gives 6d. to agree with Henry Calf and John his son. Pledge, Robert de Hegrod.

Richard de Sausemer v. Richard Suart, for assaulting him in a place called Wodehusknol, within the bounds of Erdeslowe, and for knocking him on the head with a bow so that he fell down. Deft. denies it, and is ordered to wage his law. Pledge, Robert de Wyrunthorpe. Damages claimed, 40s. Plt. sues Adam Wymark for striking him with a sword on the same occasion.

Adam Wymark v. Nicholas de Bateley, for assault at the same time and place, and for carrying off his bow and arrows, worth 2s. He claims 100s. as damages. Deft. holds that he is not obliged to answer the complaint, because plt. has charged him with two offences, one of which may be true and the other false, and therefore seeks judgment. Plt. says one of the actions arose out of the other. The matter is respited until the next Court.

Matthew de Bosco v. Thomas de Coppeley, for seizing cattle. Pledge, Robert s. of William de Saltonstall.

HOLNE.—Nicholas Keneward gives 18d. to agree with Adam s. of Adam de Wlvedale, Adam s. of Nelle, Thomas s. of Waryn, and Thomas [sic], his brother.

John Waryn gives 2s. to agree with Nicholas Keneward and his sons.

Robert Stirk gives 2s. to agree with Peter del Peek.

John Waryn and Thomas Waryn give 2s. to agree with Adam de Scoles.

ALVIRTHORPE.—German Swerd *v.* John Schirlok, for debt. Pledge, William the Clerk.

Richard Gerbot *v.* William s. of John Hoskel, for trespass. Pledge, Philip Thorald.

HOLNE.—John s. of John de Holne gives 12*d.* to agree with Gilbert de Alstanley. Pledge, Henry the Grave.

Sir William le Flemeng made default. William de Locwode, his attorney, appeared ; therefore he goes quit.

SANDALE.—William de la Grene gives 18*d.* to agree with John le Parmenter and William s. of William le Vacher (twice). Pledge, Thomas s. of Pelle.

ALVIRTHORPE.—Hannecok le Nunne *v.* William Attebarre, for seizing his cattle and wrongfully demanding 4*s.* rent of him, for he owes him nothing. An inquisition of the neighbours finds that the plt. does owe the 4*s.*; which he is to pay. Fine 6*d.* Pledge, Philip Thorald.

William s. of John Hoskel gives 3*d.* to agree with Richard s. of Gerbot, in a plea of debt. Pledge, Henry del Bothem.

John Schirlok gives 6*d.* to agree with German Swerd, in a plea of debt. Pledge, Adam Gerbot.

HOLNE.—Margery da. of William the Shepherd of Wlvedale gives 6*d.* to take ¼ of a bovate of land, with buildings, from John del Holme, for ever. Pledges, John s. of Gilbert and John de Holm.

Robert de Alstanley gives 6*d.* to take one acre of land from Richard s. of Elkoc.

William de Locwode and Walter de Tofteclyve have a love-day.

ALVIRTHORPE.—Agnes widow of Hugh de Alvirthorpe *v.* Robert Wyles, for ousting her from a parcel of meadow, in which she was not dowered. Deft. says she was dowered therein, because she was dowered in the whole of the holding of her late husband, and afterwards Agnes gave the meadow to Quenild, her daughter, who demised it to William Wyles for a term not yet expired ; he asks for an inquisition as to William's entry by license of the Court. At the next Court Agnes comes, and will not submit to the inquisition. Robert is therefore to hold in peace.

STANLEY.—Emma da. of Alexander Waltheu *v.* Mariota la Bele, for calling her a thief and a harlot before the chief people [*coram communitate capitali*] of Sandale, and assaulting her. Deft. denies it, and they refer to the verdict of William de Castelford, who was present, who confirms plt. Mariota is therefore fined 3*d.*, and must pay damages. Pledge, Roger le Bele.

Master Robert de Barneby sues Alice da. of the Chaplain for seizure of cattle. Pledge, William Wodemus.

COURT there on Friday before the Feast of St. Thomas the Apostle [Dec. 21], in the year abovesaid, etc. [1297].

ESSOIGNS.—Maude de Birstall, from suit of Court, by Robert the Cobbler. Pledge, Robert de Mirefeld.

Isabel da. of Thomas the Cook, by Robert the Clerk of Sandale. Pledge, Edmund le Normaund.

Alan Almod, attorney of the lady Margaret de Nevill, by William Scot. Pledge, Edmund le Normaund.

William de Schipeden, by Symon de Schipeden. Pledge, Thomas de Thorneton.

Richard de Staneley, by Robert de Ledes. Pledge, John de Querneby.

John de Trimigham, by William de Staynland. Pledge, William de Castelford.

Baldwin de Seyvill, by Hugh, his son. Pledge, Thomas de Thorneton.

John s. of John de Haldewrth, by Thomas de Yllingwrth. Pledge, John de Haldewrth.

John de Croslande, by John Gurdon. Pledge, Peter Swerd.

Nicholas s. of Robert de Bateley, against Adam Wymark, in a plea of trespass, by William s. of William de Erdeslowe. Pledge, Robert de Wyrunthorpe.

Dom. Robert de Barneby, against Alice da. of the Chaplain of Thurstanland, for seizing cattle, by Richard Pees. Pledge, William Wodemus. Alice essoigns by Symon s. of the Chaplain. Pledge, Richard Ossan.

Walter de Tofteclif, against John, his brother, for trespass, by Richard de Salsa Mara [Saltmarsh].[1] Pledge, William de Castalford.

Matthew de Bosco and Thomas de Coppeley have a love-day.

Thomas de Hopton gives 12*d.* to agree with Thomas Badde.

Richard Suart wages his law against Richard de Salsa Mara, who is fined 12*d.* for false claim. Pledge, John de Thyngelawe.

----

[1] Probably identical with the Richard de Sausemer, who occurs frequently.

B

The like against Adam Wymark, who is fined 6*d.*

Thomas s. of Michael de Yllingwrth fined 6*d.* for obstructing a road. Pledge, John de Haldewrth.

William de Locwode gives 3*d.* to agree with Walter de Tofteclyve.

John de Panhale gives 12*d.* to agree with Adam s. of Martin and Adam s. of Richard, in pleas of debt.

HOLNE.—Margaret widow of Matthew de Heppewrth *v.* William s. of the Grave, for ⅓ of a bovate of land, with buildings, as dower. Deft. says that her husband held the said land without right, and lost it under an inquisition, wherefore she apparently has no title to dower therein. An inquisition is called of the neighbours, viz. John de Holne, Richard de Alstanley, Robert de Alstanley, Robert del Scoles, John del Scoles, Richard de Buttreley, John s. of Adam de Heppewrth, William s. of William de Heppewrth, Richard s. of John de Heppewrth, Robert s. of John, Thomas de Billeclyve, and Matthew de Barneby, who say that her husband died seised as of fee in the said tenement. Therefore she is to recover seisin. William's fine is forgiven, because he is poor.

THORNES.—Robert de Thornes gives 12*d.* to take ½ bovate of land and ½ a toft in Thornes from John Malin, for ever. Pledge, Philip de Mora, the Grave.

SOUREBY.—Robert Rotel gives 6*d.* to take ½ bovate of land in Soureby fields (one messuage excepted) from William de Wales, for ever.

HOLNE.—Matthew de Scoles gives 3*s.* to take 6 acres in Fugeliston from Adam s. of Richard de Fugeleston, for ever. Pledge, John s. of Adam de Heppewrth.

SOUREBY.—John s. of Thomas the Webster [*tixtor*] gives 2*s.* to take half a bovate from William s. of Adam de Werloweley, for ever. Pledge, Thomas de Roaldesete.

ALVIRTHORPE.—Richard de Colley, for vert, 4*d.*

THORNES.—Philip de Snaypethorp, the like, 6*d.* Pledge, John de Flansowe.

John Graffard and Thomas Viron's wife, the like, 6*d.* and 3*d.*

ALVIRTHORPE.—Juliana Tyan and John s. of Margery, living in Juliana's house, for dry wood, 1*d.* each. Pledge, Richard de Colley and Philip the Grave.

STANLEY.—The maid [*ancilla*] of Walter Salie, the like, 3*d.* Pledge, William s. of Thomas Ode.

The young daughter [*ancilla filia*] of Thomas Ode, the like, 1*d.* Pledge, William, her brother.

Walter del Spen, the like, 2*d.* Pledge, Hugh Typet.

Robert Pescy, the like, 2d. Pledge, Hugh Skayf.

Richard del Bothem's maid, 4d. Pledge, Hugh the Forester.

WAKEFEUD.—The sons of Alan Fisc and Richard s. of Jonne, the like, 1d. each. Pledge, John s. of John the Leche and Peter the Sadelar.

Anota le Lene, the like, 2d. Pledge, her husband.

STANLEY.—Philip le Syur, for traps set by his son, 6d. [pro laqueis positis].

ALVIRTHORPE.—Richard s. of Broun, for venison found in his house, 12d.

WAKEFEUD.—Walter Bylle, for a hare taken by his dog, 4s.

William de Lewynthorpe and others unknown killed a doe in Wyrunthorpe field. Pledges, for their satisfying the will of the Steward thereupon, Robert de Wyrunthorpe, Monk of Eccleshill,[1] and Robert de Rachedale of Schelf.

Adam Nacke the Forester v. Richard, servant [garcio] of the Prior of St. Oswald, whom he found off the road within the great wood, and required a pledge of him; whereupon Richard assaulted and beat him.

STANLEY.—John Poket and Hugh Tagge, for vert, 4d.

Robert le Rollere, John de la Sale, Robert s. of Ralph de Stanley, living in Wakefield, acknowledged that they were bound to pay 16s. to the Prior and Convent of St. Oswald at Easter next.

Walter de Tofteclyve v. John his brother, for trespass. Pledge, William Hardegrip.

John the Milner of Schelfley v. Elias de Schelfley, on an agreement. Pledge, Richard Osan. Deft. is attached by Adam de Heley.

STANLEY.—Juliana de Uchethorp v. Alice wife of Thomas s. of Symon de Stanley, for trespass. Pledge, Robert Gos.

HIPERUM.—Wille the Pipere v. Alcok the Waynwricht and Adam s. of John, for trespass. Pledge, William de Hiperum.

SANDALE.—William the Dykere v. William del Okes, for trespass. Pledge, John Kukewald.

ALVIRTHORP.—John Schirlok v. Adam Gerbot, for trespass. Pledge, Richard s. of Broun.

---

[1] Doubtful. The text reads monc'. Probably the Christian name has been omitted.

Richard s. of Broun gives 2s. to go in peace regarding a sheep, which he had wrongfully and maliciously marked.

Ralph de Colley v. John Wythehundes. Pledge, Philip the Grave.

William s. of John v. Richard de Colley, for trespass. Pledge, Adam Gerbot.

COURT there on Friday after the Epiphany of our Lord [Jan. 6], in the year abovesaid [1298].

ESSOIGNS.—Edmund le Normaund, from suit, by Henry de Chyvet. Pledge, Robert de Mirefeud.

Maude de Birstal, the like, by Robert the Cobbler. Pledge, Adam Hod.

John de Trimigham, the like, by Matthew de Bosco. Pledge, Robert de Wyrunthorpe.

Richard de Staneley, the like, by Thomas the Webster. Pledge, John le Flemeng.

John de Crosseland, the like, by John Gurdon. Pledge, John de Haldewrth.

Adam Wymark, plt., v. Nicholas s. of Robert de Bateley, by William s. of John de Erdeslowe.

Master Robert de Barneby, plt., v. Alice da. of the Chaplain of Thurstanland, by William de Bately. Deft. afterwards pays 6d. to agree. Pledge, Henry the Grave of Holne.

John the Milner of Schelfley v. Elias de Schelfley, by Richard de la Haya. Pledge, John le Flemeng. Elias asks a free law against the said John, because he is free. [*Et petiit liberam legem pro eo quod ipse liber est contra dictum Johannem.*]

Alice widow of William de Cardoil v. John Mollan, for debt, by Richard the Serjeant. Pledge, William the Clerk.

John de Tofteclive and Walter his brother have a love-day.

Matthew de Bosco (whose fine is forgiven) has license to agree with Thomas de Coppeley with regard to a seizure of cattle, on the following terms :—That both are to inclose and make fences about their demesnes in close time, and if the cattle of either happen to stray, they are to be driven back, and not impounded; in open time they ought to inter-common.

HIPERUM.—William the Pipere gives 12d. to agree with Alcok the Waynwrith [Wainwright] and Adam s. of John, for trespass. Pledge, William s. of Hugh.

SANDALE.—The land of William de Chevet is in the Earl's hands, because he is dead.

Elias s. of Yvo replevies 2 cows, an ox, and a heifer. Pledges, Thomas de Roaldesete and Hugh s. of Reynold, who pledge themselves that he shall enter the said cattle at the next Court.

THORNES.—John Tasse gives 3*d.* to take ½ acre by the Kirkegate towards Thornes, for 6 years, from Richard s. of Jonne. Pledge, William de Castelford.

OSSETE.—Adam de Chykenley, for brush-wood, 4*d.* Pledge, Swayn de Ossete.

Ralph de Northwode's wife, the like, 3*d.*

THORNES.—John Graffard, for 3 trespasses for vert and dry wood, 18*d.* Pledge, John de Haghe.

The wife of Thomas s. of Hawe, for dry wood, 2*d.*

ALVIRTHORPE.—William s. of John Hoskel, for vert, 3*d.* Pledge, Richard s. of Gerbot.

STANLEY.—John Yssabell, the like, 2*d.* Pledge, Adam s. of Cote.

Richard Spink's son, for dry wood, 2*d.* Pledge, Adam Spink.

John Walhot's son, for vert, 6*d.* Pledge, Richard del Ker.

Eva da. of Thomas s. of Nalle, for dry wood, 4*d.* Pledge, Hugh the Forester.

SOUREBY.—William del Bothem, for vert, 6*d.* Pledge, William s. of Alcok.

John s. of John the Webster *v.* Thomas s. of John, for trespass. Pledge, Ote....[1] Deft. is attached by William s. of Robert Haldewrth.

ALVIRTHORPE.—Walter s. of Richard del Bothem *v.* Walter s. of Adam, for trespass. Pledge, Henry del Bothem.

———

COURT there on Friday before the Purification of the B. V. M. [Feb. 2], in the year abovesaid, etc. [1298].

ESSOIGNS.—Alan Almod, from suit, by Jordan del Ker. Pledge, Robert de Mirefeud.

John s. of John de Haldewrth, the like, by Richard le Fogeler [Fowler]. Pledge, John de Trimigham.

Thomas de Thorneton, the like, by Henry s. of Gilbert. Pledge, John de Tofteclyve.

William de Lyvershege, attorney of Thomas de Langefeud, the like, by Richard s. of William de Lyvershege. Pledge, Peter Swerd.

Nicholas s. of Robert de Bateley, deft., *v.* Adam Wymark, for trespass, by William de Erdeslowe.

———

[1] Query, Greenman, *ho' vir'.*

John le Mouner of Schelfley *v.* Elias de Schelfley, in a plea of agreement, by Robert de Mirefeud.

Maude de Birstall gives 12*d.* for respite of suit until Michaelmas. Pledge, Roger Malet.

John Mollan is fined 6*d.* for default at the last Court. Pledge, William de Castelford.

Alice widow of William de Cardoil and John Mollan have a love-day.

Adam de Hopton gives 4*s.* to go in peace from the charges brought against him at the Tourn.

John de Tofteclyve *v.* Walter, his brother, for assaulting and wounding him in the hand with a caltrop[1] [*cum uno tribulo*] at Birkeley grene; he claims 40*s.* damages. Deft. says that he acted in self-defence, as the plt. hit him on the back with a stone, and he claims 40*s.* damages. An inquisition is ordered for the next Court.

William del Okes gives 6*d.* to agree with William the Dykere. Pledge, John Patrik.

Richard de Staneley gives 2*s.* for respite of suit till Michaelmas. Pledge, Thomas de Coppeley.

STANLEY.—Thomas s. of Simon gives 6*d.* to agree with Juliana de Uchethorpe, for trespass. Pledge, Richard le Lepere.

Nicholas de Werloweley, arrested for an offence presented at the Tourn at Halifax, finds Thomas de Coppeley, William the Grave of Soureby, William de Lyvershegge, Elias s. of Yvo, William de Coppeley, and Andrew de Werloweley, as manucaptors.

ALVIRTHORPE.—Adam Gerbot *v.* John Schirlok, for carrying away his hay in the Morcroft, worth 2*s.* Deft. says that there was an agreement that he [Adam] should give him [John] 2 acres of land in le Morcroft, so that the whole meadow should remain to him [John]. An inquisition is taken by the oath of Robert de Flansowe, Henry le Nonne, Alexander Waltweyf, Richard de Colley, William, servant [*garcio*] of Gerbot, and Philip de Mora, who say that the meadow was divided between them at the same time as the [arable] land. Therefore Adam is to hold his meadow, as it was divided, and John must pay damages for the hay, which are taxed at 12*d.* Fine, 6*d.* Pledge, Richard s. of Broun.

The same inquisition finds that Walter s. of Adam de Alvirthorpe demised certain land to Walter s. of Richard del Bothem for one

---

[1] Translation doubtful; *tribulus* means a caltrop, a kind of thorn, and a kind of thistle; *tribulum* means a threshing sledge.

crop, which Walter [s. Richard] did not have last year, because Walter [s. Adam] sold the grass. Therefore Walter [s. Richard] is to have the crop this year. Walter [s. Adam] is fined 6*d*. Pledge, Philip the Grave.

SANDALE.—Malina de Plegewyk pays 2*s*. relief on the land of William de Chyvet[1] for ever. Pledge, John Monke.

John s. of Swayn gives 5*s*. to take 1½ bovates of land from the said Malina, for ever. Same pledge.

Henry s. of William de Plegewyk gives 12*d*. to take ½ bovate from the said Malina, for ever. Same pledge.

STANLEY.—Richard del Bothem gives 6*d*. to take a perch of land from Robert de Bateley, and 6*d*. for three perches from John Yssabell, both in Stanley, for ever. Pledge, Henry, his brother.

HOLNE.—Adam the Waynwricht gives 5*s*. to take 13 acres of land from Thomas Ferenhoule, with Eva, his daughter, in marriage, to himself and their joint heirs.

ALVIRTHORPE.—The widow of Ralph de Uchethorp, for vert, 4*d*.

Emma da. of Alexander, for dry wood, 1*d*. Pledge, her father.

STANLEY.—Henry Lewyn, the like, 2*d*.

The maid of Robert s. of Geppe, the like, 2*d*. Pledge, Richard del Ker.

Thomas s. of Simon, the like, 2*d*.

The wife of Walter s. of Adam, the like, 2*d*. Pledge, William Albrey.

Simon Tyting's son, the like, 2*d*.

Emma de Lofthus, the like, 2*d*. Pledge, Richard le Lepere.

Roger le Bele, the like, 1*d*. Pledge, John Isabell.

WAKEFEUD.—Amabel le Leche, the like, 1*d*. Pledge, John Thorald.

Richard Drake's son, the like, 1*d*. Pledge, Hugh Bille.

The son of Margery [? *Marior*'] de Rachedale, the like, 1*d*.

John Leche junior, the like, 1*d*.

Agnes da. of Gelle de Stanley, for buying brush-wood, 2*d*. Pledge, John Colle.

Robert Pollard, the like, 3*d*. Pledge, William Benne.

THORNES.—Philip del Hill of Snaypethorpe, the like, 4*d*.

---

[1] Relationship not stated.

ALVIRTHORPE.—Richard s. of Brun, for dry wood, 3*d*. Pledge, Adam Wlf.

Adam Wlf's son, the like, 1*d*. Pledge, Richard Broun.

John Schirlok, for throwing down . . . . . [*quia prostravit blottron*[1]], 12*d*.

SOUREBY.—Maude da. of Nicholas *v*. Elias s. of Yvo de Worloweley, for trespass. Pledge, William the Grave. Deft. is attached by his cattle.

SANDALE.—William le Vacher and Cicely his wife *v*. William de la Grene and Agnes his wife, for trespass. Pledge, William del Overhall.

———————

COURT there on Friday after Ash Wednesday, the year abovesaid, etc. [1298].

ESSOIGNS.—Edmund de Chyvet, from suit, by Henry Waryn. Pledge, Robert de Mirefeud.

John le Flemeng, the like, by Richard de Erdeslowe. Pledge, Robert de Wyrunthorpe. He afterwards came.

John de Trimigham, the like, by John de Miggeley. Pledge, Robert de Wyrunthorpe.

John de Crosland, the like, by John Gurdon. Pledge, Adam Hod.

William de Schipeden, the like, by Symon de Schipeden. Pledge, John de Miggeley.

Thomas de Thorneton, the like, by John de Thorneton. Pledge, John de Tofteclyve.

Walter de Tofteclyve *v*. John, his brother, for trespass, by John de Erdeslowe. Pledge, William Hardegripp. John prays that an inquisition may be taken, and it is so ordered, as Walter has not come. It is taken by the oath of Walter de Doniglawe, William Child, Adam s. of Almod, Thomas de Thyngelawe, William Hardegripp, Walter Franceys, Richard s. of Huske, Thomas s. of William, Robert the Smith of Heton, Hugh de Chideshill, and Nicholas de Thofteclyve, who say that Walter struck John, to his damage of 5*s*.; fine, 12*d*. Pledge, William the Clerk.

Nicholas s. of Robert de Bateley *v*. Adam Wymark, for trespass, by Richard s. of William. Pledge, Robert de Wyrunthorpe.

John Mollan gives 6*d*. to agree with Alice, widow of William de Cardoil, for debt.

———————

[1] I cannot suggest any meaning for this word.

Nicholas de Werloweley, arrested for an offence presented at the Tourn at Halifax, finds Thomas de Coppeley, William the Grave of Soureby, William de Lyvershegge, Elias s. of Yvo, William de Coppeley, Matthew de Bosco, and Richard de Bouderode, as sureties for his appearance at the next Tourn at Halifax.

SOUREBY.—Maude da. of Nicholas de Werloweley *v.* Elias s. of Yvo de Werlowely, for 7 sheep detained by him. An inquisition is ordered.

Sir William le Flemeng makes default at this Court, and is to be distrained.

HIPERUM.—The land of Henry de Schipeden is in the Earl's hand, because he is dead.

OSSETE.—Richard de Lynne, for escape of 4 oxen in Dewysbiry wood, 6*d.* Pledge, Richard s. of Adam, who also pays 3*d.* for the like.

John s. of Malyn, for the like, 6*d.*

Alcok de Boudere [Bouderode], for putting a mare in the grass of his own accord [*spontanea voluntate*], 3*d.* Pledge, Adam de Boudere [Bouderode].

Roger de Hecmundewyk, for 2 oxen, 6*d.* Pledge, Alcok de Bouderode.

William de Dewysbiry, for 2 oxen, 3*d.* Pledge, John Malyn.

WAKEFEUD.—Robert de Stanley's wife, for dry wood, 4*d.* Pledge, John Beek.

John Beek's wife, the like, 2*d.* Pledge, Robert Lorimer.

Philip Filche's son, the like, 1*d.* Pledge, Robert de Motterum.

Henry Schorthose's maid, the like, 2*d.* Pledge, Hugh the Forester.

Geppe de Aula's daughter, and the sons of Richard Drake and Alan Fisc, the like, 1*d.* each. Pledge, Geppe de Aula.

Magota da. of Ellen, the like, 4*d.* Pledge, John Thorald.

Eva de Brameley, the like, 6*d.* Pledge, Robert Pollard.

Agnes Danyel's son, the like, 1*d.* Pledge, John Thorald.

ALVIRTHORPE.—Richard Broun's son, the like, 2*d.* Pledge, Richard s. of Philip.

STANLEY.—The son of Adam s. of Cote, for taking dry wood for sale, 2*d.* Pledge, his father.

Hugh Tipet, the like, 2*d.* Pledge, Richard del Ker.

The son of Richard le Lepere, the like, and Walter Bateman, 3*d.* each.

Eva Albrey's son, 2*d.* Pledge, William Albrey.

The son of Thomas s. of Simon, the like, 2*d.* Pledge, Robert s. of Geppe.

HIPERUM.—John del Rode, for dry wood, 6*d.* Pledge, Adam de Briggehuses.

Alcok del Clif, for vert, 4*d.* Pledge, Henry de Northwode.

Walter s. of Mocok, the like, 6*d.* Pledge, William de Schipeden.

William de Heley, for escape of 2 oxen, 2*d.* Pledge, Peter de la Lache.

Malkyn de Haldewrth, for escape of one ox, 1*d.* Same pledge.

WAKEFEUD.—Isabel de Honley, Geppe de Aula's son, the wife of John s. of Sibbe, and Amabel the Laundress [*lotrix*], for breaking the pale, 1*d.* each. Pledges, Philip the Parker, John le Leche, William Pede, and Philip the Forester.

SOUREBY.—Richard de Barkeseye, for escape of pigs, 8*d.* Pledge, John de Barkeseye.

Hanne de Luddinggedene, for 3 oxen in the broom [*in husseto*], 3*d.* Pledge, John the Milner.

HOLNE.—William Pileman, for an escape, 1*d.* Pledge, Thomas s. of Cicely.

Adam Benne and Agnes del Clif, for dry wood, 3*d.* each. Pledge, Richard the Forester.

Adam s. of Nelle the Smith and John del Dam, for a bull [*? pro uno bul*], 6*d.* Pledge, Richard de Stansefeud.

William the Skinner, for dry wood, 2*d.* Pledge, Richard the Forester.

THORNES.—Ivo the Smith gives 2*d.* to agree with William the Forester, for trespass.

Magge Wytlof sues Adam s. of Walter for ⅓ of a bovate of land, which he took from the heir of John Witlof. Deft. calls John s. of John Wytlof to warrant that he took the land in Court. They afterwards agreed; fine forgiven, because the plt. is poor.

STANLEY.—Richard del Bothem, for grinding [corn] elsewhere than at the Earl's mill, to which he owes suit, and Hugh Skayf, for the like, are both in mercy. Nothing done here, because it belongs to the perquisites of the town of Wakefield, and they are to be fined there.

THORNES.—Philip de Mora and Ivo the Smith, pledges for the appearance of John Graffard to answer the charges of Thomas de Garderobe, are fined 3*d.* because he does not come. John is to be distrained.

ALVIRTHORPE.—Ralph de Colley and John With-the-hounds [*cum canibus*] have a love-day.

The suit between William s. of John and Richard de Colley is respited till Richard returns from Scotland.

HIPERUM.—Maude widow of Ivo the Smith is fined 6d. for drawing blood from Adam s. of Ivo. Pledge, William del Bothes. Richard Boton, her son, is to be attached to answer for the same.

SANDALE.—William le Vacher and Cicely, his wife, sue William de la Grene and Agnes, his wife, because Agnes assaulted Cicely very seriously [valde male] and drew blood, for which she claims 6s. 8d. Agnes says that Cicely came to her door and called her a harlot, and her husband a thief. An inquisition is ordered.

ALVIRTHORPE.—William Attebarre gives 12d. to take 6 acres of land in Alvirthorpe from Henry le Nunne for ever. Pledge, Adam Gerbot.

THORNES.—Alice da. of Thomas, servant [garcio] of Lecia, surrenders ½ bovate of land in Thornes, and Richard s. of Thomas Pegere, and the said Alice, pay 12d. to take the said land to themselves and the heirs of their bodies. Pledge, Thomas Pegere.

Robert s. of William Pymerich gives 12d. to take 2 tofts in Thornes, between the land of John s. of Nalle and William Proudfot, from the said John and William, for ever. Pledge, Philip the Grave.

WAKEFEUD.—A stray heifer is sold to the Grave for 3s. Pledge, John Nelot.

ALVIRTHORPE.—Henry de Swynlington gives 6d. to take ½ bovate and 2 acres of land in Neuton fields from Robert Daneys, for ten years.

ALVIRTHORPE.—Adam Gerbot v. Maude, relict of Gerbot, in a plea of land. Pledge, Richard Gerbot.

Joan wife of Bate de Waleton v. Nicholas[1] de Wyston, for trespass. Pledge, Robert at Well.

SANDALE.—Cicely Wythor v. William Attegrene, for trespass. Pledge, William le Vacher.

COURT there on Friday after the Feast of St. Gregory [March 12], in the year abovesaid, etc. [1298].

ESSOIGNS.—John de Querneby, from suit, by John le Fraunceis of Staynland. Pledge, John le Buteller.

John de Crosland, the like, by John Gurdon. Pledge, Adam Hod.

John de Trimigham, the like, by Elias de Werloweley. Pledge, William de Castelford.

---

[1] Called Colyn in the record of postponement at the next Court.

ALVIRTHORPE.—Emma Walthew, Quenild, and Letice da. of Philip, for thorns [*pro spinis*] carried off from the new park, 4*d.* each. Pledge, Philip Thorald.

John le Mouner gives 6*d.* to agree with Elias de Schelfley, in a plea of agreement. Pledge, Hicke the Serjeant.

SOUREBY —Maude da. of Nicholas de Werloweley, fined 12*d.* for not prosecuting her suit against Elias s. of Yvo.

SANDALE.—Thomas Tubbing of Chyvet, for vert, 12*d.*   Pledge, Robert the Clerk of Sandale.

SOUREBY.—John s. of John the Webster, fined 6*d.* for not prosecuting his suit against Richard s. of John.

Sir William le Flemeng gives 2*s.* for defaults, and 3*s.* for respite of suit till Michaelmas.

HIPERUM.—John s. and heir of Henry del Dene gives 12*d.* relief on his deceased father's land. Pledge, William del Bothes.

HOLNE.—Nicholas de Littlewode, for an escape in the broom [*in husseto*], 6*d.* Pledge, Margery, his daughter.

Henry, servant of the cow-keeper [*garcio vaccarii*], for vert, 4*d.* Pledge, his father.

Thomas de Billeclif and Adam del Boure, for dry wood, 6*d.* and 2*d.* Pledges, Adam del Rode and Richard de Stansefeud.

THORNES.—John Graffard's maid, the like, 4*d.* Pledge, Adam le Hunte.

ALVIRTHORPE.—Adam Gerbot, for vert, 4*d.* Pledge, Adam le Hunte.

Margaret Swan, for dry wood, 1*d.* Pledge, Alexander Hulcote.

WAKEFEUD —Magge de Rachedale's son, Henry Schorthose's maid, and Robert de Soureby's son, the like, 1*d.*, 3*d.*, and 2*d.* Pledges, John s. of Sibbe and John Colle.

Isabel de Honley's son, the like, 2*d.* Pledge, John Lauedyman.

Malina da. of Richard de la Haye, the like, 3*d.* Pledge, William the Goldsmith.

Eve de Ayketon's son, the like, 2*d.* Pledge, William Brighelbayn.

The maids of Henry de Gouton and John Beek, the like, 1*d.* each. Pledges, Robert Pollard and John Beek.

The sons of Robert Slenge and Nabbe Brodeye, the like, 1*d.* and 2*d.* Pledges, Walter de Alvirthorpe and Henry Archur.

The wife of Richard the Serjeant, for cursing the forester [*quia maledixit forestarium*], and for dry wood, 3*d.* Pledge, John s. of Sybbe.

Adam le Wyte's son, for dry wood, 1*d.* Pledge, John Thorald.

STANLEY.—Richard s. of John Bulloc, for dry wood, and Philip s. of Agnes, for thorns, 2*d.* each. Pledge, John Thorald.

Adam Cote's wife, for cutting away the pale, 6*d.* Pledge, John Bulloc.

Adam Cote, for not making the pale, 6*d.* Pledges, Gelle Cussing and Nicholas de Bateley.

William de Neuton, for a cartload of brush-wood, 4*d.* Pledge, Hugh the Forester.

Hugh Typet and Adam his brother, 6*d.* each for the like.

Thomas s. of Simon, for dry wood, 2*d.* Pledge, Hugh Skayf.

ALVIRTHORPE. — An inquisition finds that John Wythehundes wounded Ralph de Colley in the hand with a sword; he must pay damages, assessed at 3*s.*, and 6*d.* fine. Pledge, William s. of John.

Also that Richard de Colley struck William s. of John with a mattock [*vanga*], and broke his pot, full of ale; damages, 12*d.*; fine, 12*d.*

Also that Adam Gerbot sold an acre of land to Agnes de Bretton for 1½*d.* a year, and not 6*d.*, as he says; fine, 3*d.*

SANDALE.—Also that William de la Grene's wife assaulted Cicely Wythor; damages, 6*d.*; fine, 12*d.* Pledge, John Munk. They are under a pain of 3*s.* if they break the peace.

Also that William Attegrene assaulted the said Cicely; fine, 6*d.*

THORNES.—Ralph Bate gives 12*d.* to take ½ bovate of land in Thornes to himself and the heirs begotten between him and Margaret da. of Richard Gerbot, his wife, from the said Richard Gerbot; with reversion, in default of such heirs, to Richard Gerbot and his heirs.

SANDALE.—William s. of Robert del Holmes is elected forester in Westwode.

Richard Beausire is elected warrener at Crigeliston.

ALVIRTHORPE.—Robert Estrild gives 6*d.* to take 1½ acres of land in le Fal from William s. of Walter de Neuton, for 30 years.

STANLEY.—Robert Gunne gives 10*s.* relief on the land of Agnes de Uchethorpe, whose heir he is.

ALVIRTHORPE.—John Schirlok gives 6*d.* to exchange all his share of the meadow in le Morcroft for ⅔ of a rood of arable land, with Adam his brother.

Adam Gerbot *v.* Malle relict of Gerbot for his share, as heir, in 2 acres which his father took for a term. Deft. says that her husband gave them to her in open Court for the term, and appeals to the Rolls of Peter de Lundo, the steward, which are to be inspected.

Adam Gerbot has license to take all the land his father held in le Rodes towards le Leyes, for ever. Pledge, John Schirlok.

WAKEFEUD.—Robert Peger v. German s. of Philip, for trespass. Pledge, William de Castelford.

Joan da. of German Swerd v. Adam Gerbot, for trespass. Pledge, Reynold de Swynlington. He is attached by Henry le Nunne.

Magota da. of Reynold de Swynlington v. Adam Gerbot. Pledge, German Swerd.

STANLEY.—From the chattels of Agnes de Uchethorpe, deceased, intestate, 13s. 4d.

Thomas s. of John de Fekesby gives 12d. for respite from a distraint.

————

COURT there on Friday in Easter Week, in the year abovesaid [1298].

William de Bello Monte gives 13s 4d. for entry into the lands that Robert de Hoderode held in chief from the Earl in the town of Fekesby,—to hold to himself and his heirs for ever. He does fealty and suit of court.

ESSOIGNS.—William de Schipedene, from suit of court, by Thomas de Schipedene. Pledge, Robert de Mirefeud.

Edmund le Normaund, the like, by Henry de Chyvet. Pledge, John de Crosland.

Sir John de Horbiry gives 2s. for respite of suit till Michaelmas.

SANDALE.—Colin[1] de Wyston gives 6d. to agree with Joan widow of Bate de Walton, for trespass.

WAKEFEUD.—Robert Pegere fined 3d. for not prosecuting his suit against German s. of Philip.

Emma da. of Alexander de Morley v. Adam, servant [garcio] of Roger de Clyvelande, with regard to a horse found in his cart. Pledge, John de Tofteclyve.

ALVIRTHORPE.—Henry le Nunne, pledge for Adam Gerbot, at the suit of Joan da. of German Swerd and Magota da. of Reynold de Swynlington, is fined for not producing him; but he is forgiven, because he has nothing in goods.

Adam Gerbot fails to prosecute his suit against Malle widow of Gerbot; pardoned, because he has nothing in goods.

STANLEY.—Juliana Moye gives 6d. to take 2 acres of land from Thomas de Garderobe, for ever. Pledge, Simon de Monte.

————

[1] Called Nicholas : *ante*, p. 27.

SOUREBY.—Cicely widow of John s. of Elias *v.* Hugh s. of Reynold, for dower.

HOLNE.—Robert s. of Matthew del Scoles gives 6*d.* to take 2 acres of land in le Scoles from William le Parmenter, for 12 years. Pledge, Adam del Scoles.

HIPERUM.—William de Hagenewrth gives 6*d.* for license to marry Alice, widow of Robert s. of William le Chapman, and to come into the Earl's land. Pledge, William the Grave.

STANLEY.—Richard del Bothem gives 6*d.* to take 1½ acres of land in Stanley from John Walhot, and 3 roods from Symon Tyting, for ever. Pledge, Hugh Skayf.

John Bullok keeps a dog that has strangled two does. He finds pledges for satisfying the Steward therein, viz. William Attebarre, Hanecok le Nunne, William Archur, and Philip Wlf; fine, 2*s.*

Eve Ded and Adam Cote's son, for dry wood, 1*d.* and 2*d.* Pledge, Richard Spink.

William s. of Hugh de Lofthus, for thorns, 3*d.* Pledge, Henry Schorthose.

Walter del Spen, for an escape, 4*d.* Pledge, William le Lacer.

Adam de Uchethorp, for an escape into the grass of lands in the lord's hands, 12*d.* Pledges, Richard le Lepor and Walter s. of Bateman.

Richard del Bothem, the like, 3*d.* Pledge, Hugh Skayf.

Hugh s. of Bateman, the like, 1*d.* Pledge, Adam de Uchethorp.

Walter del Spen, the like, 3*d.* Pledge, Robert Pescy.

WAKEFEUD.—Richard Mayk's maid, for dry wood. Pledge, John Thorald.

John Cussing's servant [*garcio*], for breaking the gate towards Lofthus, 6*d.* Pledges, Walter Bille and Simon de Monte.

Eve de Ayketon's son, for dry wood, 3*d.* Pledge, John Don.

Maude, her maid, the like, 3*d.*

Robert de Castelforth's maid, Hugh Bille, and the son of German le Gardiner, for broom [*pro hussel*], 6*d.*, 2*d.*, and 2*d.*

The maid of Ralph s. of Mille, the like, 2*d.* Pledge, Hugh Bille.

ALVIRTHORPE.—Juliana Tyan's son, for dry wood, 2*d.* Pledge, Adam Gerbot.

OSSETE.—Robert Soneman, Sosanna de Goukethorp, Adam de Goukethorp, and John de Chykenley, for breaking the pale, 6*d.*, 2*d.*, 2*d.*, and 2*d.*

Richard s. of John de Ossete, for the like and for broom, 6*d.* Pledge, John Coynel.

THORNES.—John Graffard, the like, 6*d.*　Pledge, Richard Costel.

SOUREBY.—Richard s. of Anabel, for escape of 10 oxen in the broom blown down [*in husseto prostrato*], and Hannecok Coltenete, for the like, 12*d.* each.　Pledges, John de Miggeley and Richard s. of. Alot [?].

John Hodde's wife, for broom, 6*d.*　Pledge, Matthew de Bosco.

John the Milner, for cutting broom immoderately [*ultra mensuram*], 12*d.*　Pledge, Hanne de Ludingdene.

Margery wife of Sthephen [*sic*], for escape of 3 beasts in the herbage of Saltonstall, 3*d.*　Pledge, William Pelet.

Ivo the Milner, for 2 beasts in Werloweley wood, 2*d.*　Pledge, Ivo s. of Richard.

Hugh de Lictheseles, for cutting 5 hazels [*corulos*] and a cartload of vert, 5*s.*　Pledge, Adam s. of Dode de Skyrecotes.

ALVIRTHORPE.—Henry de Swynlington *v.* Adam Gerbot and Richard, his brother, for trespass.　Pledge, William de Castelford.

Nicholas de Bateley gives 6*d.* to agree with Adam Wymark, for trespass.　Pledge, Robert de Wyrunthorpe.

HOLNE.—John Waryn *v.* Adam s. of the Grave of Scoles, for trespass.　Pledge, Peter del Peek.

SOUREBY.—Richard s. of Cicely de Holgate *v.* Thomas de Connhale, William s. of Agnes de Halifax, Richard s. of Bateman, and Adam Migge, for debt.　Pledge, Thomas s. of Cicely de Holgate.

Richard Thorstel of Ryley *v.* Richard le Syveman, for trespass. Pledge, Adam de Heley.

WAKEFEUD.—German Filcoke gives 4*d.* for license to lengthen his booth by 4 feet to the south, paying 1*d.* a year.

———————

COURT there on Friday the Morrow of St. Philip and St. James [May 1], in the year abovesaid, etc., in the time of John de Donecaster, the Steward [1298].

ESSOIGNS.—John le Flemeng, attorney of Sir John de Heton, from suit, by William de Bateley.　Pledge, John de Tofteclyve.

Edmund de Chyvet, the like, by Henry de Chyvet.　Pledge, Peter Swerd.

Alan Almod, the like, by Jordan del Ker.　Pledge, John de Tofteclyve.

Thomas de Thornethon, the like, by Henry s. of Gilbert.　Same pledge.

John de Trimigham, the like, by William de Werloweley. Pledge, William de Castelford.

Emma da. of Alexander de Morley withdraws her suit against Adam, servant [*garcio*] of Roger de Clyveland; fined 2*s.*, because she is poor. Pledge, John de Tofteclive.

John Patrik *v.* Henry the man [*homo*] of Hugh de Serleby, by Jordan del Ker. Pledge, John de Tofteclyve.

HOLNE.—Adam s. of the Grave gives 6*d.* to agree with John Waryn, for trespass.

Robert del Sthorthes and Emma his wife *v.* William de Floketon, for debt. Pledge, William de Castelford.

SANDALE.—Thomas and John, sons of Thomas de Holgate, give 12*d.* to agree with Thomas Beusire, for trespass. Pledge, John Monk. A pain of 6*s.* 8*d.* to be paid by the first to offend again.

Richard Beusire *v.* Adam s. of Adam Tubbing, for trespass. Pledge, Adam Sprigunel.

Peter Lewelyn gives half of 9*d.* for help to recover that sum against Roger Tubbyng, who acknowledges the debt before the constable. He is to be distrained for satisfaction.

ALVIRTHORPE.—Adam Gerbot acknowledges that he has offended against Joan da. of German Swerd. He is to satisfy her; the fine is pardoned, because he is poor.

Henry de Swynlington *v.* Adam Gerbot and Richard, his brother; they let him an acre of land in le Fal for 3 crops [*ad tres cropp'*], and he manured it; and afterwards Agnes de Bretton recovered the land against him as her own, whereby plt. lost two crops [*vesturas*] and his manure. Adam acknowledges it, and must satisfy the plt. His fine pardoned because he is poor.

STANLEY.—Robert Pesci and Robert s. of Walter give 2*s.* to take 14 acres of land from Philip Bille's heir, for 10 years. Pledge, Richard del Ker.

THORNES.—Ivo the Smith gives 6*d.* to take an acre of unoccupied land, formerly held by Adam Beske, for ever.

Thomas Pegere and Alice his wife *v.* John s. of Richard s. of Geoffrey, in a plea of land. Pledge, Robert Pegere.

William s. of Thomas Ode gives 6*d.* to farm from the Earl 3 acres at Wodehall, formerly held by Gode, at 3*s.* rent. Pledge, Richard del Ker.

STANLEY.—Richard del Ker gives 6*d.* to take 2½ acres of unoccupied land in Uchethorpe, next near the land formerly held by Philip Bille, for 10 years. Pledge, Robert Pesci.

c

WAKEFEUD.—John Nelot has license to take ½ acre of land in Codenelcroft from John Theuet, for ever. Pledge, William Nelot.

HOLNE.—Pawe de Emmeley and Thomas Beaufrere, fined 3*d.* each for making a path unlawfully [*pro injuste via*].

Thomas Pridecan, for the like, 3*d.* Pledge, the Grave of Heppewrth.

Thomas Elcok, for vert and dry wood, 3*d.* Pledge, Elcok de Barnedeside.

Hawe del Stockes, for dry wood, 3*d.* Pledge, Matthew, her husband.

OSSETE.—The wives of Hugh de Chideshill, John Peny, and John Fox, 2*d.*, 2*d.*, and 4*d.*, for dry wood. Pledges, William s. of Jordan, Hugh de Chydeshill, and Hugh the Carter.

THORNES.—Thomas the Brounsmyth, for vert, 12*d.*

WAKEFEUD.—The sons of William Benne, Richard Drake, and Alan Fisc, 2*d.* each, for dry wood. Pledges, John s. of Libbe and Haget.

Peter Tirsy's maid, the like, 4*d.* Pledge, Peter Tyrsy.

ALVIRTHORPE.—Adam Gerbot and Richard his brother, for cutting thorns, 12*d.*

Hannecok le Nunne and John Bullok, for ivy [*pro hedera*], 6*d.* and 1*d.* Pledges, John Thorald and John Yssabbell.

————

COURT at Birton on Sunday after Ascension Day [May 15], in the year abovesaid, etc. [1298].

HOLNE.—Juliana da. of Gilbert de Alstanley *v.* John s. of John de Holne, for cutting her arm with a knife. He says that he did so unintentionally. An inquisition finds that he struck her through her father's door [*percussit ipsam per medium hostium patris sui*]; damages, 6*d.*; fine, 2*s.* Pledge, his father.

Matthew de Farnely gives 3*s.* for help to recover 7*s.* against John s. of John de Holne; and in case he fails [*si contingat quod cadat*], he will give 12*d.* fine. Pledge, Thomas the Shepherd of Thurstan-land. He sues John for 7*s.* for 4 skeps of oats. John comes, but does not defend it properly [*non defendit verba Curie debito modo*]. He must therefore pay the 7*s.*, and 12*d.* damages, which is given to the clerks; fine, 6*d.* Pledge, Adam s. of Nelle.

Adam s. of Matthew de Farneley *v.* John s. of John de Holne says that he delivered to him a wether [*multo*] to keep during the winter for 1½*d.*, and when shearing-time came he refused to give up the fleece to Adam; damages claimed, 3s. John is ordered to pay 2s. 6d. for the sheep; fine, 6d.; damages assessed at 6d., and they are given to the clerk.

John s. of Adam de Heppewrth gives 2s. 6d. to take 5¼ acres of land, with buildings, from Adam, his brother, for ever. Pledge, Adam s. of the Grave.

[The top of the dorse of the Roll has formed the outer covering, and the first court (a short one) is so rubbed as to be practically illegible.]

TOURN at Rastrik the Monday following, etc. [1298].

JURORS.—Robert del Stockes, John le Barn, Adam de Locwode, John le Flemeng, John de Locwode, John . . . . Hertesheved, John de Percy, Alcok del Frith, Henry de Northwod, John de Birstall, and John de Hertesheved.

John Saylle [?] drew blood from Adam Gyge [?]. Fine, 6d.

Geoffrey de Lynley drew blood from Hugh s. of Isabel. Fine, 6d.

Simon s. of Jordan de Bosco, from Thomas le Tollere. Fine, 6d.

Thomas le Tollere, from the said Simon; 6d.

William s. of William Attetonhende of Ovenden is a thief, and stole 4 bullocks, viz. one from Michael de [Sundreland], one from John his son, one from Cicely de Holgate, and one from Robert de Ovenden; and afterwards he offered John de Sundreland 6d. to withdraw the charge as to his bullock [?]. The same William stole a heifer belonging to Roger s. of Agnes de Helistanes, and sold it for 6s. He is to be arrested.

Hugh s. of Reynold v. Amabel del Bothem, for debt. Pledge, Adam Migge.

John del Westwode v. Elias s. of Yvo, for debt. Pledge, William the Grave of Soureby.

COURT at Halifax the Tuesday following, etc. [1298].

Celia widow of John s. of Elias, the late Grave, sues Hugh s. of Reynold for ⅓ of land sold to him by her late husband. Deft. says that her husband is still alive. Postponed till after Whitsuntide.

Richard s. of Cicely de Holgate fined 6d. for not prosecuting his suit against Thomas de Connhale, William s. of Agnes, Richard Bateman, and Adam Migge. Pledge, Thomas his brother.

Hugh s. of Reynold sues Amabel del Bothem for 10s., for which she was pledge. She says that she could not be pledge for anyone while her husband was alive. It appears that the liability in question was incurred while Adam [?], her husband, was alive. Plt. fined 6d. for false claim. Pledge, William the Grave.

Agnes widow of Nicholas Stute sues Hugh de Lictheseles for unjustly detaining her dower, viz. 6 acres of land. He admits it. She is to recover it. He is fined 6d.

Elias s. of Ivo gives 12d. to agree with John de Westwode, for trespass.

Adam le Crouther gives 12d. to take 6 acres of land from Agnes widow of Nicholas Stute, for her life, he doing service therefor. Pledge, William the Grave.

Richard del Wytelie sues Elias s. of Yvo for 8s., for an ox sold to him. Deft. is to pay 8s., and 12d. fine. Pledges, John Hodde and Hanne del Holgate.

Elias s. of Yvo sues Adam s. of William de Miggeley for 6s. 6d., due to him for an ox. Deft. says that the plt. requested him to pay the money to Michael de Wyteley. Plt. wages his law. Deft. is to pay the 6s. 6d., and 6d. fine. Pledge, Henry de Holgate.

Nicholas de Werloweley gives 12d. to agree with Elias de Werlowley. Pledge, William the Grave.

Elias s. of Yvo sues Adam s. of William at Town-end [ad finem ville] for 5s. 1d., for a cow sold to him. Deft. denies it, and wages his law. Elias fined 12d. Pledge, William the Grave.

HIPERUM.—Henry del Rode gives 12d. to take 3 acres of land in Hiperum from John le Barn, for ever. Pledge, William de Bothes.

SOUREBY.—Hugh de Lictheseles gives 12d. to take 6 acres of land from Adam le Cruder (viz. the 6 acres which Agnes widow of Nicholas Stute recovered from Hugh as dower, for her life); to hold to him and his heir for ever.

Adam le Cruther gives 2s. to take half of all the land, with buildings and appurtenances, at le Helm in Sourbyshire, left on the Lord's hands by William Coltenote, William de Rastrick, and Jordan s. of Agnes,—to him and his heirs for ever. Pledge, Hugh de Lithheseles. He shall begin to pay rent at Michaelmas.

HIPERUM.—Adam the Waynwrith, for vert, 6d.

John de Holewaye and Adam le Eyr, for escapes, 4d. each.

Henry de Coppelay, for vert, 6d. Pledge, Adam Horre.

Thomas s. of Elias, the like, 6d. Pledge, Richard de Sunderland.

John s. of William, the like, 6d. Pledge, Walter s. of Elias.

Henry del Rode, for dry wood, 6*d*. Pledge, Henry the Grave.

Roger s. of Walter, the like, 6*d*. Pledge, William de Schep'.

William the Carpenter, for an escape, 4*d*. Pledge, Adam the Milner.

Roger de Briggehuses the elder, for dry wood, 4*d*. Pledge, Adam, his brother.

SOUREBY.—Robert the Tanner and Diana Gunnild 4*d*. each, for escapes. Pledge, William de Stodeley.

Hanne del Schawe and Hanne de Stodeley, 6*d*. each, for the like Pledge, Richard del Estwode.

Hanne de Holgate, for escape of 20 beasts, 5*s*. Pledge, John de Miggeley.

Agnes de Luddingdene, for 3 beasts, 6*d*. Pledge, Richard s. of Alcok.

Richard de Wyteley, the like, 6*d*. Pledge, William de Balne.

William Swaype, for vert, 4*d*. Pledge, William s. of Yvo.

Thomas s. of Christiana, for brush wood, 3*d*. Pledge, Thomas de Aula.

Thomas de Langfeud and Adam s. of Nalk de Heptonstall appoint William de Castelford, their attorney, against Thomas de Coppeley, for debt.

John s. of Henry de la Haye *v*. Thomas de Hopton, for debt. Pledge, William de la Haye.

SOURBY.—Richard de Gledeholt *v*. Elias s. of Yvo, for trespass. Pledge, John del Westwode.

SANDALE.—Walter de Heselwell *v*. Nicholas de Wyston, for trespass. Pledge, Robert de Wodussme.

The old irons for marking the Earl's cattle are given to Thomas de Garderobe to keep, under the Steward's seal.

STANLEY.—John s. of Philip the Tailor [*cissor*] *v*. Richard s. of John and John Poket, for trespass. Pledges, Hugh s. of Bateman and Philip the Tailor. They are attached by Richard the Grave.

Robert s. of Adam de Erdeslowe *v*. William s. of Geoffrey de Erdeslowe, for trespass. Pledge, Robert de Wyverumthorpe. He is attached by William Luvecok.

SANDALE.—Richard the Smith of Sandale *v*. Henry the Chaplain of Sandale, for trespass. Pledge, John Best. He is attached by Robert the Clerk.

John Mollan *v*. Raymund de Danecastre, for debt. Pledge, William de Mounckton.

THORNES.—The land of William de Luppesheved is in the Earl's hands, because he is dead.

COURT at Wakefield on Friday after Pentecost [May 25], in the year abovesaid, etc. [1298].

ESSOIGNS.—John de Querneby, from suit of Court, by John le Boteller. Pledge, Robert de Wyrunthorpe.

Peter Swerd, the like, by Henry Gurdon. Pledge, Adam Hod.

John de Trimigham, the like, by William s. of William de Castelford. Pledge, William de Castelford.

William de Schipeden, the like, by Jordan de Schipeden. Pledge, John de Thyngelowe.

Henry the Chaplain of Sandal v. Richard the Smith, for trespass, by William the Goldsmith. Pledge, Thomas the Lister.

William s. of Geoffrey de Erdislawe v. Robert s. of Adam de Erdislawe, for trespass, by John de Erdeslawe.

John Patrik gives 6d. to agree with Henry, Hugh de Serleby's man. Pledge, John le Buteller.

Richard Thorsteld gives 12d. to agree with Richard the Syveman. Pledge, Adam de Heley.

Adam de Denton, Richard de Middelton, William de Heukeswrth, Robert de Bayldon, and Ralph s. of Roger de Denton, were found in Sourebyschyre Chase with a hind [bissa]; they give 33s. 4d. to go in peace concerning the same. Pledges, John de Pudeshey, Thomas de Thorneton, Henry de Hiperum, Henry s. of German, Thomas de Coppeley, and Walter de Heukeswrth.

The same men, indicted at the Tourn at Halifax for many thefts, put themselves on the verdict of Thomas de Thorneton, John de Tofteclyve, Richard de Sausemer, John de Haldewrth, Henry de Hiperum, William de Hilton, Adam de Hillingwrth, Robert de Mirefeld, John de Crosland, Adam Hod, John de Mora, and William del Okes, who say that they are all good and faithful. They therefore go quit.

William s. of William Attetunhende, indicted at the Tourn at Rastrik, and Hugh de Cartewrth, indicted at the Tourn at Birton, for many thefts, put themselves on the verdict of the above jurors, who say they are good and faithful. They therefore go quit.

HOLNE.—Adam de Fugeleston sues John de Holne for 3s., for a sheep carried of in Scotland in the 24th year [1295-6]. An inquisition is to be held.

William de Bello monte gives 8s. relief on the land which Robert de Hoderode held of the Earl in the town of Fekesby.

THORNES.—Robert s. and heir of William de Lupesheved gives 6s. 8d. relief on his father's land. Pledge, Philip de Mora.

Maude widow of William de Lupesheved gives 4*s*. (because she is a free-woman) [*quia libera*], to hold her dower for life. Philip de Mora is surety for her not removing her chattels from the Lord's land.

[STANLEY[1]].—Richard s. of John and John Poket each give 6*d*. to agree with John s. of Philip.

John Mollan, plt., and Raymund de Donecastre and Alice wife of William de Cardoil, have a love-day.

Isabel the Cook *v*. William de Ayketon, for trespass. Pledge, John le Beste. Deft. is attached by Robert Attewelle.

Robert Slenge *v*. Adam de Wodusme, for trespass. Pledge, German s. of Philip.

It is presented that Richard the Chaplain of Dewysbiry broke the door of Richard s. of John de Ossete, in the Lord's fee and demesne. He has moved all his chattels from the Earl's land, therefore distraint is to be made when it can be found.

ALVIRTHORPE.—Robert Gune *v*. Richard Bunny of Neuton, in a plea of land. Pledge, Adam Gerbot.

STANLEY.—Gelle Quintin *v*. Richard del Ker, for trespass. Pledge, John Kay.

ALVIRTHORPE.—William At-bar [*ad barram*] *v*. Hannecok le Nunne, for trespass. Pledge, Henry del Bothem.

WAKFEUD.—William de Sandale's maid, the wives of Robert s. of Dia [?], and Robert Haget, the sons of Alan Fisc and William Benne, for dry wood; fines, 2*d*., 6*d*., 4*d*., 1*d*., and 1*d*. Pledge, John s. of Libbe.

William At-bar's son, the like, 2*d*. He pledges his tunic.

Walter Bille, for a cartload of wood [*bosci*], 6*d*. Pledge, Adam le Hunte.

The sons of Robert Chobard and John s. of Libbe, for brush wood, 1*d*. each.

STANLEY.—Richard Spink's son put fire in an oak, which was burnt. Pledges for his making satisfaction at the will of the Steward, John Yssabbell and Roger le Bele. Fine, 2*s*.

William de Lofthus' son, for escape of 4 oxen, 6*d*. Pledge, John Walhot.

THORNES.—Thomas s. of Hawe, for dry wood, 6*d*. Pledge, Ivo the Smith.

Philip del Hill, for an escape, 4*d*. Pledge, Richard Costel.

ALVIRTHORPE.—Juliana Tyan's son, for vert, 2*d*. Pledge, Adam Gerbot.

---

[1] Torn off.

OSSETE.—Agnes Scot of Chideshill, for an escape, 4*d.* Pledge, Adam de Goukethorp.

John Spink of Sothill and Henry de Sothill, the like, 2*d.* and 4*d.*

HOLNE.—John s. of Mary de Calthorne, for an escape, 4*d.* Pledge, Richard de Buttreley.

Dobbe de Smaleschawe, the like, 4*d.* Pledge, John de Heppewrth.

Adam Strekayse, the like and for vert, 4*d.* Pledge, William Strekayse.

John de Alstanley, for an escape, 6*d.* Pledge, John de Holne.

John del Grene, the like, 4*d.* Pledge, Adam de Cartewrth.

William Strekayse, the like, 4*d.* Pledge, Michael de Holne.

———

COURT there on Friday after the Feast of St. Barnabas the Apostle [June 11], in the year abovesaid [1298].

ESSOIGNS.—Edmund le Normaund, from suit of Court, by Henry de Chyvet. Pledge, Peter Swerd.

John s. of John de Haldewrth, the like, by John del Stones. Pledge, Peter Swerd.

John de Crosland, the like, by John Gurdon. Same pledge.

Thomas de Thorneton, the like, by Henry s. of Gilbert. Pledge, John de Thyngelowe.

Robert s. of Adam de Erdeslowe *v.* William s. of Geoffrey, for trespass, by Thomas s. of Henry. Pledge, Robert de Wyrunthorpe.

SOURBY.—Richard de Gledeholt fined 12*d.* for withdrawing his suit against Elias s. of Yvo.

ESSOIGNS.—Henry the Chaplain of Sandale *v.* Richard the Smith of Sandale, for trespass, by Thomas s. of Ralph the Lister. Pledge, William del Okes.

Robert de Storthes and Emma his wife *v.* William de Floketon, for debt, by Jordan del Ker. Pledge, Adam de Heley.

Thomas de Langefeud, plt., *v.* Thomas de Coppeley, for debt, by Richard the Serjeant. Pledge, William de Lyversegge.

Adam s. of Nalke, plt., *v.* the same, by William the Serjeant. Same pledge.

John Mollan *v.* Raymond de Donecastre and Alice, his daughter, executors of the will of William de Cardoil.

Thomas le Geildehirde and Richard his brother, indicted at the Tourn at Halifax for theft, put themselves on the verdict of Robert de Mirefeud, Peter Swerd, John de Tofteclyve, William del Okes, Adam Hod, John de Mora, John de Trimigham, Thomas de Fekesby,

Hugh de Lictheseles, Hugh s. of Reynold, William de Schypeden, and John de Miggeley, who say that they are true men and faithful. They therefore go quit.

The said Thomas and Richard were found in the Earl's chace with a hind [*bissa*]; they give 40s. to go quit thereof. Pledge, Richard de Waddeswrth, John de Miggeley, Elias s. of Yvo, and Hugh de Litcheselis.

Elias de Birton, s. and heir of William de Birton, gives 40s. relief on the land and the whole tenement that his father held in chief of the Earl; and does fealty and homage, and will do suit at Wakefield Court every three weeks.

SOURBY.—Michael s. of Richard de Todmereden gives 2s. to take half of all the land at le Helm, left unoccupied on the Earl's hands by Jordan Peule, for ever. Pledge, Hugh de Lictheseles and Adam le Crouther.

Cicely widow of John s. of Elias recovers as dower ⅓ of all the land bought by Hugh s. of Reynald, from John, her late husband. Hugh is fined 6d.

HOLNE.—An inquisition finds that John de Holne owes Adam de Fugeliston 2d. only, and not 3s., as Adam said; he is to pay the 2d., and 12d. fine. Adam is fined 6d. for false claim.

STANLEY.—John Tricke sues Ralph s. of Nicholas in a plea of land. Pledge, John Kyde.

Robert Wyles is chosen Bailiff of the Liberty by the Earl, and receives his bailiwick at this Court.

COURT there on Friday after the Feast of the Apostles Peter and Paul [June 29], in the year abovesaid, etc. [1298].

ESSOIGNS.—Peter Swerd, from suit of Court, by John Kyde. Pledge, John de Crosland.

Elias de Birton, the like, by Edmund his brother. Pledge, John de Tofteclyve.

John de Querneby, the like, by Richard the Serjeant. Pledge, John le Buteller.

Edmund de Chyvet, the like, by Henry de Chyvet. Pledge, Robert de Wyrunthorpe.

John s. of John de Haldewrth, the like, by Richard le Vegelor. Pledge, Richard de Sausemare.

John le Flemeng, attorney of Sir John de Heton, the like, by Richard de la Haye. Pledge, Walter de Tofteclyve.

John de Trimigham, the like, by Thomas de Werloweley. Pledge, Henry de Rissewrth.

William Drake de Schypeden, the like, by William de Werloweley. Pledge, Robert de Wyrunthorpe.

Thomas de Thorneton, the like, by Henry s. of Gilbert. Pledge, William del Okes.

Robert s. of Adam de Erdeslawe *v.* William s. of Geoffrey, for trespass, by Robert s. of Robert de Rypon. Pledge, Robert de Wyrunthorpe.

William de Floketon against Robert de Thorthes [*sic; i.e.* Storthes] and Emma his wife, for debt, by Richard de Hopton. Pledge, Robert de Mirefeud.

Richard the Smith of Sandale *v.* Henry the Chaplain of Sandale, for assaulting him in John le Beste's curtilage, and breaking his head with a stone he held in his fist; he claims 20s. damages. Deft. is ordered to wage his law. Pledges, Thomas s. of Ralph the Lister and John Mollan.

John Mollan sues Raymond de Donecastre and Alice his daughter, executors of William de Cardoil, for 3s. 6d., for the custody of 7 beasts of the deceased, in his keeping by order of the Earl's bailiff. Defts. hold that they are not bound to answer, because they made no such contract with plt. The plt. is fined 6d. for false claim. Pledge, Colyn de Wyston.

Thomas s. and heir of Philip de Burgh, not yet of age and in the Earl's custody, gives £20 to have the manor of Waleton out of the Earl's custody, which he holds from him in chief; and the said £20 is assigned to the Grave of Thornes by the Earl to improve the Earl's manor [?; *ad manerium Comitis emd'*].

SANDALE.—An inquisition finds that Richard Beusire brought a false claim against Adam s. of Adam Tubbyng. Fine, 6d.

John s. of Henry de la Haye and William de la Haye, executors of the will of William de la Haye, sue Thomas de Hopton for 18s. for 2 oxen, sold to him in the 19th year of Edw. [1290-1], for which he ought to have paid in the 21st year. Deft. asks if they have any instrument by which they were [appointed] executors, either the will or letters of the Dean. They say they have not. It is therefore held that deft. is not obliged to answer. The Steward pardons plaintiffs' fine because they are poor.

An inquisition finds that Nicholas de Wiston did not graze his cattle on Walter de Heselwell's grass, as alleged, but he cut down a piece of hedge, Walter's damages 1d., and keeps him out of herbage belonging to his wife's dower, damages 6*d.*, which Nicholas is to pay; fine, 6*d.* Pledge, John le Parmenter. Walter is fined 3*d.* for his false claim. Pledge, William s of Hugh the Milner.

Henry de Rissewrth *v.* Thomas de Hopton, for debt. Pledge, John Kay. He appoints Robert de Mirefeud in his place.

SANDALE.—Richard Beausire gives 6*d.* to take 3 roods of land on the Hallested from Adam Sprigonel, for ever. Pledge, John Monk.

STANLEY.—Richard s. of William Issabell has license to take a rood of land from Roger le Bele, for ever.

John s. of Roger de Walton sues Raymond de Doncastre, Alice wife of William de Cardoil, and John Mollan, executors of the will of William de Cardoil, for 17*d.* for their cattle in his custody, taxed for 12*d.* to the King. They admit it, and are ordered to pay the 17*d.*, and 6*d.* fine. He also sues for 3*s.* 6*d.* for the keep of 7 beasts belonging to William de Cardoil, which they agreed to pay. They deny the agreement, and must wage their law.

SOURBY.—Richard del Bothes, for an escape, 3*d.* Pledge, Bate del Bothes.

Alcok del Clif, Henry del Ryding, and John s. of Dobbe de Overom, the like, 6*d.*, 4*d.*, and 3*d.* Pledge, William Pelet.

John del Cloych and John s. of William, the like, 3*d.* and 6*d.* Pledge, John s. of John.

John s. of Alan de Barkeseye and Thomas de Buttrewrth, the like, 2*d.* and 3*d.* Pledges, Roger Rotel and John s. of John.

Thomas Turnage of Rachedale, the like, 12*d.* Pledges, William the Smith of Soland and Adam de Soland.

HOLNE.—Ralph s. of Robert de Deneby, the like, 6*d.* Pledge, John s. of Gilbert.

Ralph de Carlecotes, the like, 2*d.* Pledge, Adam s. of Nicholas.

STANLEY.—Adam s. of Cote, for watching with his dog in the fields at fawning-time, 6*d.*; and for carrying away fern at the same time, 6*d.*

John s. of Philip, for watching with his dog at the same time, 6*d.*

Isabel the Cook, for not prosecuting her suit against William de Ayketon; fine pardoned, because she is poor.

Adam de Wodusme gives 6*d.* to agree with Robert Slenge. Pledge, Robert de Wodusme.

ALVIRTHORPE.—Robert Gunne fined 12*d.* for not prosecuting his suit against Richard Bunny in a plea of land.

Simon de Monte does not come; his fine pardoned, because he is the forester.

STANLEY.—Gelle Quintin *v.* Richard del Ker, says that he or his people killed his horse in the common pasture. An inquisition finds that the horse was struck by Richard or his men. Richard must pay damages, taxed at 21*d.* Fine, 12*d.* Pledge, Philip s. of Geoffrey.

Hugh Skayf gives 6*d.* to take 1½ rods of arable land and meadow in Stanley from Walter del Spen, for ever. Pledge, Simon de Monte.

Richard del Ker *v.* Richard del Bothem, Gelle Quintyn, Thomas s. of Simon, and Henry Lewyn for trespass. Pledge, Simon de Monte.

ALVIRTHORPE.—Robert Prest *v.* Hannecok le Nunne, on an agreement. Pledge, Philip Thorald.

An inquisition finds that Hannecok le Nunne sold to William Attebarre land which he had previously leased for a term, and afterwards leased one acre and ½ rood for a longer term. He must satisfy William either with the land or its value. Fine, 6*d.*

STANLEY.—It is also found that Ralph s. of Nicholas wrongfully turned John Tricke out of his land. Fine, 6*d.*

TOURN there on Sunday after St. Swythin's Day [July 15], in the year abovesaid, etc. [1298].

JURORS.—Richard de Bretton, Baldwin de Seyvill, Morice de Ecclishill, Michael de Floketon, Robert de Wodusme, William de Dewysbiry, Hugh Kay, Richard de Sausemare, Robert de Rypon, Adam Wytlof, Walter de Tofteclyve, and John de Tofteclyve.

Richard Byghel of Northmanton did not come. Fine, 6*d.*

Robert de Hegrode of Walton and Gregory the Grave of Walton did not come; by license.

Dom Richard the Chaplain of Dewysbiry, in pursuit of Ralph le Peddere, came to the house of Richard s. of John de Ossete, where Ralph had taken refuge. Dom Richard could not find Ralph, but found and badly beat the children of Richard s. of John, and drew blood from them; Richard's wife raised the hue; Richard s. of John was then in the fields, and came to the hue, and found Dom Richard in his house, and asked him what he did there. He made no answer, but drew a long knife and almost stabbed him, and then made off. And afterwards he kept on returning, and, breaking in the door, entered the house and broke the utensils [*vasa*], and then went away. He is to be attached, but cannot be found.

The wives of Adam Tubbing, Richard Hamond, and Robert Lorimar, fined 6*d*. each for brewing weak ale.

Richard the Milner of Wodekyrk and Adam Brodto, his servant [*garcio*], stole a bushel of groats from Robert Wygehale's sack.

Adam Brodto broke into the house of the Master of Wodekyrk,[1] and stole clothes belonging to the Master's shepherd.

John de Maynigham drew blood from Henry, the servant of Sir John de Sothill, whereby he lost his arm. It is found that he belongs to the Liberty of the Earl of Lincoln. Therefore nothing is done.

John s. of Richard Broun stole a tanned hide, worth 16*d*., from the garden and tannery of Henry de Swynlington.

Robert Dammesone, William Dodeman, and Osbert de Clopton drew blood from a certain clerk of Letheley. Fined 6*d*.

Juliana Swan, the Earl's villein [*nativa*], was deflowered; fine of 6*d*. for lecherwyte.

Nicholas de Wyston received many times a strange harpist [*extraneum cytheristam*], who is believed to have been since beheaded; the last time he left Nicholas's house he gave a harp into his keeping, which Nicholas is to produce.

John Cussing and Walter Hog dug earth [*terra*] on the West moor of Wakefeud, so that the King's highway is made impassable in winter. They are each fined 6*d*.

COURT there on Friday, the Feast of St. James the Apostle [July 25], in the year abovesaid, etc. [1298].

Essoigns.—Alan Almod, attorney of Lady Margaret de Nevill, from suit, by William Scherewynd. Pledge, Robert de Mirefeud.

Adam Achard, the like, by William de Erdeslawe. Same pledge.

Elias de Birton, the like, by Adam de Birton. Pledge, John de Thingelawe.

John de Querneby, the like, by John le Buteller. Pledge, Henry de Schefley.

John de Trimigham, the like, by John de Halifax. Pledge, William del Okes.

Sir John de Heton, the like, by Robert de Erdeslawe. Pledge, John de Haldewrth.

---

[1] Woodkirk or West Ardsley was a cell to Nostell Priory; the heads seem to have been called indifferently Priors or Masters. John, Earl of Warenne, relieved them of service at the Wakefield Court, due in respect of the lands at Ardsley, given by Robert Brito of Denningley. (*Mon. Ang.*, vi, 99.)

William Drake, the like, by Matthew de Schipeden. Pledge, Peter Swerd.

John de Crosland, the like, by John Gurdon. Same pledge.

Dom Henry the Chaplain of Sandale v. Richard the Smith of Sandale, by Thomas the Lister of Wakefeud. Pledge, Adam Hod.

William de Floketon v. Robert de Storthes and Emma his wife, for debt, by John Mollan. Pledge, Robert de Mirefeud. They do not come, and are fined 6d. William goes quit.[1]

William s. of Geoffrey de Erdeslawe v. Robert s. of Adam de Erdislawe, by William de Bateley. Pledge, Robert de Mirefeud.

SANDALE.—Robert de Donecastre sues John the Skinner, for trespass. Pledge, Adam s. of Roger. He is attached by William de Pleggewyk. When called, Robert does not come, and John craves judgment by default, which is given. Robert's fine forgiven, because he has nothing in goods.

HOLNE.—Cicely widow of Adam de Lecht [sic] sues Adam de Lecth [sic] and John Wyther, her husband's executors, for half an ox, bullock, mare, and foal, ⅓ of 13 goats, a sow and 9 hogs, 6 sheep, 4 lambs, and half the wool of the sheep; and gives the lord half thereof for help to recover the same. Pledge, the Grave of Holne.

Richard Norre of Erdislawe, indicted at the Tourn, as appears above [sic], finds the following manucaptors for his coming at the next Court:—Walter de Tofteclif, John his brother, William At-kirk of Erdeslawe, William de York, Richard de Dewysbiry, and William Child the elder.

ALVIRTHORPE.—Hannecok le Nunne gives 6d. for an inquisition between himself and Philip Thorald. An inquisition of the neighbours finds that whereas Hannecok said that Philip took his sheep to keep under all contingencies, Philip did not in any way undertake to guarantee them. Plt. is therefore fined 6d. for false claim.

The aforesaid inquisition, as a body, complain that Hannecok le Nunne's wife said before the Court that they were all perjured. She admits it, and must satisfy them for the defamation. Fine, 6d.

Adam Gerbot sues Hancok le Nunne for saying that he would perjure himself at any inquisition for a gallon of ale. Deft. acknowledges that he said it maliciously, and must satisfy plt., and pay 6d. fine. Pledge, Philip Thorald.

Adam s. of Walter gives 6d. to take ½ acre of land in the Morcroft from Adam Gerbot, for 12 years. Pledge, William At-bar.

---

[1] He was the defendant.

STANLEY.—Ralph s. of Nicholas *v.* John Tricke, in a plea of land. Pledge, William s. of Eve.

WAKEFEUD.—William Wlmer *v.* William s. of Walter de Neuton, for trespass. Pledge, Robert Wyles.

Henry Schorthose *v.* John de la Foreste of Floketon, for debt. Pledge, William the Goldsmith.

William the Clerk *v.* John s. of John de Holne and John his father, for debt. Pledge, Richard the Serjeant.

STANLEY.—Richard del Ker *v.* Thomas s. of Simon [and others, as above], and Alice At-town-head [*ad caput ville*], for trespass. Pledge, Simon de Monte.

Geppe the Pinder *v.* Thomas de Stanley and Philip his son, for trespass. Pledge, Richard le Lepere.

Nicholas de Cailli holds freely a carucate of land in Wakefeld called Bothom.

ALVIRTHORPE.—Adam Gerbot *v.* John Schirlok, for trespass. Pledge, Henry le Nunne.

Henry de Swynlington *v.* Richard s. of Philip, for trespass. Pledge, William the Clerk.

SOUREBY.—Robert s. of William de Lyngarthes gives 2*s.* relief on his father's land. Pledge, Hugh de Lictheseles.

William de Swynesheved, for escape of a horse, 6*d.* Pledge, Richard del Sandforth.

William s. of Molle, the like, 6*d.* Pledge, William de Stodley.

Peter Swerd, the like, 3*d.* Pledge, Robert At-Brig.

Wilkoc de Mancanholes, the like, 3*d.* Pledge, Henry de Stodley.

Robert at-Brig, the like, 3*d.* Pledge, William de Stodley.

Hanne del Schaghe, the like, 3*d.* Pledge, Hugh del Hagwe.

Adam del Schawe, the like, 3*d.* Pledge, Robert At-Brig.

William de Stodley, the like, 6*d.*, and for 12 oxen, 6*d.* Pledge, Hanne de Stodley.

Hanne de Stodley, the like, 6*d.* Pledge, William de Stodley.

Hugh de la Lawe, the like, 8*d.* Pledge, Hanne del Schawe.

Thomas de Coppeley, for escape of 6 pigs, 6*d.* Pledge, William son-in-law of the Priest.

WAKEFEUD.—John s. of William Attebarre, for broom bark [*pro cortice husseti*], 6*d.* Pledge, William, his father.

ALVIRTHORPE.—Hannecok le Nunne's son, the like, 6*d.* Pledge, William s. of Walter de Neuton.

Thomas Bunny, the like, 6*d.* Pledge, Philip Thorald.

COURT there on Friday next before the Feast of St. Bartholomew [Aug. 24], in the year aforesaid, etc. [1298].

ESSOIGNS.—Peter Swerd, from suit of Court, by John Wodekyrke. Pledge, John de Trimigham.

Edmund de Chyvet, the like, by William s. of Nicholas de Erdeslawe. Pledge, Robert de Mirefeud.

Dom Henry the Chaplain of Sandale v. Richard the Smith of Sandale, for trespass, by William the Goldsmith. Pledge, Thomas the Lister.

John de Crosland, from suit, by John Gurdon. Pledge, William the Goldsmith.

John de Haldewrth, the like, by Richard le Debler. Pledge, John de Trimigham.

Thomas de Langefeud v. Thomas de Coppeley, for debt, by William de Livereshegge. Pledge, William the Grave of Werloweley.

Adam s. of Nalke de Heptonstall v. Thomas de Coppeley, for debt, by William the Serjeant. Pledge, John Kyde.

Thomas de Stanley v. Richard del Ker, for trespass, by William le Tayllur. Pledge, William del Spen.

STANLEY.—Philip s. of Thomas de Stanley v. Geppe the Pyndere, for trespass, by John Kyde. Pledge, Robert de Mirefeud. Geppe, the plt., does not come, and is therefore fined 3d. Philip goes quit.

Thomas de Stanley v. the same Geppe, in the same plea, by German s. of Philip. Pledge, John le Buteller.

Henry de Rissewrth v. Thomas de Hopton, by Robert de Mirefeud.

Robert s. of Adam de Erdeslawe v. William s. of Geoffrey de Erdeslawe, for assaulting him at the Merebrigge in Erdeslawe, breaking his head and the small bone of his arm with a club; he claims 20s. damages. Deft. is to wage his law. Pledge, Walter de Tofteclyve.

ALVIRTHORPE.—William Wlmer sues William s. of Walter de Neuton for carrying 5 sheaves of oats off his land, as though for distraint, and for striking him on the head with a club; he claims 5s. Deft. says that he took the sheaves in distraint for ½d. due to him by resolution of the whole Byrrelaghe [*per consideracionem totius Byrrelaghe*], and that the plt. agreed thereto. He denies this, and is to wage his law. Pledge, Robert le Rollere. Deft. admits the assault, but says it was in self-defence, because plt. drew a knife. He must satisfy plt., and is fined 6d. Pledge, Adam Gerbot.

John s. of Richard Broun, indicted at the Tourn, finds these manucaptors:—John Graffard, Philip the Tailor, John the Tailor, Thomas s. of Stephen, John the Turner, Richard s. of Broun, Ralph de Colley, and Adam Gerbot.

STANLEY.—Ralph s. of Nicholas sues John Tricke for withholding from him 3 acres of land, which he says are his lawful inheritance, because his father died seised thereof. Deft. says the land is part of his mother's inheritance, and was divided between them [*inter eosdem*] in the time of William de London, and that he paid relief for it. An inquisition is ordered.

HOLNE.—William the Clerk sues John s. of John de Holne and John, his father, for 12*d.*, which Matthew de Farneley gave him in the Court at Birton for his damages. They admit it; their fine is pardoned by the Steward.

ALVIRTHORPE.—An inquisition ordered between Adam Gerbot and John, his brother, whom he charges with carrying off the crop of ½ acre of meadow in the Morcroft, which he had let to plt. for 6 years.

SANDALE.—Isabel widow of William de Chyvet gives 13*s.* 4*d.* for license to marry, and to withdraw from the Earl's land, and to hold her dower so long as she does service and suit therefor. Pledge, Ralph the Smith.

ALVIRTHORPE.—Richard s. of Philip de Alvirthorpe gives 12*d.* to take a bovate of land from Walter s. of Adam de Alvirthorpe, for 8 years. Pledge, Henry del Bothem.

SOURBY.—John s. of Hugh de Schepeley gives 12*d.* to take a bovate of unoccupied land in Soland, and 5 perches in Ulfkelrode, and a messuage under the Bromehill, for ever. Pledge, William the Grave.

ALVIRTHORPE.—Thomas de Garderobe has license to take a perch of land from Hannecok le Nunne, for 20 years, Hannecok doing service; and another perch for the same term from Adam Gerbot, on the same terms.

Adam Gerbot sues John Schirlok regarding a curtilage. Pledge, John Nelot.

SOURBY.—Thomas[1] de Coppeley, for an escape, 6*d.*

Hanne de Holgate, the like, 3*d.* Pledge, William the Grave.

Hugh de Lictheseles, the like, 6*d.* Pledge, Michael de Routunstall.

Thomas Lyly, the like, 6*d.* Pledge, John de Stansefeud.

---

[1] First written *Edm'*, but appears to have been altered.

D

Thomas, his son, for shooting at a hind [*bissa*], 2s.

William de Aveneley, for an escape, 6d. Pledge, John de Miggeley.

John del Clogh, the like, 6d. Pledge, William de Aveneley.

Nicholas de Werloweley, the like, 6d. Pledge, William the Grave.

John Fildingmayster, the like, 3d. Pledge, William de Saltonstall.

Hugh de Hillingwrth, the like, 3d. Same pledge.

Matthew de Sundreland, the like, 2d. Pledge, Richard de Saltonstall.

William s of Agnes de Halifax, the like, 3d. Pledge, William de Saltonstall.

John de Nuteschawe, Richard de Chesewaldeley, and Ivo de Chesewaldeley, the like, 3d., 6d., and 6d.

William Swaype and Adam le Crouther, the like, 3d. and 2d.

HOLNE.—Adam le Warde, the like, 3d. Pledge, John de Holne.

Symon de Thurstanland, the like, 3d. Pledge, John the Smith.

Nelle Geseling, the like, 2d. Pledge, Hanne Warde.

Thomas Pokerebyn, the like, 2d. Pledge, Elias de Schelfley.

Thomas de Schepeley, the like, 4d. Pledge, Thomas Pokerebyn.

William Ferenhoule, the like, 1d. Pledge, Thomas, his son.

STANLEY.—Adam de Uchethorp, because his dog took a hare, 6s. 8d. Pledge, Richard del Ker.

WAKEFEUD.—William Attebarre, because his dog ran in the fields, 6d. Pledge, Hannecok le Nunne.

Emma le Baggere v William Wlmer,[1] for trespass   Pledge, John Beek.

John Cukewald v. William de Ayketon, for trespass.   Pledge, John Pollard. Deft. is attached by Robert the Serjeant.

William de Floketon v. Thomas de Hopton, for debt.   Pledge, William s. of Peter.

HOLNE.—Parnell [*Petronilla*] da. of Benet v. Adam s. of John de Holne, for trespass. Pledge, Benet, her father. Deft. is attached by his father.

Juliana da. of John de Holne v. the said Parnell, for trespass. Pledge, Michael de Holne.

Adam Benne v Nicholas s. of Nicholas Keneward, for trespass. Pledge, John de Donecastre. Deft. brings a cross-suit; and another against Adam Benne and Malina, his wife.

---

[1] The defendant's name was originally written as Isolde daughter of Geoffrey Scalle. The note remained uncancelled, that she [*ipsa*] is attached by her father.

Robert de Mirefeud *v.* Thomas le Coverur of Schepeley, for trespass. Pledge, Hugh de Thornicthel [?].

THORNES.—Peter the Sadeller *v.* Robert de Thornes, for trespass. Pledge, Robert the Serjeant. Deft. is attached by Thomas del Spen.

COURT there on Friday before the Exaltation of Holy Cross [Sept. 14], the year abovesaid [1298].

ESSOIGNS.—Peter Swerd, from suit of Court, by William de Erdeslawe. Pledge, John de Crosland.

William de Bellomonte, the like, by William de Lepton. Pledge, John le Flemeng.

William de Schipeden, the like, by Matthew his son. Pledge, William s. of Hugh de Rastrik.

John de Trimigham, the like, by Richard the Smith of Werloweley. Pledge, John de Querneby.

Alan Almot, the like, by Robert de Mirefeud. Pledge, Richard the Serjeant.

John de Haldewrth, the like, by Richard le Debler. Pledge, John de Tofteclyve.

Baldewyn de Seyvill, the like, by Hugh s. of Symon. Pledge, Adam Hod.

SANDALE.—Richard the Smith of Sandale gives 6*d.* to agree with Dom Henry the Chaplain. Pledge, John Monk.

STANLEY.—Richard del Ker sues Thomas de Stanley, for twice seizing his horse in his [? own] corn [*bladum*]. Deft. admits it. Fine, 6*d.* Pledge, Robert s. of Simon.

William Wlmer gives 6*d.* to agree with Emma le Baggere, for trespass.

William de Ayketon and his pledge are in mercy, for not coming to answer John Cukewald.

Richard the Milner of Wodekirke and John s. of Richard Brun, indicted at the Tourn at Wakefeud, put themselves on the verdict of John Wythehundes, Adam Hod, William At-kirk, Walter Fraunceis, William Child, William the Hayward [*Messor*], William Broun, John s. of Alan, Thomas de Ekynton, Peter the Carter, Nicholas de Doniglawe, and Adam de Doniglawe, who say that they are good men and true. They therefore go quit.

STANLEY.—Geppe the Pinder fined 3*d.* for refusing to prosecute his suit against Thomas de Stanley. Pledge, Simon de Monte.

Cicely widow of Adam de Leche, and John Wyther and Adam de Leche, the executors of her husband, have a love-day.

The inquisition between Ralph s. of Nicholas and John Tricke, touching 3 acres of land, is taken by the oath of Richard del Bothem, Robert Pescy, Richard le Lepere, Philip le Syur, Robert Daneys, Robert s. of Walter, Robert s. of Simon, Adam Gerbot, Richard Gerbot, Thomas Pegere, William Prudfot, and Philip de Mora, who say that when their father and mother died, 40 years ago, in the time of William de London, Steward, the land was divided between them, with Ralph's consent, and that John has been in seisin ever since. Ralph fined 6d. for false claim.

Nicholas s. of Nicholas Keneward and Adam Benne give 18d. to agree. Pledge, Robert Stirks.

ALVIRTHORPE.—It is found by reference to the Court Rolls that John Schyrlok demised to Adam Gerbot ½ acre of land in le Morcroft, which Henry de Swynlington had sown with corn, and that John afterwards carried off the crop in the night. Adam is to have the land for the term, 6 years. John must pay him for the crop, and is fined 6d.

Adam Gerbot is fined 3d. for a false claim for a curtilage which he claimed against John, his brother. He admits that their father gave it to John in open Court.

HIPERUM.—William s. of Walter de Schepeley gives 2s. to take a bovate of land in Hiperum from Roger, servant [garcio] of Richard de Clifton, for 16 years, he doing service, and keeping the houses and buildings in repair. Pledges, Adam the Grave of Rastrik and Roger s. of John.

HOLNE.—John de Holne, for escape of 24 sheep, 12d. Pledge, Peter del Peck.

SOUREBY.—Hanne de Northland, for dry wood, 3d. Pledge, Hugh de Northland.

Alote del Wytelie, for escape, 6d. Pledge, John the Milner.

Cicely de Baggehill, the like, 3d. Pledge, Richard de Salsa Mara.

WAKEFEUD.—Peter the Sadellere's maid, for dry wood, 1d. Pledge, John Bule.

William Benne's daughter, the like, 2d. Pledge, John the Tailor.

The son of Nanne Roschauke [?], the like, 2d. Pledge, John s. of Sibbe.

John Beek's maid, and the daughter of John s. of Sibbe, the like, 1d. and 2d.

Robert Estrild's maid, the like, 2d.

STANLEY.—John Cort, for nuts, 6*d.* Pledge, Philip s. of Agnes.

Idonea Tyan, for dry wood, 3*d.* Pledge, William, her husband.

The son of Thomas s. of Ode, the like, 1*d.* Pledge, William, his brother.

Philip s. of Nalle *v.* Alice wife of John Graffard, and John s. of John Graffard, for trespass. Pledge, Alan de Bordens. She is attached by Thomas the Brounesmyth. They bring a cross-suit against Philip. Pledge, Philip s. of Alan.

WAKEFEUD.—John Cussing has license to build an oven in his booth, which shall be common to everyone, on the following conditions, that he shall pay the lord 6*s.* 9*d.* at the three terms, viz.:—2*s.* 3*d.* at Michaelmas, 2*s.* 3*d.* at the Purification of the Blessed Virgin Mary, and 2*s.* 3*d.* at Whitsuntide, for all service. And for faithful payment of the said rent, John pledges all his tenements in the town of Wakefeud, both in burgages and in booths, the said rent to be levied out of them if the oven does not suffice.

====

ROLL FOR 34 AND 35 EDWARD I AND 1 EDWARD II, 1306–7.

[Part of the top membrane has been torn away.]

[TOURN held in October or November, 1306.]

[JURORS].—. . . . . Thomas de Fekysby, John de Locwode, John Percy, John the Clerk of . . . . William del Bothes, Ralph de Guthlacharwes, John le Flemeng . . . .

. . . . drew blood from Adam, the man [*homo*] of Master Thomas de Dalton.

. . . . de Seleby drew blood from Isabel, his sister.

Adam s. of John de Hiperum appropriated to himself the lord's waste in Hiperum.

Alice the Mercer and . . . . . . Bradeley sold contrary to the assize.

Robert s. of Adam drew blood from Henry the Hirde.

Agnes wife of Richard de Shelf sold contrary to the assize.

Roger Senior of Briggehuses has appropriated the lord's waste.

Roger de Briggehuses, Adam the Milner, Roger s. of Wylimot, and the wife of John Specth, sold contrary to the assize.

William s. of John de Roaldesete stole an ox in Marcheden, from the cattle of the Countess of Lincoln. He is to be arrested.

The townships of Hiperum, Northuuerum, Rastrik, Fekesby and Staynland, say upon oath that [if] any one makes his will, his executors cannot administer his goods without first making a fine with the Vicar, and Richard, his chaplain.   Therefore, etc.

[COURT held] the same day.

. . . . Roger s. of John the Milner sues John s. of Richard. He says that deft. and his father sold him 3 roods of meadow for 6s. 6d., and failed to fulfil the agreement.   Deft. acknowledges it, but refuses to surrender the land.   He is therefore to return the 6s. 6d., and is fined 6d.

Cicely de Briggehuses gives 6d. to hold a toft in Briggehuses and 1¾ acres in Rastrik, which Adam the Milner her late [husband] held, for the term of her life.   Pledge, Roger de Breggehuses.

Peter de Suthclif v. Adam s. of John, says he paid 4s. for him for a customary aid, because he [? Adam] holds ⅓ of all his [? Peter's] land as dower with his [? Peter's] mother, whom he [? Adam] married. Adam says he was taxed before the Steward by his neighbours for the whole tenement he holds; reference is to be made to the Rolls.[1]

Thomas de Tothill v. John Spillewod; he says that he holds at will of the deft. a certain tenement in le Briggehuses, from which tenement he [deft.] has removed [irradicavit] a certain house, to his damage of 13s. 4d.   Deft. says that the plt. has no rights in the tenement, except a rent of 6d.   An inquisition finds for plt.   Deft. must pay the damages and 12d. fine.

Alcok le Waynwrith gives 6d. to take ½ acre of land from Adam s. of Alote, for ever.

An inquisition finds that Malina widow of Ivo offended against Peter del Barm; she is to satisfy him, and pay 2d. fine.

Richard the Smith gives 12d. to take 3 acres of waste land in Werloweley, for ever.

Simon de Tothill, elected Grave, gives 12d. not to serve this year.

John s. of Walter gives 2s., Roger s. of John the Milner gives 2s., and John de Sundreland gives 18d., not to be Grave this year.

TOURN at Birton the Wednesday following.

Jurors.—[? John] Wyther, Richard de Thornicthel, Henry de Birton, Richard Osan, John de Braythetweyt, Thomas the Shepherd,

---

[1] It is difficult to distinguish clearly between the numerous pronouns.

Thomas Ferenhoule, John de Heppewrth, Richard de la Grene, Adam del Scoles, and John s. of Gilbert.

Maude wife of John de Schepeley sold contrary to the assize.

Nicholas le Baggere and Thomas Throstel drew blood from one another.

Emma la Baggere and Cristiana de Schelfley sold contrary to the assize. Also Diana Crabbe.

Robert Botun does not come; fine 6d.

The wife of John s. of Gilbert sold contrary to the assize; 6d.

William Wodemus drew blood from Henry his son; 12d.

Jordan the Milner's wife sells contrary to the assize, 6d.; also .... de Wytestones.

[Richard] del Merse, indicted at the Tourn at Birton before Peter de Lundo, then Steward, for stealing 5 heifers from .... de Mirefeld, and not yet acquitted, is said to be guilty, and is to be arrested.

COURT there the same day.

Richard del Merse, indicted as above, gives 6s. 8d. to be under the mainprise of Matthew del Merse, Robert s. of ...., Gilbert de Birton, Robert del Merse, Thomas s. of Robert, Thomas Russell, Elias de Brocholes, Matthew Bibby, Robert s. of Margery, William the Milner, Adam de Thornyctheley and Thomas the Shepherd, until the first delivery of York Gaol.

HOLNE.—Adam de Heppewrth sues Robert de Elwardeholes, for 6s. rent for 3 years, due to the Earl for certain land. Deft. denies it, saying he took 9 acres from a certain man, for which he did fealty :...... to the Earl, and all things belonging to the said land. An inquisition finds the remaining part of the land, 9 acres, is unoccupied [*jacent vaste*] on the Earl's hands, and that .... pays 16d. a year to him from whom he took the land. And because the remaining part lies unoccupied, he must henceforward pay the rent of 16d. to the Grave; fine, 6d.

Margery widow of Richard de Thwong *v.* John de Holne, says that he and Juliana, his daughter, put obstacles in the way of the execution of the will of Thomas, her son, husband of the said Juliana. An inquisition is to be taken. Margery appoints her son Hugh her attorney.

Henry s. of Thomas *v.* William s. of Richard de Heppewrth, in a plea of land; he gives 5s. for an inquisition.

Richard de Gris *v.* Robert Botun, for debt. Deft. fined 6*d.* for not coming.

An inquisition finds that Nicholas Keneward maliciously charged William de Storthes with killing a stag. Fine, 12*d.*

Richard de la Grene gives 2*s.* to take ¼ of a bovate of land and ½ a barn in Holne for ten years, from Adam s. of Jordan the Milner.

Thomas de Bouderode owes Jordan the Milner 19*d.*, which he is to pay; fine, 2*d.*

Henry Mous gives 12*d.* to take a messuage and 3 acres in Fugheleston from Adam s. of Benne, for ever.

Thomas s. of John de Fugheleston, heir of Elias, his brother, gives 2*s.* relief on 7½ acres of land with buildings in Fugheleston. Pledge, Adam the Grave.

Adam s. of Simon de Fugheleston gives 12*d.* to take 3 acres and half a house for 9 years from Hugh del Hole. Pledge, Adam de Alstanley.

Richard s. of Elias de Alstanley gives 18*d.* to take 4¼ acres from Adam de la Grene, for 11 years.

Robert s. of Gamel gives 6*d.* to take ½ rood of land from Adam de la Grene in Alstanley, for ever. Pledge, Gilbert de Alstanley.

Thomas the Shepherd [*le Bercher*] gives 12*d.* to take a rood of meadow in le Sparch' from Thomas s. of Sarah, for ever.

Macok s. of Gilbert de Alstanley gives 18*d.* to take 2 acres in Alstanley from Gilbert de Alstanley; one half acre thereof lying in the Kylnacre, which he is to receive at once, one acre on Symmerode and half an acre in Emmerode, which he is to receive after Gilbert's death, also a curtilage in Alstanley.

Matthew Bybby *v.* John the Fuller, for debt. Pledge, Thomas Brounschanks. He is attached by Thomas Throstel, but does not come; wherefore both he and Thomas are fined 6*d.*

Thomas de Billeclif, for contempt, 12*d.*

Hugh del Hole, elected Grave, gives 2*s.* not to serve this year. John de Heppewrth gives 6*d.* for the like.

John s. of Hugh de Littlewod is elected Grave and admitted. The whole township will answer for him if need be.

TOURN at Wakefeud the Thursday following.

JURORS.—Walter de Grimiston, Robert de Wyrunthorpe, John Patrik, William de Dewysbiry, John de la More, William de Floketon, Paulin de Emmeley, Richard s of John de Ossete, Henry de Heton, Walter Scot, William Grenehod, and William the Goldsmith [*Orfeure*].

Walter Marmion of Northmanton and Henry Marmion, his brother, drew blood from one another. Fined 12d. each.

Henry Marmion, for unjustly raising the hue by night on said Walter and Emma, his sister, 12d.

SANDALE —John s. of Robert Lorymer drew blood from Margery the Wricth [Wright]; 12d.

Alice Trubbe drew blood from Cicely wife of William Trubbe; 12d.

The wives of William the Fuller and Richard Beausire, and Margery Hamond, sell contrary to the assize. The first has left the Earl's land, and cannot be distrained; the others pay 12d. and 4d.

WAKEFEUD.—Robert Dernelove fined 4d. for not coming to the Tourn.

John the Barkere does not come, but nothing is done, because he is indicted.

Thomas the Brounesmyth's wife raised the hue without cause on William s. of Jerman, as stated by the four sworn men of the town of Wakefeud.

Jerman Kay drew blood from William Tirsy. Fine, 6d.

John, servant [*serviens*] of the late Henry de Swynlington, stole an ox-hide from John de Ferie the younger, worth 3s. 4d., in the beck at Thornes [*in rivulo de Spin'*]; also a hide worth 15d. from Wodekirk Fair. He is to be arrested.

WAKEFEUD.—Robert Liftfast fined 4d. for not coming.

William s. of Robert s. of Hugh made a pit in his garden [*ortum*], the garbage from which flows into the common well⁻ [*fons*] of the town of Wakefield. He is to be attached.

Christiana wife of William Terri received as her guest Agnes de Nunnewyke, who is attainted of theft (to the value of 4d.) in Wakefeud Court; and common report says she receives other malefactors.

STANLEY.—Maude da. of Walter de Flanshowe, the Earl's villein [*nativa*], married Geoffrey s. of Robert the Chapman, without license. She is pardoned, because poor.

Isolda Ro, the Earl's villein [*nativa*], has been deflowered. Fine, 3d.

WAKEFEUD.—Juliana da. of John s. of Sibbe, 6d. for the like. Pledge, William the Tayllur.

ALVIRTHORPE.—Richard the Tanner v. John Rate, for trespass. Pledge, Adam Gerbot. He is attached by Richard s. of Broun.

Matthew de Lyntweyt v. John de Lyntwayt, John de Locwode, Alice de Lyntweyt and Margaret, her daughter, for trespass. Pledge, John de Querneby. They are attached by John de Locwode, Elias de Lingarth, John de Crossland and Richard his son.

Agnes da. of Dye de Lyntweyt *v.* John de Lyntweyt, for trespass. Pledge, Ralph de Gouthlacharwes.

HOLNE.—Jordan the Milner *v.* Nicholas s. of Nicholas, for trespass. Pledge, Thomas Ferenhoule.

Richard le Syur *v.* John de Lethe, for debt. Same pledge.

Magge wife of Elias *v.* Elias s. of Hanne the Grave, for trespass. Pledge, John the Grave.

———

COURT there on Friday, the Feast of St. Katherine the Virgin [Nov. 25], in the year abovesaid [1306], in the time of the aforesaid [Steward].

ESSOIGNS.—Robert de Wyrunthorpe, from suit, by John his son. Pledge, John Kay.

William de Schipeden, the like, by William the Serjeant. Pledge, Richard de Birstall.

Nicholas de Caylly, the like, by Robert del Spen. Pledge, John de Tofteclyve.

Nicholas le Normaund, the like, by Adam Fox. Pledge, Adam Hod.

Thomas de Thorneton, the like, by Hugh de Thorneton. Pledge, John de Tofteclyve.

Nicholas de Bateley is to be distrained afresh to hear judgment, as above.

Sibil widow of John the Leach [*Medicus*] is fined 6*d.* for withdrawing her claim against Hugh the Carter, for dower in a certain booth.

Thomas the Brounesmyth and Emma his wife, plts., and William s. of German, deft., have a love-day.

German Kay essoigns against William Tyrsy, for trespass, by Henry s. of Jerman [*sic*]. Pledge, Henry Erl.

German Philcok, for contempt committed in Court, before the Steward, 20*s.;* he went from the Court, and would not answer the charge against him until the last Court, when he submitted [*decendebat*] to an inquisition. This is now taken by the oath of Thomas de Wakefeud, William . . . . , Robert de Wyrunthorpe, Robert de la Grene, John de Mora, William del Okes, Richard de Bristall, Thomas de Wytteley, William de Dewysbiry, John de Tofteclive, Hugh de Seyvill and Richard del Ker, who say that he made a fosse [*fossatum*] in Stanley fields, without the Earl's license; but it was not to the injury of the neighbours, because it is always open in open time. They also say that Robert s. of Anote de Stanley held 2 bovates of land in the ville of Stanley, for which he did suit at the Earl's Court every three weeks; and that Philip the Mercer, father of the said German, formerly held 3 acres of land out of the said bovates, and afterwards Thomas de Garderobe bought the rest; there was a dispute between Thomas and German; Thomas would not do suit, but German did suit for his holding; and afterwards German gave the 3 acres to Mariota, his daughter, and she entered and did suit every three weeks; and when German was the Earl's bailiff they arranged their differences, and the suit was withdrawn from that time. They also say there was a dispute [*contumelium*] amongst certain people of the lord's town of Wakefield, which dispute was fostered by German, who hindered an agreement between the parties.

John the Tanner, indicted, as it appears, at the Tourn at Wakefeud, gives 6s. 8d. to be under the mainprise of William the Tayllur, William the Serjeant, Thomas de Wytteley, William the Lacer and German Swerd until the next delivery of York Gaol.

Richard del Bothom, and Elizota his wife *v.* Richard Kay, for trespass. Pledge, Robert de Bateley.

ALVIRTHORPE.—William s. of Robert s. of Simon *v.* William s. of Walter and Robert s. of Ralph, in a plea of land. Pledge, Gemme Campion.

Sir William Fitz William [*filius Willelmi*] to be distrained for many defaults.

WAKEFEUD.—Robert Pegere fails in waging his law against Henry le Erl. Fine, 6d.

STANLEY.—Thomas de Lofthus had a day for acquitting himself of breaking the lord's fold. He does not come, and is to be distrained.

SOURBY.—The forester charges Richard del Rodeker with breaking the Earl's fold, and taking his cattle away. An inquisition is ordered.

William the Cowehirde and Juliana his wife give 2s. to have an attaint of 24 on an inquisition of 12 jurors before Dom. Ranulf at the Court at Rastrik in the 34th year [1306], concerning land from which they are ousted by Elias s. of John.

ALVIRTHORPE.—John Rate gives 4d. to agree with Richard the Tannur. Pledge, Richard s. of Broun.

SANDALE.—Agnes Attehelm and John her son *v.* Nelle de Donecastre; they say that they demised land to him for five years, and he is digging sea coal [*carbones maris*] therein; damages, 6s. 8d. Nelle admits it, is to pay the damages, and 6d. fine.

HOLNE.—John de Holne and Juliana his wife, fined 2s. for impeding the execution of the will of Thomas s. of Marjory.

The inquisition between Henry s. of Thomas, complainant, and William s. of Richard, in a plea of 10 acres of land, is taken by the oath of Richard de la Grene, John de Holne, Richard de Cartewrth, Adam de la Grene, Simon s. of Adam, Thomas de Billeclyve, Thomas de Elwardeholes, Matthew de Mora, William de Buttreley, Thomas s. of Sarah, Nicholas del Clif, and Hogge de Langeley, who say that one Maude de Fugheleston, who was right heir of the said land, surrendered the land in Court, in her free virginity, in a way [*per modum*] which, the plt. claims, ought not to exclude him from his right. The jury find for the deft., who may hold to him and his heirs in peace. Henry's fine is forgiven, because he is poor.

The jury say that Nicholas s. of Nicholas fraudulently broke an agreement made between him and Jordan the Milner, with regard to a portion of tithe [*de quadam portione decime*]. Fine, 12*d.*

Nicholas s. of John s. of Gilbert de Heppewrth gives 12*d.* to take 2 acres 1 rood of land from John s. of Richard del Rode, for ever. Pledge, John s. of Hugh.

Magge wife of Elias gives nothing for a license of concord, because she is poor.

Joan da. of Walter de Heton *v.* Henry s. of Baldewyn de Sayvill, for trespass. Pledge, John Graffard.

WAKEFEUD.—Gemme Campion and Magge Witlof, his wife, *v.* William the Tayllur, with regard to a booth. An inquisition is ordered. [A note in the margin says the matter was not prosecuted further.]

HOLNE.—Richard le Syur gives 3*d.* to agree with John de Lecthe, for debt.

STANLEY.—Hugh Tagge, Robert de Mickelfeld, Robert s. of Geoffrey de Stanley, Sibbe Hamond, and John, servant [*garcio*] of Watte, for dry wood; fines, 4*d.*, 3*d.*, 2*d.*, 2*d.* and 2*d.*

OSSETE.—Robert Soneman, for escape of 5 pigs, 6*d.*

Richard Greneholm, John Alayn, Hugh Pees, John Peny, Hugh de Chideshill, Adam Luvelavedy, and Jordan Scot, 2*d.* and 1*d.* each, for dry wood.

Richard de Heton, for an escape, 6*d.*

HORBIRY.—Elias Raton, Thomas Elyne, Adam Hoperlorn, Silver-counte, and John Dipsy, for dry wood; fines, 3*d.*, 3*d.*, 3*d.*, 2*d.* and 4*d.*

WAKEFEUD.—Robert Grenehod, John de Sculebrok, Gemme the Gardiner and John le Surreys, for dry wood; fines, 2*d.*, 2*d.* and 1*d.*

William Nelot *v.* Robert Goes [?], for debt. Pledge, William the Tayllur. He also sues John Cussing, John Kay, and others of the lord's tenants, for debt.

SOURBY.—William s. of Hugh de Lictheseles *v.* Adam le Crouther, in a plea of land.

Henry the Milner *v.* John de Locwode, for trespass. Pledge, John de Querneby.

COURT there on Friday after the Feast of St. Lucy the Virgin [Dec. 13], in the 35th year, in the time of William de Wakefeud, the Steward [1306].

ESSOIGNS.—John de Willeys, from suit of Court, by Thomas de Wytteley. Pledge, Henry Erl.

John de Pudesheye, attorney of Lady Margaret de Nevill, the like, by Thomas de Seyvill. Pledge, Edmund le Normaund.

Thomas de Heton, the like, by Roger Assolf. Pledge, William del Okes.

William de Schipeden, the like, by William del Okes. Pledge, Richard de Birstall.

Peter Swerd, the like, by William the Serjeant. Pledge, William del Okes.

Nicholas de Caylly, the like, by Roger de la Mere. Pledge, John de Tofteclyve.

Nicholas le Normand, the like, by Edmund de Chyvet. Pledge, John de Mora.

William Wyldebor, the like, by Thomas the Brounesmyth. Pledge, Robert de la Grene.

WAKEFEUD.—William Tirsy *v.* German Kay, for assaulting him and cutting off his thumb with a misericorde;[1] damages, 100*s.* An inquisition is ordered. It is to be determined in the Town Court of Wakefeud.

HOLNE.—Matthew Bybby fined 6*d.*, and Thomas Brounschanks, his pledge, fined 4*d.*, for not prosecuting his suit against John the Walker.

Joan da. of Walter de Heton *v.* Henry s. of Baldewyn de Seyvill, for coming to the house of Walter de Heton, and there breaking the lock of a chamber which her father had lent her; damages, 20*d.* Deft. is ordered to wage his law. Pledge, Hugh de Seyvill.

Hugh de Seyvill *v.* Walter de Heton, for trespass. Pledge, Colyn de Caylly.

John de Locwode was charged with ejecting[2] the Earl's men from the free tenement of which he was seised, whereby the Earl was

---

[1] The text has *cum una m'ia.* A misericorde was a small dagger.
[2] Quere : *quod ipse debuit ejecisse.*

disseised; and when the Earl's Grave wished to have seisin, John came with others unknown, and refused to deliver seisin, but would have killed the Grave, who barely escaped with his life; and afterwards he tried to kill William the Tayllur, the Earl's bailiff, in the same way. John denies the charge. An inquisition is ordered.

John de Lyntweyt, charged with the same trespass, submits to the same inquisition.

Elkoc de Lyntweyt to be distrained to answer the same charge.

John de Querneby gives 2s. to have respite of suit till next Michaelmas.

SOURBY.—The inquisition between William s. of Hugh de Lictheseles, plt., and Adam le Crowther, taken by the oath of John s. of John Roger s. of Anabel, Elias s. of Yvo, Richard de Saltonstall, John del Westwode, William s. of Yvo, John Swyfte, John de Waddeswrth, Adam Migge, Richard the Smith, Thomas de Roaldesete and William the Milner, who say that William has no right to the three quarters of a bovate for which he sues, but only to ½ a bovate and 3 roods; he is therefore fined 6d. for a false claim, and pays 12d. for the inquisition. They say also that Hugh de Lictheseles, his father, demised the land for 12 years to one Soyer[?] de Sourby, who afterwards died, and Hugh received the land back again, and afterwards left it unoccupied on the Earl's hands for two years and more; and the Earl made proclamation as to the land, and no one came to claim it; so the Steward farmed the said land to Adam le Crowther, who thus had entry. Sentence is postponed till the next Court. They say that at the time of the proclamation William was 24 years old and more

WAKEFEUD.—Richard Mayk (4d.), Robert Prest junior (4d.), Henry de Gonton (4d.), John the Leche (4d.), Peter de Acom (4d.), and John le Rasede (6d.), summoned on the inquisition, are fined for not attending.

Roger le Bele and Mariota his wife, fined 4d. for not appearing at the inquisition summoned between them and William de Wakefeud.

ALVIRTHORPE.—Richard Wythehundes, for dry wood, 3d.

John Rate, for vert, 4d. Pledge, Adam Gerbot.

Richard s. of Broun, for dry wood, 2d. Same pledge.

The wife of Richard Gerbot, for an escape, 3d.

WAKEFEUD.—Alice widow of William Yllewyly, the like, 2d. Pledge, Adam Gerbot.

Henry de Sculebrok, Richard the Clerk's maid, Henry Lanpere's wife, Gilbert le Tinkere's maid, Walter Scot, Gemme the Gardiner and John Swerd, for dry wood, 3d., 2d. and 1d. (5).

Henry the Nouthirde, for an escape, 2d.

HIPERUM.—Richard s. of Walter, Walter s. of Elyot, the wife of Ivo the Milner, Roger de Briggehuses, Henry the Milner, Cicely the Milner and Ralph de Schipeley, for escapes; fines; the first five 2d., the others 1d.

STANLEY.—Juliana de Uchethorp (2d.); the wife of Robert de la Dale (4d.), and Richard Poket (4d.), for dry wood. Pledges, Robert Goes, Robert de la Dale, and John brother of Richard Poket.

SANDALE.—William de Felton, for an escape, 6d. Pledge, Robert de la Grene.

OSSETE.—The maids of Richard Passemer and Wyldebor, for dry wood, 2d. each.

John Alayn and Hugh Pees, the like, 1d. each.

THORNES.—Roger Traylment (3d.), John de la Haye (1d.), John Gour's wife (1d.), for the like.

The widow of Philip del Hill, for an escape, 2d.

An inquisition finds that Ivo the Smith's cattle damaged William the Tayllur's corn [bladum]. Damages 16d., fine 6d. The like is found against Magge Hawe.

Thomas the Brounesmyth's wife fined 12d. for raising the hue wrongfully after William de Wakefeud.

OSSETE.—Henry s. of Richard the Grave v. William s. of Jordan, for trespass. Pledge, Richard Broun of Heton.

STANLEY.—Gelle Quintin v. John Walhot and Emma his wife, in a plea of land. Pledge, Robert de Mickelfeld.

THORNES.—John Tasse v. Robert the Grave of Thornes, Marg' his wife, and Roger Traylment, in a plea of land. Pledge, William the Clerk.

———

COURT there on Friday, the Feast of St. Hilary [Jan. 13], in the year abovesaid [1307], in the time of the aforesaid [Steward].

ESSOIGNS.—John de Willeys, the common essoign [de communi],[1] by Thomas de Wytteley. Pledge, Thomas de Bellehus.

John de Pudeshey, the like, by John s. of Gelle de Stanley. Pledge, Henry de Schelfley.

Peter Swerd, the like, by Matthew de Linthweyt. Pledge, Richard de Birstall.

William Wyldebor, the like, by John de Birstall. Pledge, Robert de la Grene.

———

[1] The common essoign is that from suit of Court.

Thomas de Thorneton, the like, by Hugh de Thorneton. Pledge, Richard de Waddewrth.

Henry s. of Baldewyn de Seyvill wages his law against Joan da. of Walter de Heton, and goes quit. She is fined 12*d*. for a false claim. Pledge, John de Heton.

Richard Boton gives 12*d*. to agree with Richard de Gris. Pledge, Hugh de Thornicteley.

Peter the Chaplain gives 2*s*. for help to recover 6*s*. from Walter the Clerk of Dewysbiry and Matthew de Tothill, his pledge. They are to be distrained for it.

An inquisition finds that John de Locwode ejected Matthew de Lintweyt, etc., according to the charge entered above. Fine, 40*s*. Pledges, Adam de Colleresley, John the Smith, Thomas de Locwode and John the Harper. John de Lintweyt is found guilty of the same. Pledge, John de Locwode. Fine (?). Elcok de Lintweyt found Thomas de Aldeneley as pledge for his coming to this Court to answer the same charge, and did not come; fine, 12*d*.

Henry the Milner gives 6*d*. to agree with John de Locwode, for trespass. Pledge, John de Querneby.

SOURBY.—Elias s. of Ivo gives 6*d*. to agree with Richard Hodde in a plea of land. Pledge, John Hodde.

John de Tothill *v*. Robert Pes, for debt. Pledge, William the Clerk.

Thomas the Forester gives 2*s*. to take a bovate of land in the ville of Sourby from Agnes, his mother, for ever, reserving her dower therein. Pledge, Roger s. of Anabel.

Adam s. of Roger de la Lone *v*. John de Miggeley, in a plea of land. Same pledge.

SANDALE.—Margery and Alice, daughters of Robert the Carpenter, *v*. Master Robert de Ketelisthorp, in a plea of land. Pledge, John Monk.

HOLNE.—Juliana de Cartewrth pays 40*d*. for license to marry.

THORNES.—John the Tailor [*cissor*] *v*. Thomas the Brounesmyth, for breaking a fence running from defendant's house towards William the Clerk's barn in close time, whereby cattle of defendant and other neighbours got into plaintiff's corn; damages, 6*s*. 8*d*. Thomas is ordered to wage his law.

Matthew de Lintweyt is fined 18*d*. for withdrawing his suits against John de Locwode, John de Lyntweyt, Alice de Lyntweyt and Marg[aret], her daughter.

WAKEFIELD.—William Nelot, plt., and John Kay, Robert Estrild, William Wyles and John Cussing, defts., for debt, have a love-day.

HIPERUM.—Simon del Dene (4*d.*), William s. of Ode (2*d.*), Malina wife of Ivo (2*d.*) and Othos de Heyley (4*d.*), for dry wood.

STANLEY.—Alice the Schiphird of Metheley, 6*d.*, and Maude her daughter, 2*d.*, for the like. Pledge, Hugh Skayf.

The wives of Nicholas the Carpenter and Adam the Shepherd, the sons of William the Dykere and Walter del Spen, Benet de Stanley junior, William del Rodes, the wife of Hugh s. of William, Maude de Heyleys, Richard the Pynder's maid, William s. of Bateman, Robert Typet, and Hugh his brother, 2*d.* each, for dry wood.

William Don's wife, 1*d.*, for the like.

OSSETE.—Richard Suart, 3*d.*; William Wyldebor, 2*d.*; Mocock de Ossete, Hugh Pees and John Alayn, 1*d.* each, for the like.

ALVIRTHORPE.—Adam Gerbot, 2*d.*; the wife of Richard Gerbot, 6*d.*; and Richard s. of Philip, 2*d.*, for escapes of pigs.

SOUREBY.—William de Sothill, Adam at Town's-head [*ad caput ville*], William de Sothill and William de Chesewelleley, 6*d.* each for not coming.

STANLEY.—William s. of Richard del Ker *v.* Adam s. of Cote, for trespass. Pledge, William s. of Walter.

HOLNE.—Adam del Mere *v.* Hanne Wade, for trespass. Pledge, Adam s. of Emma.

THORNES.—Richard le Westren *v.* William le Westren and Richard de Lupesheved, in a plea of land. Pledge, Thomas Lyleman.

ALVIRTHORPE.—John Dade *v.* John With-the hounds, for debt. Pledge, German Swerd.

William Grenehod *v.* Robert the Clerk of Sandale, Robert de Hegherode, John the Clerk of Walton, and Adam Gerbot, for debt. Pledge, William the Tayllur.

COURT there on Friday after the Conversion of St. Paul [Jan. 25], in the year abovesaid [1307], and in the time of the aforesaid [Steward].

ESSOIGNS.—William de Schipeden, the common essoign, by Thomas de Wytteley. Pledge, William del Okes

William de Rastrik, the like, by Thomas de Thothill. Pledge, Walter de Tofteclyve.

Nicholas de Caylly, the like, by William the Serjeant. Pledge, Peter Swerd.

Nicholas le Normaund, the like, by Thomas de Wytteley. Pledge, John de Tofteclyve.

E

Thomas de Heton, the like, by Henry de Heton. Pledge, William Wyldebor.

Thomas de Thorneton, the like, by Hugh de Thorneton. Pledge, John de la More.

Thomas de Bellehus, the like, by William de Holdewrth. Pledge, William del Okes.

Robert de la Grene, the like, by Richard s. of John. Pledge, Richard de Birstall.

Hugh de Seyvill fined 6d. for withdrawing his suit against Walter de Heton. Pledge, Nicholas de Caylly.

Matthew de Lyntweyt is pledge for Elcok de Lyntweyt's submitting to an inquisition on the charge of abetting John de Locwode against the liberty of the Earl.

SOURBY.—An inquisition finds that Richard del Rediker did not break the Earl's fold, as alleged.

THORNES.—Thomas the Brounesmyth wages his law against John le Tayllur; he therefore goes quit, and John is fined 4d.

Agnes da. of Dye, plt., against John de Lyntweyt, is called, and does not come; she is fined 6d., and deft. goes quit.

William Wyldebor gives 12d. for respite of suit till Michaelmas.

Ralph de Lupesheved fined 3d. for not coming.

ALVIRTHORPE.—Adam Wlf gives 6d. to take to himself and his heirs ½ acre of new land in a lane leading towards the New Park, at 2d. rent.

Margaret de Nevill fined 40d. for making default at this Court.

Thomas de Dronesfeld made default. [No fine entered.]

Jordan de Lyille and John de Sayvill, 12d. each for default.

John de Trimigham, 6d.

ALVIRTHORPE.—John s. of Henry le Nunne gives 12d. to take 2 acres of land in Neuton field from his father, for ever. Pledge, Hannecok le Nunne.

STANLEY.—John s. of Philip le Syur gives 3s. to take 6 acres of land in Stanley fields from his father, for ever. Pledge, Adam Gerbot.

RASTRIK.—Beatrice da. of Thomas de Fekesby gives 3s. 4d. as relief on 3 acres of land in Fekesby, after her father's death. Pledge, Thomas del Wode.

HOLNE.—An inquisition finds that Hanne Wade demised to Adam del Mere, certain land which he had for a term, until the end of the

term ; he is therefore only bound warrant for that term. Adam fined
6*d.* for claiming general warranty [*in omnibus*].

It is presented that Sir Thomas de Burgh retains two stray
cart-horses [*affros*]. He is to be distrained, because no one has
waif in the Earl's liberty, save the Earl himself.

SOURBY.—A stray heifer is to be taken into the Earl's hand, which
is in the custody of Hugh de Lictheseles.

A filly [*pultra*], supposed to be a stray, remains in the custody
of Robert de Saltonstall, Grave of Sourby; valued at 2*s.*

RASTRIK.—A cow worth 6*s.* 8*d.* remains in the custody of the
Grave of Rastrik.

STANLEY.—Gelle Quintyn sues John Walhot and Emma his wife,
for 12 acres of land, as his right, which he took to himself and his
heirs from Alexander Lucas, then Steward, after it had lain unoccupied
for a year and more, and due proclamation had been made for the
heir. Defendants deny this. An inquisition is taken by the oath of
Robert Gunne, Robert de Flanshowe, Hugh Bateman, John Poket,
Richard Poket, Richard del Ker, Robert Bateman, Henry del Bothem,
Henry le Nunne, Robert de Uchethorp, Richard de Colley and William
Hoskel, who say that the land was unoccupied for 7 years, and confirm
plaintiff. Gelle gives 5*s.* for seisin [?]. Defts. fined 4*d.*

WAKEFEUD.—William Nelot withdraws his suit against John Kay
and Robert Estrild for debt ; fine, 6*d.* He also sues Robert Gros
for debt.

OSSETE.—Henry s. of Richard the Grave of Ossete sues William
s. of Jordan for a bovate of land, which he says belonged to Richard
his father. Deft. says that he bought the land from Richard, and took
it in open Court. An inquisition is taken by the oath of Richard s.
of John, Richard Passemer, Richard del Dene, Adam del Dene,
William Child, John de Chykenley, Jordan Moyses, Adam de
Goukethorp, Walter s. of Eva, Richard Armerew [?], Adam de
Chykenley, and Richard s. of Walter, who confirm deft. Plt. fined 6*d.*

WAKEFEUD.—William Nelot offers himself against William Wiles,
who does not come. He is to be distrained for not attending after
a love-day.

William Nelot sues John Cussing for 4*s.* 2*d.*, and 4*s.* under two
several agreements, made in the 31st and 32nd years [1302–4], that
he would be Grave for the whole community of the whole Graveship

[*quod ipse deberet esse propositus pro tota communitate totius propositure*]
and 2s. . . . . Deft. denies the debts, and must wage his law.
Pledge, William Wlmer.

SANDALE.—William Grenehod sues Robert the Clerk of Sandale
for 2 stones of wool, value 10s.   Deft. admits the debt.   He must
pay the plt.   Fine, 4d.

THORNES.—An inquisition of the neighbours finds that Thomas
Hawe had demised to John Tasse an acre of land, for 4 crops, of
which he had two before Thomas's death; after which Magge, his
widow, demised it to him for 2 crops (which he has not had), and
also half an acre of land for 3 years, which he has not had.   Robert
the Grave of Thornes, who married the said Margery [*sic*], denied
[John's] right thereto.   It is decided that John is to hold for the
terms specified, because he took them from Magge; but he is fined
4d. for taking them from Thomas Hawe, who had no right therein
except by custody, and he must lose the term which he has of
Thomas's demise.   Robert is fined 6d. for unlawful detention.

William the Tayllur sues John de la Haye for 6s. 8d., for damage
done by his cattle to plaintiff's corn; deft. denies it, and wages his
law.   Plt. is in mercy, but is pardoned because he is the bailiff of
the liberty.

STANLEY.—An inquisition finds that Robert Gos was pledge for 5s.
owed by Adam de Maladr' to William Nelot.   Robert must pay 5s.
and damages, and is fined 4d.

SOURBY.—Adam s. of Robert de la Lane sues John de Miggeley
for an acre of land, which he claims as his right.   They have license
to agree, Adam quitclaiming the said land to John and his heirs, and
John paying the Court and 6d. fine.

The case between Beatrice Kay, plt., and Nicholas de Bateley,
deft., for trespass, is respited until she returns from Rome.

The case between Thomas the Brounesmyth and Emma his wife,
plts., and William de Wakefeud, deft., is respited till the coming of
Sir John de Nevill, the chief Steward [*capitalis seneschallus.*].

ALVIRTHORPE.—William Grenehod sues Adam Gerbot for a stone
of wool, price 5s., due to him; damages, 2s.   Deft. admits it.   He
must pay the wool or the price, and the damages.   Fine, 4d.

ALVIRTHORPE.—Robert s. of Ralph de Uchethorpe, 3d., and Richard
s. of Robert de Bateley, 4d., for dry wood.

HIPERUM.—John del Wro, 4d., William de Thorp of Hiperum, 4d.,
and Malina Peti, 2d., for escapes,

SANDALE.—Robert de la Grene, 2*d.*, William de la Grene, 2*d.*, and John Monk's son, 1*d.*, for dry wood.

ALVIRTHORPE.—Adam Gerbot sues Alice da. of Alice wife of Adam the Forester, in a plea of land. Pledge, Robert de Alvirthorpe.

The sworn bailiff presents that Robert de Hegherode made a rescue; also that Quenilda de Alvirthorpe broke the Earl's fold.

ALVIRTHORPE.—William Pegere *v.* Roger Bele and Mariota his wife, Adam Gerbot, and Thomas de Wytteley, for debt. Pledges, German s. of Philip and Richard Pegere. He also sues Henry le Nunne and Adam Gerbot, for debt. Same pledges.

STANLEY.—Robert Goes *v.* William Nelot, for trespass. Pledge, Richard del Ker.

Adam Tagge *v.* Hugh Tagge, in a plea of land. Pledge, Richard Poket.

ALVIRTHORPE.—Robert le Mareschal *v.* Richard s. of Broun, for trespass. Pledge, John Tasse.

HOLNE.—Richard le Syur *v.* Thomas s. of Sarah, in a plea of land. Pledge, Matthew del Merse.

ALVIRTHORPE.—Emma Bunny *v.* John Bunny, for trespass. Pledge, John s. of Sibbe.

Thomas de Tothill *v.* Thomas s. of Modde de Lynley and Henry s. of Thomas, for debt. Pledge, Peter de Barkesland.

ALVIRTHORPE.—John Broun *v.* Richard the Cobbler [*sutor*], in a plea of land. Pledge, Richard s. of Broun.

Robert de Castelford *v.* Richard s. of Broun, for slander.

COURT there on Monday before St. Peter in Cathedra [Feb. 22], in the year abovesaid [1307], in the time of the aforesaid [Steward].

ESSOIGNS [Common].—Peter Swerd, by William the Serjaunt. Pledge, William de Schipeden.

John de Crosland, by Henry Gurdon. Pledge, Thomas de Bellehus.

Nicholas de Caylly, by Thomas Dynes. Pledge, John de Tofteclyve.

Richard de Birstall, by Thomas de Birstall. Pledge, Thomas de Thorneton.

William Wyles essoigns against William Nelot, for debt, by William the Goldsmith [*orfeure*]. Pledge, John de Tofteclyve.

Robert s. of John the Grave gives 6d. for custody of a filly [*pultra*], thought to be a stray, which he proves to be his. Pledge, Richard the Smith of Ossete.

Sir Thomas de Burgh, charged with detaining two stray horses [*affros*], finds two pledges, Robert de Wodesme and Henry de Biry, to do what right shall decree at the next Court.

John de Lascy finds pledges, Jordan del Ylle and Thomas de Tothill, to produce at the next Court a horse worth 8s., which was in the custody of Alcok del Frith, and is thought to be a stray.

An inquisition finds that Elkoc de Lyntwayt was not guilty of abetting John de Locwode.

ALVIRTHORPE.—John With-the-hounds essoigns against John Dade, in a plea of debt, by Thomas the Brounesmyth. Pledge, Richard s. of John With-the-hounds.

RASTRIK.—An inquisition finds that Matthew de Totehill was distrained by two oxen, as was presented, and did not break the fold.

SOUREBY.—Adam s. of Ivo gives 12d. to agree with Hugh de Lucheseles, as to a heifer in Hugh's custody.

HIPERUM.—Saundre de Briggehuses gives 3s. 4d. to take a messuage and 6 acres of land from Hanne s. of William de Brigge- huses, for ever. Pledge, John le Barn.

Peter del Barm sues Malina widow of Ivo, for land. Pledge, Alexander the Grave of Rastrik.

SOUREBY.—William the Cowehird and Juliana Wade sue John s. of Elias for ⅓ of two bovates of land, which he unlawfully deraigned against them at the Court at Rastrik last year, by an unjust inquisition, seeing that they took the land from lands which had lain unoccupied on the Earl's hands for a year and more. The deft. says that the inquisition was a true one. The attaint is taken by the oath of Hugh s. of Reynald, Richard de Saltonstall, John del Westwode, Henry de Holgate, John le Mouner, Adam Migge, John the Webster [*tixtor*], William the Grave of Worl', William the Smith, Thomas de Roaldesete, Elias s. of Ivo, William Horsecnave, Roger the Shepherd [*le Bercher*], John s. of Henry, Ivo de Werl[oweley ?], Michael del Lom, Adam s. of Elias the Milner, Thomas de Licthe- seles, Thomas le Crouther, Adam de Heytf', John s. of Evote, John Swyft, Adam s. of Ivo, and Henry s. of Beatrice, who find for the plaintiffs. They are to recover seisin to themselves and the heirs of Juliana, and pay 12d. for seisin. John is fined 6d. The former jury of twelve are to pay to the plaintiffs' damages, assessed at 6s. 8d.; and as it is attainted by the 24 that they made a false oath, they, namely, William s. of Ivo (40*d.*), Roger s. of Amabel (20*s.*), John s. of John de Soland (13*s.* 4*d.*), Henry s. of William (2*s.*), Richard s. of Alote (12*d.*), Henry del Dene[1] (40*d.*), William Attetoun[2] (2*s.*), Robert de Saltonstall (5*s.*), Thomas s. of Elias (2*s.*), Thomas del Feyld (2*s.*), Henry de Soland (4*s.*), and John s. of Jordan (12*d.*), are to be imprisoned; they are redeemed from prison by pledges of redemption; one being surety for another. They are fined the amounts put over their names, altogether 60*s.* [59*s.*].

WAKEFEUD.—William Nelot fined 6*d.* for withdrawing suit against John Cussing, for debt.

STANLEY.—Adam s. of Cote gives 4*d.* to agree with William s. of Richard del Ker. Pledge, Robert the Grave.

ALVIRTHORPE.—Adam Gerbot gives 2*s.* for an attaint as to an acre of land assigned to Alice da. of Alice, by an unjust inquisition.

THORNES.—William the Tayllur withdraws his suit against Agnes widow of Roger. His fine is pardoned, because he is the Serjeant.

ALVIRTHORPE.—Quenilda de Alvirthorpe, for breaking the Earl's fold, 6*d.* Pledge, William Tulle.

William Pegere sues Roger le Bele and Mariota his wife for 2 quarters of oats, price 3*s.*, for which Adam Gerbot and Thomas de Wytteley were their pledges. Adam comes and admits it, and must pay the oats or their price. Thomas does not come, and is to be distrained. Adam also admits that he was surety for one quarter of oats, price 18*d.*, which Henry le Nunne owes them; he must satisfy the plaintiffs. Fines, 6*d.* and 4*d.*

SOUREBY.—A messuage and an acre of land in the ville of Werloweley are in the Earl's hands as an escheat, because William de Roaldesete, who held them, has been hanged.

Juliana Wade gives 6*d.* to take half a messuage in Soureby from Roger s. of Amabel, to the use of Beatrice da. of William the Cowehirde, and her heirs. Pledge, Adam le Crowether.

OSSETE.—William Hirning gives 40*d.* to take a bovate of land in the ville of Ossete from Raulin his brother, for ever. Pledge, Robert Soneman.

ALVIRTHORPE.—An inquisition finds that Richard s. of Broun detained Robert Marescall's pigs; he is fined 6*d.*

WAKEFEUD.—Robert de Castelford sues Richard s. of Broun for calling him Robert le Brus, to despite him. Deft. denies it, and wages his law. Plt. fined 4*d.*

---

[1] Called *de Luddingden* in the list of fines.   [2] *Del Toun, ibid.*

ALVIRTHORPE.—Emma Bunny gives 12*d.* to agree with John Bunny.

Christiana Terry, indicted at the Steward's Tourn for theft, is committed to prison; afterwards released on the mainprise of John de Ferie and Roger Bele.

An inquisition acquits Robert de Hegerode of making a rescue against the sworn serjeant.

THORNES.—John the Tailor fined 4*d.* for withdrawing his suit against Alice widow of Philip.

WAKEFEUD.—Robert Goes *v.* William Nelot; Robert was surety for 5*s.* for one Adam de Maladria, and William distrained upon him [Robert] for this amount; Robert then went to Adam, and made him put a mare in the fold, at William's disposal; William then released him. An inquisition finds for Robert, who therefore goes quit. William is to pay 7*s.* 6*d.* damages, and is fined 4*d.*

STANLEY.—Adam Tagge sues Hugh his brother for 2 acres of land, which he claims after his father's death, as his heir. Hugh says that he had entry by Robert Typet, his elder brother. An inquisition is taken by the oath of Gelle Quintyn, John Walhot, John Poket, William Albrey, Adam s. of Cote, Robert Goes, Richard del Bothem, Robert s. of Robert, John Cockespore, Roger Traylment, Robert Pescy, and John s. of Alice, who say that Bateman Tagge, their father, held 18 acres of land, and that Hawe, his wife, had dower in 6 acres after his death; after Hawe's death, Robert Tipet paid relief on the 6 acres, as next heir, and he sold the 6 acres to Hugh and William Tagge, as was lawful, and they took them in Court. Adam is fined 6*d.* for a false claim.

HOLNE.—Richard de la Grene sues Peter de Brus for maliciously slandering him to the Earl and others; damages, 100*s.* An inquisition finds for the plt.; damages, 6*s.* 8*d.* Fine, 6*d.*

ALVIRTHORPE.—Juliana Swan *v.* John Thorald, in a plea of land. Pledge, Richard de Colleye.

THORNES.—John Tasse *v.* Ivo the Smith, Agnes wife of Roger, Roger Traylment, and John del Haghe, for trespass. Pledge, Alexander de Aula.

STANLEY.—William Tagge *v.* Robert Gunne, for trespass. Pledge, Robert de Mickelfeld.

Robert le Rollere *v.* John s. of Philip de Wodehall, for trespass. Pledge, Nicholas de Bateley.

Robert Gunne complains of Master John of the Schools [*de Magistro Johanne Scolarum*], for trespass. Pledge, Robert Pescy.

ALVIRTHORPE.—Thomas s. of Launce *v.* Richard s. of Philip de Alvirthorpe, in a plea of land. Pledge, William de Uchethorpe.

Robert de Stodeley is elected Bailiff of the Liberty in the Soke of Wakefield, in the place of William the Tayllur. Pledges, German Philecok, Henry Erl, and Robert le Rollere.

- - - - - -

COURT there on Friday before the Feast of St. Gregory [March 12], in the year aforesaid [1307].

ESSOIGNS.—Elias de Birton, the common essoign,[1] by John Daunsel. Pledge, John de Tofteclyve.

Nicholas Normaund, the like, by William the Serjeant. Pledge, John de la More.

Thomas de Heton, the like, by Roger Assolf. Pledge, Richard de Birstall.

John de Crosland, the like, by Henry Gurdon. Pledge, John de Tofteclyve.

Peter Swerd, the like, by William the Serjeant. Pledge, Richard de Birstall.

Thomas de Bellehous, the like, by Robert de Stodeley. Pledge, William the Serjeant.

John de Wylleys, the like, by Robert de Soureby. Pledge, Hugh de Sayvill.

William de Schipeden, the like, by William de Werloweley. Pledge, Robert de la Grene.

William de Rastrik, the like, by Thomas de Tothill. Pledge, ... de Thorneton.

John With-the-hounds against John Dade, for debt, by Richard his son; and John Dade against him, by John Kay. Pledges, Robert s. of Jordan del Grene and Thomas de Wakefeud.

HOLNE.—Richard le Syur sues Thomas s. of Sarah for 3 acres and one rood of land in Fugheleston, which he claims as his inheritance, because Henry s. of Peter, his uncle, whose heir he is, demised the land for a term of 3 years, now ended. Thomas says that his mother took the land from the Earl's waste [*de vasto Comitis*] before Thomas Cok, then Steward, in open Court. An inquisition is taken by the oath of Thomas Ferenhoule, Henry s. of Thomas, Richard s. of Michael, Matthew de Mora, Robert de Elwardeholes, Simon de Heppewrth, William s. of Wylke, Nicholas

---

[1] From suit of Court.

Keneward, Adam his son, Jordan the Milner, Thomas s. of Juliana, and Matthew s. of Thomas, who say that one Thomas s. of Peter is the next heir, as nephew by a brother, whilst Richard le Syur is a sister's son; they say also that the said land lay waste for three years and more, before Sarah, mother of the defendant, took it. But, as it was taken before proclamation was made, it is held that the next heir ought not to be excluded from his right; he is therefore to recover seisin, and pays 2s. for entry. Thomas is fined 6d.

John de Lascy proves that a horse (worth 8s.) is his.

Thomas de Tothill, keeper of the goods of the Blessed Mary [*custos catallorum Beate Marie*] in the parish of Halifax, *v.* Thomas s. of Modde and Henry s. of Thomas, for debt.

ALVIRTHORPE.—Adam Gerbot sues Alice da. of Alice for an acre of land, which he claims because Gerbot, his father, bought the land and took it in open Court, and never surrendered it. Alice says that Gerbot, [? his or her] father, bought the land to her use with her own goods. An attaint is taken by 24, viz.:—Philip de Mora, Robert de Lupesheved, William s. of Thomas, John Malyn, Thomas Lyleman, Richard Pegere, Richard s. of Broun, Robert Hod, Richard Bunny, Henry del Bothom, Walter del Hill, Robert Pille, Philip le Syur, Richard del Bothom, John Bullok, Robert Gunne, Walter Bateman, William Albray, Simon de Monte, John de Chykenley, Adam del Dene, William Child, John s. of Eva, and Adam de Chykenley, who find that Gerbot de Alverthorpe bought the land with Alice's chattels and for her use. She may hold in peace. Adam is fined 4d.

The land which Philip Thorald held in Alvirthorpe is in the Earl's hands, because he is dead.

An inquisition finds that Richard s. of Philip ousted Thomas s. of Launce from ½ acre of land which he [Thomas] took from Anote [?], maid of Hugh Kay, for a term of years before Anote sold the land to the deft. Thomas is to recover for his term, 2 years, and Richard is fined 4d.

Juliana Swan sues John Thorald for 3 roods of land and a small piece of meadow, from which she asserts that he is ousting her. He says that John Swan demised him the land for 2 years not yet expired. Juliana says that it was previously demised to her and her heirs before deft. had entry for his term. An inquisition finds that defendant's term of 2 years is expired; he is fined 4d.

STANLEY.—Robert Gunne sues Master John of the Schools [*Magistrum Johannem Scolarum*] for deforcing him from ½ acre of land belonging to his bovate. Deft. says that one Magge Mote demised him the land for a term of years. An inquisition is taken by the oath of Simon de Monte, Robert s. of Walter, Richard del Ker, Adam s. of Cote, Gelle Quintin, John s. of Philip, Richard Poket, Robert Goes, Robert Pescy, Adam Gerbot, Robert Richard, and Andrew Pogge, who find for deft. Robert fined 6d.

William Tagge, when called as plt. against Robert Gunne, does not come; he is therefore fined 4d., and deft. goes quit.

ALVIRTHORPE.—John Broun sues Richard the Cobbler, who had demised him a rood of land for a term, with warranty; he is now distrained for rent in arrear. An inquisition finds that the deft. demised the land in the same way as he took it, and not otherwise. Plt. fined 6d.

Richard del Bothem and Elizota his wife, plaintiffs, do not appear against Richard Kay, who therefore goes quit. They are fined 6d.

STANLEY.—William Tagge v. Robert Gunne, for trespass. Pledge, Robert s. of Bateman.

OSSETE.—Anabel wife of Hanne de Heton v. William s. of Jordan, for trespass. Pledge, Richard del Dene.

SANDALE.—John Tropinel and Adam de la Grene are fined 3d. each for not coming.

ALVIRTHORPE.—John Rate v. John Swan, for trespass. Pledge, Richard s. of Broun.

STANLEY.—Robert le Rollere sues John s. of Philip, for throwing down the fence [sepem] which he had made about his meadow. Deft. justifies it, saying that he ought to have a common way there. An inquisition finds for the deft. Robert is fined 6d. for false claim.

OSSETE.—Anabel wife of Hanne de Heton sues William s. of Jordan for unlawfully levying an aid of the lord of 40d. upon her, instead of upon Henry s of Richard s. of Jordan. Deft. says that [the aid was due] from Hanne de Heton. An inquisition finds that Hanne was assessed at 12d., and Henry s. of Richard s. of Jordan at 40d. Deft. is ordered to pay 6d. damages, and 2s. 4d. which he levied in excess, and 6s. 8d. fine.

STANLEY.—An inquisition finds that Robert Gunne damaged William Tagge's corn with his geese, and cut down his wood; damages, 6d.; fine, 6d. William fined 4d. for wrongfully charging Robert with carrying earth away from his ditch [extra fossatum].

THORNES.—Adam s. of Thomas and Margery his wife give 5s. to take a bovate of land in Thornes from Ellen and Joan, daughters of

Richard s. of Jonne, and from Christiana their mother, who has dower therein; paying them 40*s.* in two instalments. Pledges, Robert s. of Simon de Flanshowe, Robert his son, and Richard de Colleye.

SANDALE.—William s. of Robert de Holynes gives 40*d.* to take 5 acres 1 rood of land between Bysmarerowe and Holinthorp from Thomas Erneburgh, for ever. Pledge, John Monk.

STANLEY.—Richard del Bothem gives 12*d.* to take an acre of land in the town of Stanley from Eva de Ayketon, for ever. Pledge, Richard Longschanks.

ALVIRTHORPE.—Richard s. of Broun *v.* Robert Mareschall, for trespass. Pledge, John his son.

SOURBY.—Nelle s. of Ivo, for vert, 12*d.* Pledge, Adam de Heytford. Hanne s. of William, for dry wood, 4*d.* Pledge, John the Milner.

WAKEFEUD.—The sons of Hugh Bille (2*d.*), William s. of Eva (3*d.*), Richard s. of Jonne (2*d.*), John Gurdon (1*d.*), and Robert Prest the elder (1*d.*), for dry wood. Pledges, their respective fathers.

William Attekyrke, for an escape, 4*d.* Pledge, Roger Bele.

Thomas de Lofthus, for dry wood, 6*d.* Pledge, Thomas the Forester.

German the Gardiner's son (3*d.*); the maids of John le Southeren (2*d.*), John de Sculebrok (2*d.*), and John Swerd (1*d.*); Walter Bylle's son (1*d.*); the maids of William s. of Godith (1*d.*), Richard le Wayte (4*d.*), and Reynald de Swynlington (2*d.*); the sons of Magota Prest (1*d.*), and Hugh Bylle (4*d.*), for dry wood. Pledges, their respective fathers and masters.

OSSETE.—The sons of William Wyldebor (2*d.*) and John Alayn (4*d.*), the maids of John Hirning (3*d.*), John the Walker (4*d.*), Richard s. of John (3*d.*), and Richard s. of Jonot (3*d.*), for dry wood. Pledges, as above.

John Mansel, for an escape, 12*d.* Pledge, Richard his brother.

THORNES —Thomas the Brounesmyth's son (1*d.*), Thomas Vyrun's son (4*d.*), and the maid of John Graffard (3*d.*), for dry wood.

STANLEY.—William the Dyker's son (2*d.*), Walter del Spen's son (2*d.*); the maids of Robert del Spen (4*d.*), and Robert s. of Geppe (3*d.*), for dry wood.

Richard s. of Robert de Bateley, for an escape, 4*d.*

ALVIRTHORPE.—John Schirlok, for vert, 6*d.* Pledge, William Culle. Ralph Wlf and Robert s. of Ralph de Neuton, 6*d.* each, for vert. Richard the Tanner, for dry wood, 2*d.*

HIPERUM.—Alcok the Waynwricth, for vert, 6*d.*

John de Holewaye (*6d.*), Henry de Coldeley (*6d.*), William Broun of Schelf (*6d.*), Thomas del Brok (*3d.*), and Henry de Coppeley (*3d.*), for dry wood.

WAKEFEUD.—John Tupe's wife and John Theuet's wife, *2d.* each, for dry wood.

The maids of Adam Clouter (*1d.*) and Robert Broun (*1d.*); of William Nelot (*4d.*), and Adam Hod (*2d.*), for dry wood.

Michael de la Schawe, taken in the Earl's free chase in Soureby-schyre, for trespasses committed there, makes fine of 10 marks to go quit thereof. Pledges, Henry de Buttrewrth, Henry de la Schawe, Robert the Grave of Soureby, John Swyft, and John de Miggeley, who constitute themselves severally principal debtors to pay the 10 marks in two instalments.

Dom. Roger, Vicar of Rachedale, taken for the like offences, makes fine of £20 to go quit, of which he pays £10 down. He finds John de Lascy and 13 others, whose names are written in a bond, for payment of the remainder.

SANDALE.—Margery and Alice, daughters of Robert the Plogh-wricht of Ketelisthorpe, sue Master Robert de Ketelisthorpe for 7 acres of land, which their father sold and surrendered to him out of Court and without license; and 3½ acres of land which he received in like manner from Henry, their brother, then a minor. Deft. says that John, late Earl Warenne, freely enfeoffed him by his charter in 12 bovates of land (8 in Ketelisthorpe and 4 in the town of Sandale), for his life (he produces the charter in Court), and that the 7 acres are included in this grant; and he maintains he could receive the land out of Court and without license from anyone, because the Earl himself delivered it; he also says that when Henry sold him the 3½ acres he was of full age. An inquisition is taken by the oath of Elias de Wodethorpe, Robert the Clerk of Sandale, William de Abbathia, Peter the Shepherd, John s. of Ralph, Robert s. of Isolda, Adam Wylmot, Adam del Okes, Richard Beausire, Adam s. of Roger, Robert the Shepherd, Roger the Milner, Henry the servant [*garcio*] of the Constable, Elias de Donecastre, John le Beste, Richard, heir of Danda [? ; *her' Dande*], Swayn Scot, Henry s. of Roger, William s. of Robert, Robert de la Grene, Thomas de Dorkingge, William de Donecastre, Thomas s. of Bate, and John s.

of Thomas, who confirm all the defendant's statements. Plaintiffs fined 6d. for a false claim.

The same Master Robert sues the said Margery and Alice for a bovate of land and 2 acres of meadow in the town of Sandale, as his right and inheritance, because John, his father, died seised thereof, and after his father's death he himself held the same till the defendants ejected him under a false inquisition, held before John de Donecastre, the then Steward. The attaint is taken by the above 24 jurors, who say that, a long time ago, in the time of William, Earl Warenne, great-grandfather of the present Earl, 12 bovates of land were in the Earl's hands by escheat, for want of an heir, 8 bovates were in Ketelisthorpe and 4 in Sandale; and the said Earl William gave them to one William de Ketelisthorpe for his service, to hold of him freely. And afterwards came one who was the right heir, and sued the said William [de Ketelisthorpe] for the 12 bovates before Martin de Padeshill, the King's Justice in Eyre, at York; and William, understanding that he would lose the tenements, went to the Earl, who, by his counsel, made William confess before the said Justice that he was the Earl's villein [*villanus*], whereby the writ was quashed; and so the tenements from that time were held in servitude [*devenerunt in servitutem*], beginning from the time of Alexander Lucas, the Steward. And afterwards the said William [de Ketelisthorpe] died, leaving 2 sons, William and Robert; and William, the son, held the land as heir for a long time, and afterwards gave a bovate in Ketelisthorpe to Robert his brother, to hold to him and his heirs of the said William, and also gave [*accomodavit*] him a bovate of land and 2 acres of meadow in Sandale, to be held at will. William had a son and heir, John de Ketelisthorpe. And afterwards Robert died, leaving his son and heir, Robert le Plogwricht, then under age; and the said John, the son of William, had the guardianship of Robert, being his tenant; when Robert came of age, John de Ketelisthorpe delivered him the bovate granted to his father, but not the land and meadow in Sandal demised at will. John was succeeded by his son and heir, the plaintiff, and he and his father together held the said land in peace for 66 years and more, until Margery and Alice, in the time of John de Donecaster, then Steward, recovered the said land and meadow in Sandal by a false inquisition of 16 men, who said that the women had the better right to it, which was false, because the ancestors of the women held nothing except at the will of the ancestors of Master Robert. Robert is therefore to recover the said land and meadow, and pays

40*d.* for seisin; defendants fined 6*d.* The jury who gave the false return, viz.:—Thomas s. of Pelle (40*d.*), William the Grave (12*d.*), John Cukewald (40*d.*), John Munke (40*d.*), Thomas de Holgate (40*d.*), Robert At-well (12*d.*), William the Grave of Sandale (2*s.*), John de Holgate (18*d.*), Robert Attewelle, Richard s. of Hugh (12*d.*), John Malefay, Roger Tubbyng (12*d.*), John s. of William Margiry (12*d.*), Peter Leuwelyn (8*d.*), and Hugh Tubbing (6*d.*), are to be imprisoned, and are redeemed, being fined the sums put over their names. Robert Attewelle is dead, and John Malefay pays nothing, because he is poor.

Adam Achard, for many defaults;

Baldwin de Seyvill and Hugh s. of William de Northland, for default at this Court;

Henry le Campion, for many defaults; all to be distrained.

STANLEY.—Robert Gunne *v.* William Tagge, for trespass. Pledge, Andrew Pogge.

HOLNE.—Henry de Birton *v.* Matthew del Merse, for trespass. Pledge, Thomas Wodeman.

Matthew del Merse made a rescue against the forester, who was acting as bailiff [*qui fuit loco ballivi*].

William the Clerk *v.* Philip s. of Agnes and Richard Spink, for trespass. Pledge, John Damysele. They are attached by John Tasse.

ALVIRTHORPE.—Magota widow of John s. of Gelle [?] *v.* Roger Bele and Mariota his wife, for debt. Pledge, Robert the Fuller. She also sues Henry le Nunne, for debt. Pledge, John Beek.

Richard s. of Patrick [?] de St. Swythin *v.* Gilbert the Lister of Birton, for trespass. Pledge, Walter Scot.

OSSETE.—William s. of Jordan *v.* Adam de Chykynley, Richard Passemer, John Maunsel, Richard del Dene, Adam del Dene, and Richard Armerewe, for trespass. Pledge, Adam Gerbot.

COURT there on Friday, the first of April, in the year abovesaid [1307].

ESSOIGNS.[1]—William de Schipeden, by Jordan s. of Od'. Pledge, William del Okes.

John de Wylley, by Robert de Sourby. Pledge, Richard de Birstall.

Thomas de Heton, by Roger Assolf. Pledge, Thomas de Bellehus.

Thomas de Thorneton, by Hugh de Thorneton. Pledge, Richard de Birstall.

---

[1] From suit of Court, unless otherwise stated,

Robert de Bramewyth, attorney of Thomas de Schefeud, by Robert de Staynland. Pledge, John de Mora.

Robert Pees against John de Thothill, by William de Bateley. Pledge, Robert de la Grene of Ossete.

John Dade sues John With the-hounds for 15s. for a horse sold to him on All Saints' day, 1306, and which ought to be paid on S. Giles's day [Sept. 1]; damages, 6s. 8d. Deft. says that S. Giles's day has not yet arrived. Plt. fined 6d.

John Dade v. John With-the-hounds and Philip Wlf and Henry del Bothem, his pledges, for debt. Pledge, John Kay.

Henry de Birton fined 6d. for not prosecuting his suit. Pledge, Elias de Birton.

Sir Thomas de Burgh delivered 2 cart-horses [affros], supposed to be strays, to one Robert Chep of Wentebrigge. Let Robert come to the next Court, and do what is decreed; if not, Thomas must answer for them.

HIPERUM.—Peter del Barm fined 4d. for not prosecuting his suit against Malina wife of Ivo.

Robert Pees gives 6d. to agree with John le Barn, for debt. Pledge, Robert Soneman.

ALVIRTHORPE.—The land of Philip Thorald in Alvirthorpe is in the Earl's hands, because he is dead.

Thomas de Tothill v. Thomas s. of Modde and Henry s. of Thomas, as keeper [custos] of the chattels of Blessed Mary in the parish of Eland. They did not come, and are to be distrained.

THORNES.—John Tasse sues Ivo the Smith, Agnes wife of Roger, and John de la Haghe, for trampling ½ acre of land sown with rye [siligo] with their cattle; damages, 2s. They say that the damage was done before the Purification, and not afterwards, and that they ought to be quit by punchet [quod debent esse inde quieti per punchet]; they put themselves on a jury. The plaintiff's damages are taxed at one . . . . . . [poncell'] before the Purification and 2 garbs of rye after the Purification, which deft. must satisfy. Fine, 9d.[1]

STANLEY.—Robert Gunne gives 6d. to agree with William Tagge.

William the Clerk sues Philip s. of Agnes and Richard Spinck, for putting up a pale [palicium] within his free tenement; damages, 6s. 8d. John Tasse appears for them, but makes no answer, and asks for a love-day. He may have it on condition of finding pledges

---

[1] This case is very puzzling. I am unable to find the words *punchet* and *poncell'* in any dictionary. The latter would seem to be a measure of some sort, and is perhaps akin to the English word *punchion*.

for their submitting to the consideration of good men. He finds Peter de Acom and John de Mora. Pledges for William the Clerk, John Kay and John Patrik.

ALVIRTHORPE.—Lance the Clerk *v.* Robert s. of Richard Gerbot; he claims 6 acres of land as his inheritance, because Ellen, his mother, died scised thereof. Deft. says that Ellen held them for her life only, by the Earl's grace, and that all right therein descended to him [Robert] after her death. An inquisition is taken by the oath of Robert s. of Simon, Henry del Bothem, Richard s. of Broun, Richard s. of Philip, Alexander Waltweu, William Hoskel, Richard Bunny, John de Flanshowe, Adam Wlf, John s. of Alan, William s. of Walter, and Philip le Syur, who say that one Gerard le Double, at that time the Earl's chief Forester, bought the land of one Richard Lambot, the Earl's villein [*nativus*], and afterwards gave it to Ellen, mother of the plt.; Ellen was afterwards married to Hugh the Tanner, and they had a son, the plt. Immediately afterwards Hugh sold the land to one Gerbot de Alvirthorpe; after Hugh's death, Ellen recovered the land from Gerbot in Court, and afterwards demised it again to him for his life; Gerbot gave it to Richard, his son, and his heirs. After Gerbot's death, Ellen recovered it again in Court from Richard; Richard then went to the Earl, and complained that Ellen had recovered that land from him, and said that she was a free woman, and this was villein land [*terra nativa*], and asked the lord if he would allow his villein land to become hereditary in the hands of any free person; the Earl caused Richard to be re-seised [*fecit reseisire predictum Ricardum*] of the land, because he was his villein [*nativus*]. Afterwards Ellen prayed the Earl, of his special grace, to return the land to her, because she was a poor woman, and he thereupon ordered that she should have it for her life. Richard entered after her death, and held it all his life; and after his decease, Robert his son entered, and now holds it. They say that the rent of the land is 2*s.*, and that it is villein land, because it owes aid [*auxilium*] to the lord like other villein land, and [the holder] has to be grave [*? facere ppm.*]. Asked if it is part of the villein bovates [*? de bovatis (?) nativis*], they say it is not, but it is called rodeland, because it was cleared [*assartata fuit*] from growing wood . . . . The matter is submitted to the Earl's pleasure.

STANLEY.—Margaret da. of Thomas s. of Nalle gives 6*d.* to take a house containing 40 feet from Simon Tyting, for ever. Pledge, Robert Pescy.

F

Roger s. of Thomas Nally surrenders a bovate of land in Stanley to the use of Margaret, his sister, Gilbert de Methley, and Isolda, his sister, in equal shares, for ever. They give 5s. for seisin and entry. Pledge, Robert Pescy.

ALVIRTHORPE.—William s. of Robert s. of Simon sues Robert s. of Ralph de Uchethorpe, and William s. of Walter de Neuton, for 2 bovates of land in Neuton fields, as his right and inheritance; and he craves an inquisition, because he is the next heir. Defts. say that they took the land from the Earl because it had been lying unoccupied [vasta] for a long time. An inquisition is taken by the oath of Robert s. of Simon de Stanley, Richard s. of Broun, Alexander Waltweu, Henry del Bothem, Richard s. of Philip, William Hoskel, John de Flanshowe, Richard Bunny, Adam Wlf, John s. of Alan, Philip le Syur, and Adam Gerbot, who say that the land was unoccupied a long time for want of heirs; one Alan the Forester, a free-man, came and took it in Court; Alan had a son Robert and a daughter Edith. Alan died, and Beatrice, his widow, married one German de Wyrunthorpe, who took both the children and the land into his keeping; after a long time, he left one bovate unoccupied on the Earl's hands, and the other he retained all his life; but after his death the other also lay unoccupied. One William Ferthyng afterwards took the first bovate to himself and his heirs; he was succeeded by Juliana, his daughter and heir, who gave the bovate to Robert [the deft.], who now holds it. The other bovate lay unoccupied for a long time, and the Steward for the time being compelled [coegit] one Walter s. of German to take it, and he took it in open Court, to himself and his heirs. Walter gave half of it to Margaret, his daughter, on condition that she maintained him for the rest of his life, and left the other half to William, his son [the deft.], who now holds it. The said Robert s. of Alan afterwards claimed the 2 bovates from the said tenants [the defts.], as his right and inheritance, but lost his suit, because the tenants had entry through the Earl, and also because Robert was a freeman, whilst the land was villein land. Edith da. of the said Alan married one Robert s. of Simon, by whom she had a son, the plt. The land first lay waste before Alan the Forester bought it, about 40 years ago, in the time of John de Hille, the Steward; and the second time, after the death of German, was about 30 years ago. William, the plt., is the next heir of blood of Alan, the Forester, unless Robert, his son, is alive. William, the plt., is a freeman, as Robert was. The matter, therefore, lies at the Earl's pleasure.

Robert Pees gives 6*d.* to agree with John de Tothill, for debt.

OSSETE.—William s. of Jordan sues Adam de Chykenley, Richard Passemer, John Maunsell, Richard del Dene, Adam del Dene, and Richard Armerowe, for slandering him by saying that he took 40*d.* from Henry s. of Richard de Heton, and 12*d.* from Henry s. of Richard de Ossete, as an aid for the lord, whereby he lost 2*s.* 10*d.* to Hanne s. of Richard de Heton, and was fined 6*s.* 8*d.*;[1] damages, 20*s.* An inquisition of the neighbours, and an examination of an estreat [*extracta*] which William had for the levying of the aid, proves that they made an unfounded presentment. They are fined 6*s.*; damages assessed at 10*s.*

SALE OF WESTWODE.—William s. of Ralph de Crigeliston, Robert de la Grene of Crigeliston, William s. of Robert de Crigeliston, and Robert s. of Isolda, give 25 marks for the Westwode at Crigeliston. Pledges, Nalke de Dritker, Adam de la Grene, Thomas s. of Ralph, and Thomas de Dorkynge. They are to cut the wood as close to the ground as possible, and to clear the place of twigs [*ramuli*], so as not to impede the fresh growth of the wood.

HIPERUM.—Adam s. and heir of Henry, late Grave of Hiperum, gives 6*s.* 8*d.* as a relief on 2 bovates of land held by his father. Pledge, William del Bothes.

STANLEY.—Robert Gunne, Margery his wife, and Emma their daughter, give 12*d.* to take from Thomas Bole a croft in Uchethorpe, between the house that formerly belonged to Philip Bille and the Howeflat, to hold to Robert and Margery, for their lives, with remainder to Emma and her heirs for ever; reserving the term which John s. of Hobbe has in the same.

THORNES.—Avice widow of Henry de Holebrok *v.* William de Wakfeld, in a plea of land.

_____

[Dorse of Roll; the top is mutilated; see *ante*, p. 53.]

[COURT; probably in May, 1307.]

WAKEFELD.—John Cussing *v.* Roger Preist and Rose [?] his wife,
. . . .

Robert de Wodesom to be distrained to answer Henry Eril, for debt.

Juliana [?] da. of Richard de Chyvet, plt. *v.* John the Clerk of Walton, for trespass, comes and withdraws. She is fined 40*d.*

Ralph the Grave of Dewysbiry, deft., essoigns against John s. of Henry de Fekesby, for taking cattle, by Thomas de Wakefeld.

[1] See *ante*, p. 75.

Adam s. of Ivo to be summoned to answer Henry de Luddigdene, in a plea of land.

John de Grenegate [?] sues John de Flansowe, Walter s. of Adam, and Robert his brother, for . . . .; they are fined 6d. Pledge, Adam Gerbode.

STANLAY.—Thomas Bule [?] claims 2 acres of land in Ouchethorpe from Robert Goys and Juliana . . . ., of which Philip Bole [?], [Thomas's] grandfather, died seised, whose heir he is. Robert says that he claims no interest. Juliana says that Philip Bule [?] did not die seised, but that he gave the land first to Hugh Bulle [?], who held it for a long time, and afterwards to Thomas de Warderobe, who gave it to [? Juliana], who now holds it. An inquisition is ordered.

SANDALE.—Agnes da. of Bate v. William de la Grene, for trespass. Pledge, Robert s. of Isolda.

William Margeriknave v. Henry le Nonne and Adam Gerbode, for debt. Also v. John de Flansowe, William de Neuton, and Robert s. of Ralph.

WAKEFELD.—William Nelot to be distrained for breaking the Earl's fold, and taking away his cattle, and for depasturing his sheep on the Earl's grass; damages, 2s. 6d.

THORNES.—John s. of Philip de Mora gives 3d. to agree with Richard del Kerre.

ALVIRTHORPE.—Walter s. of Adam de Hille v. Adam Gerbode and John de Flansowe, for detaining . . . . for Adam del Spitell. They acknowledge they owe 2s., which they must pay, with 6d. fine; but they say that Walter gave Adam a longer day [for payment]¹ . . . . An inquisition is ordered.

SANDALE.—Robert [?] Hilhor gives 12d. to take an acre of land in Sandale from Robert the Clerk, for ever.

SOURBY.—Thomas de Ovendene, for the escape of a horse, 2d. Pledge, John s. of John.

Little Hugh de Ovenden, for an escape, 2d. Pledge, Hugh de Illegwrth.

Bate del Bothes, the like, 2d. Same pledge.

Mocok de Ouerum, the like, 3d. Pledge, Richard de Saltonstall.

Henry de Holgate, for the escape of 24 oxen, 6s. 8d.

Robert s. of William de Werlouley, for 2 oxen, 4d. Pledge, Richard de Saltonstall.

¹ Apparently the defendants were sureties for a debt of Adam del Spittell.

HOLNE.—Alan de Thounges [?], for dry wood, 3*d.*   Pledge, William de Storthes.

William Wodemous, 3*d.*; Adam Benne, 3*d.*; Thomas s. of Beatrice, 3*d.*, for dry wood.

Cissota [?] Toute, 3*d.*, for dry wood.

William de Lee [?], 12*d.*, for escape of 2 oxen.

[? STANLEY.]—Richard del Bothem, for vert, 12*d.*

Robert del Dale's wife, for dry wood, 3*d.*

Gilis [?] de Ouchethorpe, 4*d.*; Magota Smale, 3*d.*, for dry wood.

John Flechard, for breaking the pale, 4*d.*

THORNES.—Robert s. of Simon, for the escape of sheep, 4*d.*

John del Haye, 4*d.*; Agnes wife of Roger, 2*d.*; Roger Trailment, 4*d.*; the maids of Thomas the Smith and Thomas Vyron, 2*d.* each, for dry wood.

SOURBY.—Thomas Caynock, 4*d.*, and Philip Ters, 6*d.*, for dry wood.

Henry le Wyte, for vert, 6*d.*

Richard s. of the Grave, for dry wood, 2*d.*

ALVIRTHORPE.—Richard de Bateley, for the escape of 4 pigs, 4*d.*

Adam Gerbode, for 2 pigs, 2*d.*

Henry del Bothem, 2*d.*, for the like.

HIPERUM.—John the Milner, 4*d.*; John del Rode, 4*d.*, for dry wood.

John de Hastay, for sheep escaped, 4*d.*

Thomas Sourmylk, for the escape of oxen, 4*d.*

Bate del Clyf, 6*d.*; Alcok s. of Walter, 6*d.*; and Thomas del Northend, 2*d.*, for dry wood.

WAKEFELD.—Elias Tirsy, for . . . . , 2*d.*

Walter the Cook, 1*d.*; the son of Eva de Bramley, 2*d.*; Adam Torketro, 3*d.*; William s. of Magota Preist, 2*d.*; Walter Scot's maid, 3*d.*; Cicely Archur, 4*d.*; Hugh le Chapman, 4*d.*; William Ilhor's son, 2*d.*; Gelle Dodde, 2*d.*; William de Sandale's son, 3*d.*; Peter Hunkel, 4*d.*; the maid of Richard s. of Mille, 3*d.*; Philip Damysell, 12*d.*; the maids of John Dun, 2*d.*; Robert the Goldsmith, 2*d.*; John Baba, 2*d.*; German the Gardiner, 2*d.*; John de Skulbrok, 2*d.*; Thomas s. of Henry, 2*d.*; William the Gardiner, 2*d.*; John Peger, 2*d.*; Robert Capon, 2*d.*; and of Richard le Wayte, 2*d.*, for the like.

William de Wakefeud, for pigs escaped, 6*d.*

John Cay, for pigs in the New Park, 6*d.*

The maids of John Best and Walter Bille, 1*d.* each, for dry wood ; John Tevet, 2*d.*; John Tasse, 4*d.*; Philip de Castilford, 6*d.*; the maids of John Leche, 4*d.*, and Halfmark, 2*d.* ; the son of John s. of Sibbe, 4*d.*; Ellen Quie, 2*d.*, for the like.

OSSETE.—John Fox, for pigs escaped, 4*d*.

WAKEFEUD.—John de Gailgrave [? Gargrave] gives 6*d*. to take a piece of land of the Earl's waste, between his own land and the Earl's hall, 162 feet long and 10 feet wide; also a piece which John the Leach [*medicus*] formerly held, for ever. Rent, 18*d*. Pledge, Robert de Northfolk.

———

COURT at Halifax on Tuesday, the Morrow of St. Boniface [June 5], in the 35th year [1307].

SOURBY.—Adam de Middelton gives 12*d*. to take 3 acres of the Earl's waste in Soureby at le Helmebothes, for ever. Rent, 15*d*. Pledge, John de Miglay.

William the Mercer gives 6*d*. to take ½ acre of the Earl's waste in Soureby, for ever. Rent, 4*d*. Pledge, Adam de Midelton.

Michael Sourmylk gives 12*d*. to take 2 acres of the Earl's waste in Sourby, under Haderschelf, for ever. Rent, 16*d*. Pledge, Roger Rotell.

Adam s. of Elias the Milner gives 12*d*. to take 6 acres in Sourby, left waste by Adam de Miglay and Alexander Pie [?], for ever. Pledge, Robert de Saltonstal. He also gives 6*d*. to take an acre of the waste in Sourby, for ever. Rent, 6*d*. Same pledge.

Henry de Luddigdene, plt., *v*. Adam s. of Ivo, in a plea of land, withdraws, and is fined 4*d*.

Adam s. of Ivo gives 6*d*. to take two acres of land in Luddigden from Henry de Luddigden, for ever. Pledge, William de Connale.

Adam de Miglay gives 6*d*. to take 2 acres in Sourby, left waste by Adam de Miglay, senior, for ever. Pledge, Robert de Saltonstall. Also 6*d*. to take an acre of the lord's waste in Sourby, paying 6*d*. rent. Same pledge.

Adam Migge gives 12*d*. to take 2 acres of the lord's waste in Sourby, for ever. Rent, 12*d*. Same pledge.

Ivo the Milner of Miglay gives 18*d*. to take 1½ acres of the lord's waste in Werlouleye Wood, for ever. Rent, 9*d*. Same pledge.

Jordan del Hirst of Miglay gives 2*s*. to take 2 acres of the lord's waste in Queteleyhirst, for ever. Rent, 12*d*. Same pledge.

John the Webbester gives 12*d*. to take an acre of the lord's waste in Werlouley Wood, for ever. Rent, 6*d*. Same pledge.

Adam s. of Ivo gives 3*s*. to take 3 acres of the lord's waste, for ever. Rent, 18*d*. Pledge, John the Webbester.

Roger s. of Amabel gives 2*s*. to take 2 acres of the lord's waste in Sourby, for ever. Rent, 12*d*. Pledge, Robert de Saltonstall.

Thomas de Roldesete gives 2s. to take 2 acres of the lord's waste in Soureby. Rent, 12d. Pledge, Roger Rotell.

John the Milner gives 6d. to take an acre of the lord's waste in Sourby, near the Milnebroke, for ever. Rent, 6d. Pledge, Robert de Saltonstall.

Henry s. of William de Werlouley gives 2s. to take 2 acres of the lord's waste in Werlouley, for ever. Rent, 12d. Pledge, Robert the Grave.

Henry del Helme gives 12d. to take 1 acre of the lord's waste in Werlouley. Rent, 6d. Pledge, Henry de Saltonstall.

Maude da. of Elias gives 4d. to take a toft, with buildings, in Werlouley from Henry de Luddingden, for 6 years.

Henry de Luddingden of Sourby gives 2s. to take 2 acres of the Earl's waste in Ryburnedene, for ever. Rent, 12d. Pledge, Robert the Grave.

Richard del Feilde gives 6d. to take 1 acre, as last above. Rent, 6d. Pledge, Thomas de Luddigden.

Richard the Smith of Werlouley gives 12d. to take an acre of the lord's waste in Werlouley, under Judderode, as above. Rent, 6d. Pledge, William the Milner.

William s. of Alcok de Sourby gives 2s. to take 2 acres of the lord's waste near Luddingdeneforth. Rent, 12d. Pledge, John Hodde.

Robert s. of William de Saltonstall gives 13d. to take 1½ acres and half a perch of the lord's waste in Sourby, as above. Rent, 13d. Same pledge.

John Hodde gives 12d. to take the same amount. Rent, 13d. Pledge, Robert the Grave.

Elias the Couper gives 3d. to take an acre of land in Sourby from John the Milner, for ever. Pledge, Roger Rotell.

Thomas the Mercer gives 12d. to take 2 acres of the Earl's waste in Astleyker in Werlouley. Rent, 12d. Pledge, Robert de Saltonstall.

John the Milner of Sourby gives 2s. to take 3 acres of the lord's waste in Ryburnedene. Rent, 18d. Pledge, Henry de Luddigdene.

William the Milner gives 2s. to take 3 acres 1 perch of the waste in Werlouley. Rent, 19d. Pledge, Robert de Saltonstall.

William de Connale gives 2s. to take 3½ acres, as last above. Rent, 21d. Pledge, Hugh del Holgate.

Henry s. of William de Soland gives 6d. for 6 acres in Soland, left on the lord by Thomas de Rachedale, for ever. Pledge, Richard s. of Alice.

Thomas s. of John de Migley gives 6*d.* to take an acre of the waste in Sourby. Rent, 6*d.* Same pledge.

Adam de Heitfeud has license to take 2 acres of the waste, as above. Rent, 12*d.* Pledge, Robert de Saltonstall.

William del Bothem gives 3*s.* to take 6 acres of the waste, as above. Rent, 3*s.* Pledge, John de Miglay.

Thomas s. of Elias de Sourby, the forester, has license to take 2 acres left on the lord by Elias the Forester; and gives 6*d.* for another acre of the waste in Sourby, at 6*d.* rent. Pledges, Robert de Saltonstall and Robert the Grave.

Robert s. of William de Saltonstall gives 6*d.* for an acre of the waste in Sourby. Rent, 6*d.* Pledge, Richard del Feilde.

Alice widow of Henry de Rissewrth gives 2*s.* to take 3 acres in Werlouley, left waste on the lord by Henry de Willeys. Pledge, Robert de Saltonstall.

Henry de Holgate gives 12*d.* for an acre of the waste in Sourby. Rent, 6*d.* Pledge, Adam s. of Ivo.

Adam le Crouder has license to take ½ acre of the waste in Lithhesles. Rent, 2½*d.* Pledge, Robert de Saltonstall.

TOURN there the same day.

JURORS.—Richard de Waddeswrth, Richard del Dene, John s. of John de Northelande, John de Langlay, John de Miggelay, Henry s. of Reynald, Thomas de Bellehouses, German del Grenewode, William del Croft, John Fox, William del Northende of Halifax, and Richard de Saltonstall.

Michael Thirlebacon drew blood from William s. of Adam de Grenehirst; fine, 12*d.*

Sarah wife of Bate de Halifax (6*d.*), Juliana wife of Thomas (6*d.*), Magota wife of Ripon (6*d.*), Cicely wife of Elias the Walker (3*d.*), and Amabel wife of Henry the Walker (6*d.*), for brewing contrary to the assize.

William s. of Henry de Godelay drew blood from William, his brother; fine 12*d.*

Richard del Feild drew blood from William del Bothem (6*d.*), and William del Bothem from Matthew de Bosco, in self-defence (2*s.*).

John del Milnehouses, Robert s. of the Chaplain of Eland, John del Castell, lister, John de Birton, and William de Birton, broke into the house of William de Stodelay, and stole goods worth £20; this is presented by the townships of Stanesfeld, Langefeld, Waddeswrth, Miggelay, Werlouley, Northeland, Sourby, Skircotes, Ovendene, and Halifax. They are to be arrested.

COURT at Rastrik, the Wednesday following.

HYPERUM.—Richard s. of Jordan de Halifax gives 6d. to take an acre of the lord's waste in the Okynbank, in the graveship of Hyperum.   Rent, 6d.   Pledge, William the Milner.

William the Milner gives 6d. to take an acre of the lord's waste near the beck side [*juxta rapam (sic) rivuli*] at Halifax. Rent, 6d. Pledge, Richard s. of Jordan.

Henry de Northclyf gives 6d. to take an acre of the lord's waste, between le Welleclogh and the land of Thomas s. of Thomas de Hiperum; as above.   Pledge, Henry the Pynder.

Roger s. of John, senior, gives 2s. to take 2 acres of the lord's waste in Cherpeleyker, in the graveship of Hiperum.   Rent, 16d. Pledge, Thomas de Rode.

Richard s. of Adam s. of John [*? fil' Jonis*] gives 2s. as a heriot on 3 acres held by his late father.   Pledge, John s. of Walter.

HIPERUM.—Geoffrey del Dene admits that he owes Beatrice de Tothill 7s.

Gilbert Bridde gives 6d. to take ½ perch of the lord's waste in the Brighouses.   Rent, 2d.   Pledge, Richard de Bosco.

Roger de Chepeley gives 12d. to take 1½ perches there. Rent, 4d.   Pledge, William the Milner.

RASTRIK.—Thomas de Lyth[er?] Rigge gives 12d. to take ½ acre of the lord's waste in Fekesby.   Rent, 4d.   Pledge, Adam Attebroke.

HIPERUM.—Peter del Suthclif and Adam Orre admit that they owe John Fox 9s. as sureties for Geoffrey the Colier, and a pair of shoes [*sotularia*]; price, 6d.

RASTRIK.—Adam Attebroke and Beatrice his wife give 6d. to take ½ acre of the lord's waste in Rastrik.   Rent, 3d.   Pledge, Henry s. of John.

HIPERUM.—Amabel da. of Henry del Dene gives 12*d.* for license to marry. Pledge, Simon de Tothill.

Dom Richard de Midelton, chaplain, and William de Sunderland give 2*s.* to take 10 acres of the lord's waste in the Blacker, on Gleg Clyff. Rent, 4*s.* 2*d.* for all service.

William de Sonderland gives 12*d.* to take 3 acres of the lord's waste between the essart of Hugh de Ovenden and the Holcan. Rent, 18*d.* Pledge, William de Bothes.

Bate del Clif of Ouerom gives 6*d.* to take a toft, with buildings, and 4 acres of land in Ouerum from Dom Richard the Chaplain, for 10 years. Pledge, Richard de Bosco.

TOURN there the same day.

JURORS.—John de Rodes, William de Bothes, John de Locwode, John le Flemyng of Dalton, Henry s. of Walter, John de Bristall, Henry de Coildelay, John de Percy, John de Hertesheved, William de Bradelay, Alexander del Frith, and Simon de Schelfley.

John s. of Adam de Locwode drew blood from Robert s. of Ralph and Adam del Brighuses; fine, 12*d.* Also from Agnes da. of Diana de Lynthayt; fine, 6*d.*

William s. of Cicely de Dalton drew blood from his mother; fine, 12*d.*

Ralph s. of Richard de Kerlinghowe drew blood from William s. of Stephen de Fekesby; fine, 12*d.*

HYPERUM.—Roger s. of John brews contrary to the assize; fine, 6*d.*

Maude del Barme, Richard le Taillour, and William the Milner, 6*d.* each, for the like.

COURT at Birton on Thursday, the Feast of St. William [Archbishop of York, June 8], in the year abovesaid [1307].

HOLNE.—Thomas s. of Sarah gives 6*d.* for an inquisition against Richard le Syur, regarding land.

Parnell de Holne *v.* John s. of John de Holne, for trespass. Pledge, Thomas s. of Gilbert. An inquisition finds that deft. broke an agreement for ploughing plaintiff's land. Damages, 8*d.*; fine, 6*d.* Pledge, Thomas del Rode.

Thomas s. of Sarah sues Richard le Syur for 3 acres and 1 rood of land in Fouleston, which his mother took from the lord as waste land. Richard says that one Richard Lynyld, his grandfather, took the land from the waste and first essarted it, and that it was never left waste on the lord. An inquisition is taken by the oath of Richard de Cartewrth, Hugh del Hole, Thomas Keneward, Thomas de Elwardeholles, Robert s. of John s. of Gilbert, Nicholas del Clif, John de Holne, William s. of the Grave, Richard s. of John, Robert Stirk, John s. of Adam de Heppewrth, and Adam del Scoles, who find for the plt. He is to recover, and gives 2s. for seisin. Deft. fined 3d. Pledge, John the Grave.

William Wodemous admits that he is bound to account to Agnes de la Grene for her children's goods and chattels; fine, 4d., for unjust detention. Pledge, Richard s. of Michael.

William Strecays fined 4d. for detaining 9d. from John s. of Adam de Heppeworth.

Richard le Syur, 3d., for contempt. Pledge, Thomas Fernehoule.

Adam de Euyas gives 2s. to take 4½ acres of land and a culture in Fouleston from Thomas Fernehoule, to hold, etc. Pledge, said Thomas.

Richard s. of Michael gives 12d. to take ½ acre of land in Fouleston from Robert s. of Bobby, for ever. Pledge, Henry s. of Thomas.

Alice de Slaghthayt gives 12d. to take a house and acre of land in Heppewrth, for ever, from Henry s. of Richard. Pledge, William s. of Wilkes.

William de Hallomschir gives 12d. to take a toft and one acre of land in Heppewrth from Richard s. of Elias, for ever. Pledge, said Richard.

Henry de Littelwode fined 6d. for detaining 14d. under his wife's will [de testamento uxoris sue].

TOURN there the same day.

JURORS.—Richard de Thorntelay, Richard Osan, Hugh de Thorntelay, John Wyther, John s. of Quenilda, John de Braythait, Henry de Birton, Thomas Fernoule, John s. of Gilbert, Adam s. of Emme, Richard de la Grene, and William Strekase.

HOLNE.—Juliana de Cartewrth, Christiana de Chelvelay, Emma la Baggere, Christiana wife of Richard de Holdernesse, and Maude wife of Gilbert the Milner, brew contrary to the assize; fined 6d. each.

Thomas de Billeclif drew blood from Thomas s. of Richard; fine, 12d.

HOLNE.—Alice wife of John s. of Gilbert brews contrary to the assize; fine, *6d.*

Cicely de Wytstanes, the like, *6d.*

Richard del Bothe drew blood from William Strekase; fine, *12d.*

Henry de Storthes drew blood from John de Stokkes; fine, *12d.*

Robert Stirk and Matthew de Langley brew contrary to the assize; fined *6d.* each.

Hugh del Hole drew blood from John the Coupere; fine, *12d.*

John the Coupere drew blood from Hugh del Hole and William s. of Matthew de Marisco; fine, *2s.*

Gilbert de Gaunt drew blood from William s. of Elias del Wode; fine, *12d.*

Gilbert Fatheuedsteppeson drew blood from John Crowe; fine, *12d.*

Mariota Pre brews contrary to the assize; fine, *6d.*

TOURN at Wakefeld the Friday following.

JURORS.—John Patrik, Walter de Grymeston, Robert de Wyromthorpe, William Ingreys, William s. of Michael de Floketon, William de Dewisbiry, Robert de Horbyry, clerk, Richard de Salsa Mara, Richard de Bristall [Birstall], Robert de Wodesom, Henry de Chyvet, and Hugh de Seyvill.

Robert le Roorer of Normanton drew blood from Henry Jose, his servant [*garcio*]; fine, *2s.*

Agnes wife of Robert the Clerk of Dewysbiry brews ale contrary to the assize, &c.; fine, *12d.*

Robert Pees of Ossete drew blood from Thomas the Mercer of Castel in Rachedale [*de Castel de R.*], and Thomas drew blood from Robert; a number of people were wounded [*vulnerati et sanguinolenti*] in the affray, but they do not know by whom each was wounded; fine, *6d.*

The wife of Matthew de Schelflay in Ossete brews bad ale; *6d.*

Henry de Hoton drew blood from William Ingreys; *12d.*

Robert Pees fined *6d.* for making known [*quia intimavit*] the council of the twelve [jurors] with regard to Matthew de Schelflay's brewing.

Adam Wytebelt and Henry s. of Gregory de Walton drew blood from one another; fined *12d.* each.

Adam Wytebelt drew blood from William s. of Gregory, *12d.*; and Gregory de Walton, from Adam, *12d.*

Robert the Harpur had baked bread to sell, weight unknown; 6*d*.

William Cort's wife drew blood from Thomas s. of Felicia.

ALVIRTHORPE.—Magge Wyntre, the Earl's villein [*nativa*], is deflowered; 6*d*.

Thomas de Boysvill of Dewysbiry baked bread to sell, weight unknown; 6*d*.

Thomas Vyron of Snaypethorpe fined 3*d*. for not coming.

John Castill's wife brews, &c.; 6*d*.

The town of Wakefeld presents that Richard s. of Nelle Hors stole a silk coffer [?; *loculum*] and a curtain [*velum*] from John Lauediman's house; value, 7*d*. He is to be arrested.

Henry Archur obstructed the common way through the hayfields [?; *per fenile*]; 6*d*.

Robert the Goldsmith junior drew blood from John Pollard; 12*d*.

Thomas s. of Hugh Bille drew blood from Thomas Bole. He has no goods.

Henry s. of Ellen drew blood from John the Webster, but not maliciously; 3*d*.

Alice wife of John Kyde of Wakefeud was abducted by night by the servant [*garcio*] of Nicholas, the parish chaplain of Wakefeud, on the chaplain's horse and by his command, and with the woman's consent; she was taken to Ayllisbiry, with goods belonging to her husband, to wit, 11*d*., taken from her husband's purse; 3 gold rings, worth 18*d*.; a cup of mazer, 12*d*.; a napkin [*mappa*], 12*d*.; a towel, 6*d*.; a gown, 6*s*. 8*d*.; a new hood, taken from her husband's pack [*de fardello*], 12*d*.; with many other things unknown. Afterwards Alice returned to her husband.

Alvirthorpe presents that Robert Mareschall turned the course of a certain stream of rain-water [*cujusdem aque pluviale*] in Snaypethorpe fields, to the injury of William the Clerk's tenement; fine, 12*d*.

William s. of Margery de Walton did not attend at the summons of the 12. He afterwards came, and was pardoned.

OSSETE.—Adam s. of Henry de Goukethorpe *v*. Robert Sunneman, in a plea of land. Pledge, John Rate. Same *v*. same, for trespass. Pledge, Walter del Hull.

SANDALE.—William Nelot *v*. John Mounk, John Cokewald, and William de Sandale, in a plea of land. Pledge, Robert de Rypon.

COURT at Wakefield on Friday, the eve of the Nativity of St. John the Baptist [June 24], in the 35th year [1307].

ESSOIGNS.[1]—Robert de Wyromthorpe, by John Cay. Pledge. John de Toftclif.

Richard de Bristall, by John Damoysell. Pledge, Adam Hod.

Thomas de Heeton, by Roger Assolf. Pledge, John de Lepton.

Peter Swerd, by William Margerikave [*sic*]. Pledge, Thomas de Langfeld.

Thomas de Bellehous, by Robert de Steynland. Pledge, William Margeriknave.

Thomas de Thorinton, by Hugh de Horbyry. Pledge, John de Toftclif.

William de Schepedene, by William de Soland. Pledge, Hugh de Seyvill.

John de Crosland, by Henry Gurdoun. Pledge, John de Toftclif.

Robert de Bramwich, attorney of Thomas de Schefeld, by Richard Pie. Pledge, John Cay.

Robert de la Grene of Ossete, by Robert Sonneman. Pledge, Hugh de Seyvill.

ALVIRTHORPE.—John Dade essoigns against John With-the-hounds, Philip Wulf, and Henry del Bothem, for debt, by John Cay. Pledge, William de Locwod.

John Rate and John Swan have a love day.

Robert Mareschall defends against Richard Broun, for trespass, by John Damoysell. Pledge, John Cay.

Henry s. of Gregory de Walton fined 12*d*. for withdrawing his suit against William Witebelt, Adam Wytebelt, and Custance Wytebelt. Pledge, Gregory de Walton.

John Costill fined 6*d*. for not producing Thomas Brounesmyth and Emma his wife, whom he had attached to answer William de Wakefield.

Beatrice Cay and Nicholas de Batelay have agreed by license.[2] Beatrice fined 6*d*. Robert de Bateley, father of Nicholas, fined 6*d*., because his son, whom he had attached for the purpose, left the Court in contempt, without answering.

Magota widow of John Colle fined 4*d*. for not prosecuting suit against Roger Bele and Mariota his wife.

Adam de Heylay, 12*d*., for not having Gilbert the Lister of Birton to answer Richard s. of the Brother of St. Swythin.

[1] From suit of Court unless otherwise stated.
[2] *Sic;* but presumably *without* license.

Henry Erle, plt., essoigns against Robert de Wodesom, by John Cay, in a plea of debt. Pledge, John Hoskell.

Ralph the Grave of Dewysbiry, against John s. of Henry de Fekesby, for taking cattle, by Thomas de Wyttelay. Pledge, John de Podesay.

SANDALE.—Agnes da. of Bate fined 6d. for not prosecuting her suit against William de la Grene.

Beatrice de Tothill, plt., essoigns against Henry del Ryding, for debt, by Thomas Filcok. Pledge, William de Locwod.

WAKEFELD.—William Nelot fined 12d. for not prosecuting his suit against John Mounk, John Cokewald, and William de Sandale, in a plea of land.

SOURBY.—John Culpen gives 15s. to take 14½ acres and one perch of land left on the lord in Mithomrode, to hold to himself and Ingelard de Miglay and their heirs; rent, 6d. per acre. It used to pay only 4d. an acre. Pledge, Robert de Saltonstall.

HOLNE.—William s. of John de Littelwode gives 2s. to take 4½ acres of land in Cartewrth from Thomas s. of Roger. Pledge, John s. of Geoffrey.

HYPERUM.—Simon de Tothill gives 6d. to take 1½ roods of land in Ouerom from Eva da. of William the Chapman, for 20 years. Pledge, Robert de Saltonstall.

SOURBY.—William de Lythesles gives 12d. to take 1½ acres of land of the waste in Lytheses [sic], paying 9d. per annum. Same pledge.

ALVIRTHORPE.—Robert s. of Richard Gerbode gives 3s. to take 4 acres of land and meadow in Flansowe, from John de Flansowe, for ever. Pledge, Adam Gerbode.

STANLEY.—Robert Gunne and Hugh Skayf give 20s. to take for ever 33 acres and ½ rood of land, and 3 acres and ¼ rood of meadow, in Wodehalle, from the lord, paying yearly 6d. an acre for the land, and 2s. an acre for the meadow; being an increase of 19s. 11¼d. on the 3s. it used to pay.

ALVIRTHORPE.—John s. of Richard Gerbode gives 12d. to take an acre and a perch of land in Alvirthorpe from John Swan, for ever. Pledge, Adam Gerbode.

WAKEFELD.—William Wyles gives 6d. to take ½ acre of meadow in Baseheyng, from Robert Pille, for ever. Pledge, John Cussing.

John Kyde fined 5s. for trespass committed. Pledges, Thomas s. of Richard the Clerk and William Taillour.

ALVIRTHORPE.—William Grenehode sues Henry Nunne and Adam Gerbode for covenant. Pledge, William Taillour.

SANDALE.—John s. of Swayn brings separate suits against Alexander de Crigeleston, John s. of Nalke, Richard Dandeheir, John s. of Hugh, Thomas s. of Hugh, Robert de la Grene, Robert s. of Isolda, William de Sandale, and John s. of Richard Hamund, for land. Pledge, Robert s. of Parnell.

German Philcoks v. Elias s. of Ivo de Werlouley, William his brother, and Robert the Grave, for debt. Pledge, Peter Hunkell.

THORNES.—Agnes Pymme of Thornes v. Magge wife of Eliot, for trespass. Pledge, William s. of Thomas.

John de Tothill v. Robert the Goldsmith, for trespass. Pledge, John Cussing.

HOLNE.—Richard de Cartewrth v. Juliana de Cartewrth, for debt. Pledge, John de Littelwode.

COURT at Wakefeld on Friday before the Feast of St. Margaret [July 13], in the year abovesaid [1307].

ESSOIGNS.[1]—Peter Swerd, by William Margeriknave. Pledge, Richard de Bristall.

Robert de Bramwith, attorney of Thomas de Schelfeld, by John Damoysell. Pledge, German Cay.

William de Chipedene, by Robert de Staynland. Pledge, Richard de Bristall.

John de Crosland, by Henry Gurdon. Pledge, John de la More.

William de Rastrik, by John de Tothill. Pledge, John de Toftclif.

ALVIRTHORPE.—John With-the-hounds [cum canibus], deft., essoigns against John Dade, for debt, by Richard Withundes. Pledge, Thomas the Brounsmyth.

John Dade, plt., Philip Wlf and Henry del Bothem have a love-day.

Henry Erle and Robert de Wodesom have a love-day.

William Margeriknave withdraws his suit for debt against John de Flansowe, William de Neuton and Robert s. of Ralph. He is pardoned the fine because he is the lord's serjeant.

Adam Gerbode admits that he owes William Margeriknave for half a stone of wool, as pledge for Henry le Nunne. Damages, 12d.; fine, 6d. Pledges, Peter de Pedder and John de Flansowe.

HOLNE.—Richard de Carteworth fined 6d. for a false claim against Juliana de Carteworth.

ALVIRTHORPE.—Walter Hogge v. William de Ouchethorpe and Robert his brother, for land. Pledge, Nicholas Hog.

[1] From suit of Court unless otherwise stated.

Adam s. of Thomas gives 2s. to take 6 acres of land in Alvirthorpe from Thomas s. of Philip Thorald. Pledge, Robert s. of Simon.

SOURBY —Adam s. of William de Lyngardes gives 3s. to take a messuage and ½ bovate of land in Soland, from Henry s. of William de Soland. Pledge, John s. of John de Northland.

SANDALE.—Hugh Cay gives 6d. to take 2½ acres of land and a rood of meadow in Sandale from Robert the Clerk of Sandale, for 18 years, and ½ acre of land for ever. Pledge, William de Castelford.

Adam de Castilford and Alice his wife give 6d to take an acre of land in Sandale fields from Thomas de Milnethorpe. Pledge, William de Everhull.

STANLAY.—Maude Pescy, the Earl's villein [nativa], gives 12d. for license to marry. Pledge, Robert Pescy.

William Takell v. Robert s. of Walter de Stanlay, for debt. Pledge, Adam le Wayte.

Thomas de Langfeld v. William s. of Ralph de Grygeleston, for debt. Pledge, Robert de Stodelay.

ALVERTHORPE.—Walter Hogg v. Henry Nunne, for debt. Pledge, Robert de Stanlay.

SOURBY.—Thomas de Saltonstall and Richard At-town-head [ad capud ville], 2d. each for escape of horses.

Richard s. of Robert de Cheswelley, 4d.; Geoffrey the Colier's wife, 2d.; John s. of Robert, 2d.; William de Haldewrth, 6d.; Thomas de Bellehous, 2d.; William Swaype, 6d.; Robert de Werlouley, 2s.; Thomas the Mercer, 8d.; Jordan de Skircotes, 4d.; Thomas Otes, 2d.; Henry del Schawe, 3d.; Richard de Waddeswrth, 4d.; William the Cowherd [vaccarius], 4d.; John the Milner, 6d.; Henry s. of Nalle, 3d.; John de Langley, 2d.; Richard s. of Stephen, 2d.; Adam s. of Ivo, 8d.; Dom Robert the Chaplain, 8d.; Adam del Schawe, 3d.; Henry de Holgate, 3d.; Adam de Kyrkeschawe, 3d.; John de Longlay, 2d.; Hannecok the Harpur, 12d.; Elias s. of Ivo, 6d.; for escapes.

William Wytebelt v. Thomas de Burgh, for trespass. Pledge, William Margeriknave.

Robert de Ketelesthorpe v. John the Skinner, and Robert and William, his sons, for trespass. Pledge, Robert de Stodleye.

William s. of John de Erdeslowe and Joan his wife v. Thomas de Heeton, for seizing cattle. Pledge, John Rased.

John Cussing v. Adam Gerbode, on an agreement. Pledge, John Chaffar'. Same v. Richard Baillif, for trespass. Pledge, John Damoysell.

ALVERTHORPE —Robert de Flansowe v. Richard s. of Broun, for trespass. Pledge, John de Flansowe.

G

Alice da. of Hugh *v.* Alice wife of Roger and Eva wife of Richard Broun, for trespass.   Pledge, John Wythehundes.

John Schirlock *v.* Alice da. of Hugh, for trespass.   Pledge, Richard s. of Broun.

COURT there on Friday before the Feast of St. Oswald the King [Aug. 5], in the first year of the Reign of King Edward, son of King Edward [1307].

Essoigns.[1]—Reynald le Flemyng, by John de Wakefeld.   Pledge, John de Podesay.

John de Lepton, by Robert de Horbiry.   Pledge, Thomas de Wakefeld.

Margaret de Nevile, by John de Podesay.   Pledge, John Damoysell.

John de la More, by John his son.   Pledge, William de Locwode.

Adam de Everingham, by John de Toftclif.   Pledge, Thomas de Thornton.

William del Okes, by Robert the Clerk of Sandale.   Pledge, Robert de Wyromthorpe.

William Drake, by Robert de Stodelay.   Pledge, John de Toftclif.

Nicholas le Normaund, by John Patrik.   Pledge, Nalk del Ker.

Elias de Birton, by John Damoysell.   Pledge, Robert de Wyromthorpe.

Thomas del Bellehous, by William Wodemous.   Pledge, Thomas de Thornton.

Nicholas de Cailly, by John Damoysell.   Pledge, German Filcok.

John de Tothill, by William Taillour.   Pledge, John Cay.

Richard de Bristall, by Robert de Normanton.   Pledge, John de Toftclif.

ALVERTHORPE.—John With-the-hounds, plt., essoigns against John Dade, for debt, by John de Fikesby.   Pledge, Robert de la Grene.

William s. of Godefrey de Dewysbiry, deft., essoigns against Robert Wyles of Wakefeld, for trespass, by William the Goldsmith.   Pledge, John Dade.

John Rate fined 6*d.* for not prosecuting his suit against John Swan.

Henry Erle and Robert de Wodesom, agreed by license; Robert is fined 12*d.*

Richard s. of Broun sues Robert Mareschall for damage done to his fallow land [*terra warectata*] by the routing of defendant's pigs; Robert says he has offered to make amends.   Judgment to be given [*Ideo ad judicium*].

---

[1] From suit of Court unless otherwise stated.

William s. of John de Erdislowe appoints William the Goldsmith of Wakefeld his attorney against Thomas de Heeton, for seizing cattle.

John the Skinner fined 12d. for not having his sons, John and William, to answer Robert de Ketelesthorpe.

Robert de Ketelesthorpe sues John the Skinner and Robert his son for cutting and carrying off his rye [siligo], in a place called Wulfgrene, in Sandale fields, value 40s., and for breaking his hedges [sepes], and doing other damage to the amount of cs. Defts. deny it, and are to wage their law. Pledge, John Patrik.

John s. of Henry de Fekesby and Ralph the Grave of Dewisbiry have a love-day.

John de Tothill, plt., essoigns against Robert the Goldsmith, for trespass, by Thomas his brother. Pledge, Peter Swerd.

John the Skinner and Robert his son are in mercy for carrying off corn when forbidden by the Bailiff [ultra defencionem ballivi].

Thomas de Burgh, attached to answer William Wytebelt, for trespass, by William s. of Gregory the Harpur, does not appear. Fine, 12d.

Adam s. of Maude de Crigeleston v. William de Burgh, Parson of Thornhill, Hervinus his man [homo], and Henry his servant [serviens], for seizing a cow. Pledge, Thomas s. of Roger.

Nicholas Nodger fined 12d. for not prosecuting his bill, attached before J. de Nevile against German Philcok.

STANLAY.—The inquisition between Thomas Bele, plt., and Juliana de Ouchethorpe, deft., for 2 acres of land with buildings claimed by Thomas as his inheritance, after the decease of Philip Bille, his grandfather, is taken by the oath of John s. of Alice, Gelle Quintyn, Robert Ricard, John Poket, Richard Poket, Richard del Bothem, Simon de Monte, Simon s. of Bateman, Walter s. of Bateman, Robert del Dale, Andrew Pogge and John Bullock, who say that the said Philip Bille acquired the land, and gave it to Hugh Bille, his son, who was seised of it for 40 days, and afterwards Philip received it back from Hugh for his life, with remainder to Hugh; after Philip's death Hugh recovered it under an inquisition held before Peter de Lound, and enfeoffed Thomas de Warderobe, who enfeoffed Juliana, who now holds it. Thomas is fined 4d. for a false claim.

SANDALE.—Thomas s. of Pelle gives 12d. to take 5 acres of land and meadow in Crigeleston fields in the tenure of Robert de Ketelesthorpe, from William the Clerk. Pledge, Thomas s. of Roger. He will pay 13s. at the next Court.

When Robert de Ketelesthorpe recovered divers tenements in Sandale and Ketelesthorpe against Alice and Margery, daughters of Robert the Ploghwrith, by an attaint taken by 24 jurors before William de Wakefeld, the then Steward, [reversing the verdict of] 12 jurors, taken before John de Danecastre, then and now Steward, the defendants informed the Earl that they suffered injury by being suddenly called upon to answer, without competent and reasonable summons, and also because the attaint was taken by men procured, such as tenants and servants of the said Robert, and tenants of the Parson of Sandale, who are strangers to the tenure of the Earl. The Earl, unwilling that they should suffer injury thereby, ordered John de Danecastre, the now Steward, to do them justice. Wherefore Alice and Margery attach their complaint again against Robert, and claim against him 7 acres of land as their inheritance, in which he had no entry save by a simple bargain [*per simplicem convencionem*] with their father, made out of Court, and without the lord's license, and never surrendered in Court, according to custom; also 3½ acres sold to Robert by Henry, their brother, while under age; also a bovate of land and 2 acres of meadow in Sandale, of which Thomas, their uncle, died seised, without heirs of his body, whereby the right descended to Robert his brother, their father, and from him to them, as daughters and heirs. Robert produced a charter of Earl John, grandfather of the present Earl, and asked the Court whether he is bound to answer for his free tenement except by the King's writ. The Steward replied that the same right by which he made Alice and Margery answer him in this Court, when he recovered the tenements, obliged him to answer them now in this Court. He wholly refused, and left the Court. In his default, the Steward took the inquisition from five Graveships, namely, William de Plegwik [?], Alexander del Wodethorpe, John s. of Swayn, Robert the Harpur, Adam le Wayte, Thomas s. of Roger, Robert s. of Adam del Neubigging, from the Graveship of Sandale; John Pollard, William Wyles, William Nelot and John Kyde, from the Graveship of Wakefeld; Adam Gerbot, Henry del Bothem, Richard de Collay, Robert de Flansowe and John Wythehundes, from the Graveship of Alverthorpe; Philip de Mora, Robert de Luppesheved, Thomas Pegere and John Malyn, from the Graveship of Thornes; Philip le Syur, Robert Pescy, Robert s. of Walter and Simon de Monte, from the Graveship of Stanley; who say that the 7 acres were never surrendered in Court by Robert, father of the appellants; that Henry, their brother, was under age when he sold the 3½ acres to Robert; also that Thomas, their uncle, died seised of a bovate of land in Ketelesthorpe, and of a bovate of land and 2 acres of meadow in Sandale; that his widow was dowered in ⅓ thereof, and held her dower peacefully as long as she remained in the Earl's fee; that Thomas died without heirs of his body, and the right descended to his brother Robert, father of the appellants, who was then under age, and fell into the wardship [*custodia*] of John de Ketelesthorpe, father of Robert, the present tenant, with ⅔ of the land, the other third accruing when the widow of Thomas married outside the Earl's fee, and went away; when Robert was of age, John de Ketelesthorpe gave him the bovate in Ketelesthorpe, but unjustly retained the land and meadow in Sandale, and continued to do so all his life; after John's death, Robert his son, the present tenant, continued to hold it, as before. And as Robert would not agree to this inquisition, the Earl is to be consulted as to what judgment shall be given; and in the meantime all the tenement, with the crops, is to be seised into the lord's hand. All the Jury of the attaint are to be imprisoned for their false oath; they are redeemed thence. The following do not come, and are fined:—William Hare, Peter the Shepherd, Robert s. of Isolda, Adam del Okys and Roger the Milner, 4*d*. each; Henry the servant [*garcio*] of the constable, and John le Best, 6*d*. each; Henry s. of Roger, Thomas de Dorkyng and Thomas s. of Bate, 4*d*. each.

WAKEFELD.—John Cussing complained to the Earl that whereas Gerard Cussing, his brother, surrendered to his use in Court 5½ acres of land in the fields of Wakefeld, to settle several debts owed by the said Gerard to divers persons, amounting to £9 13*s*. 4*d*., one Roger Preist and Rose his wife came before Ralph de Foulden, then acting for the Steward, and claimed the land as Rose's inheritance, and recovered it under an inquisition erroneous in several particulars; so that John lost the money he had bound himself to pay for the debts. The Earl therefore, both by letter and word of mouth, commanded the Steward to see that John recovered either the money or the land. And the parties now appearing before the Steward in full Court, John claims from Roger and Rose either the £9 13*s*. 4*d*., or the land. The defts. say that Gerard's goods and chattels were enough to satisfy all his debts without the land. An inquisition is taken by the oath of John Pollard, Robert the Walker, John Kyde, William Wyles, Elias Tyrsi, Philip Wlf, William de Neuton, Walter Bille, Richard de Collay, William s. of Jordan, William de Ouchethorpe and Robert Gunne, who are chosen by consent of both parties. They say that at his death Gerard's goods barely sufficed to bury him, and that he assigned

the land to John to satisfy his debts, and that John is a loser
[*careatur*] by the amount of those debts. Therefore as defendants
cannot pay the money, John is to recover the land.

HOLNE.—Matthew de Barneby gives 18*d.* to take 1½ acres of new
land from the waste in Fouleston, in the Longker, for ever; rent, 9*d.*
Pledge, Henry le Bagger.

Henry le Bagger gives 2*s.* to take 2½ acres as above; rent, 15*d.*
Pledge, Matthew de Barneby.

Adam Benne gives 12*d.* to take 1 acre as above, under Coppedhirst; rent, 6*d.* Pledge, Matthew de Mora.

Richard s. of Matthew de Mora gives 12*d.* to take an acre there,
in Stackwodeker; rent, 6*d.* Pledge, Adam Benne.

Richard s. of Thomas Bridde gives 5*s.* 6*d.* to take 5½ acres of new
land in Fouleston, in Edmundleyker and the Moreker; rent, 2*s.* 9*d.*
Pledge, Thomas his father.

Thomas de Hellewardhulles gives 2*s.* for 2½ acres of new land
there, in Langker and Eweclif; rent, 15*d.* Pledge, Richard s. of
Michael.

Richard s. of Michael gives 3*s.* to take 3 acres as above, in
Edmundleyker; rent, 18*d.* Pledge, the above Thomas.

Henry Wodemous gives 3*s.* for 3 acres there, as above, in
Wulricheleye; rent, 18*d.* Pledge, Adam Fernoule.

Adam Fernoule gives 18*d.* to take 1½ acres of new land there,
near Butterleystiel and Underhorne; rent, 9*d.* Pledge, Henry
Wodemous.

Thomas s. of Robert de Fouleston gives 4*s.* to take 5¼ acres of
new land in Fouleston, 3¼ being at Paulynbothehirst, 3 roods at the
Grene Swynstyeclif, ½ acre in the Breriker, and 3 roods at Littelwode
Lane; rent, 2*s.* 7½*d.* Pledge, Adam de Butterley.

Adam de Butterley gives 2*s.* to take 2 acres of new land in
Butterleygrene; rent, 12*d.* Pledge, Thomas s. of Robert.

Thomas s. of Herbert gives 18*d.* for 1¾ acres as above; rent, 10½*d.*
Pledge, Richard s. of Herbert.

Richard s. of Herbert gives 18*d.* for 1½ acres in Fouleston—one
acre in Edmundleye, and ½ acre in the Breriker; rent, 9*d.* Pledge,
Thomas s. of Herbert.

Matthew s. of Thomas de Fouleston gives 18*d.* to take 2 acres in
Fouleston; rent, 12*d.* Pledge, Adam the Waynwrith.

Adam the Waynwrith gives 3*s.* for 3 acres there, at Stackwodeker
and Roghloweker; rent, 18*d.* Pledge, Matthew s. of Thomas.

Peter de Bruys gives 2s. for 4 acres in the same places; rent, 2s. Pledge, Thomas s. of William.

Thomas s. of William de Butterley gives 2s. for 2 acres in Paulynbothehirst and Stackewodeker; rent, 12d. Pledge, Peter de Bruys.

Thomas de Billeclyf gives 3s. for 3¼ acres in Heppewrth, in Rolayker; rent, 19½d. Pledge, Adam del Rode.

Adam del Rode gives 18d. for 1 acre at Rolay; rent, 6d. Pledge, Thomas de Billeclyf.

Thomas s. of Richard gives 2s. for 2 acres in Heppewrth—½ acre lying round his house, and the other 1½ acres in Stitnol [?]; rent, 12d. Pledge, John s. of Adam.

John s. of Adam gives 3d. to take a rood in Schepewassegrene; rent, 1½d. Pledge, Thomas s. of Richard.

Richard s. of John gives 12d. for an acre in Heppewrth, in Eweclifker; rent, 6d. Pledge, Thomas s. of Thomas.

Thomas s. of Thomas s. of Elias gives 2s. 6d. for 2½ acres in Wlfhingandleye; rent, 15d. Pledge, Richard s. of John.

Adam the Shepherd gives 2s. for 2 acres there; rent, 12d. Pledge, William s. of the Grave.

William s. of the Grave gives 18d. for an acre in Cuntelacheker; rent, 6d. Pledge, Adam the Shepherd.

Robert s. of John gives 12d. for 1 acre there; rent, 6d. Pledge, Nicholas s. of John.

Nicholas s. of John gives 11s. for 10 acres in Heppewrth at Aldebothe, rent, 5s.; and 2 acres already ploughed, left waste on the lord by Richard de Frankysse.

Elias s. of Henry has license to take a rood of new land in Denerode; rent, 1½d.

Thomas s. of Simon gives 18d. for 1½ acres of waste in Heppewrth; rent, 9d. Pledge, Nicholas s. of Simon.

Nicholas s. of Simon gives 2s. 6d. for 2½ acres there; rent, 15d. Pledge, Thomas s. of Simon.

John s. of Thomas Keneward gives 12d. for 1 acre there; rent, 6d. Pledge, Nicholas s. of Simon.

John de Harehoppe gives 18d. to take 1¼ acres in Alstanlay; rent, 7½d. Pledge, Richard del Bothe.

Richard del Bothe gives 3s. for 2 acres there and 1 acre in Quelesbothem; rent, 18d. Pledge, John de Harehoppe.

Richard de Alstanlay gives 12d. for 1½ acres in Alstanlay; rent, 9d. Pledge, Henry Hulle.

Henry Hulle gives 2s. for 2 acres there; rent, 12d.   Pledge, Richard de Alstanley.

Richard s. of Elias gives 2s. for 2¼ acres there; rent, 13½d. Pledge, Gilbert de Alstanley.

Gilbert de Alstanley gives 2s. for 2 acres at Dobberode and the Lonehende; rent, 12d.   Pledge, Richard s. of Elias.

Geoffrey s. of William Strekayse gives 18d. for 1½ acres in Thoung; rent, 9d.   Pledge, John s. of Hugh.

John s. of Hugh gives 2s. for 2¼ acres at Welesbothem and 3 roods at Heyncheclyf; rent, 18d.   Pledge, the said Geoffrey.

Hugh del Hole gives 2s. for 2 acres in Quelesbothem; rent, 12d. Pledge, John de Bristall.

John de Bristall gives 6d. for ½ acre there; rent, 3d.   Pledge, Hugh del Hole.

John del Bothe gives 2s. for 2 acres in Roliphirst; rent, 12d. Pledge, Roger de Longleye.

Roger de Longleye gives 3s. for 3 acres there; rent, 18d.   Pledge, John del Bothe.

Adam s. of Adam de Wlvedale gives 2s. for 3½ acres in Henribrigholme; rent, 21d.   Pledge, John s. of Nicholas.

John s. of Nicholas gives 18d. for 1½ acres in Fayrhirst; rent, 9d. Pledge, the said Adam.

Nicholas s. of Nicholas gives 12d. for an acre in Stubbingker [?]; rent, 6d.   Pledge, Henry Wade.

Henry Wade gives 18d. for 1¼ acres in Wadeker; rent, 7½d.   Pledge, the said Nicholas.

Eliot At-Well gives 12d. for 1½ acres in Alcocrodende; rent, 9d. Pledge, Jordan the Milner.

Jordan the Milner gives 5s. for 5 acres in Fairbothem; rent, 2s. 6d.   Pledge, the said Eliot.

John the Couper gives 18d. for 1¼ acres in Alcokerodende; rent, 7½d.   Pledge, Adam de Langlay.

Adam de Langlay gives 12d. for 1 acre in Drycloghker; rent, 6d. Pledge, John the Couper.

Adam s. of Nicholas Keneward gives 12d. for 1 acre in Stubbingker; rent, 6d.   Pledge, Matthew de Langlay.

Matthew de Langlay gives 2s. for 3 acres in Langlay; rent, 18d. Pledge, the said Adam.

John s. of Nicholas Keneward junior gives 2s. for 2 acres in Ricroftker and Horssegatebank; rent, 12d.   Pledge, Adam s. of Nicholas.

Henry de Rastrik gives 4s. for 4½ acres in Mithomwodc; rent, 2s. 3d. Pledge, William de Storthes.

William de Storthes gives 2s. for 2½ acres in the Merkehirst; rent, 15d. Pledge, the said Henry.

William de Heytfeld, the forester, has license because he is in the Earl's service, to take 2¾ acres in the Merkehirst; rent, 16½d. Pledge, Robert Stirke.

Robert Stirke gives 12d. for 1 acre in the Rodehengker; rent, 6d. Pledge, the said William.

Adam Bray of Cartewrth gives 7s. for 7 acres in Aleynrode; rent, 3s. 6d. Pledge, Richard de la Grene.

Richard de la Grene gives 2s. for 2 acres in Wilkynker and under Rounnesdenewell; rent, 12d. Pledge, Adam Bray.

Thomas s. of Roger de Cartewrth gives 6s. to take 6 acres in the Ewyntreleye [?]; rent, 3s. Pledge, Richard de Cartewrth.

Richard de Carteworth gives 12d. for 1 acre in Drycloghker; rent, 6d. Pledge, the said Thomas.

John de Craven gives 18d. for 1½ acres in Littelwode; rent, 9d. Pledge, the said Richard.

Robert de Scoles gives 2s. for 2¼ acres in Haukehirst and Wadeker; rent, 13½d. Pledge, Adam s. of Emma.

Adam s. of Emma gives 3s. for 3 acres in Haukesker; rent, 18d. Pledge, the said Robert.

Richard s. of Henry del Rode gives 6d. for ½ acre at Wykeleyrode; rent, 3d. Pledge, the said Robert.

William del Bothe gives 2s. for 2 acres in Holne; rent, 12d. Pledge, William Wastell.

William Wastell gives 6d. for ½ acre in Holne; rent, 3d. Pledge, William del Bothe.

ALVERTHORPE.—Agnes da. of Roger s. of Christiana v. Adam Gerbode, for trespass. Pledge, Walter Scot. He is attached by Hugh Bille.

HORBIRY.—Philip s. of William de Horbyry v. Richard s. of the Grave, for trespass. Pledge, Henry le Wyte. He is attached by Hugh Danyel.

William s. of William de Mancanholes v. Adam de Kirkeschawe, for trespass. Pledge, Robert de Stodelay.

HOLNE.—Henry le Bagger of Heppewrth v. Nicholas de Clyf, for trespass. Pledge, Adam s. of Emma.

STANLAY —Richard del Bothem v. Hugh Tagge, for trespass Pledge, Richard Poket.

Richard del Ker *v.* Robert Gunne, for trespass.　　Pledge, Henry del Bothem.

Robert Gunne *v.* Richard del Ker, for trespass.　　Pledge, Robert Pescy.

————

COURT there on Friday the Morrow of St. Bartholomew the Apostle [Aug. 24], in the first year of the reign of King Edward, son of King Edward [1307].

ESSOIGNS.[1]—Peter Swerd, by William servant [*serviens*] of Margery.[2] Pledge, John de Toftclif.

Adam de Everingham, by John de Toftclyf.　　Pledge, Hugh de Seyvill.

Thomas de Thornton, by Hugh de Thornton.　　Pledge, John de Toftclif.

Margaret de Nevill, by German Estrild.　　Same pledge.

Robert de Wyueromthorpe, by John Damysell.　　Pledge, Richard de Bristall.

Thomas de Heeton, by Robert his servant [*garcio*].　　Pledge, Hugh de Seyvill.

Robert de la Grene of Ossete, by William de Langlay.　　Pledge, Robert de Stodelay.

John de Trymyngham, by Robert de Saltonstall.　　Pledge, William de Chepedene.

John de Crosland, by Henry Gurdon.　　Pledge, Hugh de Seyvill.

Thomas de Bellehouses, by Richard del Wode.　　Pledge, Elias de Birton.

William de Rastrik, by John de Tothill.　　Pledge, John de Lepton.

ALVERTHORPE.—John Dade sues John Wythehundes, Philip Wlf and Henry del Bothem for 15*s.* 4*d.*, balance of 22*s.*, the price of a horse bought of him; damages, 20*s.* Defts. deny it, and must wage their law.

Reynald le Flemang, son and heir of Sir William le Flemang, deceased, offers himself as true and lawful heir of the said William, in the tenements he held of the Earl in his fee, and of full age, as is proved. He was received to fealty, which he did; and, required by his fealty to admit the lawful services arising from the tenements he claims to hold of the Earl, he says that he holds the manor of Clifton with its appurtenances, by homage, fealty and suit every three

---

[1] From suit of Court unless otherwise stated.

[2] The William Margeryknave of other entries.

weeks in the lord's Court at Wakefeld, and by a rent of 20s. He pays 40s. for a relief, and an ox to the Steward[1] [?].

John the Skinner, Robert, John and William, his sons, are fined 13s. 4d. for contempt done against the lord's order [*ultra defencionem domini*].

John s. of Henry de Fekesby is fined 12d. for not prosecuting his suit against Ralph the Grave of Dewysbiry, for trespass.

Richard s. of the Brother of St. Swythin has license to withdraw his complaint for trespass against Gilbert the Lister of Birton, because no attachment can be found upon the said Gilbert [*quia attachiamentum non potest inveniri super predictum G.*].

William s. of William de Mancanholes is fined 12d. for not prosecuting his suit against Adam de Kirkeschawe, for trespass.

STANLAY.—Richard Isabel gives 12d. to take 6½ acres of land, with a toft and buildings, in Ouchethorpe, from Thomas Bole, for ever. Pledge, Robert Pescy.

John de Toftclif, formerly attorney of Adam de Everyngham, under a writ now quashed [*per breve quassatum*] by the death of the King, gives 2s. to retain his status without another writ.

Robert de Ketelesthorpe is fined 12d. for not prosecuting his suit against John the Skinner and his sons, for trespass.

William de Wakefeld, Thomas le Brounsmyth and Emma his wife, have a love-day.

John s. of Swayn is fined 2s. for not prosecuting his suit against Alexander de Crigeleston and others.[2]

SANDALE.—The 24 jurors of the attaint between Robert de Ketelesthorpe and Alice and Margery, daughters of Robert the Ploghwricht, are in mercy for their false oath. Swayn Scot is dead; therefore he is quit.[3]

OSSETE.—Adam s. of Henry de Goukethorpe is fined 3d. for not prosecuting his suit claiming land against Robert Sunneman.

Adam s. of Henry de Goukethorpe sues William s. of Richard Hirnyng for 2½ bovates in Ossete and Goukethorpe, as his inheritance after the death of Geoffrey his brother, whose heir he is. Deft. says that Geoffrey was convicted of felony, and hanged, whereupon the land escheated to the lord; Richard, deft.'s father, took the land from Peter de Lounde, then Steward, paying 20s. for entry, and deft. is his

---

[1] In the margin: *bos sen'*.

[2] See *ante*, p. 96.

[3] The names are given, but not the fines. See *ante*, p. 100.

son and heir; and he paid 6s. 8d as a heriot to the said Peter, then Steward. This is borne out by an examination of the rolls. Adam is fined 3d. for a false claim.

Thomas de Totehill v. John Spegth', for trespass. Pledge, Robert de Stodelay.

ALVERTHORPE.—William Grenehode sues Henry le Nunne and Adam Gerbode, his pledge, for 2s. 2d., which he had paid Henry for a rood of land for 6 years, and 16d. which he paid for manure on it. They admit it, and must satisfy him, and are fined 6d.

THORNES.—Agnes Pymme is fined 3d. for not prosecuting her suit against Magge wife of Eliot, for trespass.

WAKEFELD.—Walter Hogge, 6d., and 6d. for not prosecuting suits against William de Ouchethorpe and Robert his brother, for land; and against Henry le Nunne, in a plea of debt.

STANLAY.—Robert s. of Walter de Stanlay is fined 6d. for wrongfully detaining 4s. from William Takell, whom he had hired for work on the mill dam [quem conduxit ad opus stangni].

ALVERTHORPE.—Richard s. of Broun gives 6d. to agree with Robert de Flansowe, for trespass.

THORNES.—Juliana widow of Gerard de Thornes v. John Kyde, in a plea of land. Pledge, Richard Longschaunk.

Agnes Pymme v. Margery wife of Eliot de Thornes, for trespass. Pledge, William s. of Thomas.

ALVERTHORPE.—Adam Gerbode and John de Flansowe give 6d. to agree with Walter s. of Adam del Hill, for debt.

STANLAY.—An inquisition finds that Robert Gunne's cattle trampled Richard del Ker's sheaves of corn [tresellos]; damages, 1 sheaf; fine, 6d. For trampling on his hay, there is a second fine of 12d.; damages, 12d.

ALVERTHORPE.—John Cussing v. Henry Gauton and Richard Bailiff, for trespass. Pledge, John s. of Sibbe.

STANLAY.—Robert Gunne, fined 12d. for contempt.

ALVERTHORPE.—Adam Gerbode v. John Cussing, for trespass. Pledge, John Damysell.

WAKEFELD.—Maude widow of Peter Tirsi v. Master Robert Tirsi, for dower. Pledge, John Cussing. She afterwards withdraws.

ALVERTHORPE.—Richard s. of Philip de Alverthorpe, fined 12d. for contempt.

Thomas s. of Philip de Alverthorpe, to be attached to answer for the like.

STANLAY.—Robert Gunne and Richard del Ker have an essart, containing 40 perches, inclosed by a hedge [*sepes*], which they have to keep up in equal portions. Robert has left 14 perches of his portion unrepaired for 2 years, and Richard has had to repair it, at a cost of 2s. 4d. Robert is to pay this, and is fined 12d.

Hugh Tagge gives 6d. to agree with Richard del Bothem, for trespass.

SANDALE.—John the Skinner v. Agnes de Ossete, for trespass. Pledge, John Cokewald.

Alice the maid [*ancilla*] of Robert At-well v. William de Rypon, for trespass   Pledge, the said Robert.

STANLAY.—Robert s. of Robert s. of Walter v. Sibil widow of Nicholas the Carter and William and Robert, her sons, for trespass. Pledge, Philip le Syur.   They are attached by Simon de Monte.

THORNES.—William s. of Elias Bulneys v. Agnes Pymme, for trespass. Pledge, Robert the Grave.

John de Maynigham v. Thomas de Heeton, for detaining a horse. Pledges, William the Gardyner and Lance his son.   He is attached by Richard Sparive and Adam Bonar' [?].

William de Wakefeld sues William the Dyker on an agreement. Pledge, German Filcok.

THORNES.—William At-Elm [*ad Ulmum*] v. Henry Poyde, for trespass.   Pledge, Robert At-Elm.   He is attached by William s. of Roger.

ALVERTHORPE.—Richard the Tanner of Alverthorpe v. John Rate, for trespass.   Pledge, Robert Gerbode.

STANLAY.—Philip s. of Agnes de Wyromthorpe v. Adam s. of Cote, for trespass.   Pledge, Richard Spink.   He is attached by John s. of Philip.

COURT there on the Morrow of the Exaltation of the Holy Cross [Sept. 14], in the first year of King Edward s. of King Edward [1307].

ESSOIGNS.[1]—Reynald le Flemyng, by German Cay.   Pledge, John de Wakefeld.

Nicholas le Normaund, by Thomas de Burgh.   Pledge, William del Okes.

John de Crosland, by Henry Gurdon.   Pledge, Robert de la Grene.

Elias de Birton, by Nicholas de Birton.   Pledge, John de Toftclif.

---

[1] From suit of Court unless otherwise stated.

Robert de Wyromthorpe, by William de Castilford.   Pledge,
William del Okes.

Nicholas de Cailly, by John de Cailly.   Pledge, Thomas de
Bellehouses.

Hugh de Seyvill, attorney of Baldwin de Seyvill, by Henry de
Seyvill. Pledge, Robert de Grene.

William de Schepedene, by John Damoysell.   Pledge, John de
Lepton.

Richard de Bristall, by Robert Scot. Pledge, John de la More.

John Spegh, deft., against Thomas de Totehill, for trespass, by
John de Lascy. Pledge, John de Podesay.

Adam s. of Maude de Crigeleston, plt., against William de Burgh,
Parson of Thornhill [and others[1]], by John de Clayton.   Pledge,
Henry de Chyvet.   William de Burgh essoigns by Thomas de Burgh.
Pledge, William Ingreys.

John Wythehundes, deft., against John Dade, for debt, by Thomas
de Totehill. Pledge, Richard Wythehundes.

Philip Wlf, against John Dade, for debt, by William de Estfeld.
Same pledge.

William de Wakefeud sues Thomas the Brounsmyth and Emma
his wife, for calling him a false and faithless [*infidelem*] man and a
robber, in Wakefeud market, and raising the hue after him, and
repeating it in the four nearest townships; so that, after William had
bought a cask [*doleum*] of wine from Walter Gowere for 40s., this
scandal and infamy coming to Walter's ears, he refused to have any
dealings with him [*noluit mercuncinare*], or to keep the agreement
regarding the wine; whereby William lost 20s., which he could have
made as profit on the wine; damages, 40s.   Defts. say that the hue [is
raised where there] is a terror to the neighbourhood,[2] damages under
which lie to the King, or to other magnates who take such emends
in their fees, and that they were fined for [raising] this hue at the
Earl's Tourn, wherefore William cannot recover emends for the same.
They deny that any agreement as to the wine was broken, or profit
lost, by the hue.   William craves judgment, because they have made
no answer to the principal head of his complaint, namely the slander.
The matter is respited.

HOLNE.—Henry le Bagger withdraws his complaint for trespass
against Nicholas del Clif; fined 6d. Pledge, the said Nicholas.

---

[1] See *ante*, p. 99.

[2] Translation doubtful: *uthesium est quidam terror patrie cujus emende pertinent
ad dominum Regem.*

German Filcok is fined *6d.* for not prosecuting his suit against Elias s. of Ivo, William his brother, and Robert de Saltonstall, for debt.

William Wytebelt, *6d.* for the like against Thomas de Burgh, for trespass.

HORBIRY.—Richard s. of Philip de Horbiry gives *6d.* to agree with Philip s. of William, for trespass. Pledge, Henry le Wyte.

Peter Swerd, *6d.* for default.

OSSETE.—Richard de Heeton gives *12d.* for license to marry his daughter Margery.

ALVERTHORPE.—Alice wife of Roger *v.* Alice da. of Hugh de Alverthorpe, for calling her a thief. Fine, *6d.*

The said Alice da. of Hugh *v.* Eva wife of Richard s. of Broun, for calling her a thief and a harlot in Wakefeud Market; she [? the deft.] would have cut off her [? the plaintiff's] head, had she not been prevented by several men. An inquisition is to be taken.

THORNES.—Juliana de Thornes, *3d.* for a false claim for land against John Kyde.

ALVERTHORPE.—An inquisition finds that Alice da. of Hugh, assaulted Edusa wife of John Schirlock, led her into a snare [*tractavit eam in foveam*], threw her down and trampled on her; damages, *6d.*, which Alice is to pay, and *12d.* fine.

THORNES.—Agnes Pymme is fined *3d.* for a false claim against Margery wife of Elias Bulneys, for trespass. Margery, and William her son, are fined *3d.* for a false claim against Agnes.

ALVERTHORPE.—Adam Gerbode, *3d.* for a false claim against John Cussing; also *3d.* for beating Agnes da. of Roger s. of Christiana, damages, *6d.*

John Cussing fined *6d.*, for not prosecuting his suit against Adam Gerbode.

STANLEY.—Robert Gunne, *12d.* for a false claim for trespass against Richard del Ker.

SANDALE.—William de Ripon gives *3d.* to agree with Alice, the maid of Robert At-Well. Pledge, William del Overhall.

SOURBY.—Richard the Smith of Werlouleye gives *12d.* to take a toft with a barn in Werlouleye from Adam s. of Ivo, for ever. Pledge, John del Westwode.

William s. of John de Erdeslowe sues Thomas de Heeton for seizing 4 oxen and a bullock in the high street of the town of Heeton, causing them to be driven to his manor of Heeton, and keeping them till delivered by John Damysell, the sworn bailiff;

damages, 20s. Deft. justifies the seizure, which he says was made in his severalty, in a place called the Hyngande Rode, and not in the street. [Entry not completed.]

Thomas de Langfeld *v.* William and Henry, sons of Ralph the Smith, for debt.

STANLAY.—Richard del Kerre *v.* Robert Gunne, says that they jointly hold an acre of land in Stanlay, containing 8 butts [*butte*], of which neither of them has any certain portion; two years ago, without his consent, Robert, of his own authority, appropriated the best part of the land to himself; damages, 6s. 8d. Robert says that his father held the portion which he now holds all his life, and he holds it as his heir. An inquisition is taken by the oath of Robert del Dale, Richard del Bothem, Richard Poket, Gerard Quintyn, John Poket, Philip le Syour, Robert s. of Walter, Robert Rychard, John s. of Alice, Hugh s. of Bateman, Simon s. of Bateman and Robert Gosse, who say that the deft. holds the portion his father held, but has incroached 10 perches by 5½ feet on Richard's portion. Richard is to recover the incroachment, and damages, 1 sheaf. Robert is fined 40d. for the incroachment. Pledges, Robert s. of Walter and Robert Pescy.

John de Maynigham and Thomas de Heeton have a love-day.

ALVERTHORPE.—John Thorald *v.* Robert the Carpenter of Wakefeld, for trespass. Pledge, Geoffrey de Birkynschawe.

Alice wife of Roger *v.* Alice de Birkynschawe, for trespass. Pledge, Richard s. of Broun.

John Cussing *v.* Adam Gerbode, on an agreement. Pledge, William s. of Walter.

Henry le Nunne and Adam Spynk, for cutting vert, 6d. each. Pledge, Adam Gerbode.

Adam Spynk, for breaking the fold, 12d.

Adam Gerbode, for dry wood, 3d.

Richard the Pynder of Lofthous, for escape of cattle, 12d. Pledge, William de Neuton.

Henry le Nunne, for dry wood, 1d. Pledge, John Flachard.

John Bullock, the like, 3d. Pledge, Richard Spink.

John Schirlock, for a mare not agisted in the new park, 6d.; and for a cow sent in there during the night, 6d.

Adam Gerbode, and Richard s. of Broun, for escapes, 6d. each.

THORNES.—John de Haya, the like, 2d.

Thomas Brounsmyth, for dry wood, 2d.

Ivo the Smith, for stones broken in the new park, 12d.

John Grafford, for an escape there, 4*d.*

WAKEFELD.—Richard Baillyf, 3*d.*; Ralph Bate's wife, 1*d.*; the da. of William s. of Godith, 1*d.*; Richard s. of Henry s. of Mille, 12*d.*; Robert Dernelove, 12*d.*; Robert de Fetherston, 6*d.*; Robert de Bruys, 12*d.*; John de Skulbroke, 2*d.*; John le Sotheren, 2*d.*; Agnes Swerd, 2*d.*; Thomas s. of Henry, 2*d.*; and William Proudefot's daughter, 2*d.*; for dry wood.

HOLNE.—"Litel Dobbe" of Carlecotes, for escape of 8 beasts in Holnefrith, 12*d.* Pledge, Richard s. of Elcok.

John le Riche, 2*s.* for the like. Pledge, William de Hallomschire.

Richard the Baker, for 6 beasts, 12*d.* Pledge, Richard s. of Elcok.

HYPERUM.—John Greteword, 3*d.*, and Thomas s. of Elias, 2*d.*, for dry wood broken in Hyperum wood.

John s. of Hanne de Bayrstowe, 4*d.*, John s. of Ralph, 4*d.*, and William the Milner of Halifax, 2*d.*, for escapes.

Roger the Milner of Briggehouses senior, 4*d.*, and Richard the Tailor, 2*d.*, for dry wood.

SOURBY.—John del Rediker, for escape of 6 beasts and 5 pigs in le Frith, 6*s.* 8*d.*

Henry del Holgate, 4*d.*; Adam s. of Ivo, 6*d.*; Henry the Fuller of Sourby, 4*d.*; Thomas de Rodes of Hyperum, 3*d.*; John s. of Hugh de Northeland, 12*d.*; John s. of Hanne de Halifax, 4*d.*; for escapes.

Henry de Coildelay, for escape of a horse in Saltonstall meadows, 6*d.* Thomas de Rodes, 3*d.*; William s. of Peter de Hiperum, 3*d.*; Adam Cappe of Miggelay, 12*d.*; John de Noteschawe, 6*d.*; and William the Carpenter, 6*d.*; for escapes there.

Ingelard de Miglay, Ivo de Miggelay, Adam s. of William At-Town-head, the daughter of Maude del Okes, 2*d.* each; Richard At-Town-head of Miglay, and Thomas s. of William de Saltonstall, 3*d.* each; Richard del Wyteleye, 2*d.*; William de Monte alto, 3*d.*; John s. of Robert de Cheswelleye, 2*d.*, and Richard his brother, 2*d.*; for escapes in le Frith.

Hugh de Mixendene, for escape of a horse in Saltonstall meadows, 6*d.*

STANLEY.—Robert del Dale, Richard Poket, Philip le Syour and Hugh s. of Bateman, fined 3*d.* each for not attending as jurors.

Robert Gosse, for the like. He came afterwards.

Robert s. of Walter de Stanley *v.* Robert Soneman, William s. of Jordan, Ivo the Smith and Robert s. of Robert de Flansowe, for trespass. Pledge, Robert Richard.

H

ALVERTHORPE.—The Graveship of Alverthorpe is fined 20s. for not coming to the driving of the chase, as summoned to do [*quia non venit ad stabul' chacee ut som'*].

Walter Hogg *v.* Henry le Nonne and Robert s. of Ralph, for debt. Pledge, Robert de Stanlay.

HOLNE.—Jordan the Milner sues Robert Stirk, as a surety [*de placito plegii*]. Pledge, John de Littelwode.

ROLL FOR 1 AND 2 EDWARD II, 1307–8.[1]

. . . . and perquisites of the Soke of Wakefeud from Michaelmas in the first year of the reign of King Edward son of King Edward [1307], in the time of John de Danecastre, then Steward, until the same feast in the year following.

COURT at Wakefeud on the Friday in the octave of St. Michael, in the year abovesaid [1307].

ESSOIGNS.[2]—Reynald le Flemyng, by John de . . . .

Thomas [?] de Burgh, by Alan Almot. Pledge, Robert de Hey . . . [? Heyrode].

Margaret de Nevill, by Thomas de Seyvill. Pledge, Thomas de Heeton.

William s. of William de Bello monte, by John Bulloc. Pledge, John Patrik.

Thomas de Thornton, by Hugh de Thornton. Pledge, John de Mora.

William de Chepedene, by John del Wode. Pledge, Hugh de Seyvill.

William de Rastrik, by John Damoysell. Pledge, John de la More.

John s. of John de Solande, by Thomas de Totehill. Pledge, John de Totehill.

Richard de Bristall, by Robert Scot. Pledge, John Damoysell.

William de Burgo, Parson of Thornhill, *v.* Adam s. of Maude de Crigeleston, in a plea of seizing a cow, by Robert de H[eyrode?]. Pledge, John Patrik. Adam appeared [*optulit se*], and therefore a day is given.

---

[1] In bad condition.

[2] From suit of Court unless otherwise stated.

Hervinus, the said William's man [*homo*], *v.* the said Adam, touching the same, by John Patrik. Pledge, William del Okes.

Henry, the said William's servant [*serviens*], *v.* the said Adam, touching the same, by William del Okys. Pledge, John de la More.

William s. of Ralph de Crigeleston and Henry s. of Ralph *v.* Thomas de Langfeud, for debt, by Robert de Heyrode. Pledge, William del Okys. Thomas appeared, and a day is given.

Robert le Flemyng gives 2*s.* to have respite of suit until Michaelmas.

Thomas de Langfeud, 3*s.* 4*d.*, for the like.

John de Quernby [?], 2*s.*, for the like.

William de Wakefeud, plt., *v.* Thomas the Brounsmyth and Emma his wife, for trespass, by Robert de S . . . . lay. Pledge, John Damoysell.

ALVERTHORPE.—John Cussing *v.* Henry Gouton, for trespass. Henry made default, and is to be distrained to answer by the next Court. He afterwards came, and vouched Adam Gerbode to warrant 3 roods of land which Adam demised to him.

WAKEFEUD.—John Cussing, for a false claim of trespass against Richard Baillif, 6*d.*

Richard Baillif, 6*d.*, for doing what the lord had forbidden [*quia fecit ultra defensionem domini*].

ALVERTHORPE.—Richard s. of Ph[ilip] de Alverthorpe, 6*d.*, for not having Thomas his brother, for whom he was pledge. Thomas is to be attached for doing what the lord had forbidden.

Richard Broun, for a false claim against Robert the Mareschall, 6*d.*

William s. of Peter le Pedder, for a false claim against Margery Wyntre, ...

Agnes de Ossete to be distrained to answer John the Skinner [*pelliparius*], for trespass.

John de Thornhill gives 4*s.* to have respite of suit till Michaelmas.

ALVERTHORPE.—Eva wife of Richard Broun is in mercy for assaulting Alice da. of Hugh, whose damages are taxed at 6*d.*

John Wythehundes, Philip Wolf and Henry del Bothem come and perfect the law which they waged against John D[ade] . . . . 4*d.*, as they ought. They go quit, and Dade is in mercy for a false claim.

Beatrice de Totehill, by her attorney, *v.* Henry del Ryding, for debt. He does not come, and is to be distrained.

John de Maynigham, plt., *v.* Henry de Heeton, for detaining a horse, comes and withdraws. He and his pledges, William the Gardiner and Laurence s. of Simon, are in mercy.

William Aur' [? Aurifaber, the goldsmith], the attorney of William s. of John de Erdeslowe, *v.* Thomas de Heeton, for seizing cattle . . . . Pledge, John de Mora. Thomas appeared, and a day is given.

William de Wakefeud *v.* William le Dyker, on an agreement. Deft. does not come, though twice summoned; to be distrained.

Henry Poyde gives 6*d.* to agree with William at Elm [*ad ulmum*], for trespass. Pledge, the said William.

Robert the Carpenter, for carrying off corn, *v.* John Torald, in mercy, 6*d.*

ALVERTHORPE.—Robert the Carpenter *v.* Henry le Nonne, Adam Gerbode and William de Neuton, for trespass. Pledge, John s. of Sibil . . . .

John Rate is in mercy for refusing to be attached [*quia noluit se attac'*].

The plea between Richard the Tanner and John Rate, for trespass, is adjourned to the Tourn at Wakefeud.

Sibil widow of Nicholas Car . . . [the Carter], for herself and her sons, gives 6*d.* to agree with Robert s. of Robert s. of Walter, for trespass.

Adam s. of Cote is in mercy for preventing Philip s. of Agnes from enjoying his common [*quia deturbavit Philippum filium Agnetis ad communiam suam utendam*]. Damages, 6*d.*

The tenements late of Henry de Rodes are in the lord's hands, because he is dead.

Alice wife of Roger, 6*d.*, for a false claim against Alice de Birkynschawe.

Henry le Nonne admits that he is bound to Walter Hogg in 300 fagots. He must pay.

William s. of John de Littelwode gives 12*d.* to take 3 roods of meadow in Littelwode from Thomas s. of Robert de . . . .

Nicholas de Cailly is in mercy for default.

Thomas de Totehill is in mercy for withdrawing his plea of trespass *v.* John Spegh.

William Wildebor made default.

The tenants of the land late of Richard de Stanelay made default.

[THORNES.]—Richard de Luppesheved gives 6*s.* 8*d.* to take a bovate of land with the appurtenances in Thornes from Adam s. of Th[omas (?) s. of] Gilbert. Pledge, Robert de Luppesheved.

Richard s. of John de Chikinlay gives 4*s.* for licence to take a bovate, an essart and an acre of land, with buildings and appurtenances in Goukethorpe, as a heriot after the death of his father. Pledge, ... de Gouk[thorpe].

Robert s. of Richard Beausire gives 4s. to take . . . . [as a heriot after] the death of his father.

Thomas de Bello . . . . . . [? Bello monte] gives . . . . to have respite of suit till Michaelmas.

[*The remainder of this side is for the most part illegible.*]
mem. 1d.

The pannage of Sourbyschir is sold in gross to William del Bothem for 40s.

The pannage of Hyperum wood is sold in gross to William de Bothes and Alexander del Frith for 6li.

Lady Margaret de Nevill, by the King's writ annexed to this Roll and by his letters patent, appoints Thomas de Seyvill, her attorney, to do suit in her place at this Court; and he is received.

WAKEFEUD.—John de Amyas takes the town of Wakefeud to farm for 5 years following the date of this Roll . . . . with the farms of the town, tolls of fairs and merchants, and the perquisites of the town Court, and the tolls of the oven . . . . Sourbischir, and also the mills of Wakefeud, Sandale and Thurstanhawe . . . . of the town and of the mills, anciently accustomed to be had, for £100 a year, to be paid at two terms, viz. £40 at [? Easter] and £60 at Michaelmas. Pledges, German Philcok, Robert the Walker, John Cussing, and Robert Estre [? Estrild].

John de Totehill is attached by the mainprise of the underwritten, to come before the lord or his council when he shall be warned, to answer certain articles put against him; viz. Robert Estrild, German Philcok, Robert the Walker and William Taillour. All the tenements of which Thomas de Warderoba lately enfeoffed the said John are to be held in the lord's hands, as before.

WAKEFEUD.—John Tasse (4d.), Agnes da. of Roger (4d.), and Robert Wylis (. . .), for escapes of pigs in the New Park.

Robert Estrild (. . .), John Cay (. . .), John Dade (2d.), William the Goldsmith (2d.), Joan Whytelof (. . .), John Pollard (. . .), and Robert le Young (. . .), for escapes of pigs in the Old Park.

ALVERTHORPE.—Adam Wolf (1d.), Richard s. of Philip (2d.), and Robert s. of Ralph de Neuton (2d.), for not coming to the chase.

THORNES.—William s. of Thomas de Thornes (2d.), John Malyn (2d.), and Thomas Peger (1d.), for the like.

STANLAY.—Adam Figge (4d.) and Robert s. of Ralph (2d.), for escapes of pigs in the Old Park.

mem. 2.

COURT at Wakefeud on the Friday in the eve of the Apostles Simon and Jude [Oct. 28], 1 Edward II [1307], in the time of John de Danc[astre].

ESSOIGNS.[1]—Peter Swerd, by William Margerienave. Pledge, Richard de Bristall.

John de Lepton, by Nicholas de Lasceles. Pledge, Thomas de Thornton.

John de Toftclif, attorney of Adam de Everigham, by Walter de Thinglowe. Pledge, Thomas de Thornton.

Robert de Wyveromthorpe, by John Cay. Pledge, Richard de Bristall.

Robert de la Grene, by William de Castelford. Pledge, John de la More.

John de Crosseland, by Henry Gurdon. Pledge, William del Okys.

John de Willeys, by Robert de Saltonstall. Pledge, Robert de Stodelay.

Thomas de Burg, by Thomas de Wittelay. Pledge, Thomas de Seyvill.

Thomas the Brounsmyth and Emma his wife, defts., *v.* William de Wakefeud, in a plea of trespass, by Thomas de Wake . . . . . Pledge, William de Okes.

Adam s. of Maude de Crigeleston *v.* William de Burg, parson of Thornhill, and Hervinus and Henry, his servants, for seizing a cow, by William Scot. Pledge, Thomas de Seyvill.

William s. of Ralph de Crigeleston and Henry his brother, defts., *v.* Thomas de Langfeud, for debt, by Thomas de Wittelay. Pledge, William del Okes.

Robert de Heyrode, plt., *v.* German Filcok, for seizing a mare, by John de Sandale. Pledge, William del Okes.

William s. of John de Erdeslowe, plt., *v.* Thomas de Heeton, for seizing cattle, comes and withdraws. He is in mercy. Pledge, William the Goldsmith.

Reynald le Flemyng made default at this Court. He pays 4*d.* for his fine, and to have respite till Michaelmas.

Elias de Birton, John de Totehill, William Wildebore (6*d.*), and John s. of John de Soland (6*d.*), for default.

HOLNE.—William del Bothe (6*d.*) and William Wastell (3*d.*), for escapes of pigs in Carteworth.

---

[1] From suit of Court unless otherwise stated.

Juliana de Alstanlay (3*d.*), John s. of Geoffrey de Littelwode (4*d.*), Juliana de Carteworth (3*d.*), Adam de Dalton (3*d.*), Cicely de Carteworth (3*d.*), and Hugh de Carteworth (3*d.*), for collecting nuts.

The same Hugh for the escape of a horse in Carteworth, 2*d.*

William de Storthes, for a horse kept in le Frith, 6*d.*

Thomas de Billeclif, for the escape of a horse, 2*d.*

ALVERTHORPE.—Henry le Nonne and Richard Bullock, for dry wood, 4*d.* each.

Robert Campion, for the escape of pigs, 2*d.*

Richard s. of Philip, for beating oaks [*pro querc' verber'*], 2*d.*

John s. of Thomas Ode, for dry wood and acorns, 6*d.*   Pledge, Richard Buny.

The son of Henry le Nonne, for acorns, 3*d.*

WAKEFEUD.—The da. of Robert Broun, the da. of Roger de Silkeston, the da. of John Lattock, the da. of Malkine Godesowell, and the maids of Robert Lastfast [?] and Adam the Clouter, 1*d.* each, for dry wood.

STANLAY.—Emma Dully, 2*d.*, for the like.

ESSOIGN.—William s. of William de Bello monte, from suit of Court, by John Bulloc.   Pledge, Thomas de Thornton.

WAKEFEUD.—Robert de Fetherstan, 2*d.*, for acorns.

William de Sandale's son (1*d.*), William s. of Godith (2*d.*), John le Sotheren (4*d.*), Ralph s. of Malle (1*d.*), Ralph s. of Henry (1*d.*), the da. of William Proudefot (1*d.*), Richard Passemer (6*d.*), the da. of William Wildebore (1*d.*), and John Maunsell (3*d.*), for dry wood.

Malina de Sourby, 4*d.*, for dry brushwood.

Agnes de Bretton, 4*d.*, for her two maids breaking dry wood.

Henry de Swynligton, 6*d.*, for brushwood blown down by the wind.

Thomas s. of Philip de Alverthorpe in mercy for carrying corn put in the lord's defence [*quia cariavit bladum positum in defensum domini*], at the suit of Thomas s. of Lance, besides [his damages?].

John the Skinner withdraws his plaint against Agnes de Ossete. He and his pledges are in mercy.

Beatrice de Totehill appears by her attorney *v.* Henry del Ryding, in a plea of debt.   Henry does not come, and is to be distrained.

William de Wakefeld *v.* William le Dyker, in a plea of agreement; the like.

The plea of trespass between Richard the Tanner and John Rate is respited till the Tourn at W[akefield?].

The tenements late of Henry de Rodes are in the Earl's hands, because he is dead.

The plea of debt between Robert s. of Walter de Stanlay, plt., and Robert Sonneman, William s. of Jordan, Ivo the Smith, and Robert s. of Robert de Flansowe, is respited till the Tourn at Wakefeud.

The plea of debt between Jordan the Milner and Robert Stirk is respited till the Tourn at Birton.

The inquisition as to the alleged breaking of the Earl's fold by William Nelot is respited till the Tourn at Wakefeud. Also the charge against him of putting his sheep in the Earl's grass.

[THORNES.]—The plea of agreement between John Tasse and Agnes Peger is respited till the same Tourn. She is in mercy, and must be distrained for not coming when summoned.

The plea of agreement between William Grenehod and Agnes Pegere is respited till the same Tourn.

The plea between Quenilda de Alverthorpe, plt., and William Hoskell and Richard de Collay, for assault, is respited till the Tourn . . . .

Robert de Stanlay v. Robert s. of Ralph de Neuton, for trespass. Pledge, William Beauchant.

Same v. John Rate, for trespass. Same pledge.

William Hoskell v. Quenilda da. of Adam, for seizing cattle. Pledge, Henry del Bothem.

John s. of Swayne Scot v. Roger de la Grene of Crigeleston, for land. Pledge, Hugh Tubbyng.

Same v. William de Sandale, for land. Same pledge.

Walter s. of Elias de Ourom and Maude his da. v. John s. of Walter and Richard his brother, for assault. Pledge, Robert de Sorby [?].

———————

[COURT at . . . .] on the morrow of S. Edmund the Archbishop
[Nov. 16], 1 Edward II, [1307].

[The succeeding eleven lines, containing essoigns, are illegible.]
mem. 2d.

ESSOIGNS.—Robert de Heyrode, plt., v. German Philcok, for seizing a mare, by John de Sand[ale?]. Pledge, William de [Okes?].

The said German, deft., v. the said Robert in the same plea, by John Cay. Pledge, John Patrik.

Thomas de Langfeud, plt., v. William s. of Ralph de Crigeleston and Henry his brother, for debt, by John Patrik. Pledge, William del Okes. William appeared, and a day is given. Henry, who has twice essoigned, does not come. Therefore William del Okes, the pledge of the essoign, is in mercy for not having him. Thomas de Wittelay, the essoigner, is to be attached, and Henry is to be distrained for default.

William de Burgo, Parson of Thornhill, deft., *v.* Adam s. of Maude de Crigeleston, in a plea of seizing a cow, by John Patrik. Pledge, Richard de Bristall. Hervinus, William's man [*homo*], in the same plea, by John Damysell. Pledge, William del Okes. Henry, William's servant, in the same plea, by John Damysell. Pledge, Hugh de Seyvill.

Beatrice de Totehill, by her attorney, *v.* Henry del Ryding, for debt. Henry does not come; to be distrained.

William s. of William de Bello monte gives 2*s.* for respite of suit till Michaelmas.

ALVERTHORPE.—The plea of land between John Cussing and Adam Gerbode is respited until the Rolls have been searched [*donec fiat scrutacio rotulorum*].

THORNES.—It is found by an inquisition that Agnes Pegere has deforced John Tasse of the crop [*vestura*] of 3 roods of land, in which he has still two crops by the demise of her husband. Damages 10*d.*, which she must pay; also 3*d.* fine. John may hold the land for his term.

The same Agnes gives 3*d.* to agree with William Grenehod in a plea of land.

ALVERTHORPE.—The plea between John s. of Philip and Eugenia Daneys, his wife, plts., *v.* Peter de Acom, for trespass, is adjourned till the next Court. Peter is to be distrained.

Henry de Swynlington *v.* Adam Gerbode, complains that he unjustly detains two stone of wool, price [? x*s.*]; he was pledge that Juliana Swanne should pay at Pentecost last, and she has paid nothing. Adam admits it; he must pay, and is in mercy.

It is found by an inquisition that Robert s. of Ralph de Neuton unjustly detains from Robert de Stanlay . . . . . [*buscham de v* . . . . .]. Damages, 3*d.*

John s. of Swayn de Crigeleston is in mercy for false claims *v.* Robert de la Grene and William de Sandale, in two pleas of land.

Sir Thomas de Burgo, by the King's writ hereto annexed, and by his letters patent, appoints Alan Almot, his attorney, to do the suit which he owes to this Court; and he is received.

OSSETE.—John the Walker of Ossete (4*d.*), Richard s. of John of the same (4*d.*), Alice da. of Anote (2*d.*), Richard Suart (4*d.*), John Hirnyng (6*d.*), William le Wyte [?] (2*d.*), and Richard de Thynglowe (4*d.*), for dry wood in the New Park.

Robert de Baghill, for escape of cattle in the new coppice [? *in novo cop'*], 8*d.*

THORNES.—William [?] s. of Philip del Hill (*2d.*), Roger Trailment of Snaypethorpe (*6d.*), Agnes wife of Roger (*2d.*), John Graffard (*2d.*), Richard s. of Broun [?] (*2d.*), William Hoskell (*3d.*), Richard the Tanner (*2d.*), and Adam de Flansowe (*6d.*), for dry wood in the New Park.

WAKEFEUD.—Henry de Skulbroke (*2d.*), John le Sotheren (*4d.*), German the Gardyner (*2d.*), William the Gardiner (*2d.*), Beatrix de Aula (*1d.*), Eva de Bramlay (*6d.*), and John Thorald (*4d.*), for dry wood.

Robert de [Staynland] *v.* John s. of William de Greteland, for debt. Pledge, John de Bothem.

The tenements late of Henry de Rokes [*sic*] are still in the lord's hands, because his heir has not come and paid relief [*non dicta tenementa releviare*].

HOLNE —John s. of John de Holne *v.* Adam his brother, for seizing cattle [?]. Pledge, Richard s. of Elias.

Adam de la Grene *v.* [Gilbert] de Alstanlay, for trespass. Pledge, John the Grave [?].

[Thomas] s. of Thomas *v.* Adam de Heitfeld, for trespass. Pledge, Roger s. of Amabel.

[William at Town-head] *v.* Anabel de Chesewelley and Richard her son, [for trespass].

John s. of Robert *v.* Thomas del Feild, for debt. . . . . .

Henry s. of Thomas del Westwode *v.* John del Westwode, for trespass. . . . . .

Thomas de Connale *v.* Matthew de Bosco, for seizing cattle. . . . . .

William the Cowherd [*vaccarius*] of Sourby and Juliana Wade *v.* Thomas de Roaldessete, [for debt].

. . . . . . Werlouley, for debt. Pledge, Robert de Saltonstall.

------

mem. 3.

COURT at Halifax on Monday, the feast of S. Edmund the King [Nov. 20], 1 Edward II, [1307].

[SOURBY].—William at Town-head of Sourby withdraws his plea of trespass *v.* Anabel de Chesewellay and Richard her son. Fine, 6*d.*

Thomas s. of Thomas withdraws his plea of trespass *v.* Adam de Heitfeld. Fine, 2*d.*

Thomas del Feilde gives [? 6*d.*] to agree with John s. of Richard Hodde, for trespass. Pledge, Robert the Grave.

Thomas de Connale surrenders to John his son and his heirs a messuage, with a toft and croft, and 10 ac. land in Sourby; John gives 12d. fine for entry. Afterwards John surrenders the same to Thomas for life.

William the Mercer gives 6d. to take 2 ac. land from Thomas de Connale, for 7 years, doing service, etc.

Richard s. of Alote de Sourby gives 12d. to take 3 ac. land in Sourby from Adam s. of Elias the Milner.

William the Smith of Solande gives 12d. to take 4 ac. land in Sourby from the same Adam.

Alice de la Mere [? More] gives 12d. to take 3 ac. land in Werlouley from Margery widow of John s. of . . . . . . , for Margery's life, Alice doing service, etc.

Roger de Walsedene and Alice his wife give 6d. to take 2 ac. land in Sourby from Richard s. of . . . . . .

Adam del Hill of Lithesles gives 2s. to take 8 ac. land in Solande from William the Smith.

Henry s. of Robert del Lone gives 6d. to take half a toft in Sourby from William the Cowherd.

Nicholas le Aumbleour gives 6d. to take to himself and his heirs 2 ac. land in Benteleyrode, which William de Saltonstall left waste on the Earl 12 years ago. Pledge, Robert s. of the said William de Saltonstall.

Thomas de Roldesete, for unjustly detaining 23d. from William the Cowherd and Juliana Wade, 6d. He must pay them. Pledge, Robert the Grave.

Thomas the Soldier [*mercenarius*[1]] gives 12d. to take ⅓ bovate and 1 ac. land with 2 . . . . in Werlouley from John s. of Jordan, for 12 years. Thomas [must give it up] at the end of the term in the state in which he received it.

Hugh de Lithesles surrenders to Robert his son and his heirs a messuage with buildings and 18 [? ac. land] in Lithesles. . . . . Robert afterwards surrenders the same to Hugh for life.

Henry s. of Thomas *de* Westwode and John *del* Westwode, as to the dispute between them, put themselves on the verdict of John de Migley and Hugh s. of Roger, on Henry's part, and Richard del Dene and William his brother, on John's part. Adjourned to the Court at Wakefeud.

---

[1] *Mercenarius* is a rare word, of doubtful meaning. Ducange gives *mercator* and *presbyter* as equivalents. The English word soldier comes, through the old French *soudoier*, from the Latin *solidarius*, and is an exact synonym of *mercenarius*, *i.e.* one who serves for pay.

Henry del Helme gives 12*d.* to take three parts [fourths] of a bovate of land in Werlouley from John de Westwode, for 16 years.

MILLS.—John Swyft, carpenter, has farmed [*affirmavit*] the mills of Solande and Werlouley this year for 40*s.*, and for so small a price [*pro tam parvo precio*] because the said mills are broken [*fracta*], and cannot grind without great repairs [*sine bona reparacione*]. John has undertaken to repair and mend the mills, as to dams, wheels, and other necessaries, so that he shall give them up at the end of the year in a good and sound state [*in bono et sano statu*]. Pledges, John the Milner, Henry de Luddingtone, Richard the Smith of Werlouley, Adam del Hill of Lithesles, Adam s. of Elias the Milner, and John de Waddeswrth.

John s. of John de Northelande is chosen Grave of Sourby this year by the election of the whole Graveship, and is received.

John the Milner surrenders to the lord 8 ac. land in Solande. Afterwards John [and Maude his wife] give 3*s.* to take the same to themselves and their heirs begotten between them. If John and Maude shall die without such heirs, then reversion to the heirs of John.

TOURN there the same day.

JURORS.—Thomas de Coppelay, Richard de Waddeswrth, William s. of Molle, Peter del Crosseley, German de Grenewode, Adam Attetounhend, Richard de Saltonstall, Roger s. of Amabel, John de Noteschagh, Thomas de Bellehouses, William del Bothem, and John de Cockecroft.

William de Sothill junior drew blood of John de Hollegate ; [? 2*s.*].

Adam de Kirkeschagh drew blood of William s. of William of the same ; [? 12*d.*].

Richard s. of Ralph de Stanesfeld did not come ; [? 2*d.*].

John de Routonstall drew blood of Stephen s. of Margery of the same ; [? 12*d.*].

John de Westwode drew blood of William del Grenehir[de ?]. . . . . .

Thomas s. of Nelle drew blood of the same William . . . . . .

William Yoten drew blood of Robert s. of Thomas del Gren . . . . Pardoned, because he is in the Earl's service.

. . . . [Jordan Swain] obstructs [*deturbat*] the way between Schakehandbrig and the Northebrig. . . . . . . the Lister the like.

Magota de Rypon brews contrary to the assize ; 4*d.* The wives of Nelle the Walker and H . . . . . the Walker, for the like ; 4*d.* each.

. . . . . . del Westwode killed a deer [*damum*] in the Earl's forest.

.... chased a wounded deer with his dog in Saltonstallhayn.
Attached by ...... de Saltonstall.
...... de Sourby drew blood of Elias s. of Ivo ......

[*Several lines illegible.*]

_____

mem. 3d.

COURT at Brighouses on Tuesday, the morrow of S. Edmund the
King [Nov. 20], 1 Edward II, [1307].

HIPERUM.—It is found by an inquisition of 12 jurors that John
s. of Walter de Ouerom assaulted Walter s. of Elias of the same and
Maude his daughter, and beat and ill-treated them; damages, 5s.
He must pay them. Fine, 40d. Pledge, Richard de Bos....

The same Walter and Maude, for a false claim against Richard
brother of the same John, 6d.

The same Richard s. of Walter, for not coming to the inquisition
[?; *quia absentavit se ad procurandum inquisitione*], 6d.

John de Holegate withdraws his plea of trespass v. John the
Milner and Maude his wife; 12d.

The same John the Milner and Maude withdraw their plea of
trespass against John de Holewaye[1]; 6d.

The inquisition finds that Maude da. of Walter de Ouerom, in
the affray [*contumelia*] between her father and John s. of Walter,
broke John's head; damages, 12d. Fine, 6d.

John s. of Walter does not prosecute his plaint against Walter s.
of Elias; 12d.

Bate the Lister of Halifax gives 6d. to take ½ ac. land in
Hiperum from William the Milner of the same.

John s. of Geoffrey the Colier gives 6d. as a heriot after his
father's death, for 5 ac. land in Ouerom. John is within age; his
wardship is granted to Anabel his mother.

William s. of Adam de Hiperum gives 6d. as a heriot after his
father's death, for one acre.

It is found by inquisition that whereas Ivo the Smith formerly
took from Peter del Barnne two parts [thirds] of a bovate of land
with buildings, for six years, on the agreement that he was to sustain
the land with manure trodden in [*cum composto in dicta terra calcato*]
and the buildings with roofs [and other] necessaries,—Maude, Ivo's
widow, has left the land unmanured [*non compostatam*] and has

_____

[1] Though not so stated, it seems highly probable that John de Holegate and
John de Holewaye are the same person; gate, in the north, means a way or road,
and not a barrier.

allowed the buildings to become ruinous [*indiruta*]; damages, 15*d*. [?], and the value of all the manure [*fimus*] now on the land. Fine, 6*d*. Pledge, John the Milner.

Simon de Totehill, for unjustly detaining one rood and a third of land from Robert s. of Christiana, 12*d*.

John s. of William the Milner gives 6*d*. as a heriot on 3 roods of land in Ouerom after the death of Thomas his brother, whose heir he is.

John s. of Adam s. of John gives 12*d*. as a heriot on 4 ac. of land after the death of Adam his father. Pledge, William s. of John.

William del Hengandrode gives 6*d*. as a heriot on 3 roods of land in Ouerom after the death of William his father.

Richard the Taillour gives 6*d*. to take half a rood of land in Brighouses from Roger de Chepelay.

Rastrik mill is demised this year to William del Bothes and Alexander del Frith for [? 20*s*.].

TOURN there the same day.

JURORS.—John de Locwode, Alexander del Frith, Thomas de Dalton, John le Flemyng, John s. of Adam de Locwode, John de Hertesheved, John de Percy of Clifton, Geoffrey del Dene, John de Bristall, Henry de Coildelay, Henry [? le Fran]ceys, and Lovecok de Nettelton.

The wives of Richard de Schelf (4*d*.), William de Bradelay (. . .), Adam del Leye (. . .), Thomas s. of Modde (. . .), Roger del Brighouses (12*d*.), William the Milner (6*d*.), and Richard the Taillour (6*d*.), for brewing contrary to the assize.

Roger s. of Hanne de Fekesby, for drawing blood of Agnes wife of Thomas de Fekesby, [? 12*d*.].

Adam the Fuller of Goulayecarches, for drawing blood of Alan de Aldelay, 12*d*.

Malina de Holewaye of Northourum, for drawing blood of Malina wife of Ivo of the same, 12*d*.

. . . . [? s.] of Ivo de Prestlay, for drawing blood of William Coker, ...

. . . . of Alexander le Wayn[wright?], for drawing blood of Henry the Pynder of Hiperum. She is in mercy.

Alcok de Wodehouses, for drawing blood of William Foune, 6*d*.

TOURN at Birton on the Wednesday following.

JURORS.—Richard Osan, John W[ythe]r, John de Braythayt, Thomas Bridde, Adam del Skoles, William . . . . . , John s. of Gilbert de Heppewrth, Nicholas Keneward, Matthew de Marisco, Richard . . . . , and Hugh de Thorntelay.

Cissota de Wysstones (6*d.*), Emma la Baggere (6*d.*), Christiana del Kirke (. . .), the wife of Richard le Neucomen (. . .), and Thomas s. of John de Fouleston (. . .), for brewing contrary to the assize.

Juliana de Heppewrth drew blood of Malina wife of Thomas s. of . . . . . . , and Malina the like from Juliana.

Emma wife of Henry de Rastrik drew blood of Malina da. of . . . .

William s. of Elias de Honlay drew blood of Richard del Bothe.

Thomas de Bouderode, Gilbert de Alstanlay, William . . . . . . , [? came to the house] of Robert de Alstanlay, and furtively carried away . . . . . trunks [? ; *truncas*] and . . . . , value 40*s.*, and 2*s.* of silver . . . . . . [*Several lines illegible.*]

———

mem. 4.

COURT at Birton on the Wednesday after the feast of S. Edmund the King [Nov. 20], 1 Edward II, [1307].

HOLNE.—Jordan the Milner, for a false claim of debt against Robert Stirk, 6*d.*

William s. of William de Oldefeld and Emma his wife give 2*s.* to take to themselves and the heirs of their bodies 4½ acres land, with buildings, in Carte[wrth], from Thomas s. of Roger de Cartewrth.

The same William and Emma give 2*s.* to take 4½ acres, with buildings, in Cartewrth, from William s. of John de Littelwode, to themselves and the heirs of their bodies, with reversion to John s. of Geoffrey and his heirs, together with the reversion of the 4½ acres above taken from Thomas s. [of Roger de Cartewrth].

Richard s. of Richard del Dounes gives 5*s.* as a heriot on 13½ acres land, with buildings, in Cartewrth, after the death of his father.

Richard s. of Richard de la Grene gives 6*s.* 8*d.* as a heriot on 19 acres land, with buildings, in Holnefr[ith], after the death of his father.

Alan s. of John del Damme gives 6*d.* as a heriot on 2 acres land, with buildings, in Wlvedale, after the death of his father.

John s. of Roger de Langlay gives 3*s.* as a heriot on 8 acres land, with buildings, in Wulvedale, after the death of his father.

The inquisition finds that Gilbert de Bosco and William his brother beat and ill-treated Richard del Bothe . . . . which John the Couper made to Richard to help the said John [? . . . . . . *quem Johannes le Couper fecit eidem Ricardo auxiliando dicto Johanni*]; Richard's damage, 6s. 8d. Fine, 12d. Pledges, John de Littelwode and Elias s. of Henry.

John s. of William de Heppewrth gives 2s. to take 4 acres land, with buildings, in Wolvedale, from Henry Wad . . . .

Richard del Bothe, for an unjust deforcing [*pro injusta deforcione*] against Gilbert de Gaunte, 12d.

The same Gilbert, for a false claim against same Richard, 6d.

Margery da. of Richard de Greene gives 12d. for licence to relieve [*pro licencia releviandi*] 2½ acres land, with buildings, after the death of her father.

William s. of Roger de Hallomschire gives 2s. to take half a bovate and 5 acres land, with buildings, in Wolvedale, from Ma[tthew?] de Langlay.

Richard del Bothe gives 12d. to take 7½ acres land, with buildings, in Thoung, from Gilbert de Gaunte.

Jordan the Milner of Wolvedale farmed [*affirmavit*] Cartewrth mill for £13 6s. 8d. Pledges, John de Littelwode, the Grave, William del Bothe, Adam s. of Jordan, Thomas s. of Gilbert, Richard s. of Richard, ... de Bristall, Henry de Littelwode, John the Couper, Nicholas s. of Nicholas, Thomas s. of Richard del Rode, Henry . . . . , and Adam de Butterlay, who are all bound, jointly and severally, for the whole [*in solidum*].

———

TOURN at Wakefeud on Friday, the morrow of S. Clement the Pope [Nov. 23], in the year aforesaid, [1307].

JURORS.—Robert de Wyveromthorpe, Henry de Chyvet, Thomas de Wyttelay, William Ingreys, William de Dewysbir', W . . . [? Walter] de Grymmeston, Richard de Salsa mara, Richard de Bristall, Robert de Wodesom, John de la More, Henry Erle, and William Grenehode.

Ralph the Forester of Eckeleshill, for not coming, 2d.

Margery wife of William s. of Peter de Floketon, for drawing blood of Thomas s. of Henry of the same, 2s.

John s. of Thomas the Smith of Horbyr' and Adam s. of Adam Hoperborne fought and drew blood of each other; 6d. each.

Agnes Pegere of Thornes stole two sheep [*bidentes*] of William Maynard, and sold them to Peter de Acom and John le Leche, butchers. And afterwards William Maynard came to the house of the butchers, and knew the sheep; but what he did therein is not known [to the jury]. Let her be arrested.

The same Agnes stole a goose [*aucus*], a hen, and other little things [*alia minuta*]. She is also suspected of stealing a [*unius vernotis?*] from John . . . . [? she] entered the sheep-fold [*bercaria*] of Thomas Pegere, her father, with Thomas's sheep . . . . . and was seen by the said John. Thomas Pegere was a consenting party to all the robberies.[1]

John Pegere broke the chamber of Alice . . . . . To be attached.

The wife of Robert the Clerk of Dewysbir' brews contrary to the assize; 12*d*.

John s. of Robert Lorimar drew blood of Henry s. of Roger the Milner; 6*d*.

John Rate bought 110 boards [? *burd'*] from John Cussing, and when he took them he stole 14 more. To be attached.

Nalle de Birkenschagh has disturbed the township of Alverthorpe in their common in her croft, where they were accustomed and ought to have it, as they say, in open time. She is to be attached.

The maid of Thomas s. of Thomas de Wittelay took from the Earl's wood [*de bosco*] 4 paling boards [*iiij burd' palicii*], unknown to Thomas. To be attached.

The townships of Dewysbir', Floketon, Ossete, Horbiry, Bretton, Sandale, and Waleton, 4*s* each, for not coming as they ought.

Agnes Pegere, the lord's native, indicted at this Tourn, as above, for many trespasses, for which she has been arrested, is respited till the next Court on the mainprise of William Margeriman, Thomas Pegere, Robert [? Pegere], and . . . .

mem. 4d.

COURT at Wakefeud on Friday, in the Feast of the Conception of the Blessed Mary [Dec. 8], 1 Edward II, [1307].

ESSOIGNS.[2]—William de Rastrik, by John de Totehill. Pledge, John de Soland.

John de Toftclyf, attorney of Adam de Everingham, by William his son. Pledge, William de Castelford.

Robert de la Grene of Ossete, by Robert de Stodelay. Pledge, Peter Swerd.

Robert de Barneby, attorney of Thomas de Schefeud, by William Filche. Pledge, John Dade.

---

[1] The roll is in bad condition here.
[2] From suit of Court unless otherwise stated.

I

Thomas the Brounsmyth and Emma his wife, defts., *v.* William de Wakefeud, for trespass, by Thomas de Wakefeud. Pledge, John de Trymyngham.

William s. of Ralph de Grigeleston, deft., *v.* Thomas de Langfeud, for debt, by John Cay. Pledge, John the Clerk of S . . . . . Thomas puts in his place John Patrik *v.* the said William and Henry his brother, whom he makes a defendant. Therefore nothing.

Adam s. of Matthew de Grigeleston *v.* William, Parson of Thornhill, and Hervinus and Henry, his servants, for seizing a [cow], by . . . . . . de Clayton. Pledge, Elias de Birton.

Beatrix de Totehill appears by her attorney *v.* Henry del Ryding, for debt. Deft. to be distrained for not coming.

William de Wakefeud *v.* William le Dyker, on an agreement. Deft. has been distrained by ½ quarter of oats. To be better distrained.

ALVERTHORPE.—Richard the Tanner of Alverthorpe, plt., and John Rate, deft., for agreeing without licence, 6*d.* each.

Robert de Staynland *v.* William de Greteland, for debt. William, who is not resident, does not come, and must be distrained. [*Quia dictus Willelmus non residens non venit. Ideo dis'.*]

The tenements late of Henry del Rokes are still in the lord's hands. The Serjeant is ordered to receive the issues, as Henry's heir wishes for the tenements [*voluit dicta tenementa*].

HOLNE.—John s. of John de Holne withdraws his plaint *v.* Adam his brother, for seizing cattle; 6*d.*

The plea between Adam de la Grene and Gilbert de Alstanlay, for trespass, is adjourned till the next Court.

John del Westwode *v.* Henry s. of Thomas del Westwode, for pulling down the houses which he [? Henry] held for a term. Deft. must repair the houses; fine, 6*d.*

William Nelot was charged [*calumpniatus*] with breaking the Earl's fold, which he denied, and put himself on an inquisition. He now comes and refuses an inquisition. Let him be presented [*attinctus*], and in mercy.

The same William also refuses the said inquisition as to the charge of consuming the Earl's grass by his sheep. *Ideo quietus est.*[1] He is in mercy.

Adam Gerbode unjustly detains 3*s.* 6*d.* for a *collobium*[2] from John Tasse. He must pay; fine, 3*d.*

---

[1] This appears to refer to the inquisition, and seems to mean that the jurors are discharged without holding the inquiry.

[2] There does not seem to be any English word for this. It was a half-sleeved or sleeveless tunic or robe, worn by ecclesiastics. Perhaps a smock.

Quenylda de Alverthorpe *v.* Adam Gerbode, Richard de Collay, Henry del Bothem, and William Hoskell, complains that they assaulted and beat her, and broke the "spilebon"[1] of her arm; they also broke the hedge of her garden [?], and by their cattle consumed her grass to the value of 15*d.*; she claims 40*s.* damages. Defts. say that plt. wished to hold in severalty a certain culture in which they ought to common in open time, wherefore they entered the same with their cattle to enjoy their common, as was lawful for them to do; as to the assault, they ask for an inquiry. Adjourned, for the Steward to see the culture.

The plea between William Hoskell, plt., and the said Quenylda, for seizing cattle, is adjourned to the next Court.

John s. of John de Northeland gives 6*d.* for respite of suit until Michaelmas.

John de Crosseland and John de Trymyngham, 12*d.* each, for the like.

. . . . . . the Chapman and John de Flansowe agree by licence.

STANLAY.—[Margery] widow of John Wythehundes *v.* Robert [Gunne], in a plea of land. Pledge, Richard [? her son].

. . . . oket is elected Grave of Stanlay by the whole Grave-ship, and is received.

. . . . . s. of Robert Anote gives 6*d.* to take a rood of land in Stanlay from John Walhot.

. . . . gives . . . . to take an acre of land in . . . . from Thomas s. of Margery de Milnethorpe.

Philip Wolf to be summoned to answer Margery widow of John Wythehundes in a plea of dower [?].

ALVERTHORPE.—Richard Wythehundes gives 2*s.* as a heriot on 20 acres land in Flansowe in the Graveship of Alverthorpe, after the death of John, his father.

WAKEFEUD.—The Grave of Wakefeud must answer for 6*s.* 8*d.*, received for a stray cow.

HOLNE [?].—William de Heitfeld, the forester, has licence to take a toft and one acre of land in Wolvedale, from Richard s. of Richard de la Grene. He gives nothing for entry, because he is in the Earl's service.

Richard s. of Richard de Wolvedale gives 2*s.* to take 9½ acres land in Littelwode from John de la Grene.

---

[1] Probably the small bone of the fore-arm, the radius. Jamieson gives spull-bane, the shoulder blade, with a derivation from the French *espaule*, the shoulder, but he also gives quotations showing that the word was used for other limbs. Halliwell gives spell-bone, the small bone of the leg. Probably connected with spill, a splinter, or small piece of wood. See *English Dialect Dictionary, s.v.* spill.

Henry Wade gives 2s. to take 7½ acres land, with buildings, in Wolvedale from Richard Cheild.

John s of [? Richard] de la Grene gives . . . to take 2 acres land in Littelwode from Richard his brother.

Roger de Clifton gives 12d. to take 2 acres land in Hyperum [?] from Henry de Totehill.

STANLAY.—Richard the Leper of Stanlay surrenders 1½ bovates and 11 acres land, with buildings, in Stanlay to Robert his son and his heirs. Robert afterwards demised the same to Richard for life.

. . . . . . de Bouderode, Gilbert de Astanlay, William and William, his sons [sic] . . . . . .

mem. 5.

COURT at Wakefeud on Friday, the eve of the Epiphany [Jan. 6], 1 Edward II, [1308].

ESSOIGNS.[1]—Peter Swerd, by William Margeryknave. Pledge, John de la More.

Alan Almot, by Robert de Bergh. Pledge, Adam Hod.

Thomas de Thornton, by Hugh de Thornton. Pledge, John de Toftclyff.

William de Schepeden, by William del Bothem. Pledge, Hugh de Seyvill.

Isabel la Keu, by John Damoysell. Pledge, John de Toftclif.

Elias de Birton, by William de Castelford. Pledge, Thomas de Wakefeud.

Thomas de Seyvill, attorney of Lady Margaret de Nevill, by John Patrik. Pledge, Hugh de Seyvill.

William s. of Ralph de Crigeleston, deft., *v.* Thomas de Langfeud, for debt, by John Cay. Pledge, Robert de Heyers.

Thomas de Heeton, by Robert his man [*homo*]. Pledge, Hugh de Seyvill.

William de Wakefeud, plt., *v.* Thomas Brounsmyth and Emma his wife, for trespass, by German [Swerd?]. Pledge, German Filcok.

Same William, plt., *v.* William le Dyker on an agreement, by German Filcok. Pledge, German Swerd. Deft. had been distrained by a net [*per unum rete*].

Adam s. of Maude de Crigeleston, plt., *v.* William, Parson of Thornhill, Hervinus and Henry his servants, for the price [?] of a cow, by John de Clayton. Pledge, John de la More.

Thomas de Langfeud and Henry de Crigeleston have a love-day.

---

[1] From suit of Court unless otherwise stated.

Richard s. of Henry de Rokes gives 8s. 3d. for relief on the tenements late his father's.

ALVERTHORPE [?].—John Rate, for detaining 11d. from Robert de Stanlay, 6d.

Robert de Staynland, for withdrawing his plea of debt v. William de Greteland, 6d.

HOLNE [?].—Gilbert de Astanlay puts himself [in mercy] in a plea of trespass v. Adam de la Grene; 6d.

Juliana de Astanlay puts herself [in mercy] in a plea of land v. same Adam; 6d.

ALVERTHORPE.—John Cussing gives 12d. to take 1½ acres land in Alverthorpe from Henry le Nonne.

STANLAY.—Robert de Mickelfeld gives 12d. to take 1½ roods of land in Stanlay from Hugh s. of Ba . . . . .

OSSETE.—William s. of Hugh de Lithesles gives 12d. to take a bovate of land in Erlesheeton which lies waste, for 20 years; the reversion shall descend to the heirs of Adam Broun, who are unable to keep up the land [. . . . . *impotentes ad dictam terram sustinendam*].

[SANDALE.]—William Hilhor gives 6d. to take 1 ac. ½ rood of land and ½ rood of meadow in Sandale from Robert the Clerk of Sandale, for 12 years.

[ALVERTHORPE.]—The judgment between Quenylda de Alverthorpe, plt., and Adam Gerbode, Richard de Collay, Henry del Bothem, and William Hoskell, is adjourned to the next Court.

William Hoskell v. Quenylda de Alverthorpe, complains that she unjustly seized or caused to be seized a horse of his in his common of Alverthorpe, which horse was led away to her [?] house at Alverthorpe on Tuesday before All Saints' Day last; and she unjustly detained it until delivery of it was made by Adam Gerbode, the Earl's Grave; damages, 2s. Quenylda says that she found the horse by night in her severalty, eating her grass, as she had many times found it, and therefore she impounded it, as was lawful for her to do; etc. [*sic*].

John s. of Richard Broun of Alverthorpe gives 3s. to take a bovate in Snaype[thorpe?], which lay waste on the lord for 2 years and more.

. . . . William de Heytfeud takes 2 acres of new land in Wlfdale, viz. in Thoungeshirst, paying 12d. yearly.

. . . . Holt takes 2 acres of new land in Thounge, in H . . . . yhirst . . . . .

.... de Hooton [? Heeton] gives 8s. to take 8 acres of new land in Admundelay, on both sides of the road [ex utraque parte vie], paying 4s. yearly.

Bath'us [?] s. of Thomas gives 12d. to take one acre of new land, paying yearly 6d.

¹Henry s. of Thomas¹ gives 15d. to take one acre of new land in Admundelay and a rood in the Brerykerre, paying yearly 7½d.

Richard s. of Herbert gives 12d. to take one acre of new land in Admundelay, paying 6d. yearly.

William de Butterlay gives 12d. to take one acre of new land at Wodefalwelle, paying yearly 6d.

Henry s. of Sarah gives 2s. to take 2 acres of new land ...... near .... and upon [super] Admundelay, paying yearly 12d.

.... s. of Robert gives .... to take ... acres of new land in C ... hirst, paying yearly ....

...... Ferneoule gives 3s. 6d to take 3½ acres of new land on Elerenbanck in Stackwode, paying yearly 21d.

...... Elwardeholes gives 18d. to take 1½ acres of new land on the Coppedhirst, paying yearly 9d.

[*Four entries illegible.*]

mem. 5d.

HOLNE.—Still the new lands of Holnefr[ith].

Adam de Langlay gives 6d. to take ½ acre of new land in the Rolippehirst, near his own land; rent, 3d.

Adam s. of Adam de Dounes gives 12d. to take an acre of new land near Dunesleye; rent, 6d.

Adam Benne gives 6d. to take ½ acre of new land, near his own land; rent, 3d.

William de Gaunte gives 3s. 3d. to take 3 acres of new land in Butgapgrenes and a rood above the house of Richard the Milner; rent, 19½d.

John de Haroppe gives 6d. to take ½ acre of new land near Oldehoggelay; rent, 3d.

Adam s. of John gives 6d. to take ½ acre of new land near Spinkeswelle; rent, 3d.

John de la Grene gives 12s. to take 12 acres of new land near that of Richard de la Grene; rent, 6s.

Richard s. of Richard le Syour gives 12d. to take an acre of new land near Laysingbothem; rent, 6d.

---

¹⁻¹ Struck out.

William s. of Thomas Bridde gives 12*d.* to take an acre of new land in Wetstonleye [?]; rent, 6*d.*

John de Scoles gives 18*d.* to take 1½ acres of new land in Butterlaykerre; rent, 9*d.*

Robert s. of Gamell gives 15*d.* to take an acre and a rood of new land under Johanesrode; rent, 7½*d.*

Thomas s. of Roger gives 12*d.* to take an acre of new land in Aundene, near his house; rent, 6*d.*

Matthew de Langlay gives 18*d.* to take 1½ acres of new land under Langlay; rent, 9*d.*

[? WAKEFEUD].—William the Dyker *v.* William at Elm [*ad ulmum*], for trespass. Pledge, Walter del Spen. Removed to the Borough Court [*in Curia burgi?*].

OSSETE.—Alice widow of Adam Broun of Heeton *v.* Richard Broun, in a plea of dower. Pledge, William de Lighesles.

HOLNE.—William Wastell *v.* Adam s. of Jordan the Milner, for debt. Pledge, Thomas de Bouderode.

William s. of Ralph de Ouchethorpe *v.* Robert del Dale, in a plea of land. Pledge, Richard Poket.

mem. 6.

COURT at Wakefeud on Friday the morrow of the Conversion of S. Paul [Jan. 25th], 1 Edward II, [1308].

ESSOIGNS.[1]—John de Toftclyf, attorney of Adam de Everingham, by Walter de Thinglowe. Pledge, Thomas de Thorn . . . [? Thornton].

Alan Almot, attorney of Thomas de Burgo, by John Cay. Pledge, Thomas . . . .

Matthew de Bosco, by John de Northeland. Pledge, William del Okes.

William de Chipedene, by William de Castelford. Pledge, Hugh de Seyville.

Robert de la Grene, by William At-kirk. Pledge, Hugh de Seyville.

Peter Swerd, by William Margeryman. Pledge, Richard de Bristall.

William de Wakefeud, plt., *v.* Thomas Brounsmyth and Emma his wife, for trespass, by William de Ok . . . Pledge, John Cay.

Adam s. of Maude de Crigeleston *v.* William de Burgo, Parson of Thornhill, and Hervinus and Henry, his servants. He complains that they, on the Wednesday after the feast of S. Oswald the King [Aug. 5], 1 Edward II [1307], seized and caused to be seized a cow

---

[1] From suit of Court unless otherwise stated.

of Adam's in the town of Crigeleston, in the highway, and drove it
to William's manor in the same town, and there detained it until
the Friday following, when delivery of it was made by Robert de
Stodelay, the sworn bailiff; he claims 40s. damages. The defts.
appear by their attorney, and say that the seizure was not made in
the highway, but in a place called the Serigge, in a tenement held
of Edmund le Normaunde, by fealty and service of 12d. yearly; this
rent was in arrear for one year, and so they, as bailiffs of the said
Edmund, seized the cow for the rent, as was lawful for them to do.[1]

Thomas de Langfeud v. William s. of Ralph de Crigeleston and
Henry his brother, says that they unjustly detain 13s. 4d.; on Tuesday
after the Invention of Holy Cross [May 3rd], 34 Edward I [1306],
they bought from Thomas the herbage of 24 acres of pasture in the
Blackerre, for 13s. 4d., to be paid in William's barn [grangea] at
Crigeleston, half on S. Giles's day [Sept. 1] that year and half at
Michaelmas following; they have paid nothing, and he claims
20s. damages. The deft. William says that he bought no herbage
from Thomas, and made no such agreement with him, as stated.
He must wage his law; pledge, Henry s. of Ralph. Henry says that
he bought the herbage, as stated, but denies that he owes plt. any
money [in nullo denario ei inde tenetur]. He must wage his law;
pledge, William s. of Ralph.

William de Wakefeud and William the Dyker have license to
agree. William the Dyker puts himself [in mercy]; 6d.; pledges,
Walter de Spen and Benedict de Stanlay; he also admits that he is
bound to make a fish-stew [vivarium] for the plt. before Michaelmas
next, and finds pledges for this, viz. the said Walter and Benedict.

John s. of Philip and Eugenia his wife, plts., and Peter de Acom,
agree by license. Peter puts himself [in mercy]; 4d.

[? STANLAY].—Margery widow of John Wythehundes v. Robert
Gunne complains that he deforces her of her dower in a bovate of
land which he bought from her late husband. Deft. says that he is
not the tenant of the land, and claims nothing in it, but that Emma
his daughter is the tenant. False claim; fine, 3d.

[   ].—Roger de Fynee gives 5s. to take 9 acres of new
land and 4 acres of land of old tenure [de antiqua tenura] in
Heppewrth from Nicholas s. of John. Pledge, John s. of Gilbert.

Jordan de Fynee gives 40d. to take 8 acres of land in Cartewrth
from Hugh de Cartew[rth]. Pledge, the said Hugh.

---

[1] The entry concludes here with etc. Probably judgment was reserved. The
case comes on again at the next Court and subsequently.

Richard s. of Richard s. of Elcok gives 2s. as a heriot on 8 acres 3 roods of land, with buildings, in Heppewrth, after the death of his father.

[   ].—Henry de Northclyf gives 6d. to take two parts [thirds] of an acre in Hypcrom from William s. of Adam.

The land which Roger s. of Walter held is in the lord's hands, because he is dead.

William the Mercer of Sourby gives 6d. to take . . . . . . acres of new land of the waste in Sourby; rent, 3d.

William Nelot is elected Grave of Wakefeud by the choice of all the tenants of copyhold land [*terra nativa*], and is received.

Robert Estrild gives 12d. to take 2½ acres of land in Neuton from Henry le Nonne for 24 [?] years, including the term of 12 years which he first took [*cum duodecim annis quos habet in eadem terra ex prima capcione*]

Richard de Batelay gives 2s. to take 4½ acres of land in Stanlay from Robert de Batelay, his father.

Henry de Rastrik gives 2s. to take 2 acres of new land of the waste in Mythomwode; rent, 12d.

Adam the Waynwrith gives 3s. 6d. to take 3½ acres of new land of the waste in Stackewode; rent, 21d.

Roger de Fynee gives 6d. to take one rood of new land of the waste in Heppewrth; rent, 1d. [?].

[*Some entries torn away at the foot of the membrane.*]
mem. 6d.

HIPEROM.—Roger de Clifton gives 2s. 6d. to take 2 ac. one rood of new land of the waste in Wolveker; rent, 13½d.

Thomas [?] the Webbester gives 12d. to take one ac. of new land of the waste underhouth [?]; rent, 6d.

. . . . de Totehill gives 3s. to take 2 ac. of new land in the wood of Hiperom in le Stede; rent, 12d.

Richard de Bosco gives 6d. to take ½ ac. of new land of the waste in Chypedene; rent, 3d.

STANLAY.—Margery widow of John Wythehundes v. Emma da. of Robert Gunne, in a plea of land. Pledge, Richard her son.

[WAKEFEUD].—The inquisition to be taken between Robert s. of Robert de Flansowe and John Cussing, in a plea of debt of 16d. for the collection made in the Graveship for the mill-dam, is respited until the next Court.

HOLNE.—Richard le Syour, plt., and Richard s. of Herbert, deft., in a plea of land, agree by license. The deft. puts himself in mercy, 6d.

Adam s. of Jordan the Milner, for not coming when summoned to answer William Wastell in a plea of land, 6*d.* He is to be distrained to answer at the next Court.

OSSETE.—Richard Broun of Heeton to be summoned to answer Alice widow of Adam Broun, in a plea of dower.

STANLAY.—Robert del Dale to be summoned to answer William s. of Ralph de Oucheth[orpe], in a plea of land.

WAKEFEUD.—German Hodelyn 2*d.*, Idonea Proudfot 2*d.*, the son of Robert Grenehod 2*d.*, Richard Wayte's maid 1*d.*, Magota Benne 2*d.*, Adam Torketro 2*d.*, Geppe s. of Dobbe 2*d.*, Robert de Chedel 6*d.*, William de Sandale's maid 2*d.*, William Hilhore's maid 2*d.*, Henry Archur's wife 2*d.*, and Robert Haget's wife 2*d.*, for dry wood.

Robert de Fetherstan 6*d.*, and Agnes da. of Roger 1*d.*, for escapes.

THORNES.—John Graffard 6*d.*, Thomas Brounsmyth 1*d.*, Alice wife of Philip de Snaypeth[orpe] 1*d.*, Malyn Vyron 2*d.*, William s. of Roger 2*d.*, Roger Traylment 2*d.*, John de la Haye 2*d.*, John Maunsell 4*d.*, Amabel da. of Alexander 1*d.*, Agnes da. of Serlo 1*d.*, William Wyte 2*d.*, Agnes Collyer 6*d.* (pledge, William Hirnyng), and William Hirnyng 4*d.*, for dry wood.

ALVERTHORPE.—John Schirlock 2*d.*, for escape of sheep.

Adam Gerbode 2*d.*, and Christiana Gerbode 2*d.*, for escape of pigs.

Richard s. of Broun 6*d.*, Richard the Tanner 1*d.*, and John de Flansowe 4*d.*, for dry wood.

STANLAY.—Philip Isabell 2*d.*, Adam Cote's son 2*d.*, Robert Broun 2*d.*, Philip s. of Agnes 2*d.*, Martin Dedde 2*d.*, John Coyt 2*d.*, Mariota Bele 2*d.*, Richard de Batelay 6*d.*, Robert de Mickelfeld 2*d.*, Hugh Tagge 4*d.*, John servant [*serviens*] of Walter 6*d.*, Richard Bullock 4*d.*, and John Bullock 2*d.*, for dry wood.

Richard Poket 12*d.*, for vert.

HOLNE.—Richard de Linne 6*d.*, Adam del Waterhous 6*d.*, and Thomas de Billeclyf 4*d.*, for escapes.

Simon de Thurstanland 3*d.*, Magota de Horscroft 2*d.*, Mocok Bibby's son 2*d.*, and Thomas Schephird's son 3*d.*, for dry wood.

HIPEROM.—Richard de Ouerom *v.* Elias s. of Christiana and Robert his brother, for trespass. Pledge, William de Castelford.

ALVERTHORPE.—Adam s. of Thomas *v.* Richard Wythehundes, for trespass. Pledge, Robert de Flansowe.

John Tasse *v.* John Schirlok, for trespass. Pledge, Robert his [plt.'s] servant [*garcio*].

Thomas de Wakefeld *v.* Henry le Nonne, for debt. Pledge, Richard Isab[el].

Robert the Carpenter *v.* John de Flansowe, on an agreement. Pledge, Richard Wythehundes.

Thomas de Tothill and Thomas del Wode, of Fekesby, executors of the will of Thomas de Fekesby, *v.* John [del] Hole and [Margaret] his wife, for debt. Pledge, Thomas Talvace, of Fekesby.

Same *v.* Agnes wife of Thomas de Fekesbi, for debt. Same pledge.

Same *v.* Thomas s. of Modesta de Lynley, for debt. Same pledge.

Same *v.* John s. of Henry de Fekesbi, for debt. Same pledge.

Thomas del Wodde puts Thomas de Tothill in his place *v.* all these defendants.

mem. 7.

COURT at Wakefeld on the Friday after S. Valentine the Martyr [Feb. 14], 1 Edward II, [1308].

ESSOIGNS.[1]—Thomas de Heeton, by Roger Assolf. Pledge, William de Dewysbiry.

Thomas de Seyville, attorney of Margaret de Neville, by Richard de Bergh. Pledge, Alan Almot.

Nicholas de Caylly, by William his son. Pledge, William de Schepeden.

Richard de Bristall, by John Picard. Pledge, William del Okes.

Robert de la Grene, by William s. of Godfrey. Pledge, John Patrik.

Thomas de Thornton, by Hugh de Thornton. Pledge, Matthew de Bosco.

Robert de Bramwyth, attorney of Thomas de Schefeld, by William Filche. Pledge, William de Castelford.

Nicholas le Normaund, by Edmund le Normaund. Pledge, John Damoysell.

Adam s. of Maude de Crigeleston *v.* William [de Burg], Parson of Thornhill, Hervinus and Henry, his servants, for seizing a cow, by John de Clayton. Pledge, Alan Almot.

William de Burg, Parson of Thornhill, *v.* the same Adam, by Edmund le Normaund. Pledge, William del Okes.

Hervinus, servant of the said William, *v.* the same Adam, by Robert de Heyrode. Pledge, Edmund le Normaund.

Henry, servant of the said William, *v.* the same Adam, by Hugh de Seyville. Pledge, John Damoysell.

William s. of Ralph de Crigeleston *v.* Thomas de Langfeld, for debt, by Robert de Heyrode. Pledge, William del Okes. Thomas appeared, and a day is given.

---

[1] From suit of Court unless otherwise stated.

Henry his [William's] brother *v.* the same Thomas, by John the Clerk. Pledge, Robert de Heyrode.

William s. of Walter Bate of Castelford came and proved a stray mare [*jumentum*] and foal [*pullanus*], price 10*s*,. to be his. He finds pledges to answer within a year and a day, if necessary, viz.:— German Filcok and John Cussing. He gives 12*d.* for the escape.

Henry del Ryding to be distrained to answer Beatrice de Totehill, for debt.

STANLAY.—Emma da. of Robert Gunne to be summoned to answer Margery widow of John Wythehundes, in a plea of dower.

HOLNE.—Adam s. of Jordan the Milner to be distrained to answer William Wastell, for debt.

OSSETE.—Alice widow of Adam Broun *v.* Richard Broun, complains that he has deforced her of her dower in a house, a garden, and an essart called the Ryding. Richard comes, and says that she ought not to have any dower in that tenement, because her husband sold it to him before he married her, and he asks for an inquisition.

The same Alice complains of the same Richard for unjustly detaining a chest [*arca*], price 2*s*. He denies it. Let there be an inquisition.

The same Alice complains of the same Richard for assaulting and beating her seven years ago, and for hindering the impounding [*deturbavit imparcacionem*] of two sheep [*bidentes*], which Alice found in her corn; to her damage of 20*s*. He denies it, because he says that they made a concord; and he asks for an inquisition.

THORNES.—Robert s. of Robert de Flansowe and John Cussing are agreed by license. Robert puts himself in mercy; *6d.*

STANLAY.—Robert del Dale gives 6*d.* to agree with William de Ouchethorpe, in a plea of land. Pledge, Robert Gunne.

ALVERTHORPE.—John Tasse.*v.* John Schirlock, in a plea of land. Deft. does not come, and is amerced 3*d.*

Thomas de Wakefeud *v.* Henry le Nonne, in a plea of debt. Deft. does not come, and is amerced 3*d.*

HIPEROM.—Elias s. of Christiana and Robert his brother give 2*s.* to agree with Richard de Ouerom, for trespass.

Henry the Smith of Chepedene gives 6*d.* to take 3 roods of land in Schepeden from John s. of Wymarke.

HOLNE.—Richard s. of Matthew de Fouleston gives 2*s.* to take 4½ ac. of land, with buildings, in Fouleston from Thomas s. of . . . . . of the same.

Richard de Birton gives 6*d.* to take 1 ac. of land in Fouleston from Richard s. of Matthew.

...... —Adam the Shepherd gives 18*d.* to take 1½ ac. of new land of the waste at Heppeworth, at the Wodhenn[ly]; rent, 9*d.*

Thomas s. of Thomas gives 15*d.* to take 1 ac. 1 rood of the like land at the Wodhenly; rent, 7½*d.*

Peter del Peke gives 15*d.* to take 1 ac. 1 rood of new land of the waste in Littelwode; rent, 7½*d.*

STANLAY.—Received 3*s.* 4*d.* for a stray mare sold to Richard Issabell, for which the Grave of Stanlay shall answer.

Robert s. of Thomas del Wode came, and attached himself [*attachiavit se*] to prosecute suit *v.* John Batty of Westbretton in respect of a horse, price 6*s.* 8*d.*, stolen from him by the said John. Pledges, Thomas del Wode, his father, Thomas de Totehill, and Hugh de Lynnelay.

The said John Batty, arrested for the robbery, finds sureties until the next Court, namely Thomas de Dronesfeld, William le Heyr, William Batty, William the Webster of Br[etton?], ... s. of Henry of the same, and Henry s. of Elias of the same. They shall answer for John under a penalty of 3*s.* 4*d.*

Thomas the Forester complains of Henry Poyde and Richard Wythehundes, for trespass. Pledges, John de Flansowe and William ...... *Vacat, quia in Curia ville* [margin].

WAKEFELD.—John Cay, for his pigs sent and kept in the new coppice, 13*s.* 4*d.*; and for the like in the New Park, 6*s.* 8*d.*

mem. 7d.

[COURT held at Wakefield on Friday, March 8th, 1308.][1]

HOLNE.—. ...... Oldfeld gives 12*d.* to take ½ bovate in Holne from Adam s. of John de Holne, for a term of 5 years.

William s. of Gilbert de Alstanlay gives 12*d.* to take ½ bovate in Holne from Adam s. of Jordan the Milner, for a term of 10 years.

Adam s. of Jordan the Milner gives 6*d.* to agree with William Wastell, for debt.

Richard le Syour gives 2*s.* 6*d.* to take 2½ acres of new land in the Birchinwode; rent, 15*d.*

John s. of Adam gives 3*d.* to take a rood of new land in Dodeldene; rent, 1½*d.*

---

[1] The heading is missing; the date is supplied conjecturally, as being three weeks before the next Court, held on March 29th.

Richard s. of Matthew gives 6*d.* to take ½ acre of new land at Poulmanhirst; rent, 3*d.*

Beatrice de Thotehill *v.* Henry del Ryding, for debt. Henry does not come, and is to be distrained.

ALVERTHORPE.—The case between Quenilda de Alverthorpe, plt., and Adam Gerbode, Richard de Collay, Henry del Bothem, and William Hoskell, for trespass, is respited until the next Court.

The inquisition between William Hoskell, plt., and Quenilda de Alverthorpe, for seizing a horse, is respited until the next Court.

John Schirlock to be distrained to answer John Tasse, for trespass.

Henry le Nonne to be distrained to answer Thomas de Wakefeud, for debt.

William de la Grene *v.* Robert de la Grene, for debt. Pledge, Elias de Danecastre.

Juliana de Thornes *v.* Agnes Pegere, for dower. Pledge, Elias Bulnays.

John Cay *v.* John Rate, on an agreement. Pledge, Thomas s. of Laurence.

Henry s. of Simon Tyting *v.* Benedict de Stanlay, for trespass. Pledge, Simon Tyting. Benedict is attached by John de St. Swi . . . . [? Swithin].

William de la Grene *v.* Robert de la Grene, for trespass. Pledge, William del Okys.

The same Robert *v.* the same William, for trespass. Pledge, John Cokewald.

————

COURT held at Wakefeud on the Friday after the Annunciation B.V.M. [March 25],[1] in the year abovesaid, [1308].

ESSOIGNS.[2]—Thomas de Heeton, by Robert his man [*homo*] Pledge, William de Castelford.

Alan Almot, attorney of Thomas de Burgo, by John de Clayton. Pledge, Thomas de Seyville.

Thomas de Thornton, by Hugh de Thornton. Pledge, Richard de Bristall.

Peter Swerd, by William Margeriknave. Pledge, John de Querneby.

William de Chipedene, by William de Castelford. Pledge, William del Okes.

---

[1] March 25th fell on Monday in 1308, so that this Court was held on the 29th. See note to the last Court, *ante*, p. 141.

[2] From suit of Court unless otherwise stated.

[Matthew ?] de Bosco, by John de Soland. Pledge, William Margeriknave.

Thomas Brounsmyth and Emma his wife *v.* William de Wakefeld, in a plea of trespass, by John de Wakefeld. Pledge, Thomas de Wakefeld.

William de Burgo, Parson of Thornhill, *v.* Adam s. of Maude de Crigeleston, for seizing a cow, by John de Wakefeud. Pledge, John Patrik. Adam offers himself, and a day is given. It is recorded in the Bench [*record' in Banco*].

Hervinus, William's servant [*serviens*] *v.* the same, by John Patrik. Pledge, John de Wakefeud.

Henry, William's servant [*serviens*] *v.* the same, by William de Miglay. Pledge, William del Okes.

William de Wakefeud *v.* Thomas Brounsmyth and Emma his wife, for trespass, by William de Estfeld. Pledge, John Cay.

Henry s. of Ralph de Crigeleston gives 6*d.* to agree with Thomas de I angfeud, for debt. Pledge, the said Thomas.

Beatrice de Totehill appeared by her attorney against Henry del Ryding, for debt. Henry had been distrained by a sow, price 11*s.*; to be better distrained.

mem. 8.

SOURBY.—Robert de Saltonstall, attached for trespass and contempt done to the lord, finds pledges [*plegios*] to come before the Lord Earl at his first coming and to do the will of the lord therein, viz.: Adam de Midelton, John de Miggelay, John Hodde, John de Waddeswrth, Thomas del Feild, and John de Soland.

Elias s. of Ivo de Werlouleye, attached for the like, finds mainpernors [*manucaptores*] to come before the lord, as above, viz.: Michael del Lom, Thomas de Rothelsete, Henry de Saltonstall, Thomas the Mercer [*le Merc'*] of Willeys, Adam del Hill, and Henry s. of William de Solande.

SANDALE.—Robert de la Grene, plt., *v.* William de la Grene, for trespass, does not prosecute. He and his pledges are in mercy, and William goes quit.

STANLAY.—Henry s. of Simon Tyting and Benedict de Stanlay have a love-day until the next Court.

ALVERTHORPE.—John Cay and John Rate, the like, at the instance of Thomas de Wakefeud.

THORNES.—Juliana widow of Gerard de Thornes claims dower in 2 bovates of land with buildings in Thornes against Agnes Peger, who acquired it [*attingit*] after the death of Gerard de Thornes,

formerly her [Juliana's] husband. Agnes comes and says that she is
the guardian of her [?] children, to whom the land accrued after the
decease of Robert their father, and that Juliana was dowered of the
whole tenement except half a bovate which Malina Cappe recovered
[*vindicavit*] after the decease of her [? Malina's] brother, who had sold
it while he was under age, and for which Robert s. of Gerard, Agnes's
husband, gave Malina 14s. Juliana admits this. It is considered by
the Steward that Juliana do satisfy Agnes of 2s., that Juliana have
her dower of the whole tenement, and that Agnes be amerced 2d.[1]

. . . .—It is found by an inquisition that John de Flansowe
sold to Robert the Carpenter an acre of land for 14s.; he received
4s., and then broke his contract [*convencio*] unjustly. John must
repay the 4s., and damages assessed at 12d., and is in mercy.

[OSSETT.]—Alice widow of Adam Broun is in mercy for a false
claim v. Richard Broun as to a house and garden, in which she has
no right; 1d.

The said Richard is in mercy because he made himself a party
against the said Alice as to tenements in which [? he] has no right.
[*Idem Ricardus quia fecit se partem versus predictam Aliciam de tenementis
in quibus nihil habet, in misericordia.*]

The same Alice is in mercy for three false claims against the said
Richard for dower, trespass, and a chest; 3d.

ALVERTHORPE.—John Cussing appears against Adam Gerbode, and
complains that whereas Adam had sold 2 acres of land in Neuton to
him and his heirs, and John came and sowed the land, as well he
might, there came Henry Gouton [?] and carried off the crop of
3 roods of the said land, and Richard Baillyf the crop of one rood,
by alleging [*imponendo*] to Adam that he [Adam] had demised the
land to them for a term before John had bought the 2 acres, and
had received surrender [? *sursum reciperat*]. Adam came, and fully
admitted [*bene novit*] the demise, but says that he reserved to every
one his right and term [?, *salvavit cuidem inde jus et terminum suum*];
and thereupon he vouched the Steward's Rolls for the 34th year of
King Edward [1305-6]. John says that he [Adam] gave him full
seisin without any exception; and he vouches the Rolls. A search
of the Rolls shows that Adam gave seisin to John without any
reservation of the demise. John must recover seisin of the 2 acres
and damages for the crop of one acre; and Adam is in mercy.

---

[1] Agnes had evidently encroached in some way on Juliana's dower, hence the
fine of 2d.; but it does not appear why she was to be paid 2s.

HORBYRY.—John the Tailor [*cissor*] of Wakefeld takes the Halleflat of Horbyry, with the chamber and pigeon house, for 12 years, at a rent of 14*s*. payable at the two terms at which the tenants of Horbiry pay their rent. John shall have within the inclosure [*infra inclaustrum*] of the said essart such thorns as may be necessary to make and sustain his hedges.

STANLAY.—Marjory widow of John Wythehundes comes and claims dower against Emma da. of Robert Gunne, in a bovate of land in Ouchethorpe. Emma comes, and says that the said John Wythehundes formerly held that land for a term, and during the term left it waste on the lord, so that it lay waste for 24 years; the Earl caused proclamation to be made if any heir wished to hold the land; and as no heir came, the Earl by his Steward then demised it to Robert Gonne, Emma's father, for services and customs, as well he might. Marjory cannot deny this. Therefore Emma may hold what she has, and Marjory is in mercy for a false claim; 3*d*.

[WAKEFIELD.]—Henry s. of German gives 2*s*. for leave to "inburgage" [*pro licencia inburgagiandi*] part of a tenement which he holds in Kergate, containing the fourth part of a burgage; To hold to himself and his heirs as free burgage, with all liberties and profits that belong to the burgesses of Wakefeld; Paying yearly to the Earl 1½*d*. at the three terms appointed in the town of Wakefeld, and doing to the other lords of the fee the services which belong to them [*et aliis dominis feodi servicia que eis pertinent*].

Elias de Boseham, by the Earl's grant and permission, has taken a piece of land of the Earl's waste [in Wake]feld, 31 feet long and 16 feet wide, on which to build a booth [*selda*]; Paying yearly 6*d*. at the three terms appointed in the Earl's land.

STANLAY.—German Campyon and Margery his wife give 6*d*. to take 1½ acres of land from William s. of Bateman for 10 years from next Michaelmas.

OSSETE.—Richard s. of John 3*d*., John the Walker 3*d*., Richard Passemere 2*d*., William le Wyte 2*d*., Richard s. of Johannot 3*d*., Moke de Ossete 2*d*., Robert Pees 2*d*., William Wildebore's maid 2*d*., Richard Suart 2*d*., John Graffard 2*d*., Thomas Vyroun 2*d*., the wife of Philip s. of Alan 1*d*., and Roger Trailement 2*d*., for dry wood.[1]

STANLAY.—The son of Robert s. of Walter 2*d*., Robert s. of Geppe 2*d*., the son of Walter s. of Adam 2*d*., the maid of Robert del Dale 3*d*., and William Tagge 3*d*., for dry wood.

SOURBY.—John s. of Hugh, for escape of oxen, 6*d*.

---

[1] There are several other names, but illegible.

J

William s. of Adam de Heppewrth, for . . . . , 4d.

Michael del Lom, for vert, 6d.

. . . . [? Thomas] del Hollegate, for collecting nuts, ...

HIPEROM.—Alexander de Brighouses [?], for vert, 2s.

Megge de Brighouses, for dry wood, 4d.

RASTRIK.—Henry s. of John de Rastrik 6d., Richard s. of Malina 6d., and William s. of Nabbe 6d., for vert.

Anote de Rastrik 2d., for dry wood.

mem. 8d.

WAKEFELD.—The maid of Richard s. of Jomme [?] 1d., Hugh the Chapman's son 2d., John Rychaud's maid 2d., William Rychaud's maid 2d., the maid of Thomas s. of Molle 2d., Henry the Nauthird's daughter 2d., Anota Mogge 2d. (pledge, William Isabell), ... Torketro 3d., John Torild's daughters 4d., John Lethe's maid 4d., Robert Liftfast's maid 2d., Peter Spink's wife 4d., William Wolmer's son 2d., Elias Tyrsi's daughters 2d., Walter the Cook's son 2d., Walter Hogg's maid 2d., Nicholas Hogg's maid 2d., John Kyde's maid 6d., Hugh Bille's daughter 2d., Richard le Wayte's maid 3d., the da. of William s. of Godith 2d., the son of John s. of Jose 1d., German Skot's wife 1d., John the Couper's wife 1d., William Proudefote's daughter 2d., Richard le Wayte's maid 3d., John Swerd's maid 2d., John de Skulbroke's maid 2d., Henry de Skulbroke's maid 3d., Robert de Fery's maid 2d., Robert Pille's maid 2d., John de Wraggeby's maid 2d., the maid of Ralph s. of Malle 2d., the maid of Ralph s. of Mille 2d., John le Sotheren's maid 2d., the maid of William s. of Godith 2d., Adam de Craven's maid 4d., Robert Dernelove's son 2d., Cicely de Castelford's maid 2d., Agnes Swerd 3d., John Kyde's maid 2d., Walter Hogg's maid 1d., Nicholas Hogg's maid 1d., Elias Tirsy's maid 1d., William de Mora's maid 2d., Philip de Castelford's maid 2d., and Robert Grenehod's maid 2d., for dry wood.

ALVERTHORPE.—William Hoskell 4d., John de Flansowe 3d., and Amabel de Flansowe 2d, for dry wood.

Adam Gerbode 6d., Christiana Gerbode 6d., and Henry del Bothem 6d., for escape of pigs in the New Park.

Richard Wythehundes 12d., and William Danays 3d., for cutting dry wood.

John Schirlock 6d., for dry wood and ivy [*edera*].

Richard Bunny 12d., for cutting vert.

SOURBY.—Henry de Saltonstall *v.* William Swaype and John the Webster [*textor*], for trespass. Pledge, William de Saltonstall. Swaype is attached by John the Webster, and John by John de Gledeholte.

ALVERTHORPE.—Quenilda de Alverthorpe *v.* Henry del Bothem, for trespass. Pledge, Geoffrey de Birkenschawe.

SANDALE.—Henry s. of Ralph *v.* Thomas de Hollegate and Thomas s. of Roger, for debt. Pledge, Peter Leuwelyn.

STANLAY.—Richard del Ker *v.* Hugh s. of Robert s. of Geoffrey, for trespass. Pledge, Robert s. of Robert.

SANDALE.—Robert de la Grene *v.* William de la Grene, for trespass. Pledge, John Cokewald.

mem. 9.

COURT held at Wakefeld on the Friday in Easter Week [April 19], in the year abovesaid [1308].

ESSOIGNS.[1]—Thomas de Seyville, attorney of Lady Margaret de Neville, by John de Roclay. Pledge, William the Serjeant.

Richard de Bristall, by Robert Scot. Pledge, John de la More.

Alan Almot, attorney of Thomas de Burgo, by Jordan del Kerre. Pledge, Thomas de Wakefeld.

Thomas de Heeton, by John de Heeton. Pledge, William the Serjeant.

Thomas de Thornthon [*sic*], by Hugh de Thornton. Pledge, John de Toftclif.

Elias de Birton, by Robert de Birton. Pledge, Thomas de Wakefeld.

Nicholas de Cailly, by Henry de Methelay. Pledge, John de la More.

Thomas the Brounsmyth and Emma his wife *v.* William de Wakefeld, for trespass. Pledge, Hugh de Seyville. William appears, and a day is given.

Hugh s. of Robert s. of Geoffrey de Stanlay *v.* Richard del Kerre, for trespass, by Thomas de Wyttelay. Pledge, William Taillour. Richard appears, and a day is given.

Beatrice de Totehill, by her attorney, appears *v.* Henry del Ryding, for debt. Henry has been distrained by a pig, but does not come. To be better distrained.

John del Hole and Margaret his wife have been heavily distrained [*magna districcione*] to answer Thomas de Totehill and Thomas de Wode, executors of Thomas de Fekesby, but have not appeared. To be again distrained.

The like as to Agnes wife of Thomas de Fekesby, Thomas s. of Modesta, and John s. of Henry de Fekesby, all defts. at the suit of the said executors.

---

[1] From suit of Court unless otherwise stated.

SANDALE.—Robert de la Grene in mercy 6*d.* for unjustly detaining 2 qrs. of oats from William de la Grene. He must satisfy him.

STANLAY.—Benedict de Stanlay gives 4*d.* to agree with Henry s. of Simon Tyting, for trespass. Pledge, Simon Tyting.

ALVERTHORPE.—John Rate gives 3*d.* to agree with John Cay, for trespass.

OSSETE.—William s. of Godfrey de Dewysbiry gives 6*d.* to take 6 acres of land in Ossete from Agnes da. of Richard Hirnyng for [? his] life; the reversion is to descend to Agnes and her heirs.

HOLNE.—Thomas s. of Robert de Fouleston gives 12*d.* to take 1½ acres of land in Alstanlay from Alan s. of Richard de Alstanlay, to himself and his heirs.

STANLAY.—Alice da. of Robert s. of Walter gives 6*d.* for license to marry. Pledge, her father.

ALVERTHORPE.—Henry le Nonne, for unjust detention from Thomas de Wakefeud, 3*d.*

SOURBY.—Thomas s. of Richard de Heitfeld gives 12*d.* to take 2 acres of land in Sourby, which had escheated to the Earl after the death of Adam, [Thomas's] brother, who was a bastard.

[? HIPERUM].—Elias s. of Christiana de Northourom gives 12*d.* to take 12 acres of land in Northourom from John del Schawe. Pledge, Richard del Wode.

WAKEFELD.—John Nelot gives 6*d.* to take ½ acre of land in the Rodes, in the Graveship of Wakefeud, from John At-Bar.

HOLNE.—Thomas s. of Robert de Fouleston gives 3*d.* to take a rood of new land of the waste in Alstanlay; rent, 1½*d.*

THORNES.—Philip Wolf gives 6*d.* to agree with Marjory widow of John Wythundes, in a plea of dower.

Thomas Lyleman 3*d.*, and Roger Trailement 3*d.*, for not coming.

OSSETE.—Richard del Dene 3*d.*, for the like.

STANLAY.—Richard the Leper 3*d.*, and John s. of Alice 3*d.*, for the like.

ALVERTHORPE.—William Hoskell, plt., *v.* Quenilda [de Alverthorpe], for seizing cattle, does not prosecute; 6*d.*

The inquisition finds that Richard de Collay and William Hoskell assaulted Quenilda de Alverthorpe and struck her; damages, 18*d.* Fine, 6*d.*

Also that her complaint against Henry de Bothem and Adam Gerbode for the same is unjust. Fine 6*d.*, for a false claim.

Also that she cursed Henry de Bothem, whereupon he kicked her [*depulit ipsam cum pede suo*]. Henry is fined 3*d.* No damages.

[SANDALE.]—Robert de la Grene, for broom and ivy [*pro husseto et edera*], 6*d.*

Thomas Bate's wife 4*d.*, the wife of Adam s. of Robert 3*d.*, Thomas Soty [?] of Wollay 2*d.*, John the Mason [*cementarius*] 1*d.*, and the wife of Robert de Aula of Sandale 1*d.*, for boughs [*pro ramalibus*].

The wife of Henry de Vallibus 4*d.*, Alexander Dane 4*d.*, John de Plegwyck's wife 2*d.*, and Thomas Hulpy 3*d.*, for dry wood and boughs [?].

John de Raygate, servant [*garcio*] of William de Plegwik, 6*d.*, for vert and coal.[1]

William Hare's son 2*d.*, and Agnes de Ossete's servant [*garcio*] 3*d.*, for vert.

John Tropinell and R. le Schoter 12*d.*, for vert.

John Payne 2*d.*, for escape of oxen.

. . . . s. of John 2*d.*, for escape of sheep.

. . . . s. of Ralph 2*d.*, for escape of a horse.

John s. of Magge 6*d.*, for trespass.

John le [? R]assed 4*d.*, the maid of Thomas s. of Molle 3*d.*, Eve de la Bramelay's son 3*d.*, and Nicholas Hogg's maid . . . *d.*, for dry wood.[2]

WAKEFELD —William de Mora's maid 4*d.*, William de Ouche-thorpe's maid 2*d.*, Walter Bille's maid 2*d.*, and Robert Preist's maid 1*d.*, for [? dry wood].

Magota Preist 2*d.*, John Benne's maid 2*d.*, John Swerd's maid 4*d.*, the maid of William the Gardiner junior 4*d.*, Malkyn Danyel 2*d.*, John Pollard junior 2*d.*, Philip de Castelford's maid 3*d.*, William Proudfot's daughter 1*d.*, Robert Broun's maid 1*d.*, Eva Pollard's maid 2*d.*, John Don's maid 2*d.*, Robert the Goldsmith's maid 2*d.*, Robert Swerd's maid 2*d.*, Adam the Clouter's maid 1*d.*, Roger de Silkestan's maid 2*d.*, Adam [?] de Castelford's maid 2*d.*, Maude Wolmer 2*d.*, Malkyn Godesoul 2*d.*, and Nicholas Noddeger's maid 2*d.*, for dry wood.[2]

mem. 9d.

OSSETE.—Swayn de Ossete 2*d.*, Robert Sonneman 4*d.*, Jordan Móyses 2*d.*, and John de Chikinlay's widow 1*d.*, for escape of foals [*pulli*].

THORNES.—John Graffard 6*d.*, for escape of pigs.

STANLAY.—Robert del Spen's wife 2*d.*, Benedict de Stanlay's wife 2*d.*, John de St. Swythen's wife 2*d.*, and William the Dyker's wife 2*d.*, for dry wood.

---

[1] Charcoal. [2] Several names illegible.

Richard Cay *v.* Richard Tilly, for trespass. Pledge, Thomas de Wakefeld. Deft. is attached by Ralph Clement.

William Taillour is appointed foreign bailiff of the Liberty, and sworn.[1]

_____

COURT there on the Friday after the Feast of St. John of Beverley [   ], in the first year of King Edward [1308].

ESSOIGNS.[2]—Thomas de Seyvill, attorney of Margaret de Nevill, by Stephen Schorberd. Pledge, John de Toftclif.

Nicholas le Normaund, by John Patrik. Pledge, William de Walton.

Nicholas de Cailly, by John Damoysell. Pledge, Hugh de Seyvill.

Peter Swerd, by William the Serjeant. Pledge, John de Toftclif.

Hugh s. of Robert s. of Geoffrey de Stanlay *v.* Richard Kerre, for trespass, by German Swerd. Pledge, William s. of Marg'. Richard comes, and a day is given.

Beatrice de Totehill *v.* Henry del Ryding, for debt. Deft. has been distrained by a pig, price . . . . . , but does not come. To be better distrained.

John del Hole and Margaret his wife, who have been heavily distrained [*magna districcione*] to answer Thomas de Totehill and Thomas del Wode, executors of Thomas de Fekesby, for debt, do not come. To be better distrained, to answer to the principal plea and for many defaults.

The like as to Agnes wife of Thomas de Fekesby and Thomas s. of Modesta, at the suit of the same plts.

The same Thomas and Thomas offer themselves *v.* John s. of Henry de Fekesby; they complain that John unjustly detains one mark of silver of the will [? *de testamento*] of Thomas de Fekesby, whose executors they are; and unjustly, because John came to the house of the said Thomas deceased on Michaelmas day, 25 Edward I [1297], and obtained a loan from him of 10 marks, to be repaid at the will of the said Thomas; Thomas went to John's house on Michaelmas Day, 27 Edward I [1299], and requested the 10 marks from him; John paid nothing; after Thomas's death, his said executors went and demanded the debt, which John refused to pay, and which he still detains to their damage. John comes, and

_____

[1] The foreign bailiff, *forinsecus ballivus*, was the officer whose duty it was to do anything required outside the Liberty; he is sometimes called the "bailiff errant."

[2] From suit of Court unless otherwise stated.

defends nothing. He must pay them, and a fine of 12*d.*, and another of 6*d.* for his default at the last Court.

ALVERTHORPE.—John Schirlok *v.* John Tasse, in mercy, 3*d.*

SANDALE.—William de la Grene, for a false claim against Robert de la Grene, 3*d.*

The inquisition finds that Agnes wife of William de la Grene took from the house of Robert de la Grene two sheets [*linthia*], a towel [*manutergium*], a curtain [*velum*], and a   [*crepium*], price 12*d.* She must satisfy him, and is amerced 3*d.*

HYPERUM.—William s. of Robert de Haldewrth gives 6*d.* to take 2½ acres of land in Haldewrth, which John de Sk[ul]cotes left waste on the Earl.

John s. of Walter de Haldewrth gives 6*d.* to take 1½ acres of the same land.

STANLAY.—Richard Isabell gives 6*d.* to take ½ acre of land in Stanlay from Robert Typet.

HOLNE.—Warin de Slaghthayt gives 18*d.* to take 2 acres of land in Alstanlay from Alan de Alstanlay [*de eadem*], for 10 years.

Thomas s. of Robert de Fouleston gives 18*d.* to take 6 acres of land in Littelwode from John s. of Thomas, for 6 years.

Gilbert de Gaunte gives 12*d.* to take one acre of new land of the waste in Alstanlay; rent, 6*d.*

[STANLAY],—Gilbert de Methelay gives 12*d.* to take a rood of land in Stanlay from Robert [Typet ?].

The same Gilbert gives 6*d.* to take a piece of land in Stanlay, 40 feet long and 15 feet wide, from Walter s. of Bateman.

Thomas s. of Robert de Fouleston gives 12*d.* to take an acre of land in Alstanlay from Gilbert de Gaunte.

. . . .—The case between Richard Cay and Richard Tilly, for trespass, is respited until the next Court. The deft. is attached by Ralph Clement, chaplain.

Adam de Holne *v.* Gilbert de Alstanlay, for trespass. Pledge, Richard de la Grene . . . .

William s. of Gilbert *v.* John de Holne, for trespass. Pledge, Richard the Milner.

Same *v.* Adam de Holne, for trespass. Pledge, Robert del Skoles.

Robert Stirk *v.* William del Clif. Pledge, Henry de Rastrik.

Same *v.* Alan del Dam, for trespass. Pledge, Henry de Rastrik.

Alan del Dam *v.* Robert Stirk, for trespass. Pledge, William de . . . .

Robert the Walker *v.* Elias de Danecastre and Thomas del Holgate, for debt.

mem. 10.

COURT at Wakefeld on Friday before Pentecost[1] [May 31],
1 Edward II, [1308].

ESSOIGNS.[2]—Alan Almot, attorney of Thomas de Burgo, by Richard de Ryhall. Pledge, Thomas de Tothill.

John de Lepton, by Thomas de Witlay. Pledge, Hugh de Seyville.

Thomas de Heeton, by Robert his man. Pledge, Richard de Bristall.

Thomas de Thornton, by Hugh de Thornton. Pledge, William del Okes.

Peter Swerd, by William the Serjeant. Pledge, John de Toftclif.

Nicholas le Normaund, by John Patrik. Pledge, John de Mora.

William de Wakefeld, plt., *v.* Thomas Brounsmyth and Emma his wife, for trespass, by Thomas de Tothill. Pledge, John Patrik. The defts. appear, and a day is given.

Hugh s. of Robert s. of Geoffrey gives 3*d.* to agree with Richard del Kerre, for trespass. Pledge, William Taillour.

Beatrice de Totehill *v.* Henry del Ryding, for debt. Henry, distrained by a pig, price 2*s.*, does not come. To be better distrained.

Elcok de Lynthayt was charged [*calumpniatus*] that whereas the tenements of Matthew de Linthayt were seized into the lord's hands and retained in his protection, nevertheless he, Elcok, had with his cattle consumed the herbage and meadows of him [*ipsius;* ? Matthew[3]], and carted and carried the manure to his own manor. Elcok comes and admits it. He must satisfy him [? Matthew], and is amerced 3*s.* 4*d.* Pledges, Elias de Birton and William Taillour.

The same Elcok is charged that he seised the cattle of Maude widow of Peter de Seyville, and drove them from the Earl of Warenne's fee to the Earl of Lincoln's fee. He comes and admits it, and is amerced 3*s.* 4*d.* Same pledges.

Thomas de Totehill and Thomas del Wode, executors of Thomas de Fekesby, *v.* John del Hole and Margaret his wife, for debt. Defts., though heavily distrained, do not come. To be better distrained, to answer the principal plea and for many defaults.

The like as to Agnes wife of Thomas de Fekesby and Thomas s. of Modesta, at the suit of the same plaintiffs.

HYPERUM.—William Talvace gives 12*d.* to take 6 acres of land on Clegclif, which Henry del Lache left waste on the lord.

---

[1] Whitsunday was June 2nd.

[2] From suit of Court unless otherwise stated.

[3] It is not stated that Matthew was dead, and the words, *retenta in protectione sua*, rather suggest that he was not.

STANLAY.—Joan da. of Juliana de Ouchethorpe gives 6*d.* to take 2 acres of land in Ouchethorpe from her mother.

. . . .—Richard Tilly gives 6*d.* for license of concord with Richard Cay, for trespass.

HOLNE.—Avice widow of Adam Cosin gives 2*s.* for license to marry Adam s. of Thomas de la Grene.

[WAKEFELD].—John de Wytewode and Roger de Wytewode [*de eadem*] are fined 12*d.* for raising the hue in the town of Wakefeld. Pledge, Roger . . . .

HOLNE.—William s. of Gilbert de Alstanlay is amerced 6*d.* for not prosecuting his suit against John de Holne. The like against Adam de Holne.

Roger Stirk the like, against William del Clif, and against Alan del Dam.

Alan del Dam the like, against Robert Stirk.

STANLAY.—Robert Gosse *v.* Walter s. of Robert Gonne, for trespass. Pledge, Robert del Dale.

ALVERTHORPE.—Adam Gerbode is amerced 3*d.* for unjustly detaining 8*d.* from Geoffrey de Birkenschawe.

STANLAY.—John s. of Hobbe the Soldier [*mercenarius*[1]] gives 6*d.* to take 2 acres of land in the Graveship of Stanlay from Richard Lo[ng]schank, for 15 years from Michaelmas next.

RECOGNITION.—Richard Wythehundes comes and recognises that he has demised his tenement in Wakefeld for 20 years to John s. of Hobbe the Soldier [*mercenarius*], for a certain sum of money, as witnessed by a chirograph made between them; and by this recognition he binds himself to warrant to John against all men during the said term; and he finds pledges, under a penalty of 20*s.*, that he will keep and defend the said demise, viz: Philip Wlf, Adam Gerbode and William Hoske[ll].

. . . .—Thomas s. of Roger gives 12*d.* to take ½ acre of land on the Wytestock, ½ acre on the Cayselforeb . . . . [?], ... roods on the Lachilandes, and 2 parcels of meadow in Levenetheng, from William de Wakefeld, clerk.

John s. of Nalk gives 2*s.* to take a culture of land called Orrerode and 1 acre . . . . , from William the Clerk.

HOLNE.—Thomas de Brocholes 6*d.*, John s. of Johanot 6*d.*, Elias Abraham 6*d.*, Robert Proudfot 6*d.*, Anota wife of Richard del Grene 6*d.*, and Robert Spinck 6*d.*, for vert.

---

[1] See note, p. 123.

Matthew de Marisco *6d.*, and Emma da. of Dobbe *3d.*, for dry wood.

HYPERUM.—Adam Bythebroke *4d.*, and Roger del Clyf *6d.*, for thorns.

Thomas del Northend *3d.*, for dry wood.

OSSETE.—Adam Lovelavedy of Chideshill *6d.*, Hugh de Chideshill *6d.*, John Perry *6d.*, John de Northewode *3d.*, and Robert Perry *2d.*, for dry wood.

Robert Sonneman *4d.*, for vert.

WAKEFELD.—The maid of John Lethe *2d.*, of John s. of Jose *2d.*, and of Robert Liftfast *2d.*, for dry wood.

The maid of Elias Tirsi *3d.*, of John Lethe *3d.*, and of Robert le Young . . . *d.*, for rushes in the coppice.

[*Two entries illegible.*]

ALVERTHORPE.—Robert s. of Ralph de Ouchethorpe *6d.*, and John the Turnur *6d.*, for escape of cows.

Geppe Middenath *6d.*, for cutting vert.

Richard s. of Broun *2d.*, for dry wood.

Nicholas de Batelay *2s.*, for cutting. . . . . . . [*pro arrab' amput'*].

WAKEFELD.—The maid of John Peg[er] *4d.*, of Robert Peg[er] *3d.*, of Richard le Wayte *6d.*, of the same Richard *6d.*, of Magge Archur *4d.*, of John . . . . . ba *2d.*, of John Pollard junior *1d.*, and the son of Robert Grenehod *3d.*, for dry wood.

mem. 10d.

The Steward has been given to understand by the report of many persons that Robert the Walker of Wakefeld has boarded [*plancasset*] many buildings in the town of Wakefeld with the Earl's timber [*meremium*], which was delivered by the Earl's ministers for the repair of the mill and dam at Wakefeld; which timber the said Robert maliciously, and on many divers occasions, caused to be carried away. The Steward, wishing to certify the Earl thereof, ordered John de Wauton to make inquiry into the truth of the matter, clearly and openly. Whereupon John de Wauton, while the Steward was in the parts of London, made a secret inquiry [*inquisivit occulte*]. And the inquisition was taken by Thomas de Wakefeld, Robert le Roller, Robert de Castelford, John de Fery, Robert Swerd, Robert Dernelove, John Pollard, Nicholas Noddeger, Thomas s. of Henry, Robert the Carpenter, John Dade and William the Gardiner, who said on their oath that at the time when the old mill was pulled down and rebuilt and the dam was broken and remade, the said Robert [the Walker] by himself and his ministers on several occasions [*per vices*] stealthily and secretly [*palam et occulte*] carried away and caused to be carried away the timber from the said mill and dam, to the value of 100s. and more. They said also that the said Robert was accustomed [*custumabilis est*] to seize floating beams brought down by the excessive flow of water [*per nimiam cretinam aque*] from the western side of the bridges, mill and broken dams, by flood [*per inundacionem*], but they do not know the value of this. They said also that two pans [*due panne*]¹ of his house where he lives [*manet*] are [made] of two beams so seized.

THORNES.—Margery Wythehundes *v*. Philip Wlf, in a plea of land. Pledge, Richard Wythehundes.

The same Margery *v*. William the Goldsmith, in a plea of land. Same pledge.

The same Margery *v*. John s. of Hobbe the Soldier [*mercenarius*]², in a plea of land. Same pledge.

SANDALE.—Robert the Harpur *v*. Thomas de Hollegate, for trespass. Pledge, John Cokewald.

Thomas Alayn *v*. Robert the Grubber, on an agreement. Pledge, William Taillour. He has been distrained by two sheep.

———

mem. 11.

COURT at Halifax on Monday the morrow of Holy Trinity,³ 1 Edward II, [1308].

SOURBY.—Robert le Orgraver and Richard his brother give 2s. to agree with Elias del Bank, for trespass. Pledge, John Culp[on].

John Culpon gives 12d. to take ½ acre of land in Mithomrode from Ingelard de Miglay, which Ingelard took from the waste. Pledge, John the Grave.

Roger s. of Anabel gives 12d. to take 1 acre of new land of the waste in Sourby; rent, 6d.

The same Roger gives 6d. to take 2 acres of land in Sourby, viz. in Snaperode, which Jordan de Slaght[hwait] left waste on the Earl.

Hugh s. of Reynald gives 3s. to take 2 acres of land in Longbothem from Roger s. of Anabel, which Roger took from the waste.

Nicholas the Ryder gives 3d. to agree with Thomas de Heytfeld, for debt.

———

¹ In a timber-framed house the uprights are called *posts*, and the main horizontal beams are *pans*.

² See p. 123, note.

³ Trinity Sunday, June 9th.

William Swaype, for contemptuously [*contemptibiliter*] breaking the Earl's pound [*faldea*], whereby the cattle impounded for damage done in the Earl's grass, escaped without making emends; in mercy, 12*d*.

It is found [*attinctum*] by the inquisition of the jury that William Swaype and John the Webster [*textor*] of Werlouley assaulted Henry de Saltonstall and William his brother while they were going to their plough, and cut off the . . . .[1] of the plough, and wounded the said William de Saltonstall to his [? their] damage of ½ mark, as taxed by the inquisition. They must satisfy them, and are in mercy, 2*s*. Pledges, Richard de Saltonstall and John s. of Jordan de Saltonstall.

Escapes in Ayrikedene: Adam s. of Ivo, 2 cart-horses [*affros*], 12*d*.; Hugh de Lithhesles, 1 horse, 6*d*.; Henry s. of Nalle[2] de Northlaund, 3 beasts [*averia*], 6*d*.; Amaria de Stodelay, 2 beasts, 4*d*.; William at-Town-head, 1 horse, 2*d*.; Thomas del Feild, 1 horse, 2*d*.; William the Horsknave, 1 horse, 2*d*.; Roger del Hallestedes, 1 horse, 2*d*., pledge, William del Lone; Richard de Collereslay, 1 horse, 4*d*.; John del Lom, 1 sow and 4 hogs [*hog'*], 6*d*.; John the Milner, 4 hogs, 6*d*.; Henry del Hollegate, 3 horses, 12*d*.; Hugh the Hermit [*Hugo Heremita*], 2 beasts, 4*d*.; John s. of Richard Hodde, 2 oxen, 2*d*.; Roger s. of Anabel, 2 stirks, 2*d*.; John Culpon, 6 oxen, 6*d*.; John del Rediker, 4 cows, 6*d*.; Adam at-Town-head, 4 beasts, 6*d*.; Adam Pede of Wolfedene, 6 beasts, 6*d*.

Juliana Wade, for escape of 6 pigs in the Earl's park at Haders [?], 3*d*.

SOURBY.—Escapes in Saltonstall: Richard del Wyteleye, 2 beasts, 4*d*.; Thomas de Saltonstall, 2 beasts, 2*d*.; Elena Goisse, 1 cow, 2*d*.; Richard s. of Robert de Cheswell, 6 stirks, 4*d*.; John s. of Robert of the same, 1 horse, 2*d*.; Cicely da. of Adam, 1 horse, 1*d*.; Adam de Noteschawe, 1 horse, 3*d*.; Thomas de Ovendene, 1 horse, 3*d*.; Richard s. of Cicely of the same, 1 horse, 3*d*.; William the Smith of Ourom, 1 foal, 2*d*.; John de Astay, 1 horse, 2*d*.; Henry de Coldelay, 1 horse, 2*d*.; Adam s. of Ivo, 1 horse, 3*d*.; Hugh de Mixendene, 1 horse, 2*d*.

Eva de Godelay, for escape of 6 beasts in Bay . . . , 6*d*.; William, her son, for 6 beasts there, 6*d*.

The same William, for cutting vert, 4*d*.

Thomas de Salsa mara, for escape of three horses in Stanydene, 6*d*. Pledge, John the Grave.

---

[1] *Hardea caruce amputarunt.* Translation doubtful; Cotgrave gives *hardes*= stuff, implements, baggage. Probably *gear* of some sort is meant.

[2] Or perhaps *Malle*.

Thomas de Lithhesles, for vert, 3*d*.

Elias s. of Elias the Milner, for dry wood, 1*d*.

Robert de Saltonstall, while he was Grave in the preceding year, bought a stray horse from the Steward, out of Court, for 4*s*., with which he has not yet charged himself [*carcavit se*] in the Roll. Therefore the present Grave is charged therewith, and Robert is in mercy for the concealment, 12*d*.

Adam de Heytfeud bought a stray horse for 2*s*. 6*d*. from John de Wauton in one of his comings into Sourbishire, and the aforesaid Robert [de Saltonstall], then the Grave, was ordered to charge himself[1] therewith in the Roll at the next Court, and has not yet done so. Therefore the present Grave is charged therewith, and Robert is in mercy for the concealment, [12]*d*.

William de Locwode bought a stray filly [*pultra*] for 4*s*.

TOURN there, the same day.

JURORS.—Richard de Waddeswrth junior, John de Stodelay, William del Croft, John de Chewelleye [*sic*], Hugh s. of Reynald, John de Miggelay, Adam de Midelton, John s. of Hugh de Northlaund, Adam de Illingwrth, Adam de Miggelay, Jordan de Skircotes, and Alan del Lee.

The townships of Miggelay, Werlouley, Sourby, Rissewrth and Ovendene, are in mercy for not coming when called.[2]

Magota de Wyndehill, for drawing blood of Adam the Taillour's wife, 12*d*.

Richard s. of John Smerlof, for unjustly raising the hue on William Maunsell and Thomas s. of Peter, [? 12*d*.].

The wife of Thomas de Aula 12*d*., Amabel de Sourby . . . *d*., Magota de Rypon . . . *d*., Nelle the Walker . . . *d*., and the wife of Bate the Lister [*tinctor*] 6*d*., for brewing contrary to the assize.

The jury say that whereas the Prior of Lewes is wont and ought to have two assemblies yearly of all his tenants [*solebat et debet habere duos adventus per annum . . . . de omnibus tenentibus suis*] after the Earl's two Tourns, the same Prior, to the Earl's prejudice, from the feast of S. Peter ad vincula, 1 Edward II, [Aug. 1, 1307], up to this Tourn, has by his proctor held four Courts at Halifax touching divers pleas of trespass and without the presence and assent of the

---

[1] Robert had apparently received the 2*s*. 6*d*.

[2] The margin of the roll is in bad condition, and the amounts of the amercements, and of others below, are illegible.

Earl's ministers, and has appointed ale-tasters, as though he were lord of the liberty; and moreover the said Prior, by his said proctor, has sentenced [*inhibuit*][1] the Earl's natives and others, not dwelling in the town of Halifax, for simple trespass, which right of sentence [*inhibicio*] belongs to no one except only to the Earl, by reason of his liberty.

Richard del Wode *v.* William s. of William del Hingandrode, for trespass. Pledge, William de [? S]onderland.

COURT at Rastrik on Tuesday the Feast of S. Barnabas the Apostle, [June 11], in the said year, [1308].

HIPERUM.—William s. of Adam de Schepedene gives 12*d.* to take 1½ acres of new land of the waste in Schepedene; rent, 9*d.*

Jordan s. of Adam de Schepedene gives 6*d.* to take ½ acre of new land of the waste in Northourum; rent, 3*d.*

John s. of Adam de Hyperum gives 6*d.* to take ½ acre of new land of the waste in Hiperum; rent, 3*d.*

John s. of Adam del Wytehill gives 18*d.* to take 2 acres of new land of the waste in North Ourum; rent, 12*d.*

Richard s. of Jordan de Northourum gives 6*d.* to take ⅛ rood of new land of the waste in North Ourum; rent, 1*d.*

Thomas s. of Christiana de Lynthayt was charged that he had seized the cattle of Maude de Seyvill in Querneby, and driven them out of the Earl's fee to Almanbyry, in contempt of the Earl and to his prejudice. He comes and admits it, and is in mercy; 2*s.* Pledges, ... del Brigg and Matthew de Lynthayt.

John s. of Adam de Locwode, charged with the like, comes and denies it. Let there be an inquiry at the Tourn. Nevertheless, he is amerced 12*d.* for contempt.

HIPERUM.—It is found by the inquisition that William s. of William del Hingandrode carried off .... from the wood growing in the soil of Richard del Wode. Damage, 2*d.* Fine, 12*d.*

Thomas s. of Modesta puts himself [in mercy] against Thomas de Totehill and Thomas del Wode, in a plea of debt; 12*d.* Pledge, John s. of Henry.

Henry Abraham gives 12*d.* to take 3 roods of new land of the waste in divers places in Hiperum wood; rent, 5*d.*

---

[1] The usual meaning of *inhibio* is simply to forbid, but the context seems to imply a hearing of complaints and a consequent sentence.

RASTRIK.—John del Botherode 6*d.*, Sabina widow of John s. of Henry 6*d.*, and William Burreheved 6*d.*, for dry wood.

Henry s. of Modesta 6*d.*, Joan da. of Christiana 6*d.*, and Matthew de Tothill 6*d.*, for vert.

HIPERUM.—Walter s. of Elias de Ourum 6*d.*, Thomas his brother 4*d.*, Michael de Haddegrene 4*d.*, Richard s. of Walter 3*d.*, John the Pinder of Ourum 3*d.*, John s. of Walter 4*d.*, Richard s. of Jordan 4*d.*, John del Wytehill 3*d.*, Simon s. of Jordan 3*d.*, and Henry de Coppelay 4*d.*, for thorns.

Jordan de Haddegrenes 3*d.*, Thomas del Broke 4*d.*, John del Wroo 6*d.*, Eva wife of Thomas le Heyr 6*d.*, John del Rode 6*d.*, Thomas del Rode 4*d.*, Roger del Brighouses senior 6*d.*, and John s. of Henry de Astay 6*d.*, for vert.

Thomas s. of Roger del Clyf 4*d.*, John del Hollewaye 4*d.*, Henry de Coldelay 6*d.*, and Henry le Marwe 3*d.*, for dry wood.

Roger de Clifton gives 6*d.* to take 1 rood of new land of the waste in Hiperum wood; rent, 1½*d.*

Henry Abraham gives 12*d.* to take ½ acre of new land of the waste there; rent, 3*d.*

TOURN there the same day.

JURORS.—Alan del Frith, Thomas de Dalton, physician,[1] Ralph de Gouthelaghcharthes, Henry le Frankisse of Staynla[nd], ... Talvace, John de Bristall, John del Rode, John the Clerk of Hertesheved, Henry de Coldelay, John de P . . . . , Thomas de Wytewode, and Roger de Clifton.

HIPERUM.—The township of Hiperum is amerced 12*d.* for not coming when called.

The wife of Roger s. of John the elder [*senioris*][2] 3*d.*, Magota de Chepelay 6*d.*, Adam the Carpenter's wife 6*d.*, William the Milner's wife 4*d.*, and Richard the Taillour's wife 6*d.*, for brewing contrary to the assize.

Alexander the Milner of Brighouses 6*d.*, for not coming.

Two stray fillies [*pultre*] are in the Graveship of Hiperum; the year and day are elapsed, and [Adam ?] del Wode has sold them for 7*s.* 6*d.* The Grave of Hiperum is charged therewith.

John de Percy of Clifton 2*d.*, and [Roger ?] de Brighouses senior 4*d.*, for not coming.

---

[1] *Fisicus.* A description of this sort is most unusual in a jury list.

[2] It is possible that this is *Senior* as a surname.

Amabel . . . . . de Dalton drew blood of Agnes Rotte, her servant.

Avice the Cook [?] drew blood of Agnes da. of Adam Derling.

William the Rede of Thornhill and John the Strengfelagh burgled the house of Thomas del Wode, and took his goods, value 40s. To be arrested.

Hugh s. of William s. of Eva de Wakefeld drew blood of Richard del Lathe of Clifton. To be attached.

Robert Spillewode drew blood of Alexander the Milner of Brighouses ; 6d.

Beatrice wife of Adam the Waynwrith drew blood of Emma Pynder of Hiperum ; 6d.

The townships of Crosseland and Querneby present that John del Lynthayt and Thomas s. of Christiana seized the cattle [averia] of [Maude de] Seyville and drove them out of the Earl's fee towards Almanbiry, and this by the counsel of [John?] de Locwode, to the Earl's prejudice. John and John are to be distrained ; Thomas is amerced in Court, as above [in curia supra], 6d.

Alan de Bothemlay drew blood of Cicely da. of William de Bothemlay.

_____

mem. 12.

COURT at Birton on Wednesday the morrow of St. Barnabas the Apostle [June 11], the year [aforesaid].

HOLNE.—William del Clyf and Alan del Dam give 2s. to agree with Robert Stirk, for trespass. Pledges, John de Heppew[orth] and Adam s. of Nicholas.

Robert Stirk and Adam his son give 2s. to agree with William del Clyf and Alan del Dam, for trespass.

Adam s. of John de Holne, for a false claim v. Thomas s. of Gilbert de Alstanlay ; 6d.

It is found by the inquisition that Gilbert de Alstanlay and William, William [sic] and Matthew his sons assaulted Adam s. of John de Holne, by pursuing and chasing him with intent to do him an injury [prosequendo ipsum et fugando causa malefac' ei] ; amercement, 2s.

The case between William s. of Gilbert de Astanlay, plt., and John de Holne and John and Adam his sons, defts., for trespass, is adjourned to the Court at Wakefeld, because the said John is ill.

Adam the Waynwrith comes and surrenders to the lord a messuage and 11 acres of land in Heppewrth ; and afterwards Adam and Maude his wife received the same again from the lord, to hold to them and their heirs, doing services and customs. [Fine], 2s.

Richard s. of Michael de Fouleston comes and surrenders to the lord 10 acres of land with buildings in Fouleston; and afterwards Richard and Eva his wife received the same again from the lord, to hold to them and the heirs of their bodies, and for default of such heirs, to the right heirs of Richard. [Fine], 2s.

TOURN there the same day.

JURORS —Henry de Scheflay, John Wyther, John s. of John de Chepelay, Hugh de Thurstanland, Thomas Bridde, Adam del Skoles, John s. of Gilbert, William Strechayse, Nicholas de Littelwode, Nicholas Keneward, Richard Osan, and Richard de Birton.

The shepherd of Robert de Bardelby drew blood of Thomas s. of Adam de Langlay; 6d. And Thomas of the shepherd; 6d.

The wife of John s. of John de Chepelay, Christiana del Birketon, the wife of Richard le Neucomen, and Emma the Bagger, for brewing contrary to the assize; 12d. each.

Hanne [sic] Hogg of Chepelay drew blood of Richard le Syour of Fouleston; 12d. And Richard from the same Henry [sic]; 12d.

The wife of Adam the Bagger of Schelflay, and the wife of John s. of Gilbert de Heppewrth, for brewing contrary to the assize; 6d. each.

John s. of Malyn del Skoles did not come; 6d.

[HOL]NE.—Cicely del Wytestones, Diota widow of Adam s. of Matthew de Thurstanland, the wife of Elias de Brocholes, the wife of William del Storthes, the wife of Jordan the Milner, the wife of William the Askebrenner [Ashburner], the wife of Matthew de Langlay, the wife of Thomas s. of John de Fouleston, Malina da. of Matthew de Mora, and the wife of Hugh del Hole, for brewing contrary to the assize; 6d. each.

John s. of Roger de Langlay drew blood of Margery his sister; 12d.

Thomas s. of Gilbert de Astanlay [sic] and William his brother drew blood of John de Holne; 2s.

John de Holne drew blood of William s. of Gilbert de Alstanley; 12d.

Matthew s. of the same Gilbert drew blood of John s. of John de Holne; 12d.

Nicholas de Littelwode, one of the Jurors, disclosed the counsel [discooperuit consilium, i.e. of the jury] to Alice widow of Roger de Langlay; 12d.

K

TOURN at Wakefeld on the Thursday following.[1]

Jurors.—Robert de Wyveromthorpe, William Ingreys, Walter de Grymmeston, Richard de Bristall, John de Toftclif, Richard de Bretton, William de Dewisbiry, John de la More, Richard s. of John de Ossete, Robert de Wodesom, John del Fery and Walter Scot.

John Picard of Normanton drew blood of John [his brother?].

Jordan del Mere of the same drew blood of Roger Daundeliry; 12d.

Joan the Mason [*Johanna Cementar'*] of Emmelay drew blood of Widow Tilla; 12d.

Malina wife of Henry the Young of Emmelay drew blood of John de Farnelay's daughter. To be attached when found.

Richard Cosin drew blood of Henry the Clerk of Chepelay.

[? Holne].—William Gosse of Crigeleston drew blood of John his brother; 6d.

Thomas s. of Agnes of the same, an infant [*infans*],[2] drew blood of Henry his brother. To be attached.

[? Ossete].—William Cheild drew blood of Thomas Pees; 12d. And Thomas from William.

Richard Stuart's wife brewed weak ale.

Adam Wytebelt of Walton drew blood of John de Rachedale.

Robert the Harpur baked bread for sale, but it is not known what weight; 6d.

Thornes.—Roger the Turnur and Joan his wife and Alice Proudfot, Joan's sister, entered on a toft in Thornes, which had belonged to Idonea Proudfot, without the license of the lord or his bailiffs; 12d. The toft is to be seized into the lord's hands.

Robert s. of William the Clerk of Dewisbiry unjustly raised the hue on Godfrey of the same.

Walter the Clerk of Dewisbiry drew blood of Robert s. of William the Clerk of the same.

Agnes widow of Robert the Clerk of Dewysbiry constantly brews contrary to the assize.

mem. 12d.

Stanlay.—Richard s. of Robert de Batelay drew blood of Robert the Forester, in contempt of the Earl; 6s. 8d.

Richard Longschank drew blood of the same Robert; 12d.

Walter s. of Benedict drew blood of Hugh Croke, whereupon he raised the hue; 12d.

---

[1] The margin is much worn here, and the names of the Graveships and the amount of the fines are in many cases obliterated.

[2] Presumably in the legal sense.

ALVERTHORPE.—Richard Bonny has blocked up [*obstupit*] the common path [*semitam*] between Neuton Cross and Nicholas de Batelay's house; 12*d*. The hedge and ditch [*fossatum*] are to be destroyed [*prosternantur*].

William s. of Walter has blocked up the same path on the other part; 12*d*. The like order.

The wife of Robert Pescy, the wife of Robert s. of Robert s. of Walter, the wife of Gilbert the Theker,[1] and the wife of Robert s. of Geppe, for brewing weak ale; 6*d*. each.

Elizabeth da. of Robert de Batelay brewed contrary to the assize; 6*d*.

John Mous, Adam Torcatro, and Robert de Stanlay, for not coming to the Tourn; 3*d*. each.

[WAKEFIELD].—Philip Damoysell obstructed part of the high street in Westgate with his tan-bark [? *cum tannato suo*]; 12*d*.

Walter Bille, the like; 12*d*.

Malina de Sourby, the like, with a beam [*cum ligno suo*]; 3*d*.

Amicia [*Amic'*] de Swynlington, the like, with her tan-bark; 12*d*

Robert de Castelford, Adam s. of Walter, Thomas s. of Lawrence, and Richard s. of Mule [?], the like; 12*d*. each.

Robert the Farrier [*Mareschallus*] unjustly turned a brook [*sikettum*] before his door, to the damage of the whole town; 12*d*.

Richard de Binglay unjustly raised the hue against German Chidde; 6*d*.

Philip Damson and John de Essetoft fought, and each drew blood of the other. Both to be attached.

A stray yearling calf [*vitulus superannatus*] is detained from the custody of the Grave by German Filcok.

Henry Poyde drew blood of Thomas the Forester and fled; he has not yet come back. To be attached when found.

ALVERTHORPE.—John Rate unjustly raised the hue against Robert the Young; 6*d*.

Richard de Collay's wife brewed contrary to the assize; 6*d*.

The natives [*nativi*] of the lord of Alverthorpe have impeded the burgesses of Wakefield in the common way assigned to them through the . . . . . . [*per a . . . .*] of the lord Earl to their common in Wakefeld wood. The Steward must see to it.

WAKEFELD.—A stray pig [*porcus*], found in the bailiwick of John de Wauton a year ago, is sold to John de Wauton for 2*s*. 6*d*. The Grave. of Wakefeld is charged therewith.

---

[1] Thacker, Thatcher.

mem. 13.

COURT at Wakefield on the Friday before the Nativity of St. John
        Baptist [June 24], 1 Edward II, [1308].

ESSOIGNS.[1]—John de Totehill, by Thomas de Tothill.   Pledge,
Thomas de Wittelay.

Robert de la Grene of Ossete, by Thomas de Wittelay.   Pledge,
Richard de Bristall.

Matthew de Bosco, by William the Serjeant.   Pledge, John de
la More.

Thomas de Seyville, attorney of Margaret de Neville, by Hugh
de Chikinlay.   Pledge, William de Okes.

Beatrice de Totehill *v.* Henry del Ryding, for debt.   Henry has
been distrained by a pig, price 2*s.*, but does not come.   To be
better distrained.

John del Hole and Margery his wife put themselves [in mercy]
for many defaults *v.* Thomas de Totehill and Thomas del Wode,
executors of Thomas de Fekesby; 6*d.*   Pledge, John s. of Henry.
They have a love-day at the prayer of the parties.

Agnes wife of Thomas de Fekesby to be distrained to answer the
same executors, for debt.

Thomas s. of Modesta agreed at Rastrick Court with the said
executors, for debt, as appears at that Court.   Thomas paid no fine
there for his many defaults.   He is therefore amerced here; 6*d.*

Thomas de Heeton made default at this Court; 12*d.*

Thomas de Burgo, the like; 12*d.*

SANDALE.—Agnes da. of Bate de Wolflay, a native, gives 12*d.* for
license to marry.

John s. of Adam de Emmelay and Agnes da. of Bate de Wolflay
give 6*d.* to take 2 parts [thirds] of an acre and 3 roods of land
with buildings in Crigeleston from Eva and Cicely, sisters of Agnes,
for a term of ten years.

SOURBY.—Richard s. of Alote de Sourby gives 12*d.* to take
4 acres of land with buildings in Sourby, whereof one acre is new
land, from William the Smith.

ALVERTHORPE.—William de Wakefeld gives 6*d.* to take a large
parcel in the meadows of Alverthorpe from John Swan for a term
of 13 years, the first crop beginning at the Nativity of St. John
Baptist.

HOLNE.—Margery da. of Adam s. of John s. of Mary surrenders
½ messuage, ½ bovate, 2 acres and 1½ roods of land in Wolfdale;

---

[1] From suit of Court unless otherwise stated.

and afterwards William s. of Thomas Fernoule and the said Margery received the same again from the lord, to themselves and the heirs of their bodies [*heredibus suis de se*]. Fine, 4s.

STANLAY.—Robert Gosse, plt., v. William s. of Robert Gounne, for trespass, comes and withdraws ; 4d.

ALVERTHORPE.—John Swan gives 12d. to take ½ bovate of land in Alverthorpe from Juliana Swan, saving all terms therein.

THORNES.—William the Goldsmith gives 6d. to agree with Margery widow of John Wythehundes in a plea of land.

Philip Wolf and John s. of Hobbe to be summoned to answer Margery widow of John Wythehundes in pleas of land.

SANDALE.—Robert the Harper and Thomas de Hollegate have a love-day in a plea of trespass.

The charge against Robert the Walker [*fullo*] is adjourned until the Steward comes.

OSSETE.—Henry the Harpur of Morlay for the escape of a horse in the New Park ; 6d.

. . . .—The charge against the Prior of Lewes, which appears in the Tourn at Halifax, is adjourned until the Steward comes.

John the Rede of Thornhill and John the Strengfelagh to be arrested, when found, for burglary at the house of Thomas del Wode of Fekesby, whereof they were indicted at the Tourn at Rastrick.

Henry s. of Walter s. of Eva de Wakefeld is attached for spilling blood, as indicted at the same Tourn.

It was presented at the same Tourn by the Townships of Crosseland and Querneby that John de Lynthayt seized the cattle of Maude de Seyville, and drove them out of the Earl's fee to Almanbiry, in contempt and to the prejudice of the Earl; and this he did with the consent and advice of John s. of Adam de Locwode. They are both to be distrained.

HOLNE.—The case between William s. of Gilbert de Alstanlay, plt., and John de Holne and John and Adam his sons, for trespass, is adjourned to the next Court, because John de Holne is ill.[1]

. . . .—William del Storthes v. Robert Stirk, for seizing cattle. Pledge, Adam de Wolfday.

Malina wife of Henry the Young of Emmelay to be attached for drawing blood of John de Farnelay's daughter.

Thomas s. of Agnes de Crigeleston, the like, as to Henry his brother.

---

[1] This entry is repeated at the next Court.

Roger the Turnur, Joan his wife, and Alice Proudfot, to be distrained for intrusion. Alice Proudfot made fine at the next Court.

Philip Damson and John de Essetoft to be attached for drawing blood of each other.

German Philcok to be distrained for a stray yearling calf [*vitulus superannatus*].

Henry Poyde to be attached for drawing blood of Thomas the Forester.

WAKEFELD.—Hugh Kay . . . *d.*, William de Castilford 2*d.*, John the Clerk 4*d.*, Henry Bale . . . *d.*, John Cussing 2*d.*, the maid of Laurence s. of Simon 2*d.*, and Robert the Couper's wife 4*d.*, for rushes in the new coppice.

STANLAY.—Robert Coker, for the like [?], 6*d.*

William le Frankisse of Erdeslowe, for . . . . . , 12*d.*

Walter Gonne, for vert, 12*d.*

. . . . .—German Swerd *v.* Richard Wythehundes, for debt. Pledge, Thomas de Wittelay.

John s. of Robert the Clerk of Sandale *v.* William the Grave of Walton, for seizing cattle. Pledge, Robert . . . .

William the Dyker *v.* Phillip s. of Bateman and Beatrice his wife, for trespass. Pledge, John s. of Sibill.

Geoffrey de Birkenschawe *v.* Adam Gerbode, for debt. Pledge, William Taillour.

————

mem. 13*d.*

COURT at Wakefeld on the Friday after the Translation of St Thomas [July 3], in the beginning of the second year of King Edward [1308].[1]

ESSOIGNS.[2]—William de Schepedene, by Thomas de Wittelay. Pledge, John de Toftclyf.

Richard de Bristall, by Robert Skot. Pledge, William del Okes.

John de Totehill, by Thomas de Totehill. Pledge, John de Fekesby.

John de Lepton, by John s. of Henry de Fekesby. Pledge, Hugh de Seyville.

Peter Swerd, by William Margeryman. Pledge, John de la More.

Nicholas de Cailly, by Robert de Cailly. Pledge, Robert de Wyromthorpe.

Thomas de Thornton, by Hugh de Thornton. Pledge, William del Okes.

---

[1] The reign began on July 8th; the Court was held on July 5th.

[2] From suit of Court, unless otherwise stated.

Nicholas le Normaund, by John de Chyvet.   Pledge, Elias de Bretton.

Alan Almot, attorney of Thomas de Burgo, by Robert the Clerk. Pledge, Hugh de Seyville.   He afterwards came.   *Vacat.*

The judgment pending between William de Wakefield, plt., and Thomas Brounsmyth and Emma his wife, is adjourned to the next Court.   It is ordered that all the suitors [*sectatores*] summoned in the matter do come without essoign.

Beatrice de Totehill *v.* Henry del Ryding.   Henry has been distrained by a pig, price 2*s.*, but does not come.   To be better distrained.

Thomas de Totehill and Thomas del Wode, plts., and John del Hole and Margaret his wife, have agreed by license.   John and Margaret put themselves [in mercy], 12*d.*; they admit that they are bound to the plts. in one mark, to be paid at the Assumption of Blessed Mary [Aug. 15].

Agnes widow of Thomas de Fekesby is in mercy for many defaults, . . . *d.*

The same Agnes puts herself [in mercy] against Thomas de Totehill and Thomas del Wode, 6*d.*; she admits that she is bound to them in 8*s.* [?], to be paid at the Assumption of Blessed Mary.

Thomas del Hollegate, [deft.], *v.* Henry s. of Ralph de Crigeleston, for debt, by John Patrik.   Pledge, Henry Erel.

Thomas s. of Roger de Crigeleston [*de eodem*], [deft.], *v.* the same Henry, by Henry Erl.   Pledge, John Patrik.

Alverthorpe.—Margery widow of John Withehundes and Philip Wolf have a love-day at the prayer of the parties.

Sandale.—Thomas del Hollegate gives 6*d.* to agree with Robert the Harpur for trespass.   Pledge, John Cokewald.

Thomas Alayn *v.* Robert le Grubber, on an agreement.   Robert has been distrained by two sheep [*bidentes*], but does not come.   To be better distrained.

Holne.—William del Storthes does not prosecute his claim against Robert Stirk for seizing cattle; 6*d.*

Alverthorpe.—Richard Withehundes, for unjustly detaining 6*d.* from German Swerd, in mercy; 6*d.*   He must pay him before the next Court.

. . . . . .—William the Grave of Walton, deft., *v.* John s. of Robert de Sandale, for seizing a mare, [essoigns] by Alan Almot.   Pledge, ... de Seyville.

William the Dyker, plt., and Philip s. of Bateman and Beatrice his wife, have a love-day in a plea of trespass.

Matthew de Bosco made default at this Court; in mercy.

[THORNES].—Alice Proudfot gives 12*d.* to take a toft with buildings in Thornes from Idonea Proudfot.

ALVERTHORPE.—Walter Bille gives 6*d.* to take ½ an acre in the fields of Neuton from Henry le Nonne.

HOLNE.—John s. of William del Oldefeld gives 2*s.* to take a ¼ of a bovate and a rood of land . . . . with ingress and egress in Holne, from Parnell da. of Benedict de Holne.

SANDALE.—Robert s. of Parnell de Sandale *v.* William del Okes, for debt. Pledge, Robert the Clerk.

Juliana widow of Richard Beusire gives 40*d.* for license to marry off the lord's villein land [*extra nativam terram domini*].

The charge against the prior of Lewes, as appears at the tourn of Halifax,[1] is again adjourned.

John Tropinell *v.* Nicholas [the Smith of Croukeschagh] and John his brother, for trespass. Pledge, Richard . . . . . They are attached by Richard Cosin.

THORNES.—John Kyde *v.* John s. of Hobbe, for . . . . . . Pledge, John s. of Philip.

ALVERTHORPE.—Thomas de Wittelay *v.* John Torald, for trespass. Pledge, William Taillour.

Robert Dodde *v.* Adam Gerbode, on an agreement. Pledge, William Taillour.

. . . .—Adam s. of Maude *v.* Nicholas le Normaund, for seizing cattle. Pledge, Thomas del Hollegate.

Thomas Aleyn *v.* Robert Gonne and Hugh Schayf, for trespass. Pledge, John Torald.

John s. of Philip le Syour *v.* Joan Pescy, for trespass. Pledge, William Albray.

Ralph Wolf *v.* Robert Typet, for debt. Pledge, John Walter's-man [*garcio Walteri*].

Adam the Shepherd of Heppewrth *v.* Thomas s. of Elcok, for trespass. Pledge, Hugh del . . . .

Henry Wyvell *v.* Robert s. of Sarah, for trespass. Pledge, Adam del Mere.

Gilbert del Hill *v.* Peter [the Shepherd?], in a plea of land. Pledge, John s. of Nalk.

---

[1] See *ante*, p. 157.

Agnes de Bretton *v.* Amice de Swynlington, for trespass. Pledge, William Taillour.

Sibil widow of Thomas T . . . . . . *v.* Maude widow of Hugh Dypsy, on an agreement. Pledge, John Hode.

John [Ga]yregrave *v.* Gerbot and Henry Nunne, on an agreement·

[*mem.* 14].

COURT at Wakefeld on Friday, the Morrow of St. Peter ad Vincula [Aug. 1], in the second year of King Edward [1308].

ESSOIGNS.[1]—Robert de Wyveromthorp, by John Cay. Pledge, William Taillour.

Thomas de Thornton, by Hugh de Thornton. Pledge, Matthew de Bosco.

Thomas de Heeton, by Roger de Mirfeld. Pledge, John de Thinglowe.

Thomas de Seyville, attorney of Margaret de Neville, by John de Roclay. Pledge, Hugh de Seyville.

John de Lepton, by Robert de Horbiry. Pledge, John de la More.

Elias de Birton, by William the Serjeant. Pledge, Richard de Bristall.

William the Grave of Walton, deft., *v.* John s. of Robert the Clerk of Sandale, for taking a mare, by Henry s. of Gregory de Walton. Pledge, Alan Almot.

Thomas de Wytteley, plt., *v.* John Torald, on an agreement, by William Margery-knave. Pledge, William Taillour.

Henry Eril fined 6*d.* for not having Thomas del Hollegate, for whose essoign he was pledge at the last Court. Thomas to be distrained to answer Henry s. of Ralph de Crigeleston, for debt.

John Patrik similarly fined 6*d.* for not having Thomas s. of Roger de Crigeleston. Thomas to be distrained to answer Henry s. of Ralph, for debt.

Robert the Walker fined . . . . . for not prosecuting his suits against Elias de Danecastre, Thomas de Hollegate and John del Hollegate, for debt.

THORNES.—Margery widow of John Wythehundes and Philip Wolf have agreed; 3*d.*

A piece [*placea*] of meadow, for which the said Margery is suing John s. of Hobbe, to be seised into the Earl's hand for John's default.

---

[1] From suit of Court, unless otherwise stated.

William le Dyker, plt., and Philip s. of Bateman and Beatrice his wife, defts have a love-day.

Gilbert de Alstanley and his sons put themselves in mercy against John de Holne and his sons, for trespass.

Malina da. of Henry le Young, to be attached for shedding the blood of the daughter of John de Farnelay.

Thomas s. of Agnes de Crigeleston, to be attached for the blood of Henry his brother.

Philip Damson and John de Essetoft, attached for shedding each other's blood.

German Filcok, to be distrained for detaining a stray yearling calf.

Henry Poyde, to be distrained for shedding blood of Thomas the Forester.

Gilbert del Hill and Peter the Shepherd agree by license; Gilbert, for himself and his heirs, quitclaims to Peter all right in a bovate of land in Sandale. Peter gives 2s. for the recognition.

. . . .—William s. of Hugh de Horbiry gives 10s. to take 2 bovates of land in Horbiry as a heriot after the death of [? his father].

[*The remainder of this membrane is mutilated. The names of* Hugh Modysowel, John s. of Isabel, *and* John s. of Thomas Caynock, *can be made out*].

[*mem.* 14d.]

COURT at Wakefield on Friday the Eve of St. Bartholomew the Apostle [Aug. 24], in the second year [1308].

ESSOIGNS.[1]—Thomas de Heeton, by Thomas de Witlay. Pledge, Hugh de Seyville.

Peter Swerd, by William the Serjeant. Pledge, Thomas de Thornton.

Matthew de Bosco, by Adam de Werlouley. Pledge, John de Mora.

John de Totehill, by Robert de Kelesthorp [Kettlesthorpe]. Pledge, Robert de Wyverumthorpe.

William de Chepedene, by William the Smith. Pledge, Nicholas de Cailly.

Thomas de Seyville, attorney of Margaret de Neville, by Thomas de Derton. Pledge, Robert the Clerk.

Alan Almot, attorney of Thomas de Burgh, by John de Conyngb[urgh]. Pledge, William Taillour.

John s. of Robert the Clerk of Sandale, plt., *v.* William the Grave of Walton, for taking a mare, by Robert the· Clerk. Pledge, Robert

---

[1] From suit of Court, unless otherwise stated.

At-Well of Sandale. As William essoigned at the last Court, and does not come, he, his essoigner and pledge, in mercy.

Thomas de Holgate and Thomas s. of Roger de Grigeleston, fined 6d. each for many defaults.

Henry s. of Ralph v. Thomas de Hollegate and Thomas s. of Roger, for debt. They come, and crave the help [*auxilium*] of Anabel widow of Swayn. Let her be distrained to come to the next Court.

Philip s. of Bateman v. William le Dyker, for trespass. Pledge, William the Serjeant.

Amice de Swynlington, fined 2d. for a false claim against John de Flansowe.

ALVERTHORPE.—Henry le Nonne, fined 12d. for breaking the Earl's fold.

SANDALE.—John s. of Thomas the Carpenter of Walton does fealty for 5 roods of land in Sandale, and pays 18d. for a relief. Pledge, Robert the Clerk of Sandale.

. . . .—Richard s. of Richard de la Grene gives 6d. to take ½ an acre of new land . . . . close to his tenement ; rent, 3d.

Richard de Birton gives 5s. to take 5 acres of new land . . . . . . in different places ; rent, 2s. 6d.

Adam the Shepherd gives 12d. to take a toft, and 7¼ acres of land in Heppeworth from Robert s. of John s. of Gilbert, in exchange for 7½ acres of land there from Adam. Robert likewise pays 12d.

Alice da. of Adam de Wulvedale surrenders half of a house, a barn and 8 acres ½ rood of land in Wolvedale, and . . . . of Thomas . . . . , and the said Alice to take them again . . . .

[*The remainder is mutilated.*]

[*mem.* 15.] Still on the Eve of St. Bartholomew.

THORNES.—Agnes da. of Roger de Snaypethorp, for an escape in the new park, 6d.

John de la Haye, 6d. ; Robert s. of Robert de Flansowe, 2s. ; and Ivo the Smith of Snaypethorpe, 12d. ; for escapes.

[? ALVERTHORPE.]—Robert Gerbode, 4d. ; Richard s. of Broun, 2s. ; Alice da. of Richard Broun, 12d. ; Magge Wynter, 12d. ; Ralph Wolf, 14d. ; Robert Campion, 6d. ; Nicholas de Batelay, 6d. ; Henry del Bothem, 2s. 2d. ; Adam Wolf, 12d. ; Christiana Gerbode, 6d. ; and Henry Stirthover, 6d. ; for escapes.

. . . .—John Goure and John Costell, 3s. 6d. ; Little Adam, 6d. ; for escapes.

THORNES.—Robert le Young, 2s.; German Filcok, 3s.; Henry Dernelove, 14d.; John Rased, 6d.; Thomas de Ludeham, 5d.; John Cay, 6d.; John Wilcok, 6d.; Robert Clement, 4d.; and John Mous, 4d.; for escapes.

Walter Ape, 2d.; Sybil la Carettere, 2d.; and Adam Torketro, 3d.; for dry wood.

STANLAY.—Peter s. of Geppe de Erdeslowe, for an escape, 14d. Pledge, Robert de Wyr[umthorpe ?].

Broun de Wyrumthorpe, for dry wood, 4d.

Adam s. of Cote, 12d.; Robert de Batelay, 5d.; and Adam Spink, 3d.; for escapes.

John s. of Philip, and Gelle de Stanlay, 6d. each ; for dry wood.

HOLNE.—Peter de Wildborleyes, 2s.; Peter the Milner, 4d.; Richard the Grave, 4d.; and Emma Fabian, 3d.; for escapes.

ALVERTHORPE.—John del Grenegate v. Walter del Hill, for debt. Pledge, John Getour.

John Thorald v. John Swan, for trespass. Pledge, Adam Gerbode.

John Cussing v. Robert Archur, for trespass. Pledge, Henry le Nonne.

———

COURT at Wakefeld on Friday after the Nativity of Blessed Mary [Sept. 8], in the year, etc. [1308].

ESSOIGNS.[1]—Nicholas le Normaund, by John Patrik. Pledge, Edmund le Normaung [sic].

John s. of Henry de Lepton, by William de Lepton. Pledge, Elias de Birton.

John de la More, by John, his son. Pledge, William the Serjeant.

William de Rastrik, by John de Totehill. Pledge, Matthew de Bosco.

Peter Swerd, by William Margery. Same pledge.

Nicholas de . . . .

. . . . de Chypedene . . . .

Alan Almot, attorney . . . .

[*The remainder of this membrane is mutilated.*]

[*mem.* 15d.]

SANDALE.—Agnes de Ossete surrenders 2 bovates of land, with buildings, in Sandale, and a bovate called Rodeland, to John s. of Cicely de Sandale [?], and Agnes, daughter . . . . to them and the heirs of their bodies after her own death. Fine, 6s. 8d.

HORBIRY.—Maude da. of Philip s. of William de Horbiry gives 2s. to take a bovate of land in . . . . . . , as a heriot after the death

———

[1] From suit of Court, unless otherwise stated.

of her father. She also pays 12d. for license to marry. She afterwards surrenders the land, and Ralph Wolf and she take it again, to hold to themselves and the heirs of their bodies. Fine, 2s.

HOLNE.—William de Heitfeld gives 12d. to take a messuage and 7 acres of land in Wolvedale, from Jordan the Milner.

Nicholas the Smith of Crouschagh and John his brother, to be attached to answer John Tropenell, for trespass.

Nicholas le Normaund, to be distrained to answer Adam s. of Maude de Crigileston.

Agnes de Bretton *v.* Amice de Swynligton, for trespass.

Maude Dipsi, to be attached for contempt and to answer Sibil widow of Thomas Tope [?]

Robert de Ketelesthorp *v.* Adam s. of Stephen de Sandale.

William de Lithesles, to be attached to answer Alice widow of Adam de Horton.

OSSETE.—Richard s. of John de Goukethorp *v.* Robert Sonneman, for trespass. Pledge, Adam de Chikinlay.

SANDALE.—Warner de Carleton *v.* Robert s. of Richard Beusire, for trespass. Pledge, Thomas del Holgate.

John s. of Robert the Clerk of Sandale *v.* William the Grave of Walton, for seizing cattle. Pledge, Robert the Clerk. William is attached by John s. of Malle de Walton.

Elias de Danecastre *v.* Thomas s. of Pelle and Magota de Ketelesthorp, for debt.

Herbage.

SOURBY.—From the Herbage

of Ryburnedene, sold in gross this year, 5s.

of Mancanholemore, sold in gross . . . . . 13s. 4d.

of Cromtonstall, in gross, ... 40s.

of Marschagh and Netteltonstall, sold, . . 33s. 4d.

of Haderschelf and Sourby, ... 26s. 8d.

of Haytingges, ... 33s. 4d.

of Saltonstall, ... 20s.

HOLNE.— of Holnefrith . . . . per ann. . . . . . 27s. 5d.

DEWISBIRY.— . . . . 40s.

[*The remainder is mutilated.*]

[*mem.* 1.]

ROLL FOR 2 AND 3 EDWARD II, 1308-9.

Pleas and Perquisites of the Soke of Wakefeld from Michaelmas in the second year of King Edward son of King Edward unto the Michaelmas following; in the time of John de Danecastre, then Steward.

COURT at Wakefeld on Friday after Michaelmas, in the above year [1308].

ESSOIGNS.[1]—William s. of William de Bello monte, by Robert de Bello monte. Pledge, John de Lepton.

Robert de Wyveromthorpe, by John Cay. Pledge, William Taillour.

John s. of John de Solande, by John his father. Pledge, Thomas de Witlay.

Richard de Bristall, by William the Pinder. Pledge, John de Toftclif.

Thomas de Seyville, by Hugh de Seyville. Pledge, John de Rockelay.

Thomas de Thornton, by Hugh de Thornton. Pledge, John de Toftclif.

John de la More, by John his son. Pledge, Henry de Wakefeld.

William the Grave of Walton, for many defaults. 6*d.* Pledge, Alan Almot.

John s. of Robert the Clerk of Sandale, 6*d.*, for not prosecuting suit against the said William.

Henry del Ryding, deft., essoigns against Beatrice de Totehill, for debt, by William Margeryman. Pledge, John his son

John Cussing against Robert Archur, for trespass, by the same. Pledge, John Patrik.

Judgment given for defts. on the complaint of William de Wakefeld against Thomas le Brounsmyth and Emma his wife; plt. fined 12*d.*

Adam s. of Maude de Crigeleston, plt., essoigns against Nicholas le Normaund, for seizing cattle, by Henry s. of Gregory de Walton. Pledge, Alan Almot.

ALVERTHORPE.—An inquisition finds that John Torald ousted Thomas de Wittelay from the crop of a rood of land, worth 2*s.* 3*d.* Fine, 6*d.* Pledge, Adam Gerbode.

Walter del Hill, fined 12*d.* for unjust detention against John de Grenegate. Pledges, Adam Gerbode and Henry del Bothem.

---

[1] From suit of Court, unless otherwise stated.

SANDALE.—Robert s. of Parnell de Sandale craves license to withdraw his complaint against William del Okes, because it concerns a marriage [*quia tanget matrimonium*].[1] It is granted.

Henry Poyde, indicted at the last Tourn for shedding Thomas the Forester's blood, 6d. Pledge, William the Serjeant.

STANLAY.—Master John, Rector of the Schools, gives 2s to take a bovate of land in Ouchethorpe fields from John Wasse and Margery, his wife, for 12 years.

THORNES.—Margery widow of John Wythehundes recovers from John s. of Hobbe ½ an acre of land and 5 parcels of meadow, as her dower after the death of her husband; deft. fined 4d.

John Kyde, fined 4d. for a false claim against John s. of Hobbe.

Nicholas de Croukeschagh and John his brother, to be attached to answer John Tropenell, for trespass.

Agnes de Bretton and Amice de Swinligton have a love-day.

ALVERTHORPE.—Robert Dodde and Adam Gerbode agree by license; 6d.

OSSETE.—Richard s. of John de Goukethorpe fined 6d. for not prosecuting suit against Robert Sonneman, for trespass.

SANDALE.—Warner de Carleton and Robert s. of Richard Beusire agree by license; 6d.

Magota de Ketelesthorpe and Thomas s. of Pelle admit that they owe 2s. 6d. to Elias de Dancastre. Fine 2d.

OSSETE.—Richard the Pinder of Ossete surrenders a bovate of land in Ossete to Thomas his son; Thomas is to enter on one half at once, on the other after his father's death. Fine, 12d.

ALVERTHORPE.—William Grenehod gives 6d. to take a "brodedale" of meadow in Alverthorpe from William Hoskell, for 20 years. [*mem.* 1d.]

OSSETE.—John de Gailgrave[2] takes 4 acres of new land of the waste in Haytelay, inside the pale of the new park, for 6 years; rent, 2s. He pays no fine, because he is in the Earl's service.

HOLNE.—John s. of John de Littelwode gives 5s. for 5 acres of new land of the waste in Alstanlay; rent, 2s. 6d.

John s. of Richard s. of Matthew gives 3s. for 3 acres of new land of the waste in Fouleston; rent, 18d.

Peter del Peke gives 12d. to take 1 acre of new land from the waste in Willestubbing; rent, 6d.

---

[1] And therefore presumably had to go to an Ecclesiastical Court.
[2] *Sic;* Gargrave.

Robert de Paldeneleyes gives 12*d* to take 4 acres of land in Wolvedale from John le Dene; also 6*d*. for an acre of land there from Robert del Scoles; and 6*d*. for ½ an acre of new land from the waste there; rent, 3*d*.

SOURBY.—William de Sounderland gives 10*s*. for 34 acres of new land from the waste in Luddingdene; rent, 17*s*.;—and 3*s*. 4*d*. for 9 acres of land in Salstonstall, near the Overheyng; rent 3*s*., as he was accustomed to pay to Sir John de Horbiry.

Richard the Smith of Werlouley gives 12*d*. for 1½ acres of new land from the waste in Werlouley in Rawepithel; rent, 9*d*.

William del Bothem gives 18*d*. for 3 acres of new land from the waste in Sourby, between Riburn and Calder, half an acre lying in le Holme beyond [*extra*] Calder; rent, 18*d*.

ALVERTHORPE.—John Goure gives 3*s*. 4*d*. to take 12 acres of land in Alverthorpe from William Hoskell, at the expiration of a term of 5 years which the heirs of Henry de Swynlington have therein; with ingress and egress as William has been accustomed to have.

HOLNE.—Thomas s. of Robert de Fouleston gives 12*d*. for an acre of new land from the waste in Alstanlay; rent, 6*d*.

Gilbert s. of Richard del Bothe gives 6*s*. for 6 acres there; rent, ·3*s*.

Robert s. of Matthew del Scoles gives 2*s*. for 2¼ acres of new land from the waste under Butterlaynabbe; rent, 13½*d*.

SOURBY.—Adam s. of Ivo de Werlouleye gives 12*d*. for 2 acres[1] in Werlouleye at Longbothem; rent, 12*d*.

William the Mercer and Alice his wife give 12*d*. for 2 acres[1] in Sourby; rent, 12*d*.

John del Gledeholt gives 12*d*. for 2 acres[1] in Werlouleye; rent, 12*d*.

John del Rediker gives 2*s*. for 3 acres[1] by le Mithomrode; rent, 18*d*.

John Swift gives 12*d*. for 2 acres[1] in le Lithesles; rent, 12*d*.

William the Smith of Soland gives 2*s*. 6*d*. for 5 acres[1] in Ryburnedene; rent, 2*s*. 6*d*.

John s. of John gives 3*d*. for ½ an acre[1] in Soland; rent, 3*d*.

Thomas le Crouder gives 3*d*. for ½ an acre[1] there; rent, 3*d*.

Adam s. of Elias the Milner gives 2*s*. 6*d*. for 5 acres[1] in Werlouleye wood; rent, 2*s*. 6*d*.

Adam le Crouder gives 6*d*. for one acre[1] in Ryburnedene, under the Berecroft; rent, 6*d*.

John the Milner of Sourby gives 3*d*. for half an acre[1] in Ryburnedene; rent, 3*d*.

Thomas Lely gives 12*d* for 2 acres[1] in le Blacwode; rent, 12*d*.

---

[1] All these are new land from the waste.

Juliana da. of Henry gives 6d. for a piece of land from the waste in Sourby, 24 feet by 18 feet; rent, 1½d.

Robert s. of Robert de Baddeswrth gives 18d. to take 3 acres[1] under Helileye; rent, 18d.

[*mem.* 2.]

John s. of Roger gives 18d. for 3 acres[1] in Moildelaghton; rent, 18d.

Robert s. of John Hodde gives 2s. 3d. for 4 acres[1] in Blacwode; rent, 2s.

Richard del Feild gives 6d. for one acre[1] under Riburnedene; rent, 6d.

Henry de Luddingdene gives 12d. for 1¾ acres[1] in Riburnedene; rent, 10½d.

Margaret de Neville gives 3s. 4d. for respite of suit till Michaelmas.

Reynald le Flemaung, 4s.; Robert le Flemang, 2s.; John de Querneby, 2s.; Thomas de Langfeld, 3s. 4d.; John de Trimyngham, 12d. (because he is poor); Matthew de Bosco of Willeys, 2s.; John de Crosland, 12d.; William Wildebore, 12d. (because he is poor); and John s. of John de Soland, 2s.; for the like.

WAKEFELD.—Hugh Cay, 4d.; William Wolmere, 6d.; Joan de Aula, 4d.; John Harilull [?], 1d.; and Adam the Glover, 1d.; for escape of pigs.

Walter the Cook, 2d.; the maid of Elias Tirsi, 2d.; John the Cobbler, 4d.; John Leche, 2d.; the maids of Robert Lyftfast and Henry Nauthird, 1d. and 2d.; William Ilhore's son, 2d.; and William Beuchaunt's maid, 2d.; for dry wood.

Philip Damoysell, 12d.; and John Taillour, 3d.; for escapes of pigs.

ALVERTHORPE.—John de Flansowe, for dry wood, 2d.

Robert Gerbode, 3d.; and John Schirlock, 2d.; for escapes.

STANLAY.—Philip le Syour, 3d.; Robert s. of Walter, 2d.; Robert del Spen, 4d.; Richard Longschaunk, 2d.; Adam le Hewar, 1d.; and Richard del Bothem, 2d.; for escapes.

Richard del Kerre, because he would not come to the driving of the lord's chase [*quia noluit venire ad stabil' chacie domini*], 6s. 8d.

William del Rode, for escape of two horses, 12d.

HIPERUM.—Ralph de Bairstowe's son, 3d.; the wives of Roger de Brighouses, 3d., and Richard the Tailor, 2d.; for dry wood.

Bate del Bothes, 3d.; for an escape.

SOURBY.—A stray heifer [*pultra*] sold to William de Locwode, 3s.

Two stray heifers sold to John de Wauton, 10s.

---

[1] All these are new land from the waste.

L

ALVERTHORPE.—Richard Wythehundes *v.* William Hoskell, for debt. Pledge, Adam Gerbode.

William Wolmer *v.* Henry le Nonne, for debt. Pledge, Robert de Castelford.

THORNES.—Eva da. of Thomas s. of Hawe *v.* Robert s. of Robert de Flansowe, for trespass. Pledge, Nicholas de Batelay.

SOURBY.—Solande and Werlouleye mills are demised this year to John s. of John de Northlande and Adam de Midelton, for 46*s.* 8*d.* Pledges, William Taillour and John de Gledeholt.

COURT at Wakefeld on Friday, the Feast of St. Luke the Evangelist [Oct. 18], 2 Edward II [1308].

ESSOIGNS.[1]—John de Lepton, by Thomas de Wittelay. Pledge, Hugh de Seyville.

Alan Almot, attorney of Thomas de Burgh, by Thomas Thorald. Pledge, Thomas de Heeton.

Peter Swerd, by William Margeryman. Pledge, John de Toftclif.

Thomas del Bellehouse, by John de Toftclif. Pledge, Richard de Bristall.

William de Chipedene, by William the Serjeant. Pledge, Thomas de Thornton.

Beatrice de Totehill *v.* Henry del Ryding, in a plea of debt, by Roger de Rastrik. Pledge, William de Rastrik. Henry afterwards came, and was fined 12*d.* for agreeing without license.

John s. of Robert the Clerk *v.* William the Grave of Walton, for seizing cattle, by Robert the Clerk. Pledge, William del Okes.

Adam s. of Maude de Crigeleston, plt., *v.* Nicholas le Normaund, for seizing cattle, by John de Burton. Pledge, Richard Dandeheir.

John Cussing *v.* Robert Archur, for trespass, by William Margeriman. Pledge, Henry s. of German.

Nicholas de Croweschawe, 12*d.*, for many defaults. Pledge, William de Saltonstall.

John Tropenell *v.* Nicholas de Croweschawe, for coming to the new mill, where John was miller, and breaking the door, and assaulting him. An inquisition is ordered.

[*mem.* 2d.]

SANDALE.—John s. of Henry del Wodethorpe gives 40*d.* to take ½ a bovate of land in Sandale from Robert the Harpur.

---

[1] From suit of Court, unless otherwise stated.

Robert s. ,of Parnell gives 12d. to take 3½ acres in Sandale from Robert the Harpur.

HOLNE.—Adam the Shepherd of Fouleston gives 3s. to take 1 bovate, 2 acres, and 1 rood of land in Fouleston, as a heriot after the death of Henry, his brother, whose heir he is.

Thomas s. of Thomas gives 12d. to take ⅔ of a bovate in Heppewrth from Agnes widow of William [que fuit Willelmi], for 16 years.

ALVERTHORPE.—William s. of Thomas takes ½ a rood[1] in Alverthorpe; rent, 1½d.

HOLNE.—Alan del Dam takes one acre[1] at le Thormholme; 6d. rent, and gives 12d. for entry.

Hugh del Hole gives 3s. for 3 acres[1] in Longlayhirst; rent, 18d.

Richard s. of Michael and Eva his wife give 4s. for 4 acres[1] on the road in Stacwode; rent, 2s.

Adam de Butterlay gives 12d. for one acre[1] at Butterlay; rent, 6d.

Thomas s. of Simon gives 12d. for one acre[1] in Alaynlay; rent, 6d.

WAKEFELD.—German Philcok gives 6d. to take a piece of waste land [unam placeam de vasto] in Wakefeld market, between his two cloth booths [inter duas bothas suas drapar'], 12 feet by 5 feet; rent, ½d.

William s. of William de Bello monte and John de Totehill, to be distrained for defaults.

Order to distrain further Robert le Grubber, who has been distrained by two sheep, to answer Thomas Alayn, touching an agreement. Thomas has license to suspend his suit till Robert can be better distrained [? instriciari].

HOLNE.—Elias Walleraven v. Richard del Bothe, in a plea of land. Pledge, John del Bothe.

HIPERUM.—Roger de Clifton v. Roger del Clif, for assault. Pledge, William de Bothes. Deft. is attached by Roger de Brighouses.

Adam Gerbode v. German Filcok, for seizing a mare. Pledge, William servant of Margery.[2]

HOLNE.—William de Heitfeld v. Nicholas s. of Nicholas Keneward, for debt. Pledge, William Mous.

ALVERTHORPE.—Richard Withehundes v. Adam Gerbode, for seizing a cow. Pledge, John de Flansowe.

---

[1] All these are new land from the waste.
[2] No doubt identical with William Margeryman, who is mentioned elsewhere.

Adam Gerbode *v.* Robert the Walker, for seizing a mare. Pledge, William Margeriman [?]

STANLAY.—John the Forester *v.* Simon Tyting and Henry his son, for trespass. Pledge, John Poket.

———

[*mem.* 3.]

COURT at Wakefeld on Friday after the Feast of St. Martin [Nov. 11], 2 Edward II [1308].

ESSOIGNS.[1]—Thomas de Heeton, by Roger Assolf. Pledge, John de Querneby.

Nicholas de Cailly, by Hugh his son. Pleige, Thomas de Thornton.

Robert de Wyrumthorpe, by John Damoysell. Pledge, John Patriks.

Peter Swerd, by William Margeriman. Pledge, Richard de Bristall.

William de Chepedene, by John Thorald. Pledge, John de Toftclif.

Robert de la Grene of Ossete, by Thomas Witlay. Pledge, Hugh de Seyville.

William s. of William de Bello monte pays 2*s.* for default and for respite of suit till Michaelmas.

Thomas de Dronesfeld, 6*d.*, and John de Totehill, 2*s.*, for the like.

ALVERTHORPE.—William Hoskell, for unjustly detaining 18*d.* against Richard Withehundes; fine, 3*d.* Pledge, William Margeriman.

HOLNE.—Elias Walleraven and Richard del Bothe agree; 4*d.*

SANDALE.—Robert s. of John de Crigeleston gives 12*d.* to take ½ an acre of land in Crigeleston from William s. of Thomas.

John s. of William de Plegwik gives 3*s.* to take ½ a bovate in Neubigging from John s. of Swayn.

Hugh Cay gives 6*d.* to take one acre in Sandale from Robert the Clerk, for 20 years.

ALVERTHORPE.—William Grenehod gives 6*d.* to take 1¾ acres in Alverthorpe from John de Flansowe, for 20 years.

HOLNE.—William s. of Matthew de Mora gives 12*d.* for 1 acre[2] in le Blakebanck; rent, 6*d.*

Matthew s. of Thomas gives 18*d.* for 1½ acres[2] in le Breriker; rent, 9*d.*

Thomas s. of Herbert gives 18*d.* for 1½ acres[2] at Butterlay; rent, 9*d.*

Adam de Wolvedale gives 6*d.* for ½ an acre[2] under his garden in Wolvedale; rent, 3*d.*

———

[1] From suit of Court, unless otherwise stated.

[2] All these are new land from the waste.

John de Crouschagh, fined 6d for many defaults.

John Tropynell, plt., and Nicholas de Krouschagh and John, his brother, agree by license. Defts. fined 12d. Pledges, John de Wrtelay and William Margeriman.

William s. of William the Gardyner and Elizabeth his wife v. Elias Bulnays, for debt. Pledge, John Cay.

Robert s. of Hugh del Holgate v. Margery Hamund, on an agreement. Pledge, William Taillour.

ALVERTHORPE.—Robert de Stanlay v. Robert s. of Ralph de Ouchethorpe, for debt. Pledge, John Chaffar.

An inquisition finds that John Swayn ousted John Thorald from a crop of oats on 3 roods of land, worth 2s. 3d.; fine, 4d.

The suit between Alice widow of Adam Broun and William de Lithesles, for trespass, is respited because Alice is ill.

HOLNE.—The inquisition finds that Nicholas s. of Nicholas Keneward assaulted William the Forester in Stacwode, and maliciously charged him with sundry offences committed in his bailiwick. Nicholas must satisfy William, and pay a fine of 2s. And as Nicholas threatened him of life and limb, he is attached to keep the peace by the mainprise of Richard del Bothe, Hugh del Hole, William Wodemous, William del Dene, Richard le Syour, and Robert de Skoles.

STANLAY.—John Fox the forester, plt., and Simon Tyting and Henry his son, agree by license. Defts. pay 12d.

ALVERTHORPE.—Robert s. of Ralph de Ouchethorpe, 3d., for not coming.

William Hoskell v. Richard Wythehundes, for debt. Pledge, Adam Gerbode.

HOLNE.—Adam Strecayse v. Adam de la Grene, for trespass. Pledge, Richard de Cartewrth.

SANDALE.—Robert the Forester of Thurstanhagh v. John Tropinell, for slander, in charging him with giving away the Earl's brush wood [*buscham*] at his own pleasure, and allowing strangers and outsiders [*extraneos homines et forinsecos*] to do evil in his bailiwick, to the Earl's very great damage. An inquisition is ordered.

HIPERUM.—John del Holewaye, 6d.; Alcok le Quelewrigh,[1] 6d.; Thomas s. of Alote, 4d.; and Nabbe s. of Broun, 6d.; for cutting wood.

William del Hynganderode, Roger de Brighouses, William Scharppe, John del Rode, and Alexander de Brighouses, 3d. each; for escapes.

HOLNE.—John de Holne, 12d.; William del Bothe, 3d.; Thomas s. of Gilbert, 3d.; William del Oldefeld, 12d.; William Strekeaise, 9d.;

---

[1] Wheelwright.

Emma del Oldefeld, 3*d.*; William de Carlecotes, 6*d.*; John s. of Geoffrey, 3*d.*; John del Bothe, 3*d.*; and William de Langlay, 3*d.*; for escapes.

[*mem.* 3d.]

WAKEFELD.—Hugh the Soldier [*mercenarius*][1], 2*d.*; Richard s. of Junne [?], 1*d.*; Henry Leper, 2*d.*; Robert Hodde, 2*d.*; Henry the Nauthird, 2*d.*; and Philip de Castelford, 2*d.*; for dry wood.

ALVERTHORPE.—Robert Hode of Neuton, 2*d.*; Richard Longschank, 2*d.*; and Richard the Tanner, 1*d.*; for dry wood.

Alice da. of Robert, 2*d.*; and Christiana Gerbode, 3*d.*; for escapes.

HORBIRY.—John, servant [*serviens*] of the Chaplain, and John Caynock, 2*d.* each; for escapes.

COURT at Wakefeld on Friday, the Feast of St. Nicholas [Dec. 6], 2 Edward II [1308].

ESSOIGNS.[2]—Elias de Birton, by William Margeryman. Pledge, Adam de Helay.

John de Lepton, by Thomas de Wittelay. Pledge, Hugh de Seyville.

Thomas del Bellehouse, by John de Solande. Pledge, William del Okes.

Richard de Bristall, by William de Normanton. Pledge, William de Chipedene.

Isabel the Cook [*la Keuwe*], by John the Clerk. Pledge, Peter Swerd.

Thomas de Thornton, by Hugh de Thornton. Pledge, John de Mora.

Adam s. of Maude de Crigeleston, plt., *v.* Nicholas le Normaund, for seizing cattle. A day is given, because Nicholas appeared [*optulit se*].

William the Grave of Walton *v.* John s. of Robert the Clerk of Sandale, for seizing cattle, by Jordan del Kerre. Pledge, Alan Almot.

OSSETE.—Alice widow of Adam Broun, fined 3*d.*, for not prosecuting her suit against William de Lytheseles.

HOLNE.—Robert s. of Sarah gives 18*d.* to take 1½ acres of new land of the waste in Butterlay; rent, 9*d.*

Matthew de Langlay gives 2*s.* for two acres of new land of the waste in le Brendeleyhirst; rent, 12*d.*

THORNES.—John Graffard, 18*d.*; Alice, his mother, 2*d.*; Ivo the Smith, 4*d.*; John de la Haye, 2*d.*; Roger Trailment, 2*d.*; William s.

---

[1] See *ante*, p. 123, note.
[2] From suit of Court, unless otherwise stated.

of Agnes, 2*d.*; John Costell, 2*d.*; and Adam the Forester, 3*d.*; for escapes.

OSSETE.—Richard s. of John, 6*d.*; and Robert Pees, 3*d.*; for escapes.

Richard Passemer, 1*d.*, for dry wood.

SOURBY.—Adam Migge *v.* William Swaype, in a plea of land. Pledge, John the Webbester.

John the Webster [*textor*] *v.* William Swaype, in a plea of land. Pledge, Adam Migge.

Amabel del Bothem *v.* Thomas de Connale, for dower.   Pledge, Robert de Saltonstall.

William s. of Walter de Chepelay *v.* Henry de Godelay, for detaining a bullock [*bovettus*].   Pledge, Roger de Brighouses.

HIPERUM.—Roger del Clif *v.* John de Schepelay, in a plea of land.   Pledge, Roger del Clifton.

RASTRIK.—Thomas de Totehill *v.* Robert de Lythrige, for debt. Pledge, William s. of Peter.   And also *v.* Thomas s. of Christiana de Crosland, for trespass.   Pledge, Henry s. of John.

HOLNE.—Adam del Skoles *v.* Nicholas del Clif, for trespass. Pledge, Thomas Bridde.

Margery de Thoung *v.* Juliana da. of John de Holne, for trespass. Pledge, Hugh del Hole.

Adam Benne *v.* Adam le Waynwrith, for trespass.   Pledge, John the Grave.

HIPERUM.—Roger de Brighouses junior gives 18*d.* for license to marry Isabel and Cicely, his daughters.

HOLNE.—Jordan the Milner gives 3*s.* to take 3 acres[1] in Thoung wood ; rent, 18*d.*

Robert Stirk gives 18*d.* to take 1½ acres[1] in Thoung hirst ; rent, 9*d.*

Richard le Syour gives 18*d.* to take 1½ acres[1] in Wadehole ; rent, 9*d.*

SANDALE.—John Tropinell, fined 2*s.*, and to pay damages, for slandering Richard the Forester of Thurstanhagh.   Pledges, Thomas s. of Pelle and William s. of Robert.

ALVERTHORPE.—Henry le Nunne and Robert s. of Ralph de Ouchethorpe are fined 6*d.*, and must pay damages for detaining 400 faggots [*fagot'*] from Robert de Stanley.

STANLAY.—Andrew Pogge, fined 4*d.* for not coming.

GRAVES.—Andrew Pogge is elected Grave of Stanley, and sworn.

Richard s. of John de Chikinlay, Grave of Ossete.

---

[1] All these are new land from the waste.

John Cokewald remains Grave of Sandale, as before.

Robert s. of Ralph de Ouchethorpe is elected Grave of Alverthorpe.

Ralph Bate, Grave of Thornes.

THORNES.—Robert s. of Robert de Flansowe, fined 4*d.* for detaining 18*d.* from Eva da. of Thomas s. of Hawe. The Grave to levy [the amount].

ALVERTHORPE.—Robert Estrild gives 12*d.* to take an acre in le Fall and ½ an acre in le Morecroft, from William de Neuton.

Adam s. of Laurence del Clif gives 12*d.* to take 3 acres of land and ½ an acre of meadow in Alverthorpe, from Quenilda da. of Hugh, for 20 years.

SANDALE.—Margery Hamund gives 6*d.* to agree with Robert s. of Hugh de Hollegate, for trespass.

SOURBY.—Adam s. of Ivo de Werlouleye *v.* Hugh s. of Reynald and Thomas de Roildesceade [?], for debt.

ALVERTHORPE.—John Rate *v.* Adam s. of Henry de Goukethorpe, for trespass. Pledge, Henry del Bothem.

Quenilda da. of Hugh *v.* Adam Gerbode and John his servant [*garcio*]. Pledge, Adam s. of Lance.

mem. 4.

COURT at Halifax on Monday after the Feast of St. Nicholas [Dec. 6], 2 Edward II, [1308].

SOURBY.—Henry del Hollegate is elected Grave of Sourby, and sworn.

Amabel del Bothem claims dower in 2 acres of land in Sourby, due to her on the death of Adam de Connale, her late husband, from which Thomas de Cónnale is ousting her. He admits it, and must satisfy her; fine, 3*d.*

John the Webster and William Swaype agree by license, in a plea of land. William is fined 6*d.*

Richard del Feild gives 3*s.* 4*d.* to take 1½ bovates of land in Sourby from Thomas del Feild.

Thomas del Feild gives 2*s.* to take ½ bovate of land in the same place [*in eadem sitis*] from Richard s. of Alote.

Ellen da. of Elias de Sourby gives 6*d.* to take a rood of land from Thomas del Feild.

Henry del Hollegate, fined 40*d.* for contempt.

William Yoten is appointed Forester in Sourbischire at Wathesside. Pledges, John Hodde, Thomas del Feild, Hugh s. of Reynald de Werlouley, John de Waddeswrth, Robert de Saltonstall, John de Solande, Roger Rotell, and Hugh de Lithesles.

William de Sotehill, for an escape in Ayricdene, 16*d.*

John Culpon, 10*d.*; John del Rediker, 8*d.*; John s. of Hugh the Hermite, 6*d.*; Elias de Haderschelf, 4*d.*; John s. of Hugh de Langlay, 3*d.*; Thomas s. of John de Miglay, 1*d.*; Hancok the Harpur of Dewisbiry, 3*d.*; Henry del Hollegate, 12*d.*; Adam s. of Ivo, 6*d.*; Roger Rottell, 3*d.*; Adam At-town-head [*ad capud ville*] of Miglay, 8*d.*; William del Croft of Mancanholes, 3*d.*; Richard de Wollerenwalle, 3*d.*; Adam del Kirkeschagh, 4*d.*; Juliana Wade, 3*d.*; Nelle s. of Ivo, 4*d.*; for escapes.

Adam s. of Elias the Milner and John Swift, for cutting branches, 3*d.* each.

Thomas del Skoles, for an escape, 3*d.* Pledge, Peter de Barkesland.

William de Greteland, 6*d.*, for the like. Pledge, Hugh de Bothemlay.

Henry le Frankisse, 2*d.*; John del Toun de Northeland, 2*d.*, for the like.

Magota del Wode of Skircotes, for an escape in Saltonstall, 3*d.* Pledge, Richard de Saltonstall.

Robert del Grenehirst, 4*d.*, for the like. Pledge, William de Saltonstall.

William de Staynland, 3*d.*; Alcok s. of Simon de Ovendene, 8*d.*; John de Cheswalleye, 4*d.*; Nabbe, wife of Dobbe, 3*d.*; Ellen Goys, 2*d.*; Thomas de Saltonstall, 4*d.*; Richard del Witeleye, 4*d.*; Ivo del Hole, 6*d.*; for escapes.

TOURN there the same day.

JURORS. — Richard del Dene, Richard the Tailor [*Cissor*] of Waddeswrth, John del Rediker, German del Grenewode, William de Heyley, John de Routonstall, Peter Swerd, John de Cockecroft, Thomas de Aula, William de Skircotes, Thomas de Coppelay, and Gilbert de Halifax.

SOURBY.—Juliana Wade drew blood from William le Couhird, her husband ; 12*d.*

William and Robert, sons of Adam le Frankisse, are common thieves, and have stolen 3 oxen and 2 cows from Adam le Crouder. They have been arrested, and are in prison.

The same William and Robert and Henry de Spottelande burgled the house of John del Hirst, and stole goods worth 100*s.*; presented by the townships of Sourby and Werlouleye. Henry is to be arrested when found.

Bate the Lister, William the Milner, Henry s. of William, and Richard s. of Jordan obstructed a way that used and ought to lead to Halifax. The purpresture is to be thrown down, and the offenders attached.

Richard Drake and John s. of Ivo drew blood from one another; 12d. each.

Richard s. of Elias drew blood from Peter Swerd; 12d.

The wives of Richard Alman and Henry de Sourby brew contrary to the assize; 6d. each.

John de Hertlay drew blood from William de Stanesfeld; 12d.

Roger s. of Henry drew blood from John the Shepherd; 12d. And John from Roger; 12d. _ _____

TOURN at Rastrik the Tuesday following.

JURORS.—Alexander del Frith, Luke de Nettelton, John de Locwode, Matthew de Lynthait, Henry le Frankisse, John del Rode, Henry de Coldelay, Henry Beyontefeild, John de Bristall, Roger de Aula, John le Flemang, and John the Clerk of Hertesheved.

Adam Gigge drew blood from Richard del Lache; 12d.

William the Fisher [*piscator*], Henry de Spottelande, William s. of Adam le Frankisse, and Robert his brother burgled the house of John del Hirst; the two first are to be arrested when found.

William de Bradelay's wife brews contrary to the assize; 6d.

John s. of Roger del Clif drew blood from Roger de Clifton; 12d.

The above William and Robert le Frankysse burgled John le Bagger's house, and stole 9 lbs. of wax and other goods [*mercimonia*], worth 16s. Adam, their father, received them after the theft. He is to be arrested.

The Grangers of Bradelay broke the bridge of Bradeley, which they are of right bound to maintain. To be distrained.

Alice la Bagere and Richard Taillour's wife brew contrary to the assize; fined 4d. and 6d.

HIPERUM.—William the Milner's wife and Alexander de Brighouses, for the like, 6d. each. _____

mem. 4d.

COURT at Rastrik on Tuesday after the Feast of St. Nicholas [Dec. 6], 2 Edward II, [1308].

HIPERUM.—Roger del Clif gives 12d. to agree with Roger de Clifton, for trespass. Pledge, William Swyer.

Gilbert de Halifax gives 2s. to take 3 acres in le Roostorth, formerly held by Dom William the Chaplain.

Agnes da. of Roger de Chepelay gives 6s. 8d. for license to marry. Pledge, William the Milner.

GRAVES.—Simon del Dene is elected Grave of Hyperum.

Henry s. of John de Rastrick, Grave of Rastrick.

HIPERUM.—Thomas s. of Cicely de Holgate gives 2s. to take 4⅛ acres of land in le Blacker from Dom Richard the Chaplain.

RASTRICK.—Robert del Ligh Rigge, fined 6d. for detaining 6s. 8d. from Thomas de Totehill; he must pay it and damages, etc.

John s. of Richard de Rastrik gives 6d. to take an acre of land in Rastrik from Avice da. of Richard.

Isolda da. of Roger del Wode gives 12d. for license to marry.

Henry s. of Elias de Rastrick gives 12d. to take 3 acres of land in Rastrick from Avice da. of Richard.

Thomas s. of Christiana de Crosseland, for ill guarding [*pro mala custodia*] the sheep of Thomas de Totehill, whose shepherd he was, fined 2d.; damages, 100s.

HIPERUM.—William Swaype, fined 6d. for not attending.

William the Smith of Clifton, 6d.; Thomas the Webbester, 6d.; John Greteword, 6d.; Richard s. of Walter de Ouuerom, 6d.; Richard s. of Jordan, 6d.; John de Bristall, 6d.; John the Pinder, 3d.; Walter de Ouuerom, 6d.; Roger de Northclif, 6d.; Henry del Rode, 12d.; for vert.

Michael de Breryhaye, for thorns, 6d.

John s. of William de Ovendene, for a young oak [*querculus*], 2s.

William Fox, of Ovendene, for an alder [*alnus*], 6d. Pledge, William Swaype.

William Swyer, 6d.; John del Rode, 12d.;. Thomas, his son, 6d.; William Batte, 6d.; Robert the Smith of Wolwro, 8d.; Eva del Wolfker, 4d.; John de Bairstowe, 6d.; and John s. of Ralph, 6d.; for escapes.

William Swyer, for vert, 6d.

Gilbert Bridde, 3d.; Richard the Dyker, 3d.; Alcok the Taillour, 3d.; and Geoffrey the Colier, 3d.; for branches [*pro ramal'*].

From the smith of Staynland, for shedding Alan de Bothemlay's blood, 12d.

The town of Staynland, for concealing the same, 6s. 8d.

Adam le Frankisse, indicted and arrested, gives 10s. to have help [*auxilium*]. Pledges, William de Bradelay, Henry le Frankisse, Henry s. of John, Henry de Gledehill, John s. of William, and Peter de Barkesland.

MILLS.—William the Milner of Brighouses and Henry Abraam farmed [*affirmaverunt*] Rastrik mill this year, for £10 13s. 4d. Pledges, William de Bothes and Alexander del Frith, keepers of the said mill.

Walter de Adderigate and Simon del Dene farmed Chepeden mill, appertaining to Rastrick mill aforesaid, for 53s. 4d. Pledges, the aforesaid keepers.

———

TOURN at Birton on Wednesday after the Feast of St. Nicholas [Dec. 6].

JURORS.—Richard de Thorntelay, John Wither, Richard Osan, Henry de Birton, John de Legh, John de Braithait, Adam s. of Emma, John s. of Quenilda, Thomas Fernehoule, Gilbert de Alstanlay, John s. of Gilbert, Nicholas Keneward, and Hugh del Hole.

Richard le Bagger's wife, Christiana de Schellay, and Alice, wife of John s. of Gilbert, brew contrary to the assize; fined 6d. each.

John Knygh and Nicholas del Birkes, 6d. each, for not coming.

John s. of Matthew of the Marsh [*de Marisco*], 2s., for drawing the blood of Nicholas s. of Simon.

William s. of Matthew of the Marsh, 12d., for drawing blood of Thomas Cubbock.

Diota wife of Adam de Thurstanland, Elias de Brocholes' wife, Cicely del Wytestones, and the wife of Elias Abraam, 6d. each, for brewing contrary to the assize.

HOLNE.—Richard le Syour, for the blood of Jordan the Milner, 12d.

Adam s. of Jordan, for the blood of Richard le Syour, 12d.

Thomas s. of Lovecok, for the blood of Matthew de Fouleston, 12d.

Adam del Mere, for the blood of Thomas s. of Lovecok, 12d.

Adam s. of John de Holne, for his father's blood, 2s.

The same Adam, for selling a bovate of land to John, his brother, without making fine in Court, 12d.

The same John was fined 12d. for selling it back again to Adam; the land is to be seised into the lord's hand, and both are to be attached.

The township of Holne presents that the said Adam, the Earl's villein [*nātivus*], has for a long time received Walter de Acreland, tenant in chief [?; *architenentem*], who is constantly committing offences in the lord's free chace, and that Adam is a consenting party; and that he carried a stag that had been killed in the chace to the house of the parson of Thornhill, and received 2s. for his pains. He is to be arrested,

Nicholas s. of Nicholas Keneward finds sureties for keeping the peace with William the Forester, under a penalty of 40s., namely: William del Storthes, Nicholas Keneward, William Wodemous, Adam s. of Nicholas, John s. of Nicholas, John Keneward junior, John s. of John de Holne, William Strekayse, John s. of Geoffrey, Adam de la Grene, Robert de Scoles, and Hugh del Hole.

mem. 5.

COURT at Birton on Wednesday after the Feast of St. Nicholas [Dec. 6], 2 Edward II, [1308].

HOLNE.—An inquisition finds that Adam de la Grene owes Adam Strecayse 10s. 6d., for an ox bought of him; fine, 12d.

Robert del Scoles comes late.

Alice del Scoles gives 6d. to take an acre of land in Wolvedale, which William the Skinner left waste on the Earl. Pledge, Adam s. of the Grave.

Adam s. of Robert Strick [*sic*] gives 3s. 4d. to take 7 acres in Wolfdale from Robert Stirk [*sic*], his father, and ½ acre after his father's death. Pledges, Richard del Bothe and William Wodemous.

Nicholas del Clyf, fined 6d. for setting his dogs on to the pigs of Adam del Scoles, so that one pig, worth 2s., died, which he must pay for.

Juliana da. of John de Holne, fined 6d. for detaining utensils from Margery de Thoung, namely, one . . . . , one spit, and two hatchets [*unum craffettum, unum spite et duo hachea*]. She must satisfy the plaintiff.

John s. of Robert s. of Gamel gives 3s. 4d. to take 10 acres of land in Alstanlay from his father after his decease. If John dies without heirs of his body, the tenement to remain to William, his brother; William pays 6d. for the recognition.

John de la Grene gives 5s. to take 13 acres of land in Schaghlay from Henry s. of Alan.

Henry s. of Alan pays 2s. to take 7½ acres of land in Littelwode from John de la Grene.

Adam Fernehoule gives 6d. to take half an acre of land in Fouleston from Thomas s. of Herbert.

William de Hallomschire gives 2s. to take 3½ acres of land in Heppewrth in exchange from William s. of Thomas de Hallomschire, who pays 2s. for 4¾ acres there from William.

Adam le Waynwrith gives 3d. to agree with Adam Benne, for trespass.

Thomas s. of Robert de Fouleston gives 2s. to take 10¾ acres of land in Heppewrth from William de Hallomschire, for 10 years.

Peter de Hallomschire gives 12d. to take 3 acres of land for 6 years, and one acre for 3 years, in Littelwode, from Thomas s. of Robert.

GRAVE.—William Strecayse is elected Grave of Holne, and sworn.

Adam Strecayse, for 4 oxen in the Earl's grass, without agistment, 2s.

Matthew de Marisco, for cutting down an alder [*alnus*], 12d.

Alice da. of Simon gives 6d. to take ½ acre of land in Heppewrth from John s. of Thomas de Rodes.

John Keneward gives 6d. to take an acre of land in Heppewrth, as a heriot after the death of Thomas Keneward, his father.

John de Bristall gives 6d. to take ½ rood of land in Wolvedale from Adam his brother.

William s of John de Craven gives 4s. as a heriot on 2½ acres of land in Littelwode, after the death of John, his father. William is under age; therefore he, his land, goods and chattels, worth 20s., are given into the custody of William del Dene and Richard del Dene, his uncles, who shall honourably maintain him, and render an account when he comes of age. They must find pledges.

Richard del Dene gives 2s. to take 4¾ acres of land in Wolvedale from William del Dene, his brother.

TOURN at Wakefeld on Friday, the Feast of St. Lucy the Virgin [Dec. 13], 2 Edward II, [1308].

JURORS. — Robert de Wyromthorpe, Walter de Grymmeston, William Ingreys, Richard de Bristall, Robert de Wodesom, Richard de Salsa Mara, John Patrik, Robert Dernelove, John de Fery, Walter Scot, John Cussing, and John de Mora.

Robert de Edderikthorpe drew blood from Peter de Newland [*de Nova terra*]; 12d.

John the Walker [*fullo*] of Emmelay, for not coming, 6d.

The wives of William de Dewisbiry and Richard the Lister brew contrary to the assize; 6d. each.

John Tropinell drew blood from Gilbert the Forester of Thurstanhagh; 2s.

Adam s. of Maude obstructed a footpath in Crigeleston leading to the public well [*fons*]; 12d.

OSSETE.—Amabel wife of John s. of Alan de Ossete drew blood from Alice wife of Swain; 12*d.*

ALVERTHORPE.—Richard Wythehundes, for drawing blood of Alice wife of William Hoskell, 12*d.*

Richard s. of Broun holds an essart in severalty, in which the whole township of Alverthorpe ought to common in open time; fine, 12*d.*

Walter del Bothem, for drawing blood of Alice wife of Roger, 12*d.*

Simon the Turnur, 6*d.*, for not coming; he is to be attached on a charge of receiving at his house strange men and disturbers of the peace, who fought there at night, and shed blood.

Richard the Tailor drew blood from Richard and German Hodslyn; to be attached when found.

John s. of Robert Grenehod drew blood from Richard le Cartewricht; to be attached.

mem. 5d.

Philip Dampson, the like from Robert Dodeman; 6*d.*

Henry Archur raised the hue on John s. of Sibbe unjustly; 12*d.*

Robert Hodde drew blood from the wife of Henry Archur; 12*d.* And from Juliana Horsse; 12*d.*

John s. of Alan drew blood from German Chidde; to be attached.

Bete widow of Robert Haget commonly curses her neighbours, and makes an outcry in the town of a night, and she raised the hue on Richard Cay unjustly; to be attached.

John Leche and Robert Hod, 12*d.* each, for making their haystack [*pro faciendo fenile suum*[1]] in the common way.

Robert de Mora raised the hue on his brother Alexander; 6*d.*

The townships of Crigeleston, 40*d.*; Walton, 4*s.*; Dewisbiry, 4*s.*; and Stanlay, 12*d.*, for contempt; and Stanlay, 12*d.*, for a concealment.

STANLAY.—Juliana wife of Philip, for brewing contrary to the assize, 6*d.*

----

mem. 6.

COURT at Wakefield on Friday after the Feast of the Circumcision [Jan. 1], 2 Edward II, [1309].

ESSOIGNS.[2]—Thomas de Heeton, by Robert de Gomersale. Pledge, Thomas de Thorneton.

John de Lepton, by Thomas de Wittelay.   Pledge, Adam de Helay.

----

[1] *Fenile, locus ubi fenum ponunt.* (Ducange.)
[2] From suit of Court, unless otherwise stated.

William de Chipedene, by William le Horshird. Pledge, John de Toftclif.

Peter Swerd, by Richard Baycocks. Pledge, Richard de Bristall.

Nicholas de Caylly, by Henry de Methelay. Pledge, Robert de la Grene.

John s. of Robert the Clerk of Sandale, plt., against William the Grave of Walton, for seizing cattle, by Robert his brother. Pledge, William del Okes. Alan Almot, pledge for William, is fined 6d. for not having him at this Court.

ALVERTHORPE.—William Wolmer, fined 6d. for not prosecuting suit against Henry le Nonne, for trespass.

Adam s. of Maude, 12d., for not prosecuting suit against Nicholas le Normaund, for seizing cattle.

Margery de Plegwik claims from Robert de Ketelesthorp 3 roods of land, which she had in dower after her husband's death, 12 years ago, and of which she was peacefully seised for 12 years, until Robert unjustly disseised her. Deft. says that Robert le Ploghwrith, husband of plaintiff, had no right therein, nor has she, except at the will of himself. An inquisition is ordered.

SOURBY.—Adam Migge, fined 6d. for not prosecuting suit against William Swaype, for trespass.

HIPERUM.—Roger del Cliff, 6d. for the like against John de Chepelay, in a plea of land.

John s. of Adam de Crosseland, who married Agnes da. of Roger de Chepelay, gives 5s. to come with his goods and chattels into the land of said Agnes.

Robert Archur, for default; 6d.

Agnes de Bretton withdraws her suit against Amice de Swynlington; fine pardoned, because she is poor.

ALVERTHORPE.—An inquisition finds that Robert Archur ousted John Cussing from the crop of a rood of land in the Graveship of Alverthorpe; damages, 12d.; fine, 6d.

Alice wife of Roger the Forester, for withdrawing suit against Walter del Bothem, for trespass; 6d.

Sir Thomas de Burgh, for default, 12d.

SANDALE.—Christiana da. of Nalle de Wodethorpe gives 12d. to take the moiety of ½ bovate of land in Sandale, as a heriot after the death of her mother.

Alice da. of the said Christiana gives 12d. to take the said land from Christiana, to herself and heirs, after her mother's death.

SOURBY.—John de Gledeholt gives 3*s.* to take 6 acres of new land from the waste in Werlouleye, between Mickelassom and Colyngschagh; rent, 3*s.*

STANLAY.—Richard s. of Robert de Batelay gives 3*s.* 4*d.* to take half a messuage and 7 acres of land in Wyromthorpe from Philip le Syour.

Philip le Syour gives 12*d.* for license to marry Alice, his daughter.

HOLNE.—Adam s. of John de Holne, arrested for trespasses in the forest, whereof he was indicted at the Tourn at Birton, pays 6*s.* 8*d.* to be under the mainprise of Nicholas s. of Nicholas Keneward, William del Storthes, Adam s. of Elias, Henry Wade, Adam de Bray, Nicholas de Littelwode, John de Holne, John his son, William s. of Benedict, William del Bothe, Adam de la Grene, and Peter del Peek, until the Earl comes to these parts.

ALVERTHORPE.—Richard Wythehundes, fined 4*d.* for unlawful detention against William Hosekell.

WAKEFELD.—Adam de Castelford's daughter, 2*d.*; Roger Wasse, 2*d.*; John Tevet's wife, 1*d.*; Walter Pollard's wife, 2*d.*; Ibbote da. of Nelot, 2*d.*; Henry s. of Ellen, 2*d.*; Isabel de Honlay's daughter, 1*d.*; Alice Coly, 1*d.*; Cissote Danyel, 1*d.*; Adam the Clouter's daughter, 1*d.*; Adam Pollard's daughter, 1*d.*; John Tope's wife, 2*d.*; Robert Tope's wife, 1*d.*; Nicholas Noddeger's son, 2*d.*; and Henry Chepe's son, 1*d.*; for dry wood.

WAKEFELD.—The vicar of Warnefeld, for escape of a horse, 6*d.* Pledge, Gilbert the Turnur.

The maids of John de Skulbroke, 3*d.*; Henry de Skulbrok, 2*d.*; William Beuchaunt, 3*d.*; John de Grenegate, 1*d.*, and of Ralph s. of Mille, 1*d.*; Jordan the Mower, 6*d.*; Henry the Nautehird's maid, 3*d.*; the maid of William s. of Eva, 1*d.*; and Adam Torketro, 2*d.*; for dry wood.

ALVERTHORPE.—William Hoskell, 2*d.*, for dry wood. *mem.* 6d.

STANLAY.—John Isabell, 1*d.*, (in the Grave's estreat [*in extractum prepositi*], 2*d.*); Adam s. of Cote, 2*d.*, (in the Grave's estreat, 12*d.*); Thomas s. of Stephen, 2*d.*; Broun de Wyveromthorpe, 2*d.*; and Roger Bele, 2*d.*; for dry wood.

Symon Tyting, for vert, 6*d.*

Robert de Wyveromthorpe, for an escape, 6*d.*

THORNES.—William s. of John Malyn gives 4*s.* to take 2 bovates of land in Thornes, as a heriot after the death of his father. As he

M

has no goods, the Steward permits him to pay the fine at Whitsuntide and St. John's day.

HOLNE.—Richard de Berneslay *v.* Elias At-well [*ad fontem*] of
Wolvedale, for debt.   Pledge, Henry de Rastrik.

COURT at Wakefeld on Friday before the Conversion of St. Paul
[Jan. 25], in the second year, [1309].

ESSOIGNS.[1]—Thomas de Thornton, by Hugh de Thornton.   Pledge,
John de Toftclyf.

Elias de Birton, by Thomas de Wittelay.   Pledge, John de la More.

William de Chepedene, by Thomas de Wittelay.   Pledge, William
del Okes.

Peter Swerd, by William the Serjeant.   Pledge, John de Mora.

ALVERTHORPE.—The suit between Adam s. of Thomas, plt., and
Richard Wythehundes is respited, because the Rolls are wanting
[*pro defectu Rotulorum*].

SOURBY.—Henry de Godelay gives 12*d.* to agree with William s.
of Walter de Chepelay, for detaining a bullock.   Pledge, John de
Cockecroft.

THORNES.—Elias Bulneys, fined 3*d.* for unlawfully detaining one
wynd[2] of barley and a quarter of oats from William s. of William the
Gardyner and Elizabeth his wife.   He must satisfy them.

Amabel widow of Swayn Scot, for many defaults, 6*d.*

Thomas del Holgate and Thomas s. of Roger sue the said
Amabel for 40*d.*, as to which they were pledges for her husband
against Henry s. of Ralph, who has recovered against them.   Deft.
says that her husband could not charge [*carcare*] her therewith except
in his lifetime [*nisi tantum in vita sua*].   Plaintiffs fined 6*d* for false
claim.

SOURBY.—Adam s. of Ivo de Werlouley, fined 12*d.* for not prosecuting his suit against Hugh s. of Reynald and Thomas de Roildesete,
for debt.

ALVERTHORPE.—Adam s. of Henry de Goukethorp gives 3*d.* to
agree with John Rate, for trespass.   Pledge, Henry del Bothem.

HOLNE.—Elias At-well of Wolvedale gives 6*d.* to agree with
Richard de Berneslay, for debt.   Pledge, William Strekayse.

----

[1] From suit of Court, unless otherwise stated.

[2] Probably a *windle*, a dry measure, equalling about 3½ Winchester bushels.
Century Dictionary.)

ALVERTHORPE.—Quenilda de Alverthorpe, *3d.*, for a false claim against Adam Gerbode.

SANDALE.—Agnes da. of Henry de Vallibus gives *2d.* to take a toft and 4 acres of land in Crigeleston, as a heriot after her father's death.

HORBYRY.—Robert s. of Thore gives *4s.* to take a toft and 3 acres of land in Horbyry, left on the Earl by Margery la Portere.

HOLNE.—Matthew de Barneby gives *12d.* to take 1½ acres of land in Fouleston from Henry, his brother.

Thomas son-in-law of Warin gives *2s.* to take ⅔ of 10 acres of land in Fouleston from Robert del Scoles, for 10 years.

STANLAY.—Adam s. of Cote de Wyveromthorpe surrenders a toft and 7 acres of land in Wyveromthorpe to William, his son; William pays *12d.* for the recognition, and surrenders it to Adam for his life.

Matthew de Lynthait gives *12d.* for help [*auxilium*] to continue his term at Lynthait.

SANDALE.—Robert the Clerk of Sandale takes a rood of new land from the waste in Sandale fields; rent, *1d.*

STANLAY.—Richard s. of Robert de Batelay *v.* Philip le Syour, on an agreement. Pledge, Richard Longschank.

HOLNE.—William Strekayse gives *12d.* to take 2½ acres of land in Thoung from Robert s. of Thomas de Ryssewrth.

Richard del Bothe gives *3s. 4d.* to take 8½ acres of land in Thoung from the same Robert.

SANDALE.—Robert de Ketelesthorpe surrenders to Margery de Plegwik the 3 roods of land for which she sued; he is fined *6d.*[1]

Hugh de Rodes, arrested for trespasses committed in the Earl's free chace, pays *20s.* as a fine for respite till the Earl comes.

Thomas de Heeton and Sir Thomas de Burgh, *12d.* each, for default.

HORBIRY.—John the Grave of Horbiry, *18d.*, for a stray young sow [*suella*].

SANDALE.—John Cokewald, *5s.* for a stray cow, and *1s.* for a stray blind horse [*pro j affro ceco waivo*].

Adam s. of Maude de Crigeleston *v.* Nicholas le Normaund, for seizing a bullock. Pledge, Robert the Clerk.

William Swyer *v.* William the Proctor [*Procurator*] and Richard the Chaplain, for detaining cattle. Pledge, Roger de Clifton.

---

[1] See *ante*, p. 192.

mem. 7.

COURT at Wakefield on Friday, St. Valentine's Day [Feb. 14],
2 Edward II, [1309].

ESSOIGNS.[1]—Elias de Birton, by William, his son. Pledge, William
Taillour.

Richard de Bristall, by Robert Scot. Pledge, Robert de la Grene.

John de Lepton, by Thomas de Wittelay. Pledge, William del
Okes.

Hugh de Seyville, attorney of Baldwin de Seyville, by Adam de
Bergh. Pledge, John de Mora.

William the Grave of Walton, 6*d.*, for not appearing to answer
John s. of Robert the Clerk, for seizing cattle.

ALVERTHORPE.—Quenilda de Alverthorpe, 2*d.*, for not prosecuting
her suit against John, servant [*garcio*] of Adam Gerbode, for trespass.

STANLAY.—Philip le Syour, the Earl's villein [*nativus*], fined 4*d.*
for not appearing to answer Richard s. of Robert de Batelay, as to
an agreement. He afterwards came. Richard claims half a messuage
and an acre of land in Wyromthorpe, which he bought from Philip,
and had seisin by the Steward, but of which Philip afterwards
deforced him. Philip denies the sale and surrender. An inquisition
is ordered.

William the Proctor and Richard the Chaplain, defts., essoign
against William Swer [*sic*] for detaining cattle, by Robert de Stodelay.
Pledge, William Taillour. William Swyer [*sic*] fined 6*d.* for not
prosecuting his suit.

Adam s. of Maude de Crigeleston, plt., against Nicholas le Normaund for seizing a bullock, by John de Claiton. Pledge, William
Taillour.

Robert le Grubber, distrained by 2 sheep to answer Thomas
Alayn as to an agreement, does not come, and no other distress can
be found; therefore Thomas has license to withdraw his complaint.

ALVERTHORPE.—Robert de Castelford gives 18*d.* to take 4 acres
of land in Alverthorpe from William Hoskell.

Henry s. of Richard Broun gives 3*s.* 4*d.* to take a toft of ½ acre
and ⅓ bovate of land in Alverthorpe from his father; and Richard
afterwards takes them again for his life, with remainder to Henry.

HOLNE.—John s. of Richard de la Grene gives 2*s.* to take 16
acres and 3 perches in Littelwode from Richard s. of Richard de la
Grene, in exchange for 13 acres of land in Schaghelay. Richard
pays 2*s.* to take the 13 acres from the said John.

---

[1] From suit of Court, unless otherwise stated.

ALVERTHORPE.—Henry Gonton pays 6d. to take ½ acre of land, with the meadow adjoining, in Neuton fields, from Adam Gerbode; and 6d. for a similar piece adjoining, from Henry le Nonne; both for 12 years.

SANDALE.—William Filchc, clerk, gives 12d. to take 3 acres and 1 rood of land on the Fallebanck, from the Earl's demesne, lying waste on account of their poorness [*propter debilitatem*], for 30 years; rent, 6d. an acre.

ALVERTHORPE.—Adam Gerbode, for dry wood, 3d.

John Broun and John Rate, for vert, 6d. each.

Adam Gerbode, 12d.; Alice Gobode [*sic*], 2d; Alice wife of Roger, 2d.; Richard de Collay, 2d.; and William Hoskell, 3d.; for escapes.

John de Flansowe, 12d.; Amabel de Flansowe, 2d.; and John Schirelock, 3d.; for dry wood.

THORNES.—John Graffard, 6d.; Alice Graffard, 12d.; Roger Trail-ment, 6d.; John de Haia, 4d.; Ivo thc Smith, 1d.; and Adam the Forester, 2d.; for escapes.

John Costell, 1d.; Thomas Viroun, 3d.; Alice da. of Philip, 2d.; and Thomas Brounsmyth, 2d.; for dry wood.

mem. 7d.

STANLAY.—Emma la Longe, John Cort, and Alice Edus', 2d. each; John Bullock, 3d.; Richard Bullock, 2d.; William Dorling, 3d.; Adam le Hewer, 2d.; and Philip Issabell, 2d.; for dry wood.

[*N.B.—Membrane 8 appears to be for the most part a draft or duplicate of the last Court. The following lists are not on mem. 7.*]

OSSETE.—William s. of Gotte, 2d.; William Hernyng, 6d.; Jordan Moyses, 3d.; and Thomas Pees, 2d.; for escapes.

Hugh Pees, 2d.; William le Wyte's maid, 3d.; the wife of Adam, servant of Robert [?; *S' Roberti*], 4d.; Alot le Passemer, 2d.; Richard Suart, 2d.; Henry s. of Alcok, 1d.; and Richard s. of Joh'ot,[1] 2d.; for dry wood.

Richard s. of John, 3d.; Richard de Goukethorp, 4d.; Sonman, 2d.; and John le Folour, 1d.; for escapes.

WAKEFEUD.—Philip Damoysel, 12d.; Robert Wyles, 4d.; Richard Wayte, 6d.; Robert de Fetherston, 6d.; Jordan le Mawer, 2d.; and German le Nauthyrd, 2d.; for escapes.

William de Sandale, for vert, 12d.

Michael the Carpenter, 3d.; Hugh le Chapman, 2d.; John Rychaund, 2d.; William Rychaund, 2d.; Robert Liftefast, 3d.; John

---

[1] ? Johannot.

Leche, 2d.; John s. of Sibbe, 2d.; Elias Tyrsi, 2d.; John Sotheron, 2d.; the maids of Hugh Bille, John de Sculbrok, and Ralph s. of Henry, 1d. each; William Grenehod, 6d.; for dry wood.

ALVERTHORPE.—Richard s. of Broun v. Adam Gerbot, Richard de Colley, William Hoskel, and Richard Wythundes, for trespass. Pledge, Robert Hode.

THORNES [sic].[1]—Thomas de Wakefeud v. Ivo the Smith, for trespass. Pledge, Ralph Bate.

John Tasse v. Agnes Peger and John, her brother, for land. Same pledge.

William Grenehod v. Philip Wolf, for debt. Same pledge.

ALVERTHORPE.—Emma Bonny v. Eva widow of William de Ouchethorpe, for debt. Pledge, William s. of Walter.

Thomas the Forester v. Adam Gerbot, for debt. Pledge, William servant of Margery [i.e. Margeryman].

---

mem. 9.

COURT at Wakefeld on Friday before Mid-Lent,[2]
2 Edward [II, 1309].

ESSOIGNS.[3]—John de Lepton, by Thomas de Wittelay. Pledge, Hugh de Seyville.

William de Chepedene, by Nicholas de Batelay. Pledge, John de Toftclif.

Robert de la Grene of Ossete, by William s. of Godfrey. Pledge, Nicholas de Cailly.

Peter Swerd, by William the Serjeant. Pledge, Richard de Bristall.

Thomas de Thornton, by Hugh de Thornton. Pledge, Nicholas de Cailly.

Thomas de Bellehouses, by Hugh de Seyville. Pledge, John de Mora.

The suit of Adam s. of Maude de Crigeleston v. Nicholas le Normaund, for seizing a cow, is removed into the Bench by writ.

RECOGNIZANCE.—Henry de Schelflay enters into a recognizance in 100s. sterling to Master John de Warenna for his share of the tithes of Birton. Pledge, Elias de Birton.

---

[1] This is probably the first use of the English form; previously it has been Latinised into *Spinetum.*

[2] Mid Lent Sunday was March 9th.

[3] From suit of Court, unless otherwise stated.

Adam s. of Thomas de Flansowe, plt., *v.* Richard Wythehundes, comes. The Rolls have not yet been found. A day is given at the next Court.

THORNES.—John Tasse *v.* Agnes Pegere, for ousting him from the crop of a rood of land which he recovered against her in this Court. The Roll is searched, and it is found that he did recover. She is fined 4*d.*

RECOGNIZANCE.—Thomas de Heeton admits that he owes 5 marks sterling to Adam de Pontefract.

ALVERTHORPE.—Eva widow and executrix of William de Ouchethorpe is fined 4*d.* for unlawfully detaining 18*d.* from Emma Bonny. She must pay her.

William s. of William de Ouchethorpe gives 3*s.* as a heriot on a bovate and 10 acres of land in Neuton, after his father's death.

SANDALE.—Agnes da. of Henry de Vallibus gives 6*d.* to take 2¼ acres of land in Crigeleston from Roger s. of Geoffrey, for 12 years.

HOLNE.—Matthew de Langlay gives 12*d.* to take 5 acres of land in Wlvedale in exchange from William de Hallomschire, who gives 12*d.* to take 6 acres there from Matthew.

John s. of Robert de Billeclyf gives 3*s.* 4*d.* to take 12 acres of land in Wlvedale from William de Hallomschire.

William s. of Thomas de Hallomschire gives 12*d.* to take an acre of new land from the waste in Heppewrth, in front of his door [*ante hostium suum*]; rent, 6*d.*

William del Dene gives 2*s.* for the wardship of William s. of John de Craven, with his land and chattels, for 6 years.

STANLAY.—John s. of Gerard de Stanlay gives 4*s.* to take 8 acres of land in Stanley from Gerard, his father.

John Walehot *v.* John Godefray, in a plea of land. Pledge, Hugh Schayf.

———

COURT at Wakefield on Friday after the Feast of St. Gregory the Pope [March 12[1]], in the year abovesaid, [1309].

ESSOIGNS.[2]—William de Chepedene, by William de Sunderland. Pledge, Richard de Bristall.

Peter Swerd, by William the Serjeant. Pledge, William del Okes.

Thomas del Bellehouses, by Thomas de Wittelay. Pledge, John de Mora.

———

[1] This Court was held on March 14th; March 28th, the proper day, was Good Friday.

[2] From suit of Court, unless otherwise stated.

Alan Almot, attorney of Thomas de Burgh, by John de Clayton. Pledge, William the Serjeant.

John de Toftclyf, attorney of Adam de Everingham, by John, his son.   Pledge, Robert de Wyromthorpe.

Thomas de Thornton, by John s. of Hugh.   Same pledge.

Nicholas de Caylly, by Roger de Mara.   Pledge, Richard de Bristall.

Isabel da. of Thomas the Cook, by William del Okes.   Pledge, John de Mora.

William de Rastrick, by Thomas de Totehill.   Same pledge.

THORNES.—Thomas de Wakefeld and Ivo the Smith agree by license; Ivo is fined 6d.

ALVERTHORPE.—Amabel de Flansowe and Agnes her daughter must satisfy William Grenehod for detention of a stone of wool; satisfaction to be levied on them and Philip Wlf, their pledge, by the bailiffs.   Fine, 3d.

Thomas de Heeton, for default, 6d.

William s. of Walter de Neuton and Robert s. of Ralph de Ouchethorpe, for contempt, 3s. 4d.

OSSETE.—Adam s. of William s. of Jordan gives 5s. as a heriot on 2 bovates of land, with buildings, in Ossete, after the death of his father.

THORNES.—John s. of Robert the Drapur gives 6d. as a heriot on ½ a bovate of land in Thornes, after his father's death.

German the Gardyner gives 12d. to take in free burgage a certain tenement in Wakefeld, which he holds of the fee of James Lyvet, and to have the freedom of the town thereby, as of a free burgess; paying 3d. a year in the rental of the town of Wakefeld. *mem.* 9d.

SANDALE.—William Hillehore gives 6d. to take 5 roods of land in Sandale from Robert the Clerk of Sandale, for 20 years.

WAKEFELD.—John Cussing, 12d.; Thomas Alayn, 6d.; Robert le Young, 6d.; and Jordan le Mauwer, 6d.; for vert.

Elias Tirsy, 6d. and Robert Peger, 3d., for coal.

Michael the Carpenter's servant [*garcio*], 3d., for vert.

Robert Archur's wife, 2d.; the maids of Thomas Molle and Richard the Clerk, 2d. each; Robert Hod, 2d.; William Wolmer's son, 6d.; the sons of Hugh Bille, and Ralph s. of Henry, 2d. each; William the Gardiner senior, 3d.; German the Gardiner, 3d.; John de Sculbrok, 2d.; John le Sotheren, 4d.; Walter Bille, 1d.; Richard le Wayte, 1d.; Robert the Lister, 1d.; Robert Capon, 1d.; Walter

Ape, 1*d.*; Agnes da. of Sibil, 3*d.*; William de Mora, 2*d.*; Alice Proudefot, 1*d.*; John Baba, 1*d.*; Henry Archur, 1*d.*; Robert Lyftfast, 2*d.*; Robert de Fetherstan, 2*d.*; Robert s. of Jose, 1*d.*; Henry Cheppe, 1*d.*; Richard Anote, 1*d.*; Maude Lattok, 1*d.*; Adam de Castelford, 1*d.*; Roger Wasse, 1*d.*; Henry de Wolvelay, 1*d.*; John de Fery, 1*d.*; Amabel the Laundress [*lotrix*], 1*d.*; Robert le Hunt's maid, 1*d.*; Cissota Danyel, 1*d.*; William servant of Margery, 1*d.*; William the Goldsmith, 1*d.*; Robert the Goldsmith, 1*d.*; Idonea Pollard, 1*d.*; and Broun Robin, 1*d.*; for dry wood.

STANLAY.—Richard Bullock, 12*d.*; Adam Spink, 3*d.*; for vert.

Thomas s. of Stephen, 1*d.*; John s. of Alice, 2*d.*; Joan Pescy, 2*d.*; Simon Tyting, 2*d.*; and John Askebrenner, 1*d.*; for dry wood.

OSSETE.—Richard Suart and Jordan Eliot, for contempt to the forester, 3*s.* 4*d.* each.

Jordan Moyses, 4*d.*; and Richard de Chickinlay, 2*d.*; for escapes of pigs.

ALVERTHORPE.—John s. of Robert Mercat[1] *v.* Richard Wythehundes and Robert de Flansowe, on an agreement. Pledge, William Taillour. In the Court of the town, because they are burgesses.

Simon Tyting and Eva his wife *v.* Eva widow of William de Ouchethorp, for debt. Pledge, Richard del Kerre.

SANDALE.—John Tropinell and John Dande *v.* William de la Grene, for trespass. Pledge, Thomas s. of Pelle.

OSSETE.—Robert Sonneman *v.* Nicholas s. of Gotte, for trespass. Pledge, Richard Broun of Heeton.

Richard the Grave of Ossete *v.* Ralph Bate and Christiana Gerbot, for debt. Pledge, Robert Sonneman.

ALVERTHORPE.—Adam Gerbot *v.* Richard s. of Broun, for trespass. Pledge, Robert the Grave.

---

mem. 10

COURT at Wakefeld on Friday after the Quinzaine of Easter,[2]

2 Edw. [II, 1309].

ESSOIGNS.[3]—John de Lepton, by Thomas de Wittelay. Pledge, Richard de Bristall.

Elias de Birton, by William de Birton. Pledge, Thomas de Bellehouses.

---

[1] First written *Mercer*; ? *Mercator*.

[2] *i.e.* Friday, April 18th, three weeks from Good Friday, March 28th.

[3] From suit of Court, unless otherwise stated.

Thomas de Heeton, by William the Serjeant. Pledge, John de Mora.[1]

STANLAY.—Philip le Syour gives 6d. to agree with Richard s. of Robert de Batelay, as to an agreement.

Thomas Forester, for not prosecuting his suit against Adam Gerbot, for debt; 4d.

ALVERTHORPE.—Richard Broun, for a false claim for trespass against Adam Gerbode, Henry del Bothem, William Hoskell, and Richard Wythehundes; 8d.

SANDALE.—John Tropinell, plt., and William de la Grene agree by license; John fined 6d.

John Dande, for not prosecuting his suit for trespass against William de la Grene; 4d.

OSSETE.—Alan s. of Gotte and William Cheild, for not producing Nicholas s. of Gotte, for whom they were pledges; 12d.

Thomas de Heeton, for default; 6d.

Thomas de Drounesfeld, Sir Hugh de Elande, and Nicholas le Normaund, to be distrained for default.

ALVERTHORPE.—Richard s. of Broun, for slandering Adam Gerbode; 4d.

STANLAY.—John s. of Robert del Dale gives 12d. as heriot on a bovate of land in Ouchethorp, after his father's death.

SANDALE.—John Cokewald gives 12d. to take 7½ acres of land in Sandale, with the meadow pertaining to it, from Agnes da. of Henry Chire, for 14 years.

STANLAY.—Robert s. of Robert s. of Walter de Stanlay and Juliana his wife give 6d to take an acre of land in Stanlay from Philip le Syour, to themselves and the heirs of their bodies.

HOLNE.—John de Holne, 3s. 4d., and John his son, 6d., for cutting broom [hussetus] to feed their beasts, against the will of the forester.

HIPERUM.—Robert the Smith of Wollewro, John del Rode and his two sons, for contempt to Roger de Briggehouses, forester in Hiperum wood; 6s. 8d.

WAKEFELD.—Robert Pollard and Godeling's son, for underwood destroyed . . . . . [pro buscha prostrata cum croc']; 5d.

SANDALE.—Henry North of Wolvelay, for escape of cattle in the new coppice in Thurstanhawe; 16d. Pledge, Robert de la Grene.

John de Felton, for the like; 8d. Pledge, Robert the Forester.

---

[1] This entry is struck out, and *error* written in the margin.

John Mounk, *6d.*; Idonea Fox, *2d.*; William de Plegwik, *6d.*; Agnes the Webster, *2d.*; John the Piper, *2d.*; William Hare, *6d.*; John s. of Swayn, *2d.*; Thomas le Hunt, *8d.*; Robert de Bergh, *8d.*; Adam s. of Roger, *2d.*; Richard s. of Hugh, *2d.*; Robert de la Grene, *2d.*; John de Plegwik, *2d.*; Thomas s. of Pelle, *6d.*; for escapes there.

COURT at Wakefeld on Friday, the Morrow of SS. Philip and James [May 1],[1] in the abovesaid year [1309].

ESSOIGNS.[2]—Richard de Bristall, by Robert Scot. Pledge, Nicholas de Caylly.

John de Lepton, by John de Erdeslowe. Pledge, John de Toftclyf.

William de Chepedene, by Thomas de Wittelay. Pledge, Hugh de Seyville.

Peter Swerd, by William the Serjeant. Pledge, John de Mora.

Alan Almot, attorney of Thomas de Burgh, by Robert de Heyrode. Pledge, Adam the Forester.

Thomas del Bellehouses, by Alexander de Wodehouses. Pledge, William del Okes.

Thomas de Thornton, by John the Clerk. Pledge, John de Mora.

Elias de Birton, by William his son. Same pledge.

STANLAY.—John Walhot *v.* John Godefray and Eva his wife, claims a rood of land in Stanlay, from which he says they are deforcing him unjustly, because William Pigge, his father, died seised thereof, and after his death the plt. paid a heriot, and peaceably held it until ousted. Deft. John does not come, because he is ill, but Eva appears for them both, and says that her father, Philip le Syour, gave them the land, and she vouches him to warranty. Philip comes, and warrants, and says that neither plt. nor his father were ever seised of the land. An inquisition is taken by the oath of Robert Pescy, Richard del Bothem, Simon de Monte, Robert Gunne, William Albray, Gerard s. of Alcok, Robert de Flansowe, Richard s. of Broun, Henry del Bothem, William Hoskell, William de Neuton, and Simon Tyting, who say that neither plt. nor his father have been seised of that rood for 100 years past. Plt. fined *6d.* for a false claim.

ALVERTHORPE.—John le Rassed gives *6d.* to take a rood of meadow in Neuton from Henry le Nunne, for 25 years.

---

[1] This Court should have been held on May 9th, three weeks from April 18th; it was held a week earlier, probably because May 8th was Ascension Day.

[2] From suit of Court, unless otherwise stated.

Eva widow of William de Ouchethorp has license to agree with Simon Tyting and Eva his wife, for debt.

OSSETE.—The whole of the goods of Nicholas s. of Gotte in the Earl's fee are to be distrained, to force him to answer Robert Sonneman, for trespass.

ALVERTHORPE.—Richard the Grave of Ossete, plt., and Ralph Bate and Christiana Gerbode, agree by license. Christiana fined 6d. *mem.* 10d.

ALVERTHORPE.—William de Wakefeld has license to take a piece of meadow in Morecroft from John Thorald, for 10 years, John doing service.

SANDALE.—Thomas de Danecastre gives 12d. to take 1½ acres of land in Crigeleston from John de Vallibus.

STANLAY.—Alice da. of Philip le Syour gives 6d. to take an acre of land in Stanlay from her father.

Thomas de Dronesfeld, Nicholas le Normaund, and John s. of Hugh de Rastrick, fined 6d. each for default.

Sir Hugh de Eland is dead; his tenement is taken into the lord's hand.

STANLAY.—Andrew de Ouchethorpe v. Robert Gunde, for trespass. Pledge, William Tagge.

WAKEFELD —The maid of Hugh the Chapman, 4d.; William s. of Eva, John Rychaud, Henry le Nauthird, John s. of Molle, John the Couper, John le Lauper, Eva de Bramelay, Robert Lyftfast, Peter Spink, Robert Capon, Walter Ape, William Richaud, and Richard s. of Junne, 2d. each; William de Sandale, 1d.; Agnes Pole, 2d.; Beatrice de Aula, 1d.; Joan Dodenho, 1d.; Robert Hod, 2d.; John Baba, 2d.; Margaret Pollard, 1d.; Robert Dernelove, 6d.; John de Skulbrok, 3d.; Ralph s. of Henry, 2d.; John le Sotheron, 3d.; Hugh Bille, 2d.; Walter Bille, 2d.; Walter Ape, 1d.; John s. of Juliana, 1d.; Laurence the Clerk, 1d.; for dry wood.

John de Thorecroft, for vert, 6d.

STANLAY.—Walter s. of Bateman, 6d.; Robert s. of Walter, 6d.; John Cockspore, 4d.; Robert s. of Geppe, 3d.; Walter s. of Adam, 10d.; John the servant [*garcio*] of Walter, 4d.; Richard del Kerre, 8d.; for escapes.

OSSETE.—Richard s. of John, 6d.; John Maunsell, 4d.; Richard s. of Bate, 4d.; John le Folour, 2d.; Matthew de Ossete, 6d.; Richard Passemer, 3d.; the widow of William s. of Jordan, 2d.; Maude wife of Ralph, 2d.; Richard Suarte, 4d.; and Thomas Assolf, 4d.; for escapes.

THORNES.—John Costell, 2d.; Alice wife of Philip, 3d.; Thomas Brounsmyth, 2d.; Thomas Vyron, 2d.; Philip the servant of Ivo the Smith, 3d.; John Graffard's wife, 2d.; and the wife of John Graffard senior 2d., for dry wood.

ALVERTHORPE.—Walter del Hill, 2d.; and Henry Wolf, 1d.; for escapes.

WAKEFELD.—Henry Gonton, for vert, 12d.; and for coal, 2d.

Eva de Bramelay's son, 2d.; the maids of Robert Besk and William Ylhore, 2d. each; Beatrice de Aula, 2d.; Philip de Castilford, 6d.; Robert Capon, 2d.; Walter Ape, 1d.; and John Peger, 1d.; for dry wood.

STANLAY.—Robert s. of Geoffrey, 4d.; and William the Dyker's maid, 2d.; for dry wood.

WAKEFELD.—Thomas de Wakefeld, 12d.; Thomas s. of Lance, 12d.; Robert Wiles, 12d.; Robert de Fetherstan, 10d.; Jordan the Mauwer, 6d.; John Dade, 2d.; the parson of Wakefeld, 2d.; and John de Grenegate, 4d.; for escapes of pigs.

ALVERTHORPE.—Adam Gerbode, 18d.; and Christiana Gerbode, 4d.; for the like.

OSSETE.—Jordan de Heton, 2d.; and Richard the Grave, 4d.; for the like.

ALVERTHORPE.—Richard de Collay and John Broun, 4d. each, for escapes.

HORBIRY.—Thomas Caynock and Ralph Wolf, 3d. each, for the like.

OSSETE.—Richard s. of John, and William s. of Gotte, 3d. each, for the like.

THORNES.—Ivo the Smith, 1d.; and Roger Traylment, 4d.; for the like.

HORBYRY.—Maude widow of Adam Broun v. Hugh Lambehird, for trespass. Pledge, John Fox.

STANLAY.—Robert the Carpenter v. Andrew Pogge, for trespass. Pledge, John the Mason [cementarius].

ALVERTHORPE.—Robert Gunne v. Richard Bonny, in a plea of land. Pledge, Robert Pescy.

SANDALE.—Henry s. of Roger del Hill v. John Tropinell, in a plea of land. Pledge, Robert the Forester.

DEWISBIRY WOOD.—The herbage in Dewisbiry wood is sold this year to William de Dewisbiry, Richard de Bouderode, and Richard s. of Adam, for 43s. 4d.

SOURBY.—Alice wife of William the Soldier [*mercenarius*]¹ *v.* Henry s. of Robert del Lone, for trespass. Pledge, William At-town-head [*ad capud ville*].

Robert s. of Nabbe de Sourby *v.* Richard Selyman, for debt. Pledge, Henry de Luddigden.

Adam Migge *v.* William Swaype, Thomas de Roildesete and Adam s. of Ivo, on an agreement. Pledge, the Grave.

William de Lighesles *v.* Hugh de Lighesles, in a plea of land. Pledge, Robert de Saltonstall.

mem. 11.

COURT at Halifax on Tuesday in Whitsuntide week [May 20], 2 Edward II [1309].

SOURBY.—Richard Selyman, fined 3*d.* for detaining 15*d.* from Robert s. of Nabbe de Sourby. Pledge, the Grave.

Matthew s. of Jordan de Skircotes gives 12*d.* to take a bovate in Warlouleye, as a heriot after his father's death.

Henry s. of Robert del Lone gives 2*s.* to agree with Thomas s. of William the Soldier [*mercenarius*], for assault. Sureties for the keeping of the peace, Robert de Saltonstall and Elias s. of Ivo.

Elias s. of Ivo de Werlouley, fined 12*d.* for withholding half a stone of wax from the service of Blessed Mary, which he was fined for contempt and assault on Adam le Crouder, and evidence being given in full Tourn that Elias threatened Adam in life and limb, he is attached to keep the peace by Henry del Hollegate, William del Lighesles, Robert s. of Roger, Henry de Luddigdene, Richard s. of Alote, and Adam s. of Wilcok, who undertake to protect Adam from him.

SOURBY.—Adam Migge, plt., and William Swaype, Thomas de Roildesete, and Adam s. of Ivo, agree by license. William Swaype fined 12*d.* for them all.

John the Webster of Werlouley gives 12*d.* to take a croft of one acre there from William Swaype, for 11 years. And 6*d.* for a rood of land there from Adam s. of Ivo, for ever.

Malina sister of Simon *v.* Thomas s. of Juliana, for trespass. Pledge, John s. of Henry the Pinder. Thomas admits that he beat her. He must pay damages, and 6*d.* fine.

Michael del Lom, for cutting green broom [*hussetus*], 6*d.*

John s. of Robert de Chesewalleye, 1*d.*; Nabbe wife of Robert de Chesewalleye, 1*d.*; Ellen Goisse, 2*d.*; Thomas de Saltonstall, 4*d.*; Adam

---

¹ See *ante,* p. 123, note.

de Illingwrth, 1*d.*; John the Milner, 2*d.*; John de Miggelay, 1*d.*; Juliana de Heytfeld, 7*d.*; Hugh de Lighesles, 2*d.*; Nelle s. of Ivo, 4*d.*; John Hodde, 3*d.*; William del Bothem, 4*d.*; Henry del Hollegate, 9*d.*; Adam s. of Ivo, 4*d.*; Thomas del Feild, 3*d.*; Nelle the Couper, 2*d.*; William de Bayrstowe, 5*d.*; Nicholas the Rider, 1*d.*; William s. of Michael de Chesewalley, 1*d.*; Thomas s. of Nelle, 2*d.*; Beatrice de Totehill, 16*d.*; Eva de Coldelay, 6*d.*; and William de Coldelay, 6*d.*; for escapes.

William de Coldelay, for vert, 2*d.*

John the Milner, 1*d.*, for dry wood.

Adam del Hill, 3*d.*, for broom [*pro huss'*].

Richard de Rastrick, 2*d.*; John de Barkesland, 1*d.*; Henry Womman [?], 4*d.*; John de Cockecroft, 2*d.*; Thomas de Lighesles, 6*d.*; Robert de Stodelay, 6*d.* (pledge, William his servant); Richard del Wyteleye, 6*d.*; John s. of Robert de Chesewalleye, 2*d.*; Nabba de Chesewalleye, 2*d.*; Thomas de Saltonstall, 2*d.*; and Cicely da. of Adam, 2*d.*; for escapes.

Tourn there the same day.

JURORS.—John de Stanesfeld, Richard del Dene, William del Croft of Langfeld, John Fox of Stanesfeld, Richard s. of Richard de Waddeswrth, William de Sothill, William de Connale, John s. of John de Soland, Thomas de la Sale of Notheland [*sic*], Richard s. of Bateman, Matthew de Bosco, and John de Cockecroft.

Stephen s. of Magge de Routonstall drew blood from John, his brother; 12*d.*

John de Stainlay, 6*d.*, for not coming.

Maude de Chepedene drew blood from Thomas s. of Juliana de Ovendene; 6*d.*

Juliana Wade, from William the Couhird; 12*d.*

Henry s. of Robert del Lone, from Thomas s. of William the Soldier [*mercenarius*]; 2*s.*

Hanne del Hollegate was trying to distrain Nelle[1] s. of Ivo, for rent due to the Earl, and Nelle prevented him, and seized him by the throat. Hanne retaliated, and drew blood. Nelle fined 12*d.*

Henry s. of Nalle de Northeland drew blood from William the Gardiner of Northeland; 12*d.*

Cissota Twete, from Nabbe s. of Adam; she is to be attached.

---

[1] Nelle is masculine; ? Niel.

The wife of Richard Aleman, 6*d.*; Megota de Rypon, 3*d.*; and the wife of Henry the Walker [*fullo*], 3*d.*; for brewing contrary to the assize.

William s. of Hugh del Lawe drew blood from William s. of Cissota de Hiperum; 12*d.*

Maude Panyerbagge has been indicted several times for burgling Ellen Gose's house, and stealing a robe and a . . . . , with many jewels [*de forcerio suo furato cum pluribus jocularibus*]. She is to be arrested when she can be found.

COURT at Rastrick on Wednesday in Whitsun week, in the year abovesaid.

RASTRICK.—Joan da. of William the Carpenter of Clifton gives 12*d.* to take ½ a bovate of land and ¼ of a messuage in Rastrick, as a heriot after her father's death.

HIPERUM.—John s. of Walter de Northourum gives 3*s.* to take ½ a bovate of land (less one acre) in Northourum, from Maude da. of Henry de Northourum.

Richard s. of Jordan de Northourum gives 12*d.* to take 3½ acres of land in Northourum, from the said Maude.

RASTRICK.—Henry Steven of Fekesby was charged with concealing a certain custom of ploughing, which he owes for 12 acres of land which he holds in Fekesby. He denies the custom. An inquisition is taken by the oath of Adam Bythebroke, Matthew de Totehill, William de Totehill, Alexander de Wodehouses, William de Wodehouses, Matthew de Bosco, Adam s. of Ivo, John del Botherode, Richard s. of Maude, Alexander del Okes, Thomas del Okes, and John de Rastrick, who say that Henry's 12 acres ought to render the Earl a custom of ploughing, viz. 4*d.* for a whole plough, and 2*d.* for half a plough, yearly, and that Henry has withheld the service for 10 years, namely as to ½ a plough for 8 years, and as to a whole plough for 2 years, which amounts to 2*s.* The land is to be seized till the 2*s.* is paid; fine, 5*s.* The Township of Rastrick for not presenting the concealment at divers Tourns, 6*s.* 8*d.*

Gilbert Bridde gives 6*d.* to agree with John de Schepelay, for trespass.

HIPERUM.—Elias de Skulcotes sues Richard s. of Ivo, for 4*s.* 6*d.*, which Richard admits that he owes; fine, 3*d.* He also sues Thomas del Brok for 2 bushels of rye [*siligo*], which is admitted; fine, 3*d.* Pledge, Geoffrey del Dene.

William s. of Walter is fined 6*d.* for withholding 3*s.* from Henry de Godelay.

Alcok le Taillour, 3*d.*; Thomas the Cook, 3*d.*; and Richard Standwele, 2*d.*; for dry wood.

Eva del Wolfcar, 2*d.*; Thomas del Rode, 3*d.*; William his brother 3*d.*; Thomas del Clyf, 2*d.*; Roger de Clifton, 4*d.*; Peter del Southclyf, 2*d.*; Thomas s. of Thomas, 6*d.*; and Henry Horne, 4*d.*; for escapes.

HYPERUM.—John de Astay, Richard de Hemmygway, John de Bayrstowe, and John s. of Henry de Bayrstowe, 6*d.* each, for escapes.

Walter de Ourum, 6*d.*, for green sticks [? *pro viridis baculis*]; and Richard s. of Walter, 3*d.*, for thorns.

William de Heyley, 6*d.*; and Margaret de Haldewrth, 3*d.*; for haybote.

Agnes de Astay, 4*d.*; and Thomas s. of Thomas de Hemmygway, 2*d.*; for escapes.

mem. 11*d.*

Roger del Clyf, 6*d.*; and Jordan de Haddegrenes, 4*d.*; for dry wood.

Thomas de Bellehouses, 6*d.*; and John s. of Walter de Ourum, 4*d.*; for haybote.

Roger de Briggehouses, 4*d.*; Thomas del Rode, 6*d.*; Henry del Northclif, 3*d.*; and William de Bayrstowe, 3*d.*; for escapes.

Henry le Pinder, for dry wood, 6*d.*

Thomas del Northend of Ourum, for vert, 4*d.*

TOURN there the same day.

JURORS.—Alexander del Frith, John le Flemang of Dalton, Thomas *Fisicus* of Dalton,[1] John de Locwode junior, Roger de la Sale, Lovecok de Nettelton, John the Clerk of Hertesheved, Henry de Coldelay, John de Bristall, John del Rode, John de Sunderland, and Thomas del Wytewode.

John s. of Thomas de Barkesland stole two mares, one from William de Locwode, and one from Adam Balter of Marchedene. He is to be arrested.

The Abbat and Convent of Fountains, who are bound to make and repair Bradeley bridge, leave it unmade [*permittant dictum pontem in constructum*], in prejudice of the Earl and his liberty, and

---

[1] Called previously, "Thomas de Dalton, *fisicus*"; *ante*, p. 159.

N

to the great damage and nuisance of the whole country. They are to be distrained when found.

Robert the Smith of Wollewro drew blood from Roger de Brighouses junior; 12d.

The wife of Roger de Brighouses senior brews contrary to the assize, 12d. The wives of Richard le Taillour and Geppe Foune, 6d. each, for the like.

Richard s. of Roger del Feild stole an ox from Alexander de Rastrick, a pig from Beatrice de Totehill, and a heifer from Adam Bythebroke; to be arrested. _____

COURT at Birton on Thursday in Whitsun week,[1] in the year abovesaid [1309].

HOLNE.—William s. of Wilkes, 2d., for delivering a stirk [*stirk-ettum*], supposed to be a stray, without the Steward's permission.

Sybil widow of Henry de Fouleston gives 5s. for license to marry.

Emma widow of Thomas Keneward gives 3s. for the like.

John s. of Nicholas Keneward gives 2s. to take 3 acres 1½ roods of land in Wolvedale from Nicholas, his brother.

Matthew de Barneby gives 12d. to take ½ acre of land in Fouleston from Matthew de Mora.

John s. of Adam de Heppewrth and Elias his brother have the custody of Thomas s. of Adam, a minor, (with 5 acres of land in Heppewrth), until he comes of age. They are to feed and clothe Thomas, and maintain the land and buildings, and allow him 2s. a year; and must answer for goods and chattels, worth 8s., when he comes of age. John and Elias give 12d. for the recognition.

John s. of John de Holne gives 6d. to agree with John Baroun, for trespass.

Matthew s. of Thomas, fined 6d. for trespass in Richard de Birton's meadows; Richard, fined 6d. for a false claim against Matthew.

John s. of Thomas de Thoung gives 5s. to take 15 acres of land in Thoung, as a heriot after his father's death.

Jordan del Oldefeild gives 6d. to take a rood of land in Cartewrth from Richard de Cartewrth.

Richard le Askebrenner, for vert, 2s.

John s. of John le Loverdman and Henry Hog, 6d. each, for dry wood.

William Bogace, 2d., for an escape.

John Baroun, 3d.; Michael de Holne, 3d.; William Wastell, 6d.; and Thomas de Bouderode, 4d.; for vert.

_____

[1] Whit-Sunday fell on May 18th.

TOURN there the same day.

JURORS.—Henry de Schelvelay, Adam de Helay, Richard de Thornteley, John Wyther, John de Braythait, Simon de Thurstanland, Henry de Birton, Thomas Bridde, John s. of Alcok de Heppewrth, Adam del Skoles, Adam de Wolvedale, and Hugh del Hole.

Richard le Askebrenner drew blood from Elias s. of Adam Bray of Littelwode; 12d.

Thomas Thorstell, the like from John Crawe. To be attached.

John Crawe, the like from Thomas Thorstell; 12d.

The wife of John s. of Gilbert, 6d.; the wives of Richard Neubagg', John de Kesceburgh, and Robert Boton, 12d. each; Emma la Baggere, 12d.; the wife of Robert Lightfote, 12d.; Magota da. of John the Smith of Schepelay, 6d.; and Cissota de Wistones [?], 6d.; for brewing contrary to the assize.

William Wastel and William del Bothe, drew blood one from another; 12d. each.

The wives of Jordan the Milner and Adam le Askebrenner brew contrary to the assize; 6d. each.

[*N.B.—The Roll is in bad condition here, and the remainder of this membrane is illegible.*

mem. 12.

COURT at Wakefeld the Friday in Whitsun week, 2 Edward II, [1309].

ESSOIGNS.[1]—Thomas de Heeton, by John de Northeland. Pledge, John de Mora.

Thomas de Dronesfeld, by John de Legh. Pledge, John de Toftclyf.

Peter Swerd, by William Margeriman. Pledge, Richard de Bristall.

William de Chepedene, by Thomas de Wittelay. Same pledge.

Alan Almot, attorney of Thomas de Burgh, by Robert de Heyrod. Pledge, Thomas de Thornton.

John s. of Robert the Clerk of Sandal, fined 6d. for withdrawing his suit for seizing cattle, against William the Grave of Walton.

HORBIRY.—Maude widow of Adam Broun, fined 6d. for withdrawing her suit against Hugh le Lambehird.

STANLAY.—Robert Gunne, 3d., for his fences being broken, at the suit of Andrew de Ouchethorpe.

Alice da. of Robert s. of Walter gives 6d. to take an acre of land in Stanlay from Robert, her father, and Robert, his son, for her life.

---

[1] From suit of Court, unless otherwise stated.

Robert Sonneman, plt., and Nicholas s. of Gotte agree by license. Nicholas fined 12d. Pledge, Alan s. of Gotte.

It was presented at the Tourn at Birton that Richard de Bello Monte drew blood from Gilbert the Milner, and that Richard very often comes to Birton Church to seek a quarrel [*ad contumeliam querendam*], and will not attach himself by the constable and keeper of the peace [*et non vult se attachiare constabular' et custod' pacis*], and he has nothing in the Earl's fee. The Earl's ministers are ordered to help the constable to attach him.

SANDALE.—Robert s. of Moyses, for vert cut in Thurstanhawe, 3d.

John Tropinell, 12d.; Richard Scot, 3d.; Robert de la Grene, 2d.; and Henry North of Wolflay, 6d.; for escapes.

Thomas le Hunt and Robert de Bergh, 5s. for cutting an oak.

The above attachments for Sandale were made by Thomas de Wakefeld while he was Constable of the Castle, and were not presented till now.

TOURN at Wakefeld the same day.

JURORS.—John Patrik, Walter de Grymmeston, William Ingreys, William de Dewisbiry, John de la More, Henry de Chyvet, John de Toftclyf, Richard de Bristall, Robert de Wodesom, John de Fery, Walter Scot, and Robert Dernelove.

Richard Broun and William s. of Gotte of Dewisbiry drew blood from one another; 12d. each.

Adam le Oxhird of Sothill and Simon the Shepherd, fined 4d. each for not coming.

Nicholas de Croweschagh drew blood from Ralph the Chaplain of Emmelay; 2s.

Alice Rolle of Westbretton stole 10d. from Alice sister of the said Ralph, Parson of Emmelay, in the said Parson's house. She is to be arrested.

William de la Grene and John Tropinell drew blood from one another; 12d. each.

Agnes wife of John Dande drew blood from William de la Grene; 12d.

ALVERTHORPE.—Richard the Tanner of Alverthorpe dug a pit on the high road to put his dung in, to the nuisance of the neighbours. The pit to be filled up; fine, 6d.

The wives of Richard de Collay and William Hoskell, for brewing contrary to the assize, 12d. each.

The township of Alveithorpe, for concealing the said brewings, 2s.

Alexander the Smith received disturbers of the peace into his house, through whom affrays [*contumelia*] have very often arisen, and the hue raised. He is to be attached.

John le Turnur drew blood from Adam le Hewar and Margaret Coter; 12d. and 6d.

John Broun, the like from Thomas Tucche; 6d.

Thomas de Luda, the like from Robert Dosi; 12d.

Agnes Hogg, the like from Cicely de Castelford; 4d.

Peter de Acom obstructed the way to the draw-well [*ad puteum trahitium*] in Wakefeld market, 6d.

John Donn, for making a path illegally beyond the Burghman-toftes, 6d.

John s. of John de Fery, drew blood from John Torald; 12d.

John Torald, the like from the wife of Thomas s. of Henry; 2s.

Henry Gonton baked bread contrary to the assize, viz. "vantage-bredde," of which all the neighbourhood complains; fine, 12d.

A certain baker called Dicote, 6d. for the like; also Walter Hogg, Nicholas Hogg, John Peger, and John Chaffar, 6d. each for the like.

Ralf de Wodekirk drew blood from Richard de Wakehirst; 12d.

The whole neighbourhood complains to the twelve that the high road in Westgate is so blocked up with tan bark [? *tannata*], logs of wood and dung, put in the street, that the public passage for the neighbourhood is obstructed. The jury are to view the obstructions and present the names of the obstructors. They present the following :—

German Filcok obstructed the common passage in the town by his tan bark [?]; 12d.

mem. 12d.

Philip Damoysell, 2s.; Richard Chapman, 12d.; Walter Bille, 12d.; Robert de Castelford, 2s.; John de Grenegate, 12d.; Ralph s. of Mille, 12d.; Thomas s. of Laurence, 2s.; Richard s. of Mille, 2s.; John Benne, 12d.; John de Fery junior, 12d.; and William le Gardiner, 12d., for the like.

John de Schelvelay *v.* Richard Matel of Schelvelay, for trespass. Pledge, John Cussing. Plaintiff puts William Margeryman in his place.

SOURBY.—William Swyer of Hiperum *v.* Elias s. of Ivo de Werlouley, for trespass. Pledge, Adam le Crouder.

Adam s. of Ivo *v.* Thomas del Lom, for trespass. Pledge, Elias s. of Ivo.

ALVERTHORPE.—John Cay *v.* John Schirelock and Juliana Swan, for debt. Pledge, Robert s. of Ralph.

HOLNE.—William del Bothe *v.* William Wastell, for trespass. Pledge, Hugh del Hole.

John le Long of Cottinglay *v.* John Rate, for seizing cattle. Pledge, John de Toftclyf.

Alice da. of Philip del Hill *v.* John Graffard, for trespass. Pledge, Robert de Fery. John is attached by William Graffard and Hugh s. of Henry le Long.   _____

COURT at Wakefeld on Friday after the Feast of St. Barnabas [June 11], in the year abovesaid [1309].

ESSOIGNS.[1]—John de Lepton, by Thomas de Wittelay. Pledge, Richard de Bristall.

Elias de Birton, by William his son. Pledge, Robert de Wyromthorpe.

Nicholas le Normaund, by John Gest. Pledge, John de Toftclyf.

Thomas de Heeton, by Peter de Goulaghcarthes. Pledge, Hugh de Seyville.

Thomas de Thornton, by John de Wakefeld. Pledge, Thomas de Wakefeld.

Robert de la Grene, by William the Serjeant. Pledge, John de Mora.

HIPERUM.—William Swyer of Hiperum essoigns against Elias s. of Ivo, for trespass, by William Margeriman. Pledge, William de Chypedene.

SOURBY.—Adam s. of Ivo de Werlouley, 6*d.*, for not prosecuting suit against Thomas de Lom, for trespass.

ALVERTHORPE.—John Cay sues John Schirelock and Juliana Swan (who does not come) for a stone and 2 lbs. of wool, price 5*s.* a stone. John Schirelock admits that he is surety for the said Juliana for the wool; he is to satisfy plaintiff; fine, 4*d.*

John le Long of Cottingley, fined 6*d.* for not prosecuting suit against John Rate, for seizing cattle.

HOLNE.—William Wastell gives 6*d.* to agree with William del Bothe, for trespass.

Thomas de Dronesfeld, 6*d.*, for default.

John de Eland makes default. His tenement is in the lord's hand.

THORNES.—Alice da. of William Proudefot surrenders ½ bovate of land in Thornes; and afterwards Richard del Rode and the said

_____
[1] From suit of Court, unless otherwise stated.

Alice take it again to them and the heirs of the said Alice, paying 4s. for entry. Richard finds sureties for coming and remaining on the land with his goods and chattels, viz. Adam Wilymot and Roger le Turnur. Alice pays 12d. for license to marry the said Richard.

HOLNE.—Adam Strekayse gives 5s. to take ¾ of a bovate, with buildings, and a rood of new land, in Holne, from Adam s. of Jordan the Milner.

Thomas s. of Juliana gives 6d. to take an acre of land in Fouleston from Richard le Syour.

Adam s. of Hugh gives 12d. to take 5 roods of land in Alstanlay from Adam de la Grene; and 12d. to take an acre of land there from Henry Hulle.

STANLAY.—Richard Spink gives 12d. to take 6 acres of land in Stanlay from Juliana del Dale, for 12 years.

HIPERUM.—Richard s. of Judde de Halifax has license to take ½ acre of land in Northourum from Richard s. of Adam, for 13 years.

ALVERTHORPE.—Thomas s. of Philip de Alverthorpe gives 2s. to take 5 acres of land in Alverthorpe from Richard his brother. Richard takes 2½ acres thereof back again for his life.

HOLNE.—Adam s. of Hugh de Alstanlay gives 3d. to take a rood of new land from the waste in Alstanley; rent, 1½d.

Distrain the Abbat of Fountains for Bradelay bridge.

Attach Richard de Bello Monte, when found.

HOLNE.—The plea of land between Thomas de Querneby and William del Bothe is respited until the Steward comes.

Thomas de Langdene, 18d., for escape of 18 oxen in le Holnefrith.

Simon de Thurstanland, 4d.; John, servant of Hawe, 6d.; Richard del Nethertoun, 3d.; John de Longlay, 2d.; and Thomas le H[unt?], 6d.; for escapes.

mem. 13.

WAKEFELD.—Nicholas Noddeger, 1d.; Robert le Walker, 1d.; Adam de Castelford, 1d.; Maude Godesaule, 1d.; John Pollard senior, and John his son, 1d. each; William Wiles, 1d.; Edusa Preste, 1d.; William the Goldsmith, 2d.; Robert the Goldsmith, 2d.; Robert and John Tope, 1d. each; Henry Chepe, William Takell, Adam le Wayte, John de Fery, Beatrice Hunt, Joan Leget, Cicely Danyel, John Nelot, and Robert Swerd, 1d. each; Eva de Bramelay and John Lauediman's son, 2d. each; for dry wood.

Richard Jonne's son, 2d.; the maids of John Leche and Robert Capon, 6d. each; Marjery Archur's son, 6d.; Richard the Clerk's maid, 6d.; the son of Hugh the Soldier [*mercenarius*], 6d.; the wife of Gilbert le Tinkeler, 2d.; and Robert Archur's maid, 6d.; for rushes.

Thomas Noundy, 2*d.*; Walter Hogge, 2*d.*; Robert de Stodelay, Eva de Bramlay, Robert Archur, William s. of Eva, William Rychaude, Henry le Nauthird, and William de Wridelesford, 2*d.* each; for escapes.

Richard le Waite, 4*d.*; Alice Proudfot, 2*d.*; John Richaude, 3*d.*; the maids of John le Couper and John Molle, 2*d.* each; William de Sandale, 1*d.*; John Torald's son, 2*d.*; Maude Pole, 2*d.*; Margaret Pollard's son, 2*d.*; John Baba's son, 1*d.*; Adam Torketro, 6*d.*; Robert de Fetherstan, 3*d.*; Robert Hod, 2*d.*; for dry wood.

John Cussing, and the maids of Peter de Acom and Robert le Young, 6*d.* each, for rushes.

John Skulbrok's maid, Maude de Sourby, and Robert Dernelove, 2*d.* each; for dry wood.

John le Sotheren, 4*d.*, and Robert Estrild, 4*d.*, for escapes of pigs.

Robert Capon, 1*d.*; Richard de Mora, 3*d.*; Walter Ape, 2*d.*; Elias Tirsi, 2*d.*; Reynald de Swinlington, 2*d.*; Robert Lyftfast, 1*d.*; John Peger, 2*d.*, for dry wood.

Roger Wasse and the son of Robert Broun, 1*d.* each, for breaking the pale.

John Wolmer, for vert, 6*d.*

THORNES.—Roger Trailment, 2*d.*; Agnes widow of Roger, 1*d.*; Philip del Hill's wife, 2*d.*; and the widow of Thomas Brounsmyth, 4*d.*; for escapes.

John Graffard, for vert, 12*d.*

Thomas Viroun, 3*d.*; Alice wife of Philip, 2*d.*; and John Costell, 2*d.*; for dry wood.

HORBIRY.--John Kaynock, 4*d.*, and Hugh the Shepherd, 3*d.*, for escapes.

STANLAY.—Robert Stert's servant, 3*s.*, for green twigs [*virge*].

William Elin of Carleton, 6*d.*, for dry wood.

Robert the Carpenter of Metheley, 12*d.*, for vert.

Alice the Shepherdess [*bercatrix*], Ibbota her sister, and the son of Adam the Shepherd, 6*d.* each, for dry wood. Pledge, Richard del Bothem.

OSSETE.—John Bullock, for the like, 2*d.*

Thomas Pees, 2*d.*; Matthew de Ossete, 2*d.*; William Cole, 2*d.*; and Richard s. of Bate, 8*d.*; for escapes.

SANDALE.—William de Rypon *v.* John s. of John the Skinner, on an agreement. Pledge, Henry, the Constable's man [*homo constabularii*].

John s. of Swain Scot *v.* Alexander de Dritker, in a plea of land. Pledge, Roger Tubbing.

SOURBY.—Maude Broun *v.* Hugh le Lambehird, for trespass. Pledge, John Batin.

HOLNE.—Richard s. of Nalle *v.* Nicholas s. of Nicholas Keneward, for trespass. Pledge, John s. of Thomas.

Juliana Crabbe *v.* Thomas Thorstell, for trespass. Pledge, Henry the Smith of Skelmarth[orpe].

SOURBY.—William de Cheppedene *v.* Richard del Feild, for trespass. Pledge, Hugh de Illingwrth.

STANLAY.—Richard del Kerre *v.* Adam Torcatro, for trespass. Pledge, Andrew de Ouchethorpe.

ALVERTHORPE.—Alice, Alice, and Christiana, daughters of Robert de Alverthorpe, *v.* Richard s. of Philip, in a plea of land. Pledge, Richard de Collay.

Adam Gerbode *v.* John Bonny, for seizing cattle. Pledge, Robert s. of Ralph.

HOLNE.—John Attebarre *v.* Thomas le Rollere, for trespass. Pledge, Andrew de Ouchethorpe.

THORNES.—Ralph Bate *v.* Philip Wolf, for trespass. Pledge, William Margeriman.

. . . .—Nicholas s. of Nicholas Keneward *v.* Richard s. of Nalle, for trespass. Pledge, Richard del Bothe.

[OSSET.]—Richard s. of Adam Broun of Heeton *v.* William de Lighesles, in a plea of land. Pledge, Richard Broun.

John Rate *v.* Adam de Chikinlay, on an agreement. Pledge, Richard Longschank.

. . . .—William Grenehod *v.* William Alayn of Ecleshill, for debt. Pledge, William Margeriman.

———

COURT at Wakefield on Friday after the Feast of SS. Peter and Paul [June 29], in the year abovesaid [1309].

ESSOIGNS.[1]—John de Lepton, by Thomas de Wittelay. Pledge, William del Okes.

Peter Swerd, by William Margeriman. Same pledge.

Thomas de Dronesfeld, by John de Legh. Pledge, John de la More.

Elias de Birton, by William his son. Pledge, Hugh de Seyville.

John Graffard, deft., against Alice da. of Philip del Hill, for trespass, by Thomas de Wakefeud. Pledge, Thomas del Bellehouse.

———

[1] From suit of Court, unless otherwise stated.

William de Lighesles, fined ['6d.] for not prosecuting his suit for land against Hugh de Lighesles.

Adam Gerbode, fined . . . . . for a false claim against John Bonny for seizing cattle.

An inquisition finds that Philip Wolf charged Ralph Bate with consuming his grass and the Earl's grass [?].

The tenement which Sir Hugh de Elande held of the lord in . . . . is in the lord's hand . . . . . .[1]

mem. 13d.

SOURBY.—Robert del Gledeholt gives 5s. to take a bovate of land in Werlouley from John del Gledeholt, for the life of Avice, wife of the said Robert.

HOLNE.—Adam Strekayse gives 5s. to take 20 acres of land in Fouleston from Matthew s. of Thomas.

SANDALE.—Richard servant of Robert de Ketelesthorpe gives 6d. to marry Alice widow of Adam s. of Stephen.

Hugh Cay gives 6d. to take an acre of land in Sandale from Robert the Clerk.

ALVERTHORPE.—John Tope gives 2s. to take 1½ acres of land in the Graveship of Alverthorpe from Sibyl his mother.

SOURBY.—John de Miggelay v. Robert de Saltonstall and Henry del Hollegate, for debt. Pledge, William At-town-head.

John Maunsell v. John s. of Richard s. of John, William his brother, and Thomas le Pinder, for trespass. Pledge, Thomas de Wittelay. They are attached by Robert Pees and Richard Passemere.

William Nelot v. Robert the Clerk of Sandale and Thomas his son, for seizing cattle. Pledge, Thomas de Wittelay. They are attached by the community of the town of Sandale.

ALVERTHORPE.—John Rate v. Adam s. of Thomas, for trespass. Pledge, Richard de Collay.

RASTRIK.—Thomas de Astay, to be attached for breaking the Earl's fold.—Error.

OSSETE.—Thomas le Pinder v. John Maunsell, for trespass. Pledge, Richard le Pinder.

ALVERTHORPE.—Robert Gunne sues Richard Bonny for 2 messuages and a bovate of land in Neuton [?], as his inheritance after the decease of Henry Gunne, his father, whose heir, he asserts, he is; he says that his father held the tenements, and demised them for 10 years to one Walter de Northwode, who during his term

---

[1] The foot of this membrane is much rubbed.

unjustly alienated them to Robert Bonny, father of Richard Bonny, who now holds. Defendant says that the tenements were formerly escheated to the Earl on account of the felony of one Walter Ack, condemned for theft; that one Robert [?] s. of Reynald de Neuton, great-grandfather of the defendant, took them from the Earl to himself and his heirs, and afterwards gave them to William Gryme, his son, who held them all his life, and at his death they descended to Robert Bonny, his son and heir; Robert left the said tenements in Neuton, and lived at Wyveromthorpe, on land he received in marriage with his wife; and then Henry Gunne, father of the plaintiff, sued for the land as his right after the decease of Walter Ack, felon, as his kinsman and heir, and recovered them by an inquisition; and afterwards sold them to one Walter de Northwode; afterwards Robert Bonny recovered them under an attaint against Walter de Northwode, and held them peacefully all his life, and after his death Richard Bonny entered as his son and heir.

An inquisition is taken by the oath of Robert de Flansowe, Richard s. of Broun, Adam Wolf, Richard s. of Philip de Alverthorpe, Philip de Mora, Robert de Luppesheved, Richard del Bothem, Robert Pescy, Robert s. of Walter, Adam s. of Cote, Robert Gosse, and Roger le Turnur, who say that the tenements formerly belonged to Walter Ack, who was afterwards a fugitive, and was beheaded; and confirm the defendant, saying also that William Gryme, on account of his poverty, left the land waste for a year and upwards, whereupon Henry Gunne recovered it as aforesaid; Robert Bonny recovered it by attaint from Walter de Northwode, in the absence of Henry Gunne. Robert is to recover the land, and Richard is in mercy for unjust detention. The fine to be fixed in the Court after Michaelmas.

ALVERTHORPE.—Henry del Bothem, for escape of 5 hogs, 3*d*.

Robert Hode the Grave, for breaking the Earl's fold, 12*d*.

Walter s. of Adam, and Robert Tope, for not coming, 2*d*. each..

STANLAY.—Richard de Bothem, Hugh Skayf, John s. of Alice, Robert s. of Walter, John servant of Walter, Simon de Monte, Simon Tyting, Gilbert le Theker, Walter s. of Bateman, Richard Poket, John Poket, Philip le Syour, John Walhot, Gelle Quintyn, John Godefray, Robert Gunne, Robert Gose, the heir of Robert del Dale, William Tagge, John and Philip Isabell, Richard le Long, Richard s. of Nicholas, Robert Tersse, William s. of Nicholas, and Alice Preste; 2*d*. each, for not coming.

WAKEFELD.—William Wolmer, 2*d*., and Thomas de Warnefeld, 6*d*., for escapes.

Nicholas Noddeger, Maude Fraunceys, William Wyles, John Pollard, John his father, and William Takel's wife, 2d. each, for dry wood and fern.

Walter de Kirkeby, 8d., for escapes.

John Don, 2d.; the wives of Robert and John Tope, 2d. each; the wives of Adam le Wayte and Walter Pollard, 2d. each; for fern and dry wood.

John Tasse, 4d.; Robert Rollere, 2d.; Peter de Acom, 3d.; Robert Mareschall, 3d.; and Robert de Fetherston, 4d.; for escapes.

----

mem. 14.

COURT at Wakefield on Friday before the Feast of St. Mary Magdalene [July 22], at the beginning of the third year of King Edward [II, 1309].

ESSOIGNS.[1]—Thomas de Heeton, by Henry de Heeton. Pledge, Robert de Wyveromthorpe.

Thomas del Bellehouses, by Thomas de Wittelay. Pledge, John de la More.

Nicholas le Normaund, by William de Chyvet. Pledge, Robert de Wyveromthorpe.

Thomas de Thornton, by Hugh de Thornton. Pledge, John de Toftclyf.

Peter Swerd, by William the Serjeant. Pledge, Richard de Bristall.

Thomas de Drounesfeld, by John de Legh. Pledge, John de la More.

Nicholas de Cailly, by John Tropinell. Pledge, William del Okes.

Hugh de Seyville, attorney of Baldwin de Seyville, by John de Claiton. Pledge, William the Serjeant.

William Swyer, plt., essoigns against Elias s. of Ivo de Werlouley, for trespass, by Geoffrey del Dene. Pledge, John de Lepton.

John de Schelvelay and Richard Matel agree by license; Richard pays 6d. Pledge, Adam de Helay.

Alice da. of Philip del Hill and John Graffard agree by license; John pays 12d. Pledge, Robert de la Grene.

SANDALE.—William de Rypon and John s. of John the Skinner agree by license; William pays 6d.

HOLNE.—Richard s. of Nalle and Nicholas s. of Nicholas Keneward agree; Nicholas pays 12d. Nicholas also withdraws his suit against Richard, and pays 6d.

----

[1] From suit of Court, unless otherwise stated.

HORBIRY.—Maude Broun of Horbiry and Hugh Lamhird agree; Hugh pays 6*d.*

SOURBY.—William de Chepedene and Richard del Feld agree; William pays 6*d.*

STANLAY.—Adam Torketro has license to agree with Richard del Kerre, for trespass; fine pardoned, because he is poor.

ALVERTHORPE.—John Broun, for a false claim against Adam de Chikinlay; 6*d.*

SOURBY.—John de Miggelay, for withdrawing suit for debt against Robert de Saltonstall and Henry de Hollegate; 6*d.*

John s. and heir of Sir Hugh de Elande does fealty, and is to declare his tenement and the services due therefor at the next Court.

Sir Thomas de Burgh makes default, and is to be distrained. His attorney fined 6*d.*, because he[1] is in the King's service.

Sir Thomas de Schefeld to be distrained for the like.

Elias de Birton makes default; he is ill.

SANDALE.—The whole ville of Sandale is fined 12*d.* for not producing Robert the Clerk and Thomas his son, to answer William Nelot, for seizing cattle.

Thomas s. of Pelle *v.* William de la Grene, for trespass. Pledge, Thomas del Hollegate.

OSSETE.—An inquisition finds that Thomas le Pinder struck John Maunsell; damages, 4*d.*; fine, 6*d.* John prevented Thomas from impounding his cattle found in [Thomas's] corn. He must pay damages, and 6*d.* fine.

Robert Pees and Richard Passemere, 12*d.*, for not having John s. of Richard s. of John and William his brother, to answer John Maunsell for trespass.

HOLNE.—Henry de Hoton, Richard de Birton, and Richard s. of Michael de Fouleston, give 5*s.* to take 20 acres of land in Fouleston from Adam Strekayse; to hold to themselves and their heirs.

ALVERTHORPE.—Adam s. of Thomas, for slandering John Rate, 6*d.*, and damages.

Henry le Nonne gives 6*d.* to take 1½ roods of land in Neuton from Adam Gerbode.

Richard s. of Philip de Alverthorpe, 6*d.*, for grazing his cattle in the meadow of Alice, Alice, and Christiana, daughters of Robert de Alverthorpe; damages, 12*d.*

HYPERUM.—William de Sunderland gives 10*s.* to take 17 acres of land in Staynclif fields, lying between the house of Henry the Smith

---

[1] Presumably Sir Thomas.

and a boulder [? ; *boulum*] on the north of Staynclyf fields, together with 2 acres under the wood, from Dom Matthew, Rector of the Church of Little Sandale.

HOLNE.—Elias Walleraven quitclaims to Richard del Bothe all his right in 7½ acres of land in Thoung, bought by Richard from Gilbert de Gaunte. Richard pays 12*d.* to the lord for the recognition.

HIPERUM.—William del Bothes, forester in Hiperum wood, for 12 young oaks cut in his bailiwick, and not presented in his attachments, 10*s.* Pledge, William de Sunderland.

SANDALE.—William de la Grene, for cutting a young oak, 12*d.*

The servant of the Parson of Thornhill, for small . . . . [*arr*'], 4*d.*

William de la Grene, 16*d.*; John s. of Ralph, 6*d.*; and Robert de la Grene, 12*d.*; for escapes in the new coppice.

HOLNE.—Peter de Comberwrth, 6*d.*, and Robert de Deneby, 4*d.*, for escapes.

John s. of Nalk, 2*d.*; Henry Tubbing, 2*d.*; William Beufrere, Adam the Grave, and Baldwin de Monte, 3*d.* each; for making a path without right [*pro injusta via*].

Simon de Thurstanland, 4*d.*; John servant of Anote, 3*d.*; John de Farnelay, 4*d.*; William Moton, 4*d.*; and Thomas de Langdene, 6*d.*; for escapes.

STANLAY.—The maids of Beatrice Gunne, and of John s. of Philip le Syour, 2*d.* each, for dry wood.

Philip Isabell, for barking broom [*pro huss' excoriat'*], 6*d.*

mem. 14d.

THORNES.—Ivo the Smith, Robert s. of Robert s. of Simon, Roger s. of Alote, Ralph de Snaypethorpe, John Tasse, William s. of Roger, Robert de Thornes, Alice Proudefot, Elias de Thornes, Agnes Pegere, John s. of Richard, Richard s. of William, Adam s. of Walter, Philip Wolf, Philip de Castelford, John s. of Hobbe, Robert s. of Nalle, and John Kyde, 2*d.* each, for not coming to the new park.

OSSETE.—Maude widow of Ralph, Alice Pees, Thomas Pees, John Maunsell, Richard s. of Bate, Richard the Ferour, William Hirnyng, and Susannah de Goukethorpe, 2*d.* each, for not coming to the new park.

WAKEFELD.—The maids of John de Fery and William servant of Margery, 3*d.* each, for breaking the pale.

Walter le Turnur, 6*d.*; John le Askebrenne, 3*d.*; for escapes in the new coppice.

William Beuchaunt, 6*d.*; Hugh s. of James, 8*d.*; and Ralph Bate, 3*d.*; for cutting branches.

Robert Wyles, 12*d*., for escapes.

ALVERTHORPE.—Alice wife of Roger, 2*d*.; Henry Wolf, 2*d*.; Alice da. of Robert, 2*d*.; Richard s. of Broun, 4*d*.; Christiana Gerbode, 4*d*.; Walter del Botheum, 1*d*.; Adam Gerbode, 2*d*.; John Schirelock, 2*d*.; Adam Wolf, 2*d*.; Margery Wyntre, 3*d*.; and Anote Tyan, 2*d*.; for escapes.

John s. of Richard Gerbode, 3*d*., for vert.

Walter Bak, 3*d*., for an alder.

OSSETE.—William Coil, 4*d*.; Thomas Pees, 4*d*.; John the Walker [*fullo*], 2*d*.; Matthew de Ossete, 2*d*.; Richard Suart, 1*d*.; and the wife of William s. of Jordan, 1*d*.; for horses in the new coppice.

THORNES.—Ivo the Smith, 1*d*.; Thomas Brounsmyth, 6*d*.; and Roger Trailment, 1*d*.; for escapes.

Thomas Viron, 3*d*., for vert.

SANDALE.—Agnes da. of Henry de Ossete *v*. Robert Jangell, for trespass. Pledge, John Cokewald.

Hugh le Lambehird *v*. Henry le Wyte, John s. of Richard Johanot, and Walter del Southwode, for trespass. Pledge, John de la More.

Agnes widow of Robert the Clerk of Dewisbiry *v*. Richard s. of Walter Gates, for trespass. Pledge, John de Mora.

John Tropinel *v*. Robert the Walker [*fullo*], on an agreement. Pledge, Richard le Schoter.

Gilbert the Milner of Birton *v*. Henry del Sthorthes, for seizing 2 horses. Pledge, Adam the Shepherd.

mem. 15.

COURT at Wakefeld on Friday after the Feast of St. Oswald [Aug. 5], 3 Edward [II, 1309].

ESSOIGNS.[1]—William de Chepedene, by Richard s. of John de Ossete. Pledge, William del Okes.

John de Lepton, by Thomas de Wittelay. Pledge, Richard de Bristall.

Thomas de Thornton, by Hugh de Thornton. Pledge, Robert de Wyromthorpe.

Thomas de Heeton, by Peter de Berkesland. Pledge, William del Okes.

Isabella Keu, by Robert de Sandale. Pledge, John de la More.

William Swyer and Elias s. of Ivo de Werlouley agree. Elias pays 6*d*.

---

[1] From suit of Court, unless otherwise stated,

SANDALE.—William de la Grene, for contempt, 6*d.*

HOLNE.—Richard de Alstanlay gives 3*s.* to take 4 acres of land in Alstanlay from Henry Hulle; and 12*d.* for 2 acres there from Adam de la Grene.

John de Turton gives 12*d.* for an escape of 4 beasts in Holne Frith. Pledge, Adam del Scoles.

Hugh le Lambehird, plt., agrees with Henry le Wyte, John s. of Richard Jonot, and Walter del Suthwode. Defts. pay 3*s.*

SOURBY.—John s. of Robert del Gledeholt junior gives 10*s.* to take a bovate of land in Sourby, and 3 acres in Bentelayrode, from Thomas s. of Elias Bibby (one acre being reserved to Agnes widow of Elias Bibby, for her life), to himself and his heirs; if John dies without heirs of his body, then remainder to John [*sic*] his brother and his heirs.

Nicholas le Ryder gives 6*d.* to take ½ acre of land in Sourby from Henry the Walker [*fullo*].

THORNES.—Richard le Wayte gives 6*d.* to take an acre in Thornes from John s. of Robert le Draper, for 20 years.

HOLNE.—Robert s. of Gamel de Alstanlay gives 12*d.* to take 2 acres of land in Alstanlay from Henry Hulle.

Robert de Alstanlay gives 2*s.* to take 3 acres of land in Alstanlay, from the same Henry.

Adam s. of Hugh de Alstanlay gives 6*d.* to take one acre there, from the same Henry.

John s. of Robert de Harehoppe and Thomas, his brother, give 2*s.* to take 2 acres there, from the same Henry.

ALVERTHORPE.—Philip Damysell gives 6*d.* to take a rood of land in the Graveship of Alverthorpe from Adam Gerbode, after two crops that Robert le Young has therein.

John s. of Hobbe the Soldier [*mercenarius*] gives 6*d.* to take an acre of land in Alverthorpe from Adam s. of Base [?].

SANDALE.—An inquisition finds that William de la Grene slandered Thomas s. of Pelle, and that Thomas cursed William; 6*d.* each.

OSSETE.—John Maunsell withdraws his suit against John s. of Richard s. of John, and William his brother; fine, 12*d.*

ALVERTHORPE. — Robert de Fetherston *v.* Adam Gerbode, for trespass. Pledge, Thomas de Wittelay.

COURT at Wakefield on Friday before the Nativity of Blessed Mary [Sept. 8], 3 Edward [II, 1309].

ESSOIGNS.[1]—Nicholas de Cailly, by Henry de Cailly. Pledge, Henry de Methelay.

John de Lepton, by Thomas de Wittelay. Pledge, Hugh de Seyville.

ALVERTHORPE.—John At-bar, for not prosecuting his suit against Thomas le Rollere, 6d.

Agnes widow of Robert the Clerk of Dewisbiry, and Richard s. of Walter Gates, agree in a plea of trespass. Richard's fine is forgiven at the instance of Dom [*dompni*] John, his brother. Pledge, William de Dewisbiry.

RECOGNIZANCE.—Robert Pees, Richard Broun of Heton, and Robert Sonneman acknowledge that they are bound to William de Locwode in 28s., for corn bought of him.

HOLNE.—Thomas Thorstell, distrained by corn found on his land, delivered by the bailiff to 4 free men of the ville of Birton, does not appear to answer Juliana Crabbe. He afterwards pays 2s. to agree. Pledge, Thomas de Wittelay.

mem. 15d.

John de Rylay v. Adam de Helay, for seizing cattle. Pledge, Richard Hulle.

ALVERTHORPE.—John Dade v. Henry le Nonne, in a plea of land. Pledge, William Margeriman.

John s. of Hobbe v. Richard Withehundes and Philip Wolf, on an agreement. Pledge, William Margeryman.

Henry Wolf gives 6d. to take an acre of land in Alverthorpe from Ralph Wolf, his brother.

HOLNE.—Alexander s. of John de Bromehale gives 3s. 4d. to take 7½ acres of land in Holne from Adam Strekayse. And as he is an incoming stranger [*et quia ipse est quidam extraneus advencius*], he finds sureties for doing fealty to the lord in all things, viz. William Strekayse, Adam de Holne, Adam Strekayse, and William del Bothe.

Thomas de Heton, for default, 6d.

HOLNE.—William Strekayse, Grave of Holne, 3s., for concealing three complaints, viz. John de Holne, against the sons of Gilbert de Alstanlay; Nicholas de Littelwode, on behalf of the whole ville of Littelwode, against Adam Bray; and Jordan del Oldefeild and Henry

---

[1] From suit of Court, unless otherwise stated.

O

de Littelwode, for the ville of Cartewrth, against Adam Bray. The Bailiff of the Liberty is to cause the parties to come to the next Court.

Thomas de Burgh, for default, 2s.

The fines are to be considered, especially the fine of Alexander s. of John de Bromehale, which is insufficient, etc. [*Scrutandi sunt fines, et precipue pro fine Alexandri filii Johannis de Bromehale, qui est insufficiens, etc.*].

Richard s. of John de Ossete *v.* Robert Pees, for trespass. Pledge, William de Locwode. Robert is attached by John the Carpenter and Matthew de Ossete.

HOLNE.—Hugh de Cartewrth *v.* Henry de Rastrick, on an agreement. Pledge, Adam Strekayse.

Richard de Cartewrth *v.* Henry de Littelwode, for seizing cattle. Pledge, Adam de Dalton.

HORBERY.—Edusa da. of John Chickin *v.* Robert del Okes, in a plea of land. Pledge, Robert Godale.

John s. of Thomas the Smith *v.* Isabel la Carter, in a plea of land. Pledge, John Caynock.

William au Curneys [?] *v.* Isabel la Cartere, in a plea of land. Pledge, John the Grave.

STANLAY.—Gerard Dodde *v.* William s. of Nicholas de Tickehill, in a plea of land. Pledge, Robert Ters.

OSSETE.—Richard s. of Adam Broun *v.* William de Lighesles, for trespass. Pledge, William Cheild.

---

mem. 16.

COURT at Wakefield on Friday after the Feast of St. Matthew [Sept. 21], 3 Edward [II, 1309].

ESSOIGNS.[1]—Peter Swerd, by Thomas de Wittelay. Pledge, Thomas del Bellehouse.

William de Chipedene, by William de Heitfeld. Pledge, Richard de Bristall.

Nicholas de Cailly, by Henry de Methelay. Same pledge.

Thomas de Thornton, by Hugh de Horton. Pledge, John de Toftclyf.

Robert de Wyromthorpe, by John Cay. Pledge, John de Mora.

John de Rylay, plt., essoigns against Adam de Helay, for seizing cattle, by Henry de Wakefeld. Pledge, Thomas de Wittelay.

---

[1] From suit of Court, unless otherwise stated.

HOLNE.—Thomas de Querneby, 6d., for a false claim against William del Bothe. William is to hold in peace the ½ acre of land entered in the Rolls of Peter de Lound, which William vouched.

ALVERTHORPE.—Judgment that Robert Gunne do recover the tenement he claimed against Richard Bunny. Richard fined 6d. for unjust detention.

SANDALE.—John Tropinell is fined 6d. for not prosecuting suit as to an agreement against Robert the Walker [fullo].

THORNES.—Richard Withehundes and Philip Wolf, villeins [nativi], summoned to answer John s. of Hobbe as to an agreement, are fined 6d. for not coming. They are to be distrained.

Richard s. of John de Ossete and Robert Pees agree. Robert pays 12d. Pledge, John the Grave of Horbiry.

HOLNE.—Adam de Dalton, 6d., for not producing Henry de Littelwode to answer Richard de Cartewrth, for seizing cattle.

The plea of land between William Aucurnese [?], plt., and Isabel la Cartere is respited till the next Court.

OSSETE.—An inquisition finds that William de Lighesles assaulted Richard s. of Adam Broun at the door of the Court, seizing him by the throat; damages, 9d.; fine, 12d. Pledge, Richard de Goukethorpe.

STANLAY.—John Poket, 12d.; Robert Pescy, 4d.; Andrew the Grave, 4d.; and the son of Walter Hod, 6d.; for vert.

John Walhot, Hugh Tagge, William Tagge, Robert Gonne, and John Bullock, 6d. each, for dry wood.

SOURBY.—Henry de Cleg, 2s. 6d.; Thomas his brother, 18d.; Geoffrey de Slavedene, 18d.; John de Trivehagh [?], 12d.; Hancok de Okedene, 12d.; Magge de Ligholleres, 6d.; Richard de Byroun, 6d.; John s. of Cisse de Wassedene, 18d.; Adam Dodeman, 12d.; Adam de Coventre, 6d.; for escapes. Pledges, Roger s. of Amabel, Thomas de Lythesles, Thomas s. of Adam, William de Stodelay, and John de Miggelay.

ALVERTHORPE.—Richard Bonny v. Robert Gunne, in a plea of land. Pledges, Thomas Bonny and Richard s. of Broun. The Earl has granted him an attaint upon a jury of twelve.

Thomas de Burgh, 2s., and Baldwin de Seyville, 6d., for defaults.

HOLNE.—Nicholas de Littelwode and Adam Bray agree. Adam pays 6d.

Adam Bray gives 6d. to agree with Jordan del Oldefeild and Henry de Littelwode, for trespass.

Peter Swerd v. Richard del Sikes of Langfeld and Peter del Crosselegh of Stanesfeld. Pledge, Thomas s. of Robert.

THORNES.—John Tasse *v.* John Pegere, for trespass. Pledge, Ralph Bate.

HOLNE.—Thomas s. of Gilbert de Alstanlay *v.* John de Holne, for trespass. Pledge, John Keneward.

William s. of Gilbert *v.* John de Holne, for trespass. Pledge, Thomas his brother.

Robert del Scoles *v.* John Morolf, for trespass. Pledge, William del Scoles.

Adam s. of Jordan the Milner *v.* Robert Stirk, for debt. Pledge, William Strekase.

Henry Wade *v.* Henry de Rastrik, for debt. Pledge, Adam s. of Jordan.

Henry de Rastrik *v.* Henry Wade, for trespass. Pledge, William Strekayse

John Pollard *v.* John de Flaxhowe [?], on an agreement. Pledge, Thomas de Wittelay.

THORNES.—Juliana de Thornes *v.* John Kyde, for trespass. Pledge, Philip Wolf.

STANLAY.—Philip le Syour *v.* Robert de Mickelfeld and Robert Ricard, for trespass. Pledge, Andrew . . . .

Robert de Mickelfeld *v.* the said Philip and John his son, for trespass. Pledge, Robert Ricard.

ALVERTHORPE.—John Chirelock *v.* Christiana Gerbode, for trespass. Pledge, Adam Gerbode.

SANDALE.—Robert s. of Isolda de Grigeleston *v.* Thomas del Holegate, for trespass. Pledge, William Taillour. Thomas is attached by Hugh Tubbing.

Maude de Hopton *v.* Thomas de Burgh, for seizing cattle. Pledge, John Cussing.

John de Toftclif *v.* Walter de Grymeston, for debt. Pledge, William de Locwode.

INDEX OF PERSONS AND PLACES.

A

Abbathia, William de, 77
Abraham, Abraam, Elias, 153, 188;
  Henry, 158, 159, 188
Achard, Adam, 45, 79
Ack, Walter, 219
Ackton, Eva de, 28, 31, 76; William
  de, 39, 43, 50, 51
Acom, Peter de, 62, 81, 121, 128, 136,
  213, 216, 220
Acreland, Walter de, 188
Adam, Alice da. of, 171; Cicely da. of,
  156, 207; Elias s. of, 210; John
  s. of, 91 *bis*, 103 *bis*, 126, 141,
  158 *bis*, 164, 192, 210; Jordan s.
  of, 158; Margery da. of, 164;
  Nabbe s. of, 207; Quenilda da. of,
  120; Richard s. of, 25, 89, 205,
  215; Robert s. of, 53, 84; Simon
  s. of, 60; Thomas s. of, 161, 210,
  227; Walter s. of, 21, 23, 84, 145,
  204, 219; William s. of, 125, 137,
  146, 158, 195
——, Little, 171
Adderigate, Walter de, 188
Admundelay, 134 *pass.*
Agnes, Henry s. of, 162, 165, 170;
  Jordan s. of, 36; Philip s. of, 29,
  53, 79, 80, 109, 116, 138; Thomas
  s. of, 162, 165, 170; William s. of,
  9, 35, 50, 182-3
Aikton, *see* Ackton
Alan, Henry s. of, 189 *bis*; John s. of,
  51, 81, 82, 191 *bis*; Philip s. of,
  53, 145; Robert s. of, 82
Alayn, Aleyn, John, 60, 63, 65, 76;
  Robert, 4; Thomas, 155, 167, 168,
  179, 196, 200; William, 217
Alaynley, 179
Alaynrode, 105
Albray, Albrey, Eva, 25; William, 23,
  25, 72, 74, 168, 203
Alcock, Gerard s. of, 203; Henry s. of,
  197; John s. of, 211; Richard s.
  of, 37; William s. of, 21, 87; *see
  also* Elcock
Alcocrodende, 104 *bis*
Aldebothe, 103
Aldelay, Alan de, 126
Aldeneley, Thomas de, 64

Alexander, Amabel da. of, 138; Emma
  da. of, 23
Alice, Alice da. of, 69, 71, 74; John s.
  of, 72, 99, 112, 148, 201, 219;
  Richard s. of, 8, 87, 88
Allman, Alman, Richard, 186, 208
Almod, Adam s. of, 24
——, Almot, Alan, 1, 10, 17, 21, 32,
  45, 51, 114, 121, 132, 135, 139 *bis*,
  142, 147, 152, 167 *bis*, 169, 170,
  172, 174 *bis*, 178, 182, 192, 200,
  203, 211
Almondbury, 158, 160, 165
Alote, Adam s. of, 54; Richard s. of,
  32, 71, 123, 164, 184, 206; Roger
  s. of, 222; Thomas s. of, 181
Alstanley, *see* Austonley
Alverthorpe, 4, 16, 27, 74, 80, 93, 95,
  97, 109, 129, 130, 131, 133 *bis*,
  163, 164, 165, 175, 176, 179, 180,
  184, 191, 192, 196 *bis*, 212, 213,
  215, 224, 225; Graveship of, 100,
  114, 184, 218, 224
——, Adam de, 22, 49; Agnes de,
  16; Alice de, 217, 221; Christiana
  de, 217, 221; Gerbot de, 74, 81;
  Hugh de, 16, 111; Philip de,
  49, 73, 108 *bis*, 115, 119, 215, 219,
  221; Quenilda de, 16, 69, 71,
  120, 131 *bis*, 133 *bis*, 142 *bis*, 147,
  148 *pass.*, 195, 196; Richard de,
  49, 73, 108, 215, 219, 221; Robert
  de, 69, 217, 221; Thomas de, 108,
  215; Walter de, 22, 28, 49
Amabel of Gisburne, 11
——, Roger s. of, 8, 71 *bis*, 86, 122,
  124, 227; *see also* Anabel.
Ambler, Nicholas le, 123
Amyas, John de, 117
Anabel, Richard s. of, 32; Roger s.
  of, 62, 64, 155 *ter*, 156; *see also*
  Amabel
Anote, Alice da. of, 121; John servant
  of, 222
——, Richard, 201; Robert, 131
Ape, Walter, 172, 200-1, 204 *bis*, 205,
  216
Apecock, Walter, 12
Archer, Cicely, 85; Henry, 28, 93,
  138, 191 *bis*, 201; Magge, 154;
  Marjery, 215; Robert, 172, 174, 178,

192 *bis*, 200, 215, 216; William, 31

Ardsley, 15, 46, 48, 166; Priory, 45*n*.
——, Adam de, 11 *bis*, 15, 37, 38, 40, 46, 48; Geoffrey de, 37, 38, 46, 48; Geppe de, 172; John de, 20, 24, 38, 97 *bis*, 99, 111, 116, 118, 203; Nicholas de, 48; Richard de, 11 *bis*, 24; Robert de, 37, 38, 40, 42, 45, 46, 48; William de, 17, 20, 21, 37, 38, 45, 46, 48, 51, 97, 99; Wymark de, 11, 15

Armerew, Richard, 67, 79, 83

Arrunden, *see* Ayrikedene

Askbrenner (Ashburner), Adam le, 211; John le, 201, 222; Richard le, 210, 211; William le, 161

Assolf, Roger, 61, 73, 79, 94, 139, 180; Thomas, 204

Astay, Hastay, Agnes de, 209; Henry de, 159; John de, 3, 85, 156, 209; Thomas de, 218

Astley-ker, 87

At-Bar, *see* Bar

At-Brig, *see* Brig

At-Brook, *see* Brook

At-Elm, *see* Elm

At-Green, *see* Green

At-Kirk, *see* Kirk

At-Town, *see* Town

At-Town-end, *see* Town-end

At-Town-head, *see* Town-head

At-Well, *see* Well

Aucurneys [?], William, 226, 227

Aundene, 135

Austonley, 56 *bis*, 103 *ter*, 104 *bis*, 148 *bis*, 151 *ter*, 175, 176, 189, 215 *bis*, 224 *pass*.
——, Adam de, 56, 215; Alan de, 151; Elias de, 56; Gamel de, 224; Gilbert de, 5, 6, 16, 34, 56 *bis*, 104 *bis*, 122, 127, 130, 132, 133, 141, 151, 153, 160 *ter*, 161 *ter*, 165, 170, 188; Hugh de, 215, 224, 225, 228; John de, 40; Juliana de, 34, 119, 133; Macock de, 56; Matthew de, 160; Richard de, 18, 56, 103, 104, 148, 224; Robert de, 16, 18, 127, 224; Thomas de, 160, 228; William de, 132, 160 *bis*

Aveneley, William de, 50 *bis*

Aylesbury, 93

Ayrikedene, 156, 185

B

Baba, John, 85, 201, 204, 216

Badde, Thomas, 9, 11, 15, 17

Badsworth, Robert de, 177

Bagger, le *or* la, Adam, 161; Alice, 186; Emma, 6, 50, 51, 55, 91, 127,

161, 211; Henry, 102 *bis*, 105, 110; John, 12, 186; Nicholas, 55; Richard, 188

Baghill, Cicely de, 52; Robert de, 122

Baildon, Robert de, 38 *bis*

Bailiff, Richard, 97, 108, 113, 115 *bis*, 144

Bairstowe, Bayrstowe, Hanne de, 113; Henry de, 209; John de, 187, 209; Ralph de, 177; William de, 207, 209

Bak, Walter, 223

Baker, Richard the, 113

Bale, Henry, 166

Balne, William de, 37

Balter, Adam, 209

Bank, Elias del, 155

Bar, At-, John, 47, 148, 217, 225; William, 14, 16, 27, 31, 39 *bis*, 44, 46, 47, 50

Bardelby, Robert de, 161

Barker, John the, 57

Barkisland, John de, 207, 209; Peter de, 69, 185, 187, 223; Thomas de, 209

Barksey, Alan de, 43; John de, 7, 26, 43; Richard de, 27

Barm, Barme, Maude del, 90; Peter del, 54, 70, 80, 125

Barn, John le, 2, 7, 35, 36, 70, 80; Thomas le, 7

Barnby, Henry de, 195; Matthew de, 18, 102 *bis*, 195, 210; Robert de, 17 *bis*, 20, 129

Barnedeside, Elcock de, 34

Barnsley, Richard de, 194 *bis*

Baroun, John, 210 *bis*

Baseheyng, 95

Bate, Agnes da. of, 84, 95, 164 *bis*; Cicely da. of, 164; Eva da. of, 164; Richard s. of, 204, 216, 222; Thomas s. of, 12, 14, 77, 101
——, Ralph, 29, 113, 184, 198, 201, 204, 217, 218, 222, 228; Thomas, 149; Walter, 140; William, 140

Bateman, Hugh s. of, 31, 37, 112, 113, 133; Philip s. of, 166, 168, 170, 171; Richard s. of, 32, 207; Robert s. of, 75; Simon s. of, 99, 112; Walter s. of, 31, 99, 151, 219; William s. of, 65, 145
——, Hugh, 67; Richard, 35; Robert, 67; Walter, 25, 74

Batin, John, 217

Batley, Elizabeth de, 163; Nicholas de, 11, 12, 15, 17, 20, 21, 24, 29, 32, 58, 68, 72, 94, 154, 163, 171, 178, 198; Richard de, 76, 85, 137, 138; Robert de, 17, 20, 21, 23, 24, 59, 68, 76, 94, 137, 162, 163, 172, 193, 195, 196, 202; William de, 20, 32, 46, 80

P

INDEX TO INTRODUCTION.

INDEX OF SUBJECTS.

PRINTED BY

J. WHITEHEAD AND SON, ALFRED STREET, BOAR LANE

LEEDS.

Lightning Source UK Ltd.
Milton Keynes UK
UKOW05f2204190813

215622UK00002B/477/P